FIRE FORCE

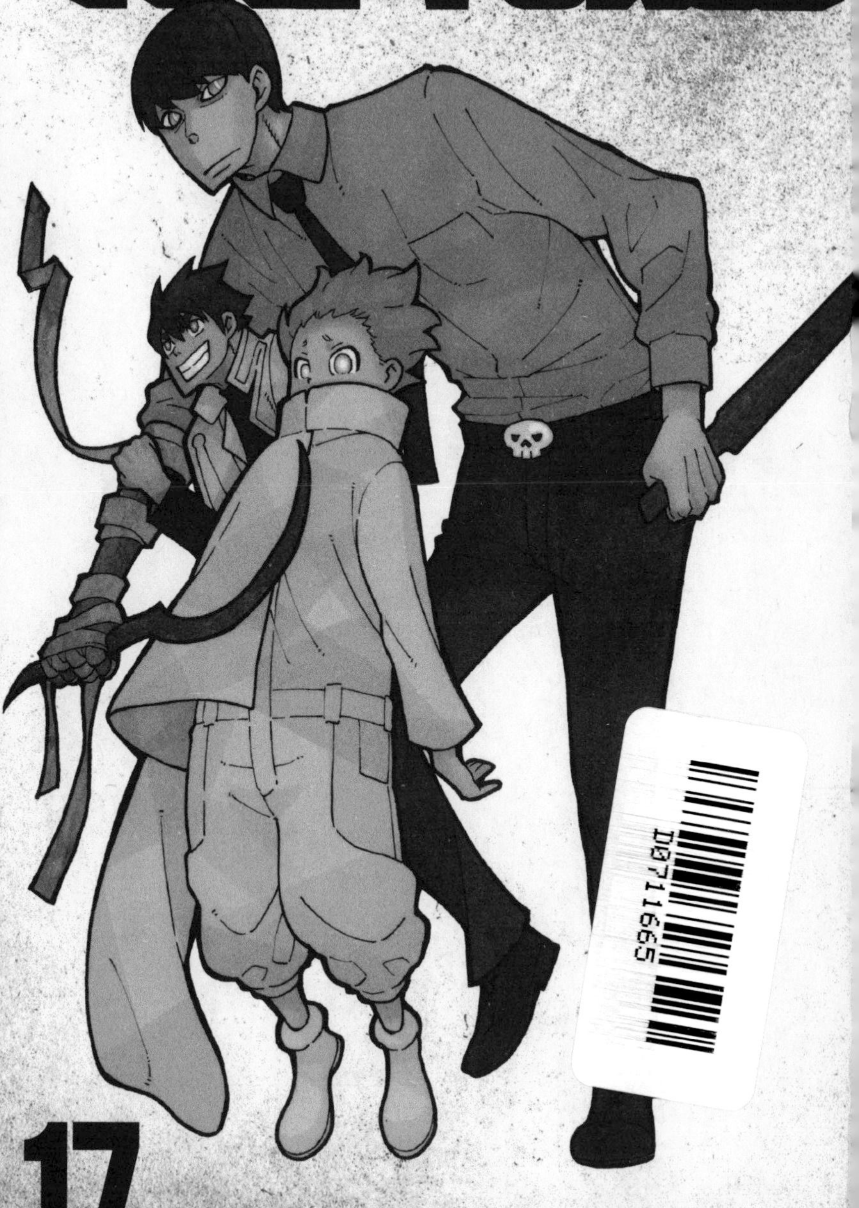

17

ATSUSHI
OHKUBO

be
tious.

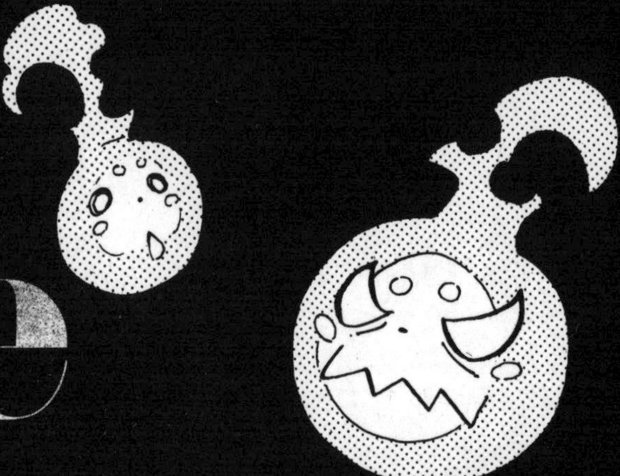

VOL. 17

ATSUSHI OHKUBO

boys,
don't
ambi

FIRE
FORCE

SPECIAL FIRE FORCE COMPANY 8

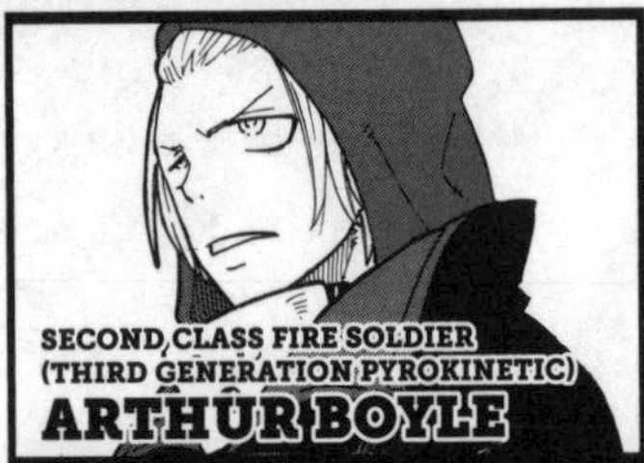

SECOND CLASS FIRE SOLDIER (THIRD GENERATION PYROKINETIC)

ARTHUR BOYLE

Trained at the academy with Shinra. He follows his own personal code of chivalry as the self-proclaimed Knight King. He's a blockhead who is bad at mental exercise. But girls love him. He creates a fire sword with a blade that can cut through most anything. He's a weirdo who grows stronger the more delusional he gets.

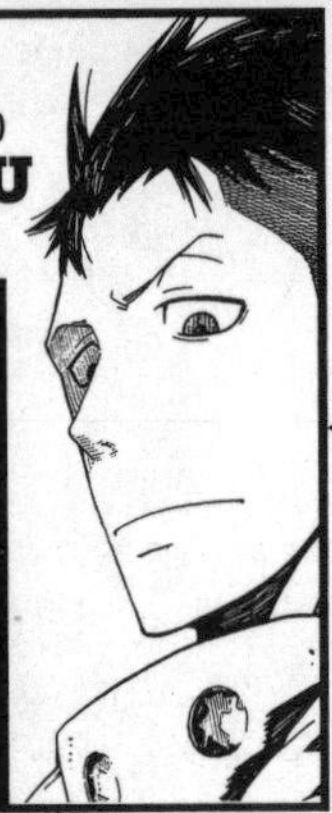

CAPTAIN (NON-POWERED)

AKITARU ŌBI

The caring leader of the newly established Company 8. His goal is to investigate the other companies and uncover the truth about spontaneous human combustion. He has no powers, but uses his finely honed muscles as a weapon in a battle style that makes him worthy of the Captain title. A man of character, respected even in other companies.

WATCHES OUT FOR

TRUSTS

IDIOT!!

WATCHES OUT FOR

TRUSTS

STRONG BOND

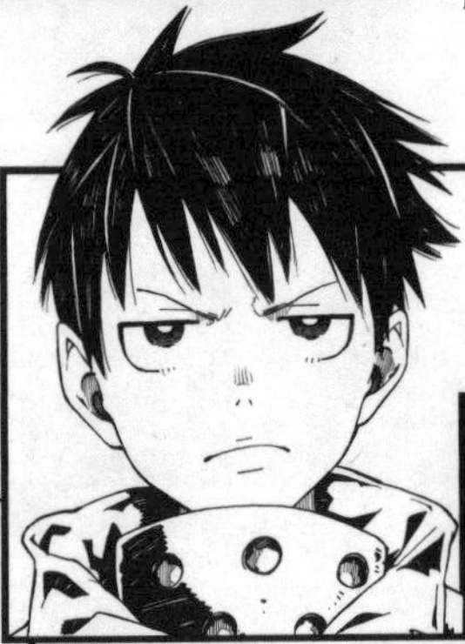

SECOND CLASS FIRE SOLDIER (THIRD GENERATION PYROKINETIC)

SHINRA KUSAKABE

The bizarre smile that shows on his face when he gets nervous has earned him the derisive nickname of "devil," but he dreams of becoming a hero who saves people from spontaneous combustion! His weapon is a fiery kick. He wields a special flame called the Adolla Burst. Before entering the training academy, he was kept in the custody of Haijima Industries' Power Development Facility.

A NICE GIRL

LOOKS AWESOME ON THE JOB

A TOUGH BUT WEIRD LADY

HANG IN THERE, ROOKIE!

TERRIFIED

STRICT DISCIPLINARIAN

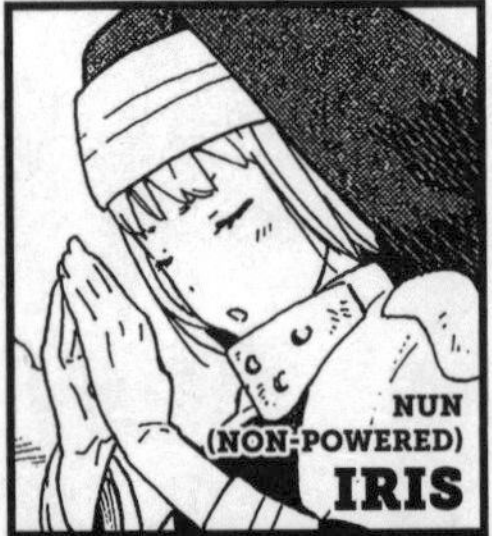

NUN (NON-POWERED)

IRIS

A sister of the Holy Sol Temple, her prayers are an indispensable part of extinguishing Infernals. Personality-wise, she is no less than an angel. Her boobs are big. Very big. She demonstrated incredible resilience in facing the Infernal hordes.

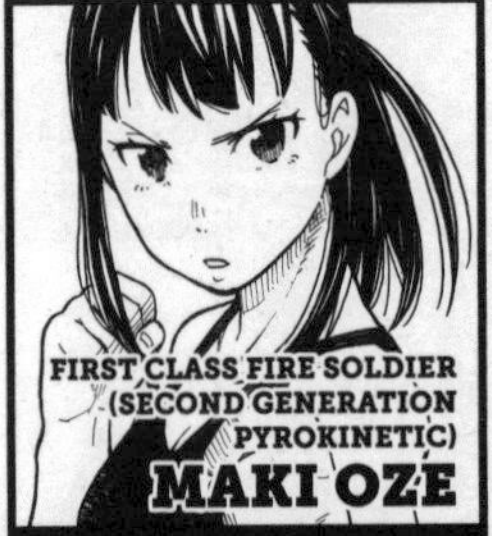

FIRST CLASS FIRE SOLDIER (SECOND GENERATION PYROKINETIC)

MAKI OZE

A former member of the military, she is an excellent fighter who controls fire. She's a cool lady, but is mad about love stories, and her beauty is overshadowed by her "head full of flowers and wedding bells." She's friendly, but goes berserk when anyone comments on her muscles. Her compatibility with Vulcan's invention, the Tekkyō, is superb.

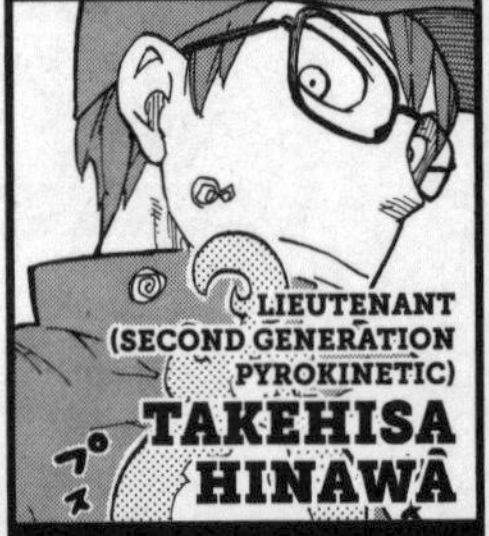

LIEUTENANT (SECOND GENERATION PYROKINETIC)

TAKEHISA HINAWA

A dry, unemotional ex-military man, whose stern discipline is feared among the new recruits. He helped Ōbi to found Company 8. He never allows the soldiers to play with fire. The gun he uses is a cherished memento from his friend who became an Infernal.

THE GIRLS' CLUB

RESPECTS

FOLLOWERS OF THE EVANGELIST

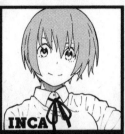

INCA

The Fifth Pillar, who gained her Adolla Burst powers in the Great Fire, which sparked her ability to predict what a fire will do. She joined the Evangelist out of her hatred of boredom.

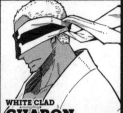

WHITE CLAD CHARON

A talkative man who specializes in question barrages. He boasts explosive offensive power and overwhelming endurance that renders Shinra's attacks virtually useless.

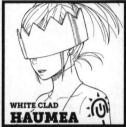

WHITE CLAD HAUMEA

One of the Evangelist's white-clad combatants. She is a troublesome opponent who can control others with her mind-jacking powers She has a foul mouth.

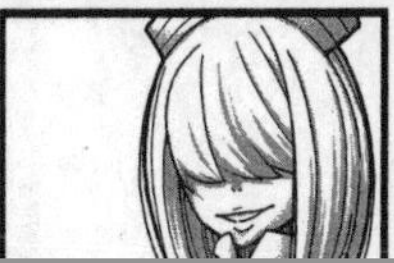

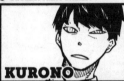

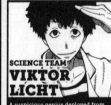

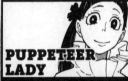

PUPPETEER LADY

The woman pulling the Dominions' strings, she rules over and disciplines children who don't yet know how to use their powers.

HAIJIMA INDUSTRIES POWER DEVELOPMENT FACILITY

KURONO

The man known as Death, he enjoys picking on those weaker than himself. He agreed to join Shinra and his company in their mission to retrieve Nataku.

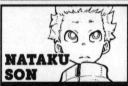

NATAKU SON

A boy whose powers were ignited by Rekka Hoshimiya's bug. He awakens as the Sixth Pillar, but gets absorbed into the Great Fiery Infernal.

SCIENCE TEAM VIKTOR LICHT

A suspicious genius deployed from Haijima Industries to fill the vacancy in Company 8's science department. Confesses to being a Haijima spy.

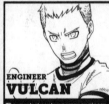

ENGINEER VULCAN

The greatest contemporary engineer, renowned as the God of Fire and the Forge. The weapons he created have increased Company 8's powers immensely.

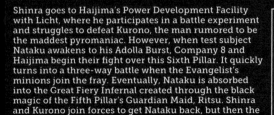

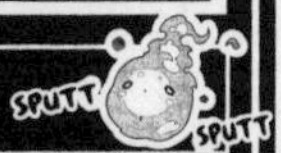

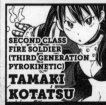

SECOND CLASS FIRE SOLDIER (THIRD GENERATION PYROKINETIC) TAMAKI KOTATSU

A rookie from Company 1 currently in Company 8's care. Although she has a "lucky lecher lure" condition, she nevertheless has a pure heart.

SUMMARY...

SPUTT
SPUTT

Shinra goes to Haijima's Power Development Facility with Licht, where he participates in a battle experiment and struggles to defeat Kurono, the man rumored to be the maddest pyromaniac. However, when test subject Nataku awakens to his Adolla Burst, Company 8 and Haijima begin their fight over this Sixth Pillar. It quickly turns into a three-way battle when the Evangelist's minions join the fray. Eventually, Nataku is absorbed into the Great Fiery Infernal created through the black magic of the Fifth Pillar's Guardian Maid, Ritsu. Shinra and Kurono join forces to get Nataku back, but then the unthinkable happens...

FIRE FORCE 17
CONTENTS

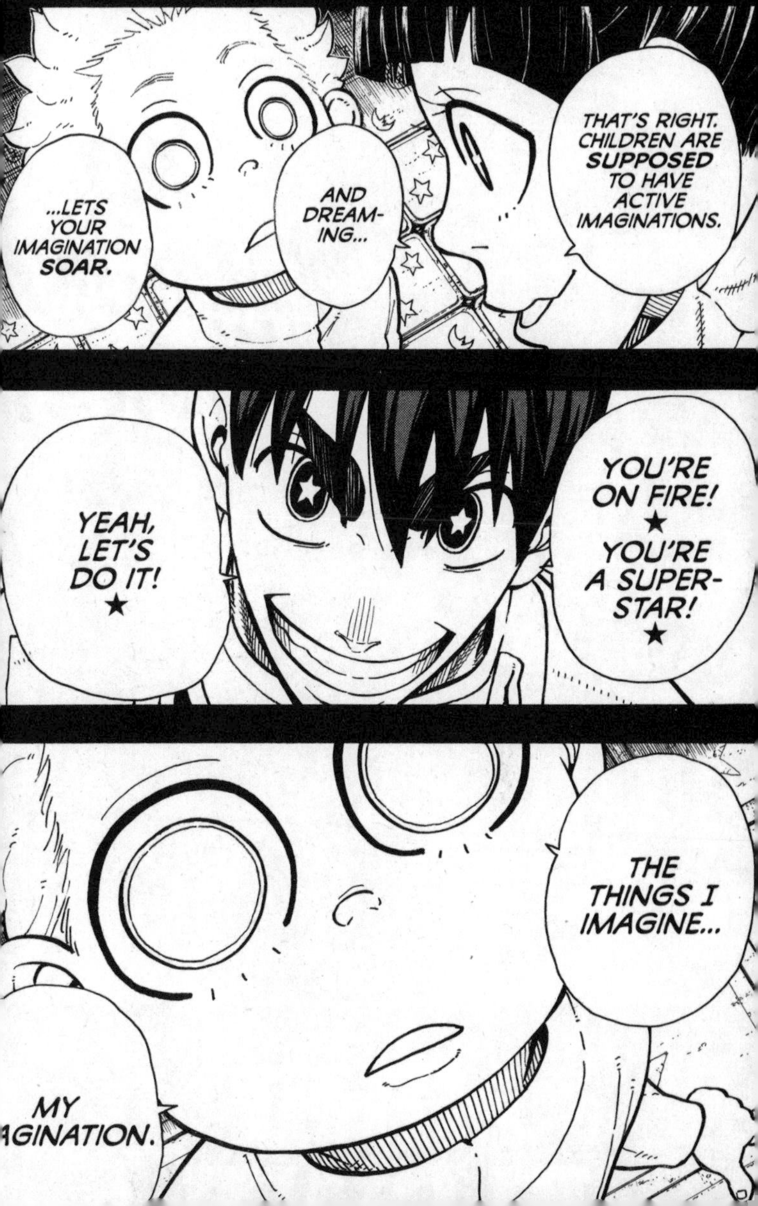
THAT'S RIGHT. CHILDREN ARE SUPPOSED TO HAVE ACTIVE IMAGINATIONS.
AND DREAMING...
...LETS YOUR IMAGINATION SOAR.
YOU'RE ON FIRE! ★ YOU'RE A SUPERSTAR! ★
YEAH, LET'S DO IT! ★
THE THINGS I IMAGINE...
MY AGINATION.

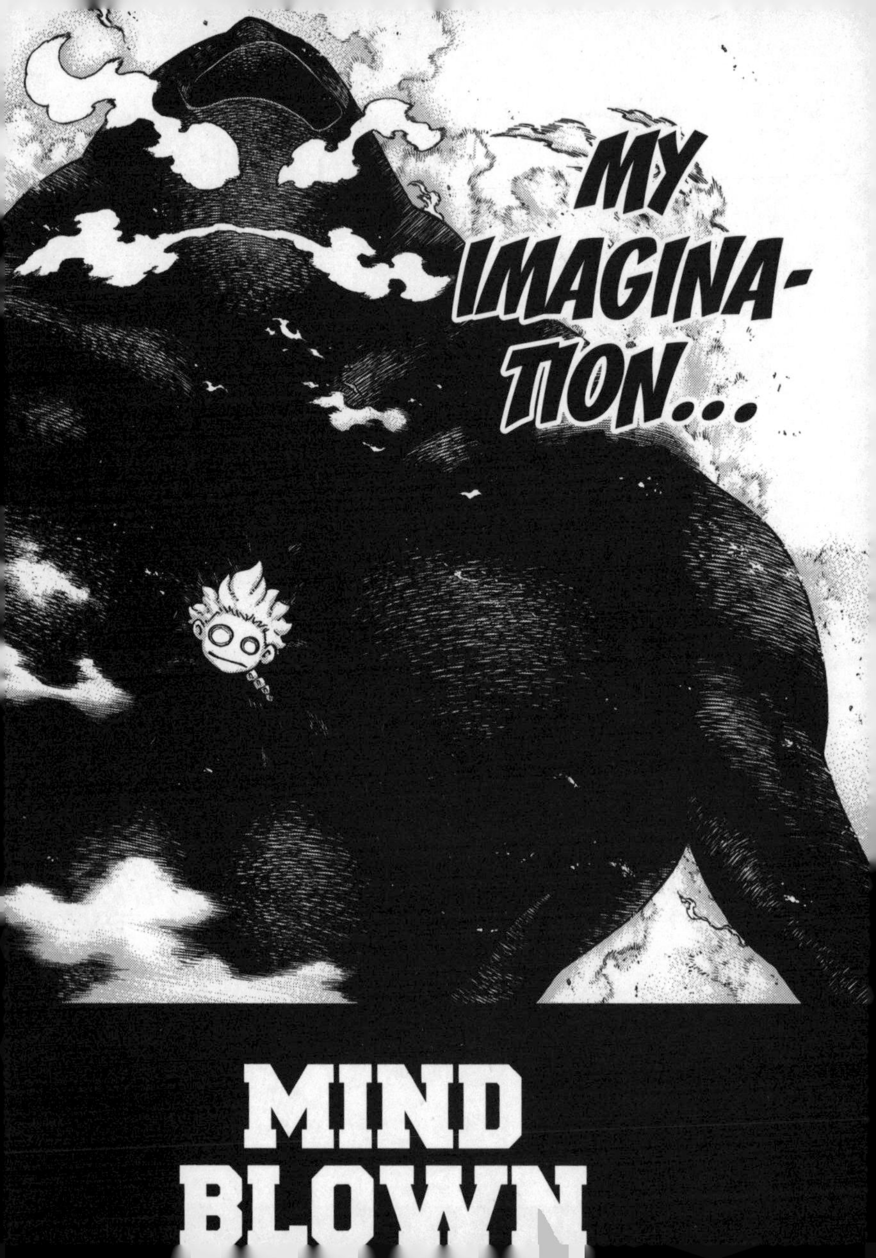
MY IMAGINA-TION...
MIND BLOWN

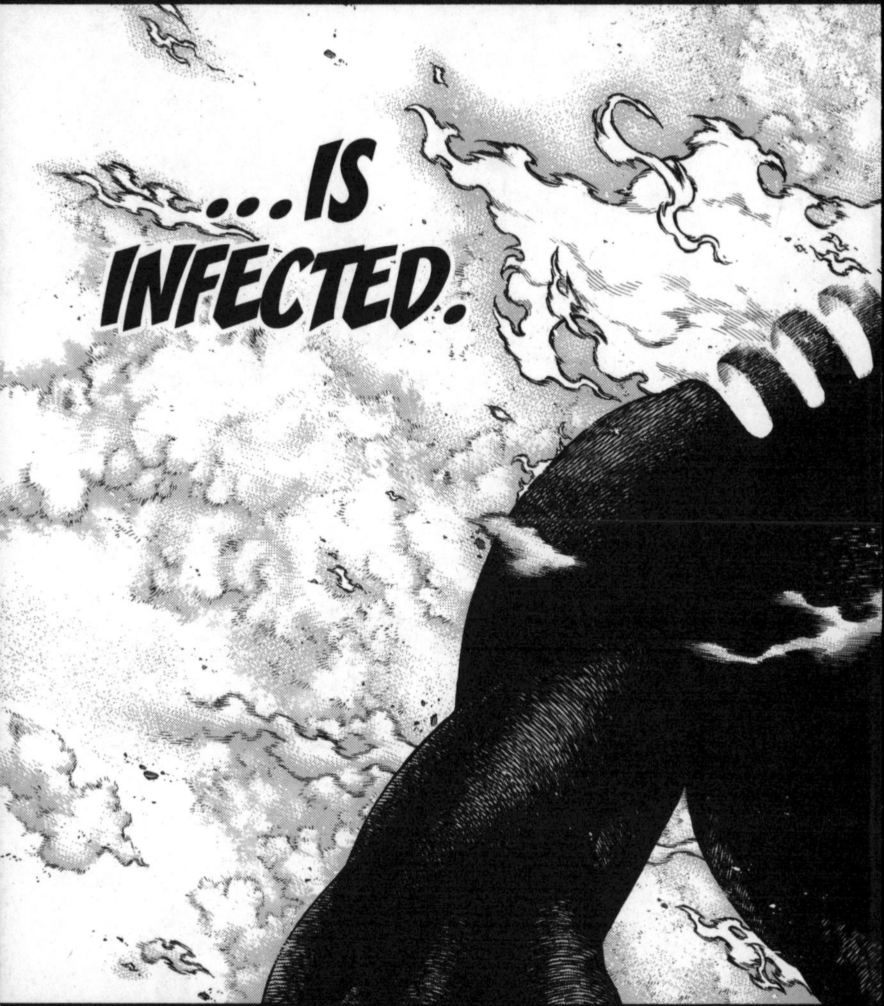

CHAPTER CXLII:

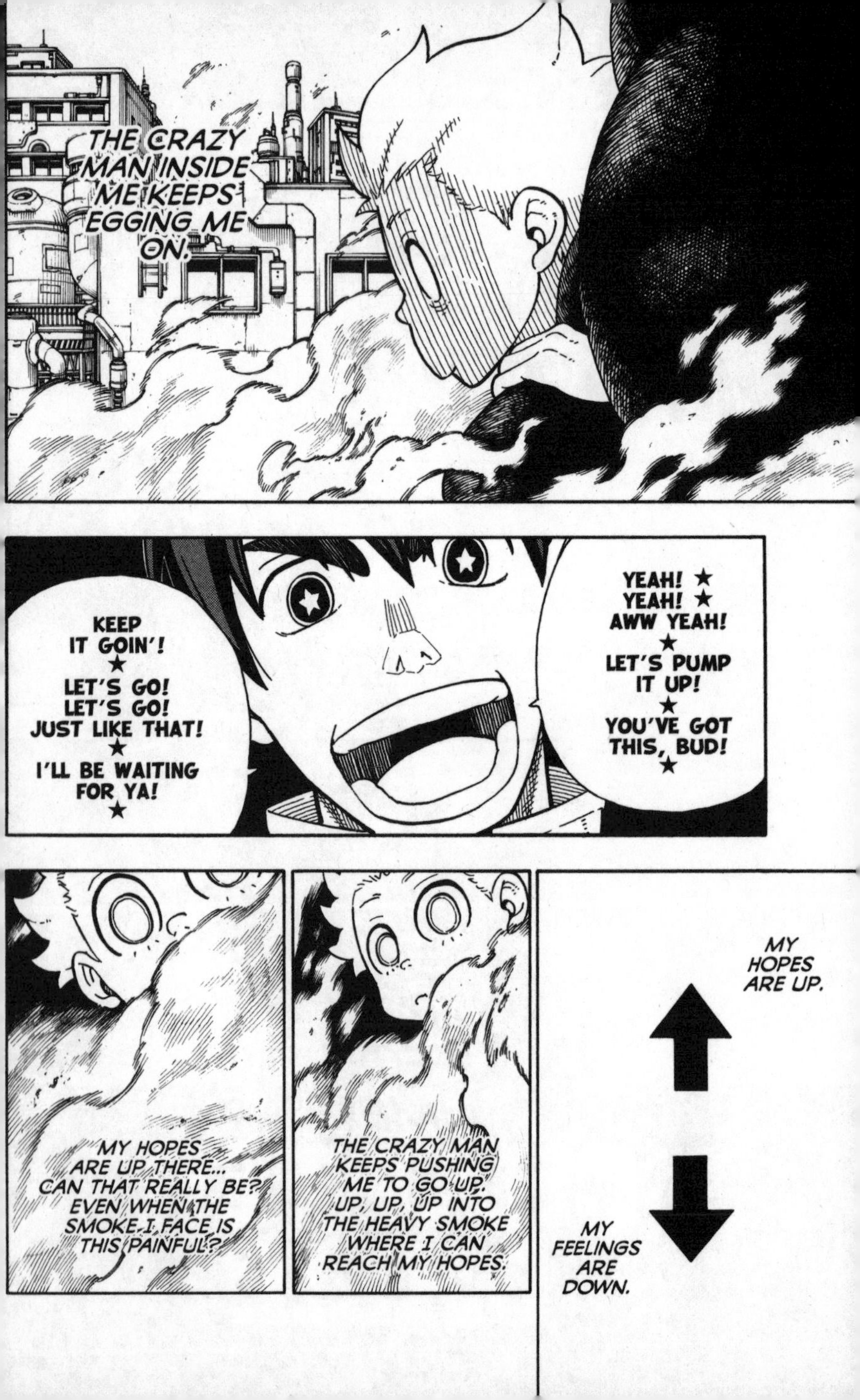
THE CRAZY MAN INSIDE ME KEEPS EGGING ME ON.
YEAH! ★ YEAH! ★ AWW YEAH! ★ LET'S PUMP IT UP! ★ YOU'VE GOT THIS, BUD! ★
KEEP IT GOIN'! ★ LET'S GO! LET'S GO! JUST LIKE THAT! ★ I'LL BE WAITING FOR YA! ★
MY HOPES ARE UP.
MY FEELINGS ARE DOWN.
THE CRAZY MAN KEEPS PUSHING ME TO GO UP. UP, UP, UP INTO THE HEAVY SMOKE WHERE I CAN REACH MY HOPES.
MY HOPES ARE UP THERE... CAN THAT REALLY BE? EVEN WHEN THE SMOKE I FACE IS THIS PAINFUL?

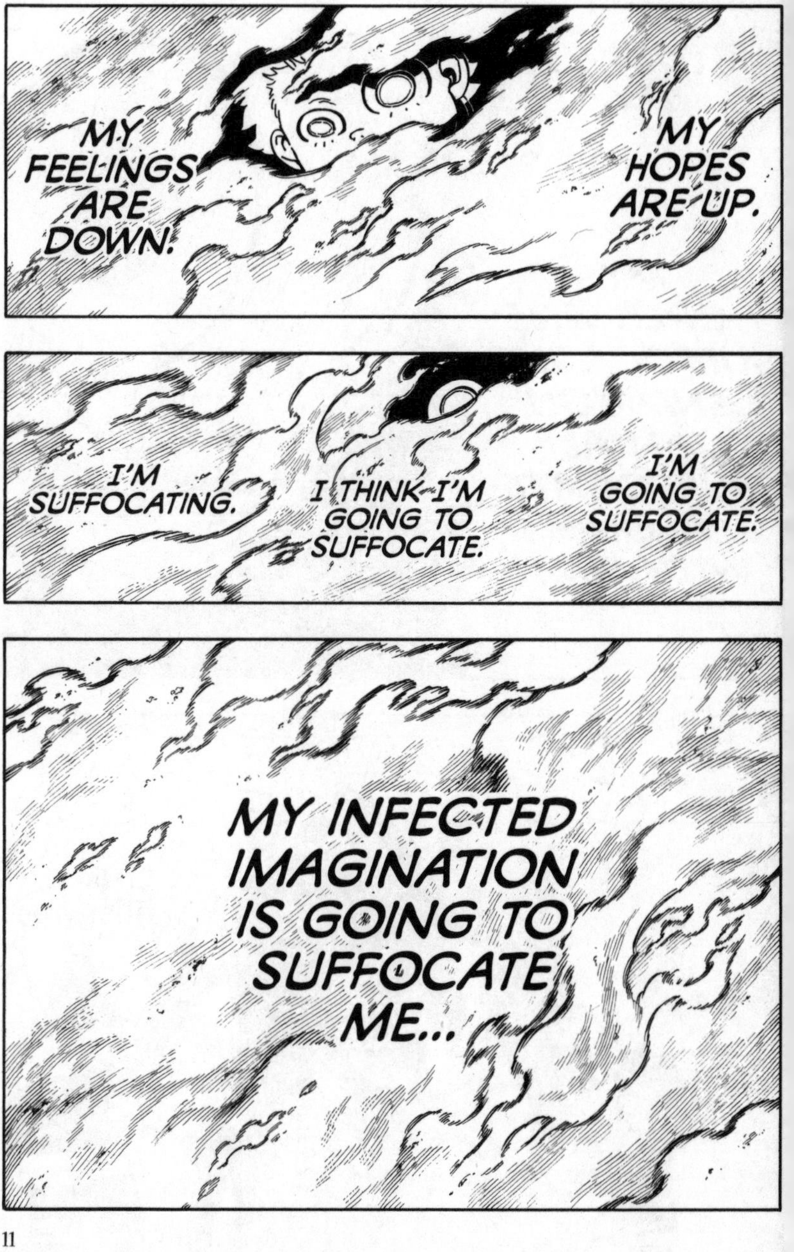
MY HOPES ARE UP.
MY FEELINGS ARE DOWN.
I'M GOING TO SUFFOCATE.
I THINK I'M GOING TO SUFFOCATE.
I'M SUFFOCATING.
MY INFECTED IMAGINATION IS GOING TO SUFFOCATE ME...

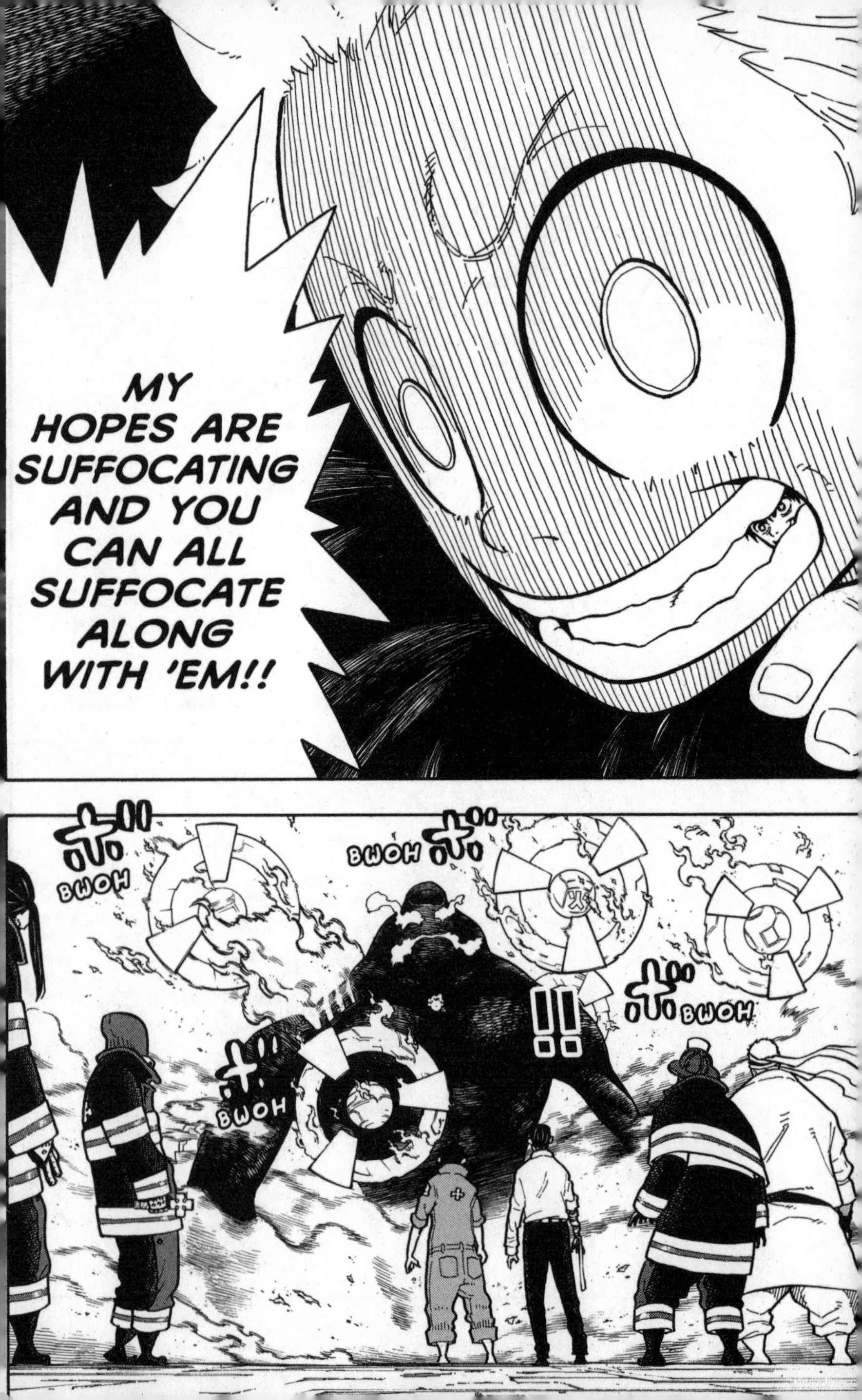
MY HOPES ARE SUFFOCATING AND YOU CAN ALL SUFFOCATE ALONG WITH 'EM!!
BWOH
BWOH
BWOH
BWOH

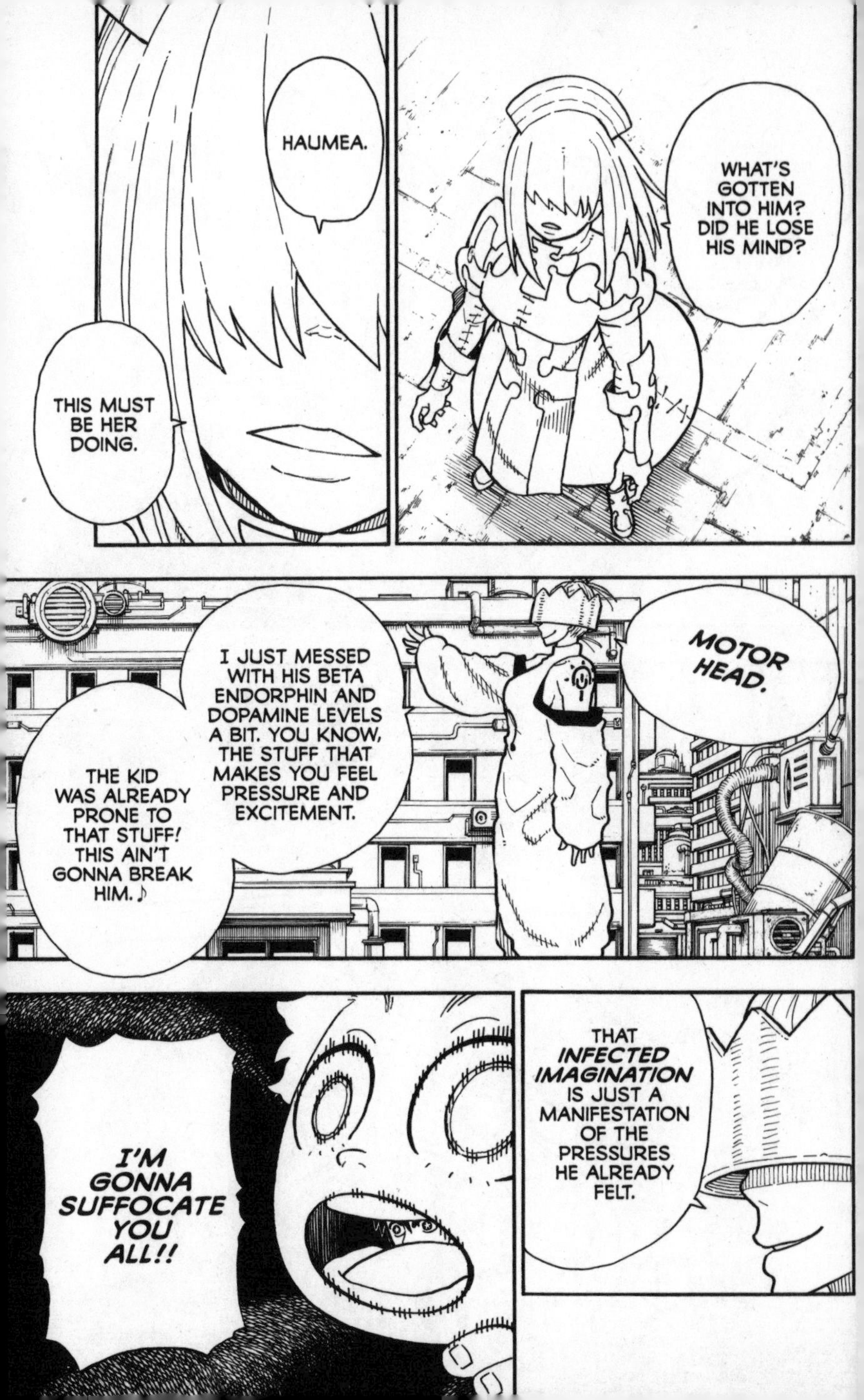
WHAT'S GOTTEN INTO HIM? DID HE LOSE HIS MIND?
HAUMEA.
THIS MUST BE HER DOING.
MOTOR HEAD.
I JUST MESSED WITH HIS BETA ENDORPHIN AND DOPAMINE LEVELS A BIT. YOU KNOW, THE STUFF THAT MAKES YOU FEEL PRESSURE AND EXCITEMENT.
THE KID WAS ALREADY PRONE TO THAT STUFF! THIS AIN'T GONNA BREAK HIM.♪
THAT INFECTED IMAGINATION IS JUST A MANIFESTATION OF THE PRESSURES HE ALREADY FELT.
I'M GONNA SUFFOCATE YOU ALL!!

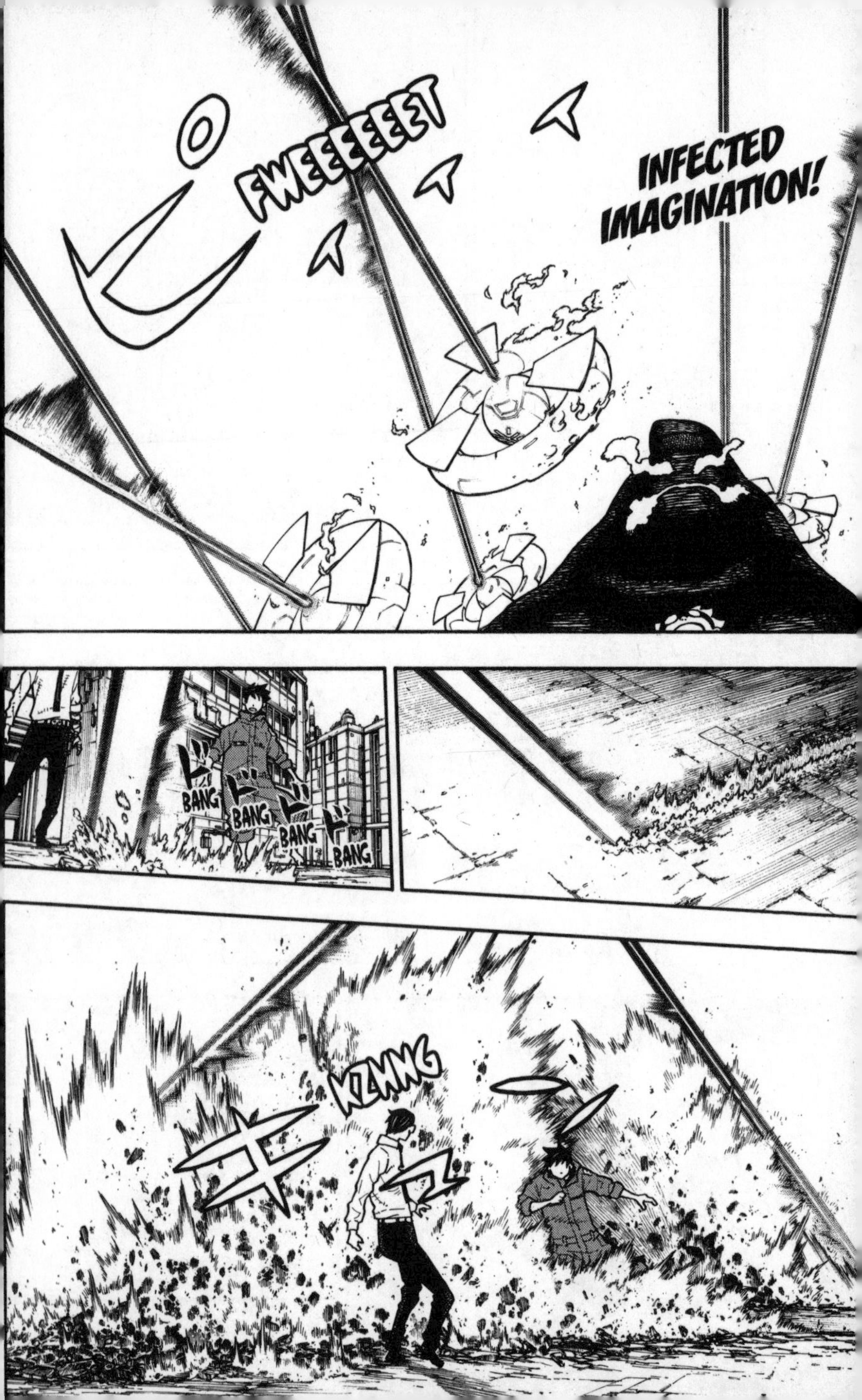
INFECTED IMAGINATION!
FWEEEEEET
BANG
BANG
BANG
BANG
KLANG

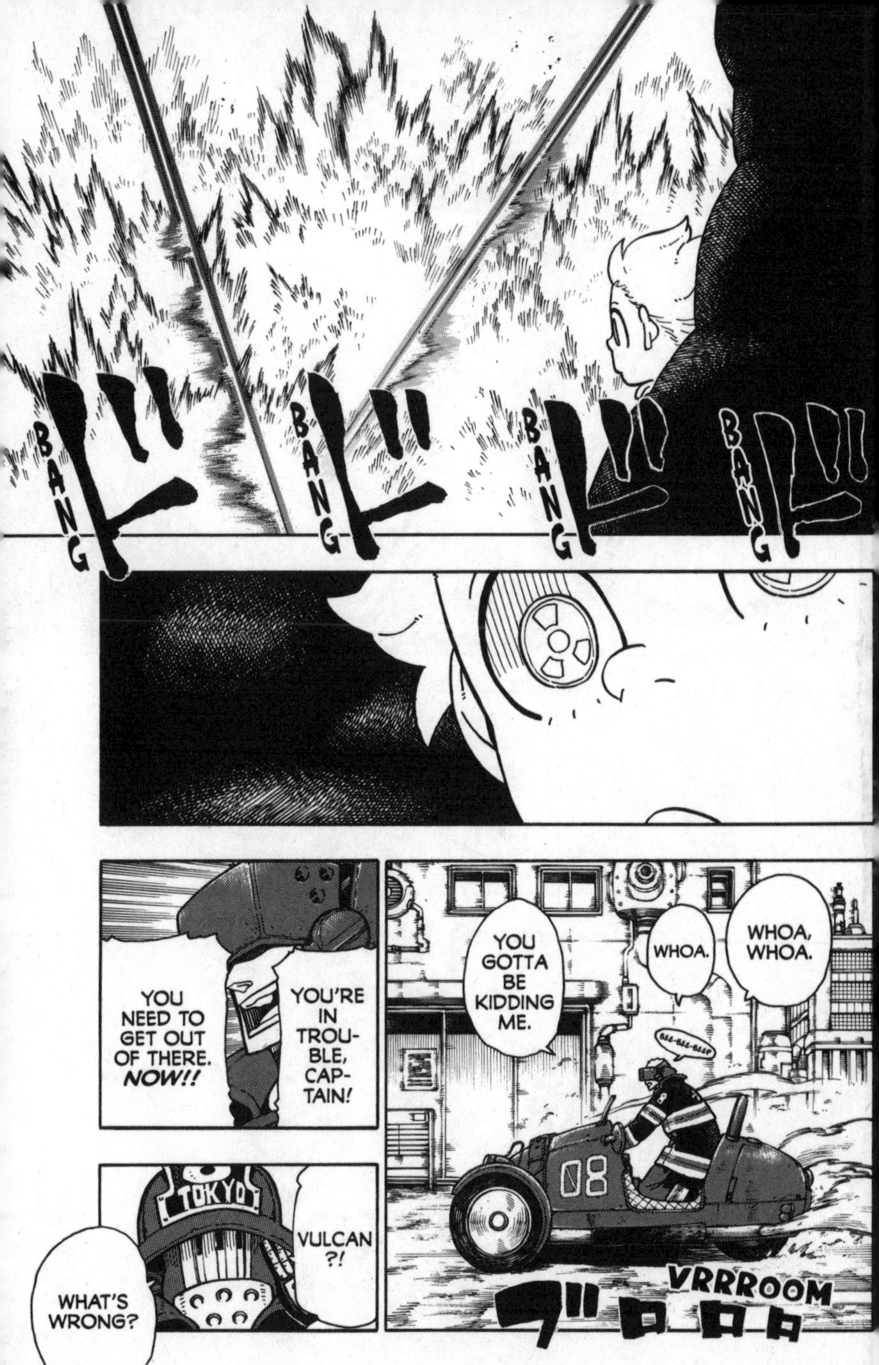
BANG
BANG
BANG
BANG
WHOA, WHOA.
WHOA.
YOU GOTTA BE KIDDING ME.
BEE-BEE-BEEP
VRRROOM
YOU'RE IN TROUBLE, CAPTAIN!
YOU NEED TO GET OUT OF THERE. *NOW!!*
VULCAN?!
WHAT'S WRONG?

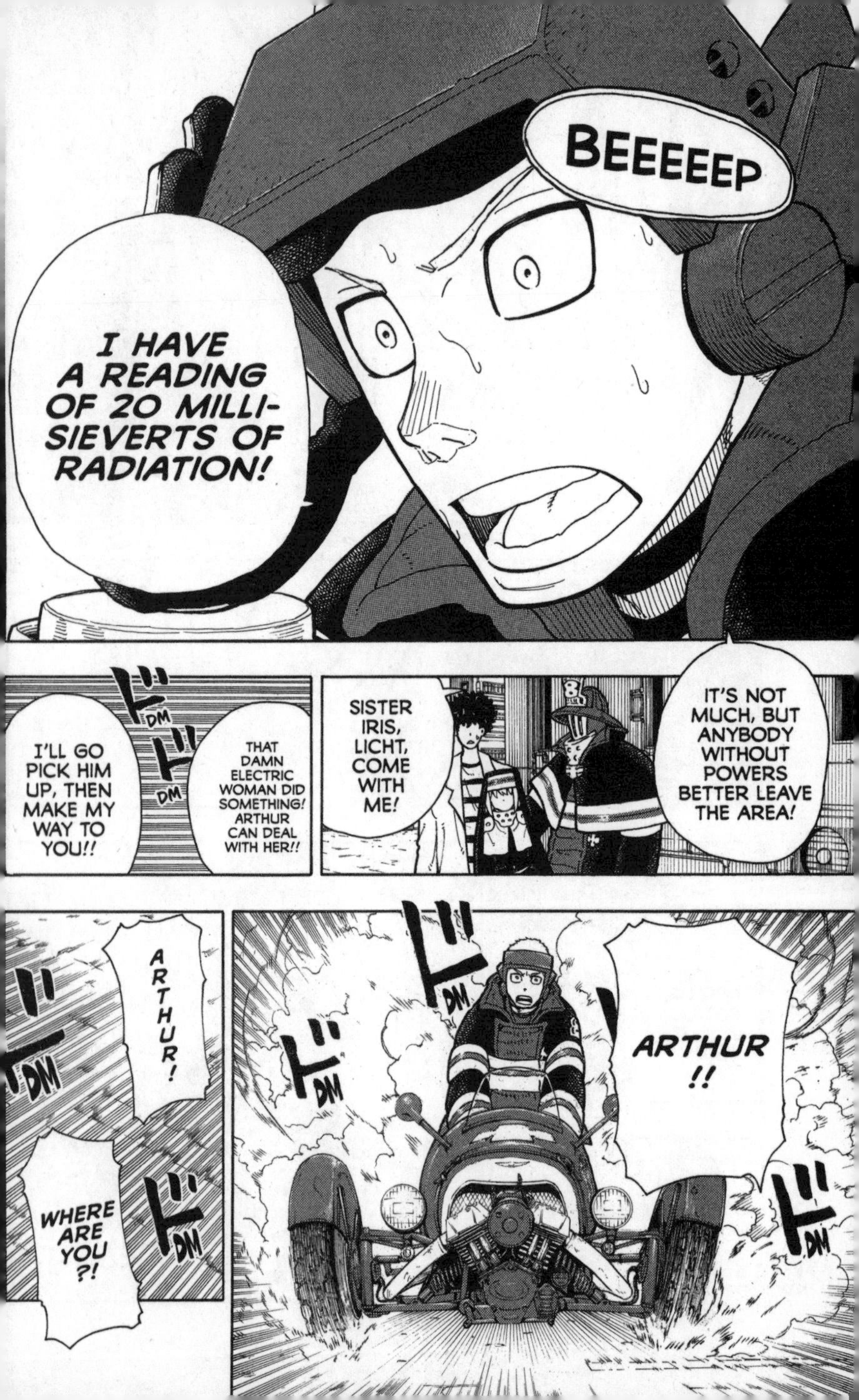
BEEEEEP
I HAVE A READING OF 20 MILLI-SIEVERTS OF RADIATION!
IT'S NOT MUCH, BUT ANYBODY WITHOUT POWERS BETTER LEAVE THE AREA!
SISTER IRIS, LICHT, COME WITH ME!
THAT DAMN ELECTRIC WOMAN DID SOMETHING! ARTHUR CAN DEAL WITH HER!!
ドDM ドDM
I'LL GO PICK HIM UP, THEN MAKE MY WAY TO YOU!!
ドDM ドDM ドDM
ARTHUR!!
ARTHUR!
ドDM ドDM
WHERE ARE YOU?!

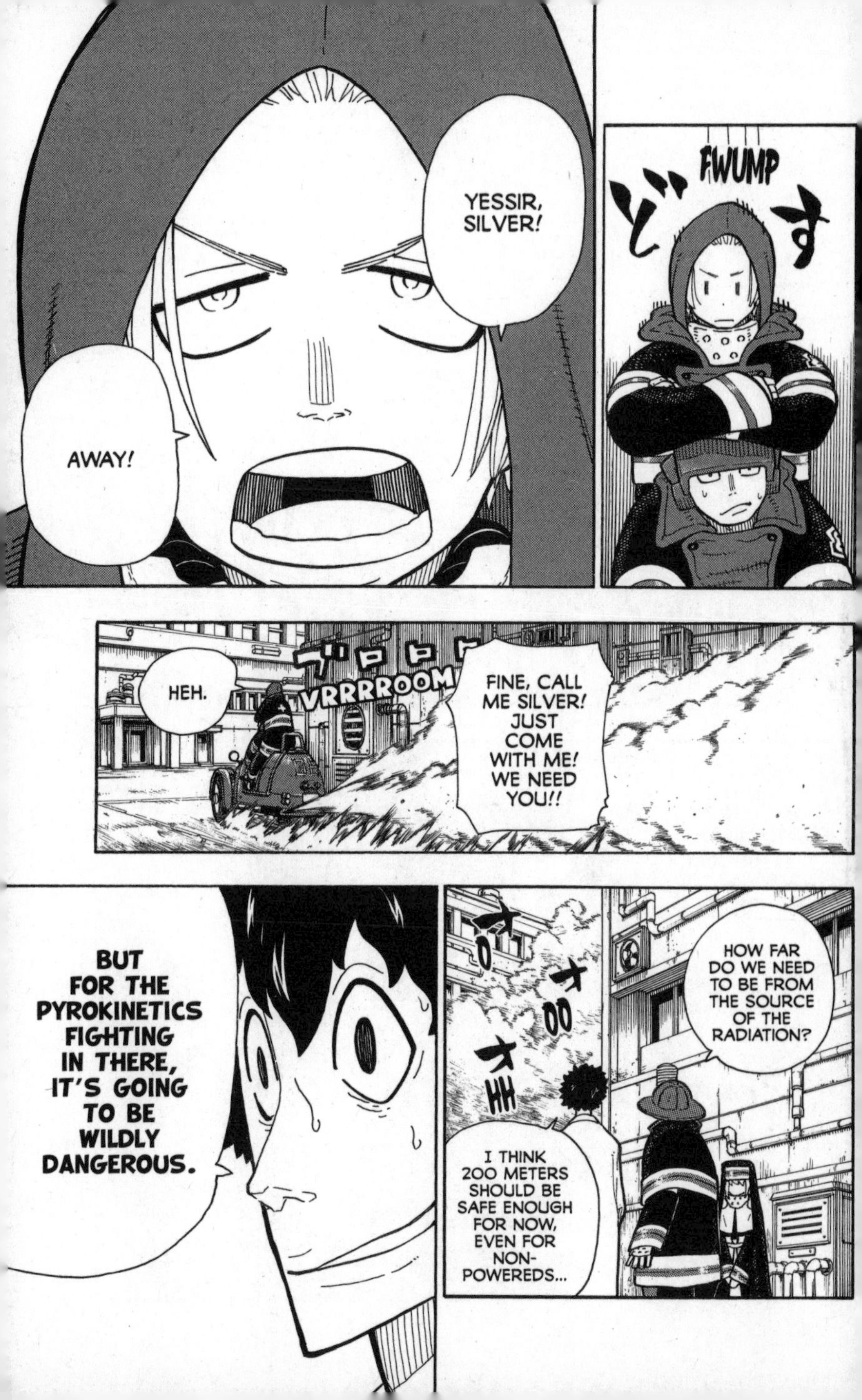
FWUMP
YESSIR, SILVER!
AWAY!
FINE, CALL ME SILVER! JUST COME WITH ME! WE NEED YOU!!
VRRRROOM
HEH.
HOW FAR DO WE NEED TO BE FROM THE SOURCE OF THE RADIATION?
I THINK 200 METERS SHOULD BE SAFE ENOUGH FOR NOW, EVEN FOR NON-POWEREDS...
BUT FOR THE PYROKINETICS FIGHTING IN THERE, IT'S GOING TO BE WILDLY DANGEROUS.

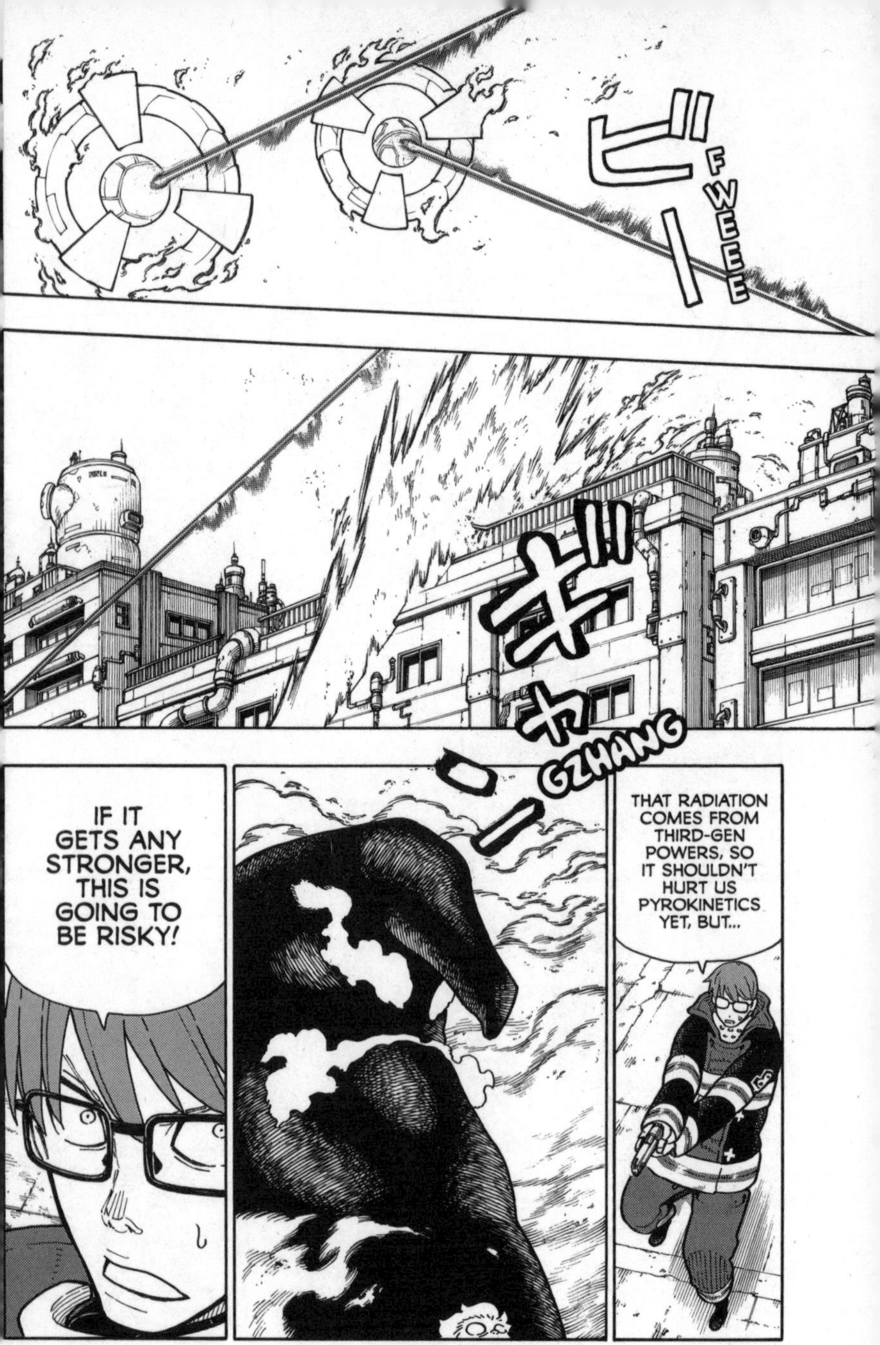
ビー
FWEEE
ギャーン
GZHANG
THAT RADIATION COMES FROM THIRD-GEN POWERS, SO IT SHOULDN'T HURT US PYROKINETICS YET, BUT...
IF IT GETS ANY STRONGER, THIS IS GOING TO BE RISKY!

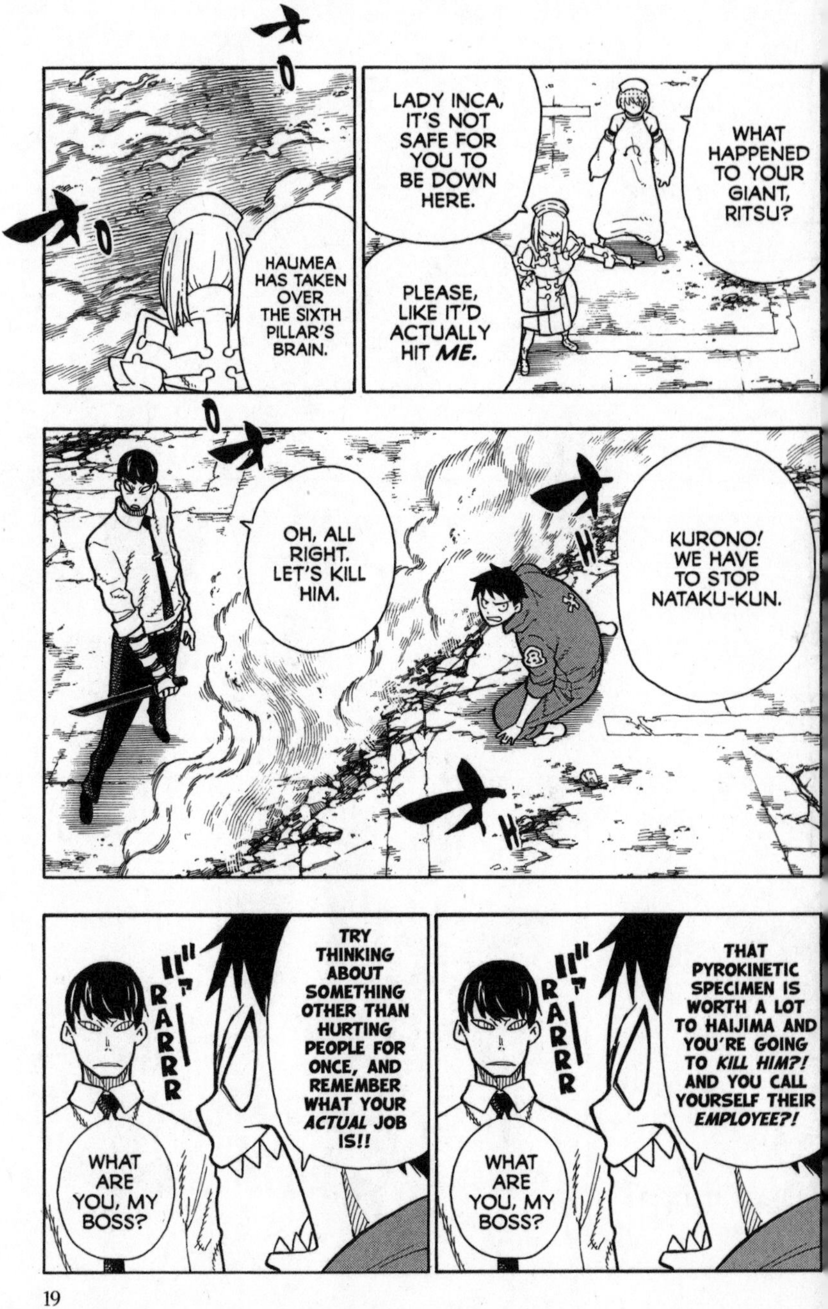
WHAT HAPPENED TO YOUR GIANT, RITSU?
LADY INCA, IT'S NOT SAFE FOR YOU TO BE DOWN HERE.
PLEASE, LIKE IT'D ACTUALLY HIT *ME.*
HAUMEA HAS TAKEN OVER THE SIXTH PILLAR'S BRAIN.
KURONO! WE HAVE TO STOP NATAKU-KUN.
OH, ALL RIGHT. LET'S KILL HIM.
THAT PYROKINETIC SPECIMEN IS WORTH A LOT TO HAIJIMA AND YOU'RE GOING TO *KILL HIM?!* AND YOU CALL YOURSELF THEIR *EMPLOYEE?!*
RARRR
WHAT ARE YOU, MY BOSS?
TRY THINKING ABOUT SOMETHING OTHER THAN HURTING PEOPLE FOR ONCE, AND REMEMBER WHAT YOUR *ACTUAL* JOB IS!!
RARRR
WHAT ARE YOU, MY BOSS?

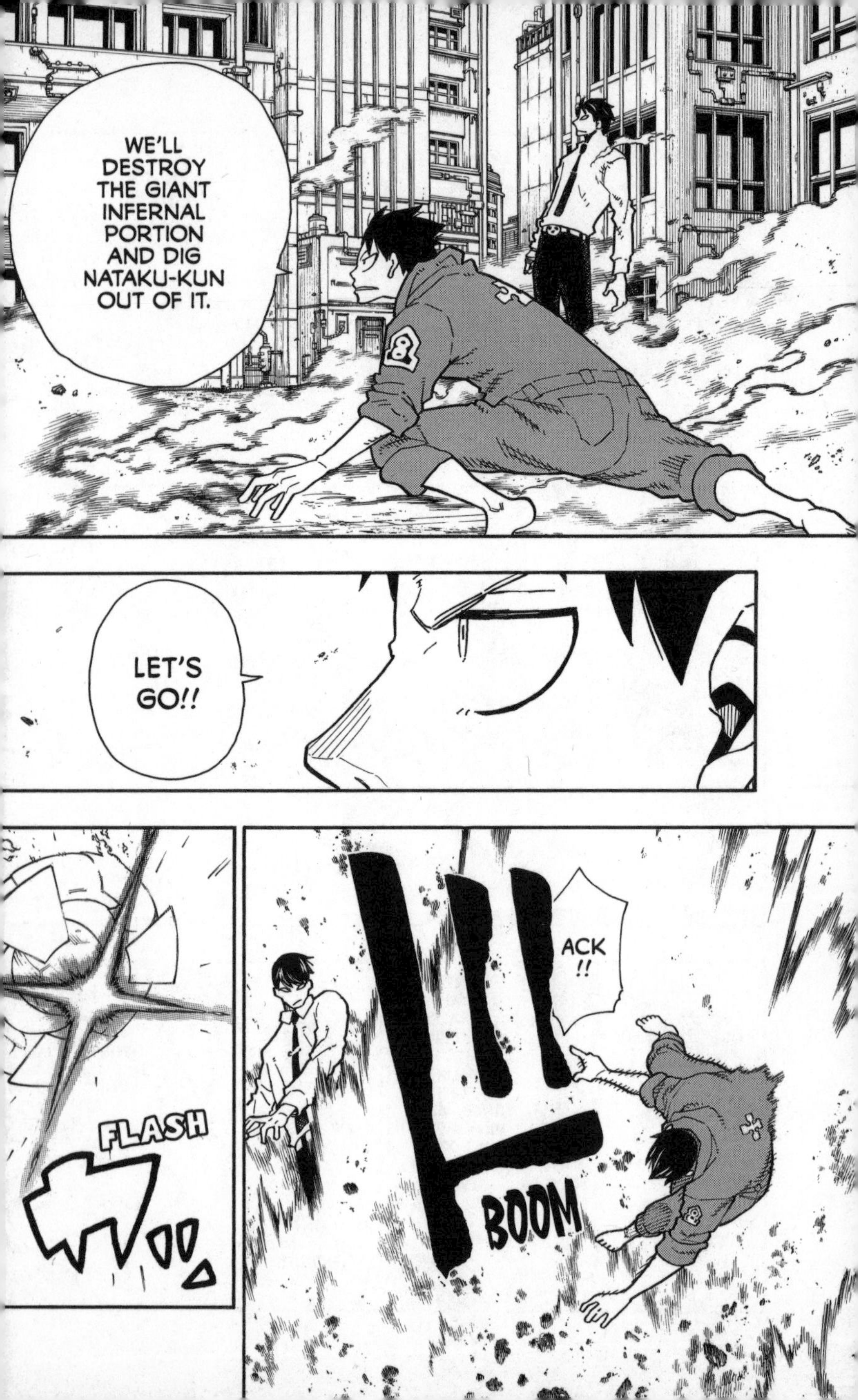
WE'LL DESTROY THE GIANT INFERNAL PORTION AND DIG NATAKU-KUN OUT OF IT.
LET'S GO!!
ACK !!
BOOM
FLASH

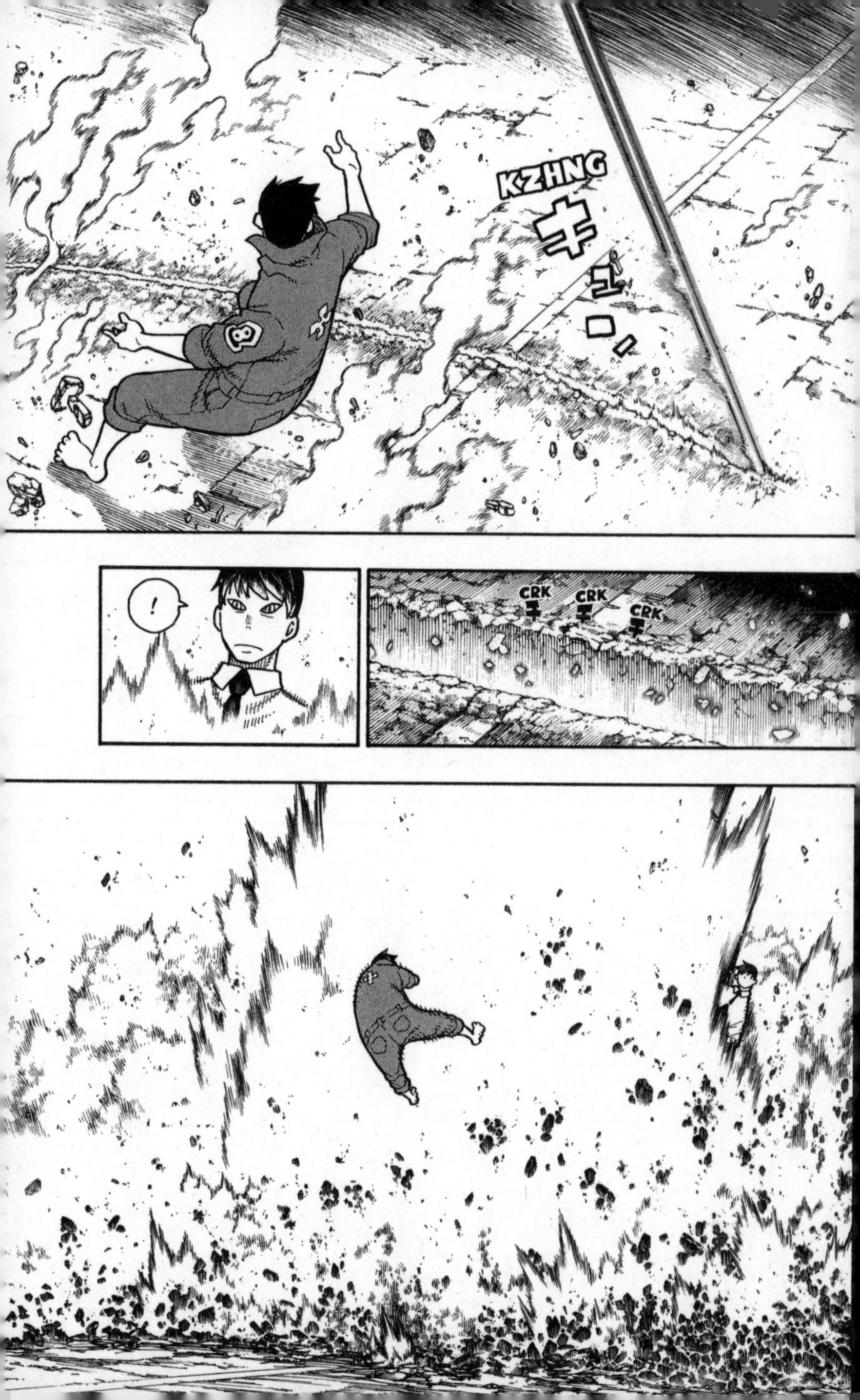

KZHNG
キュロー
CRK CRK CRK
!

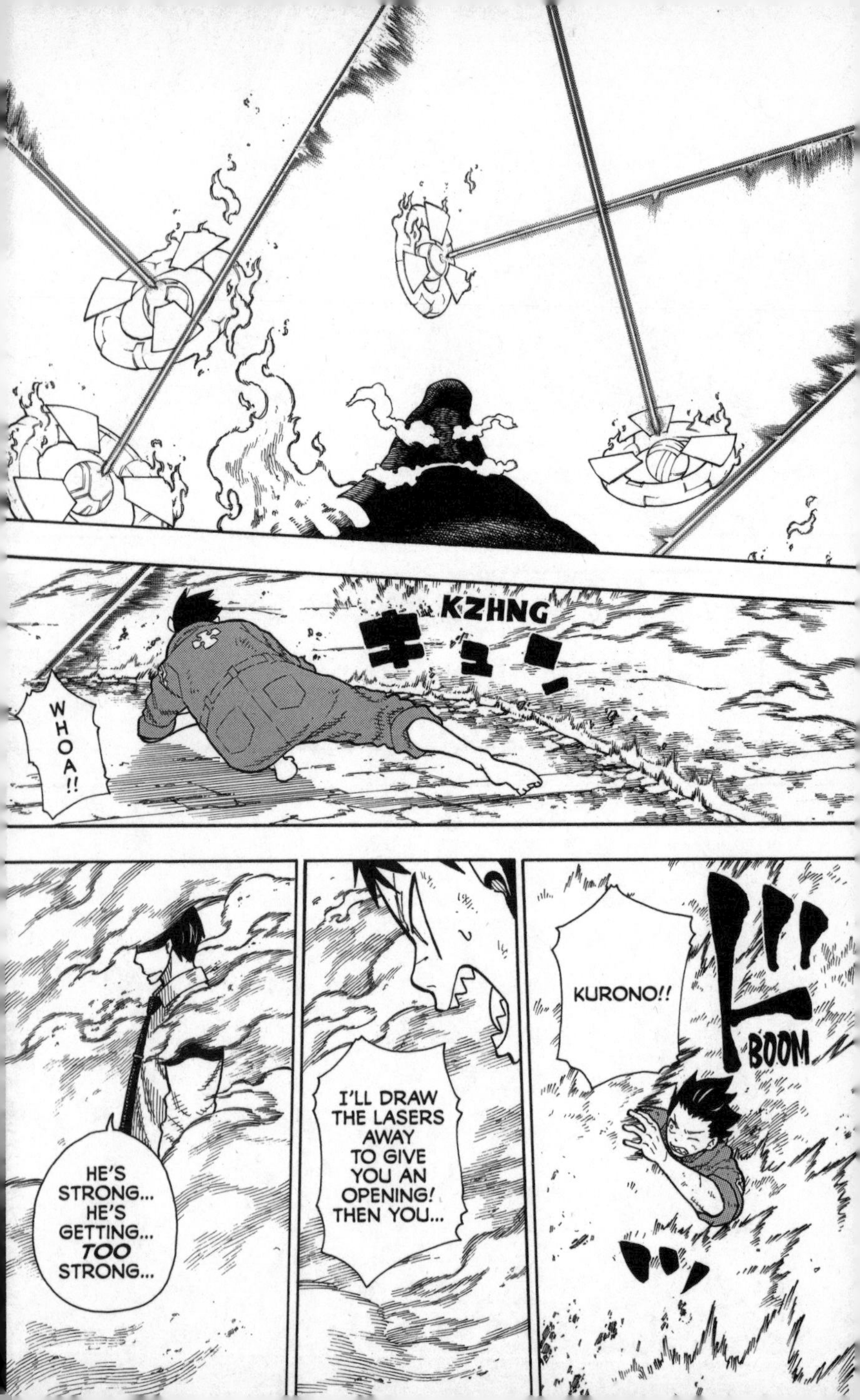
KZHNG
WHOA!!
KURONO!!
BOOM
I'LL DRAW THE LASERS AWAY TO GIVE YOU AN OPENING! THEN YOU...
HE'S STRONG... HE'S GETTING... *TOO* STRONG...

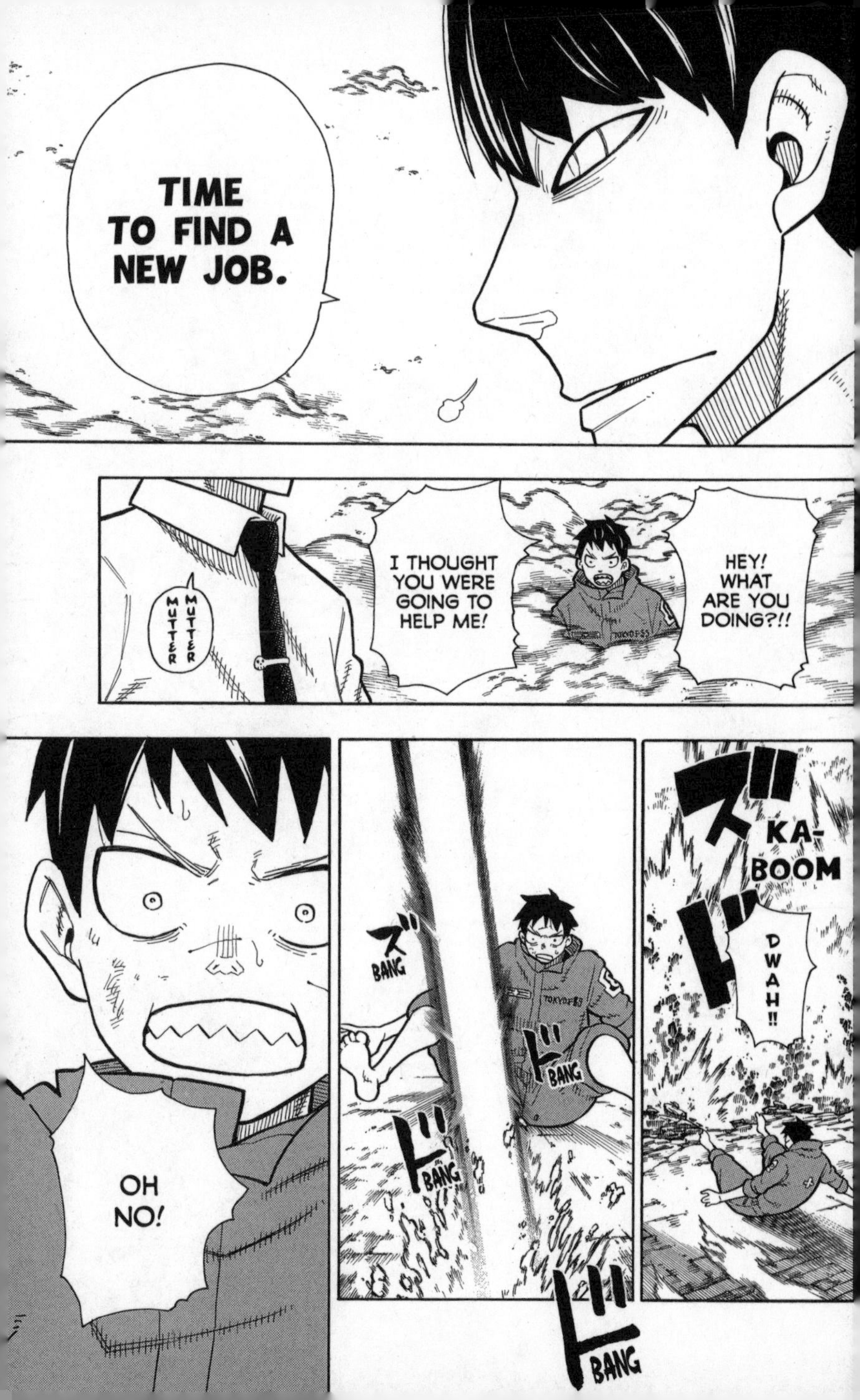
TIME TO FIND A NEW JOB.
HEY! WHAT ARE YOU DOING?!!
I THOUGHT YOU WERE GOING TO HELP ME!
MUTTER MUTTER
KA-BOOM
DWAH!!
BANG
BANG
BANG
BANG
OH NO!

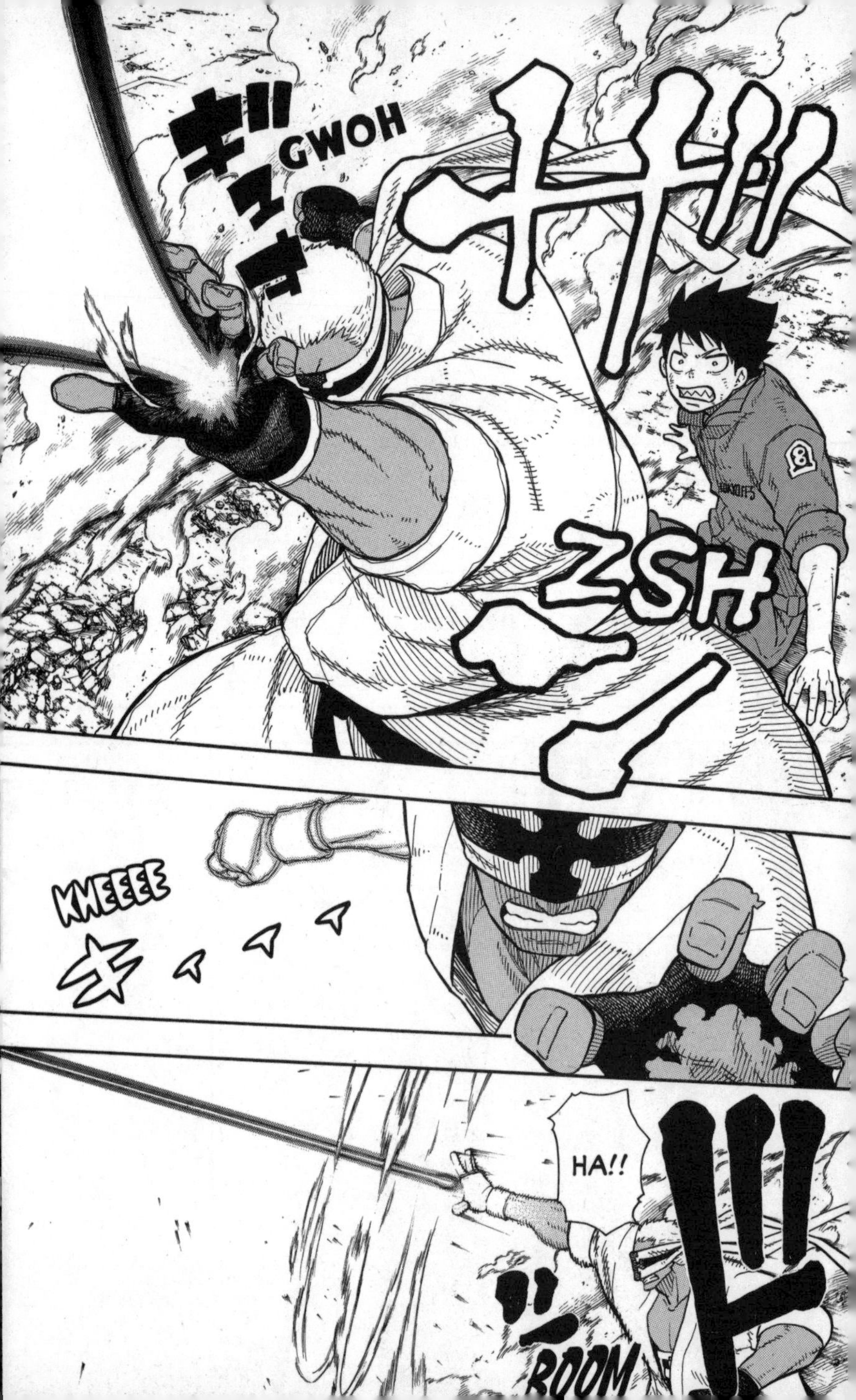
GWOH
ZSH
KHEEEE
HA!!
ROOM

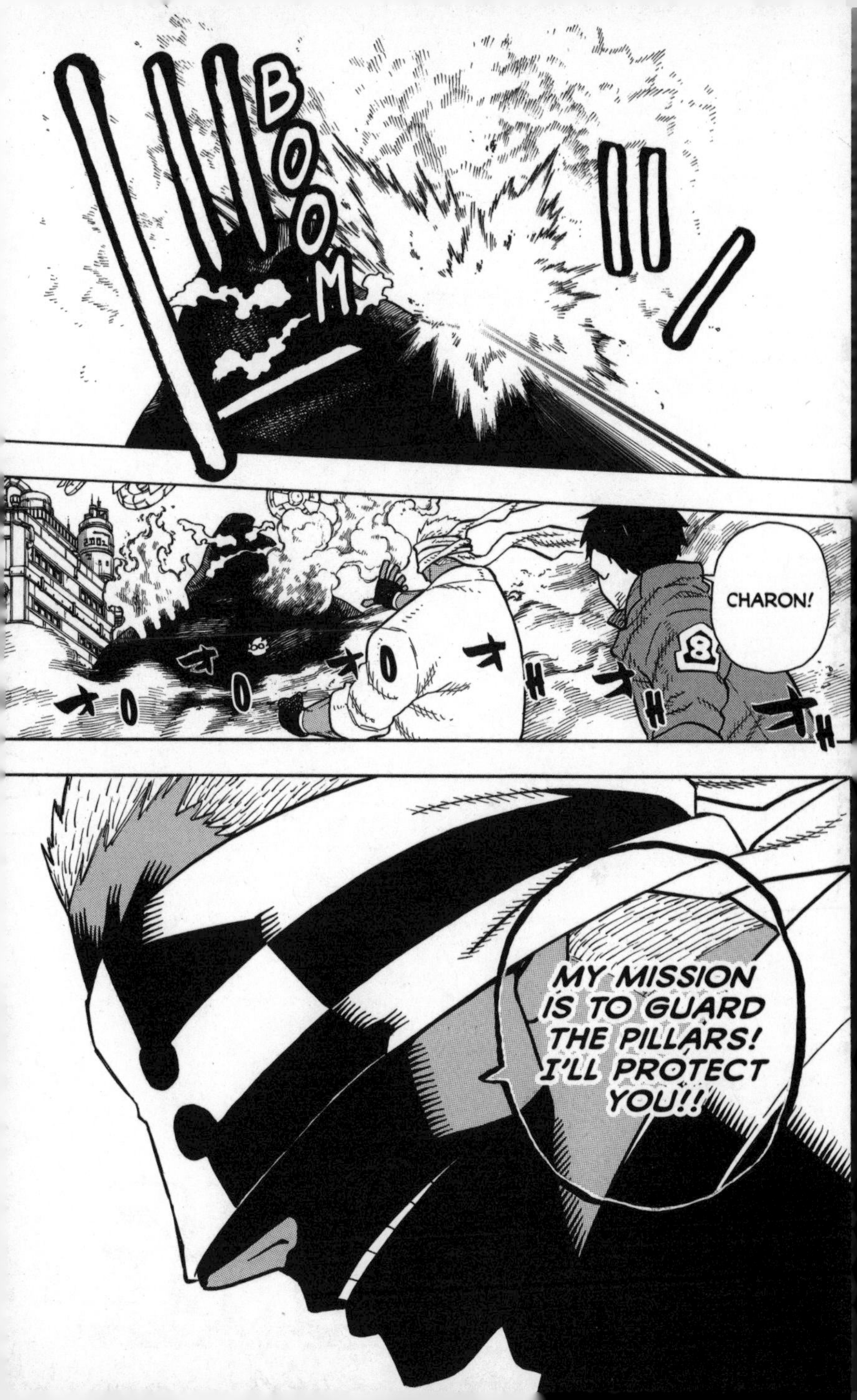
BOOM
CHARON!
MY MISSION IS TO GUARD THE PILLARS! I'LL PROTECT YOU!!

FIRE FORCE

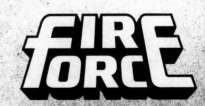

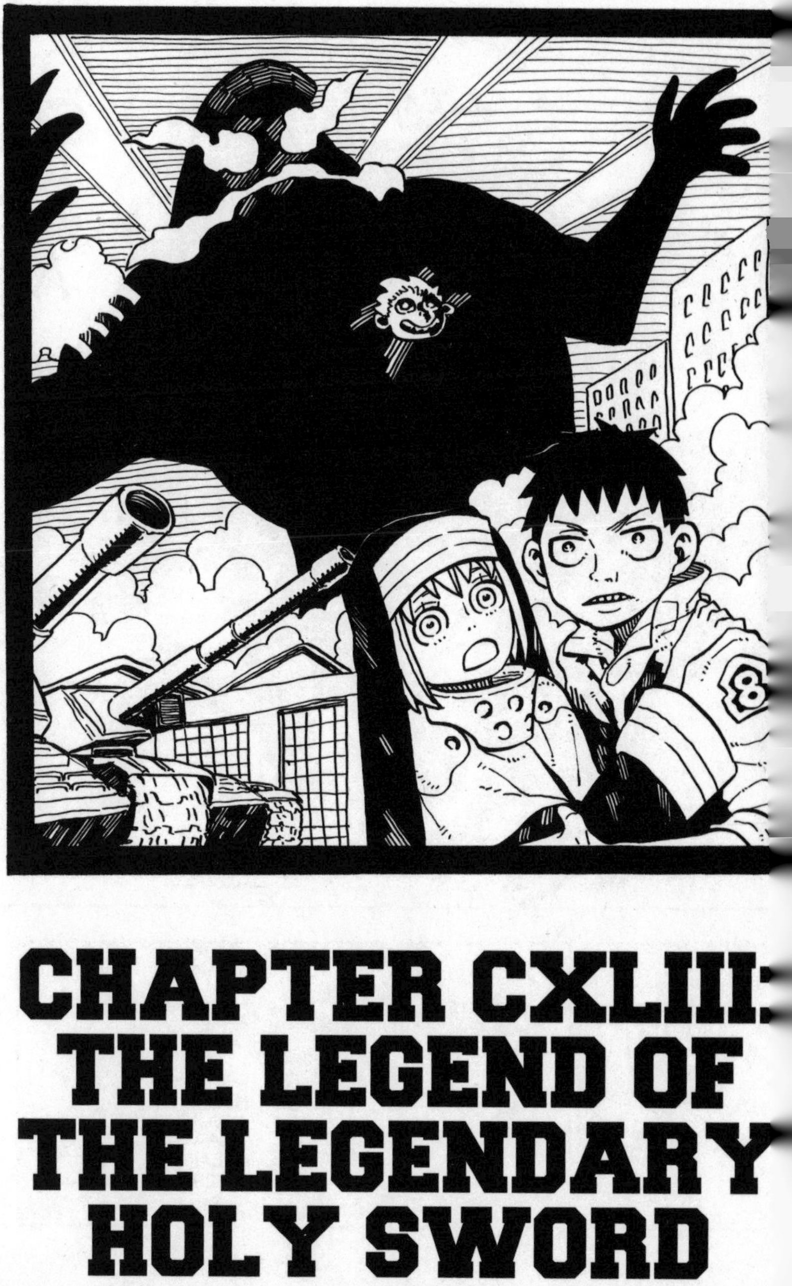

CHAPTER CXLIII: THE LEGEND OF THE LEGENDARY HOLY SWORD

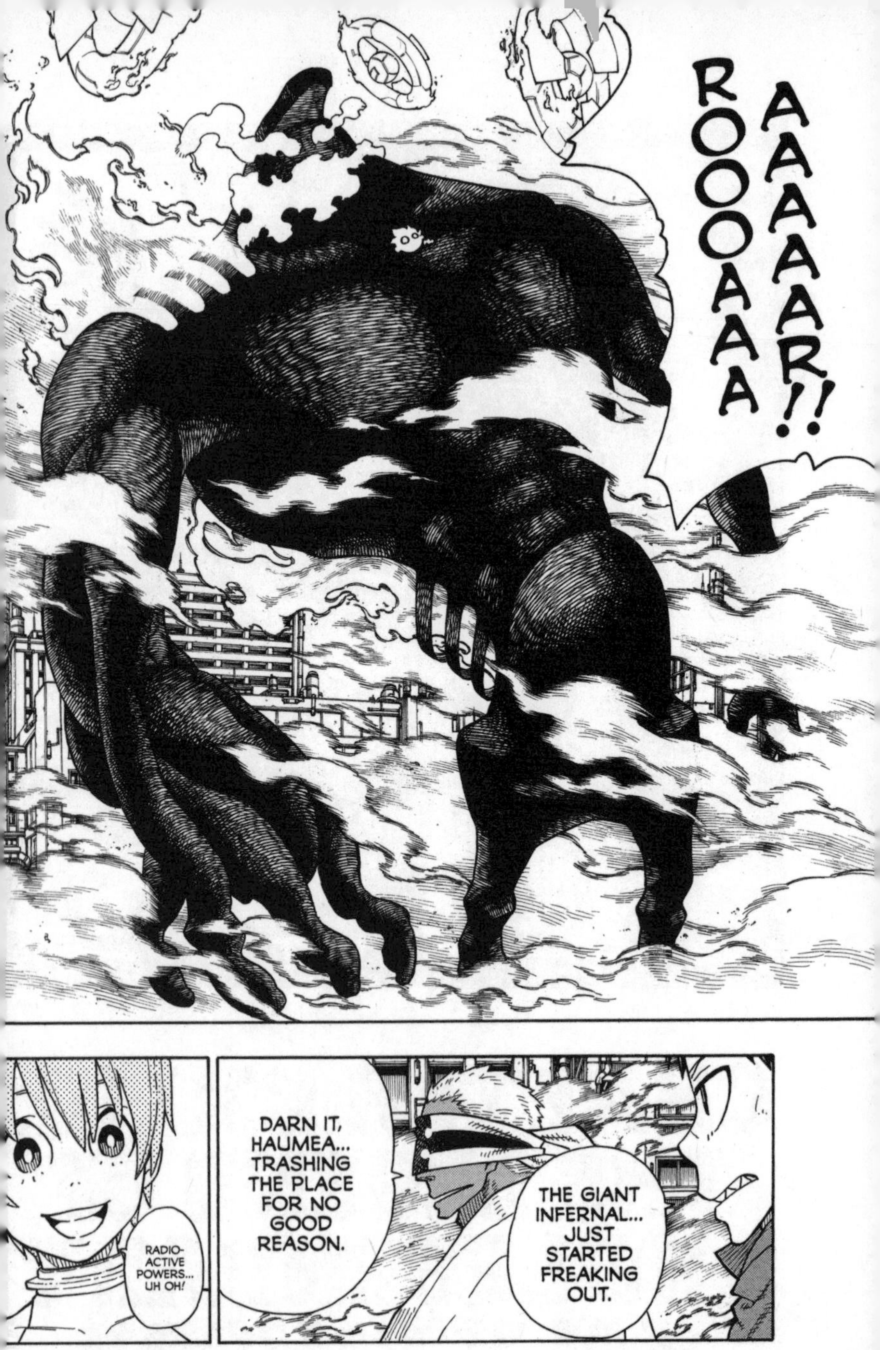
ROOOAAA AAAAAR!!
THE GIANT INFERNAL... JUST STARTED FREAKING OUT.
DARN IT, HAUMEA... TRASHING THE PLACE FOR NO GOOD REASON.
RADIO-ACTIVE POWERS... UH OH!

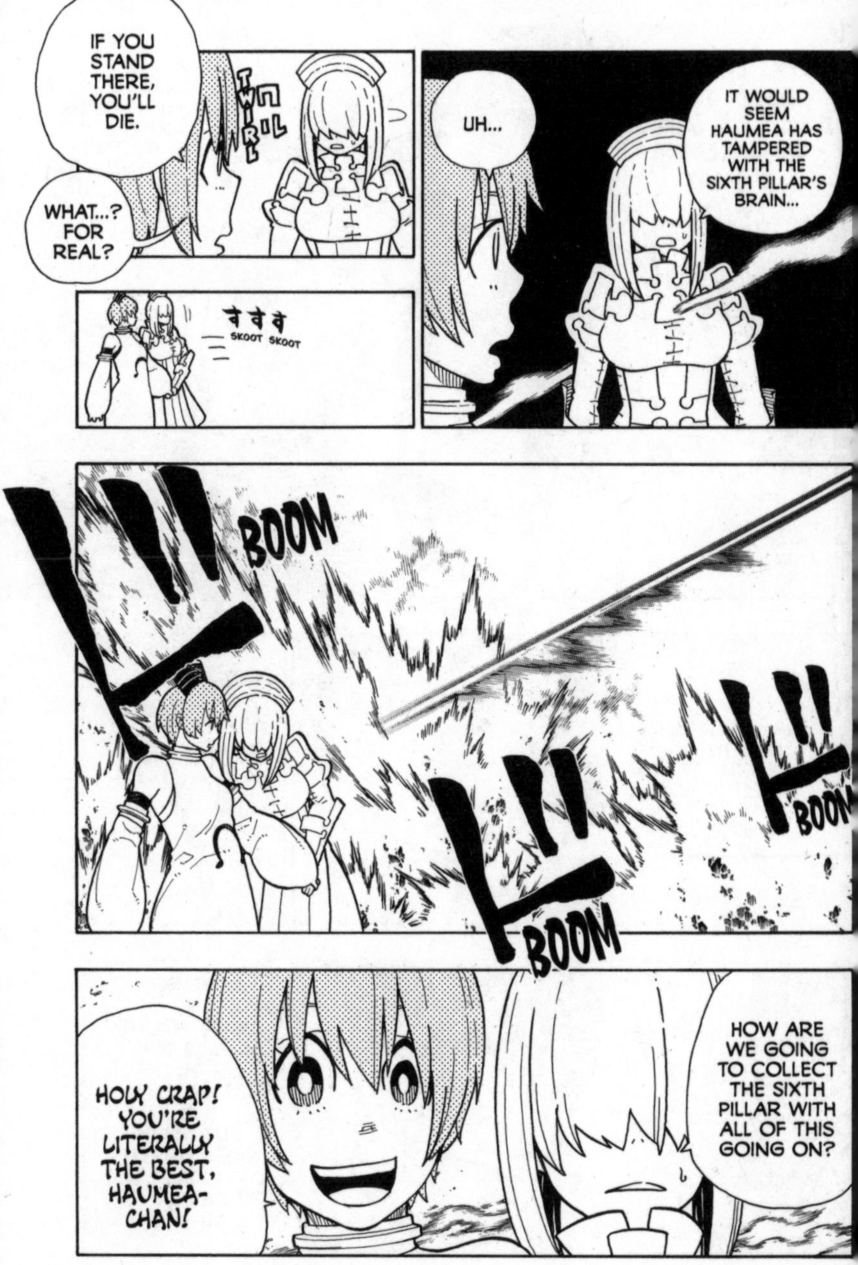

IT WOULD SEEM HAUMEA HAS TAMPERED WITH THE SIXTH PILLAR'S BRAIN...
UH...
IF YOU STAND THERE, YOU'LL DIE.
TWIRL
WHAT...? FOR REAL?
すすす
SKOOT SKOOT
BOOM
BOOM
BOOM
HOW ARE WE GOING TO COLLECT THE SIXTH PILLAR WITH ALL OF THIS GOING ON?
HOLY CRAP! YOU'RE LITERALLY THE BEST, HAUMEA-CHAN!

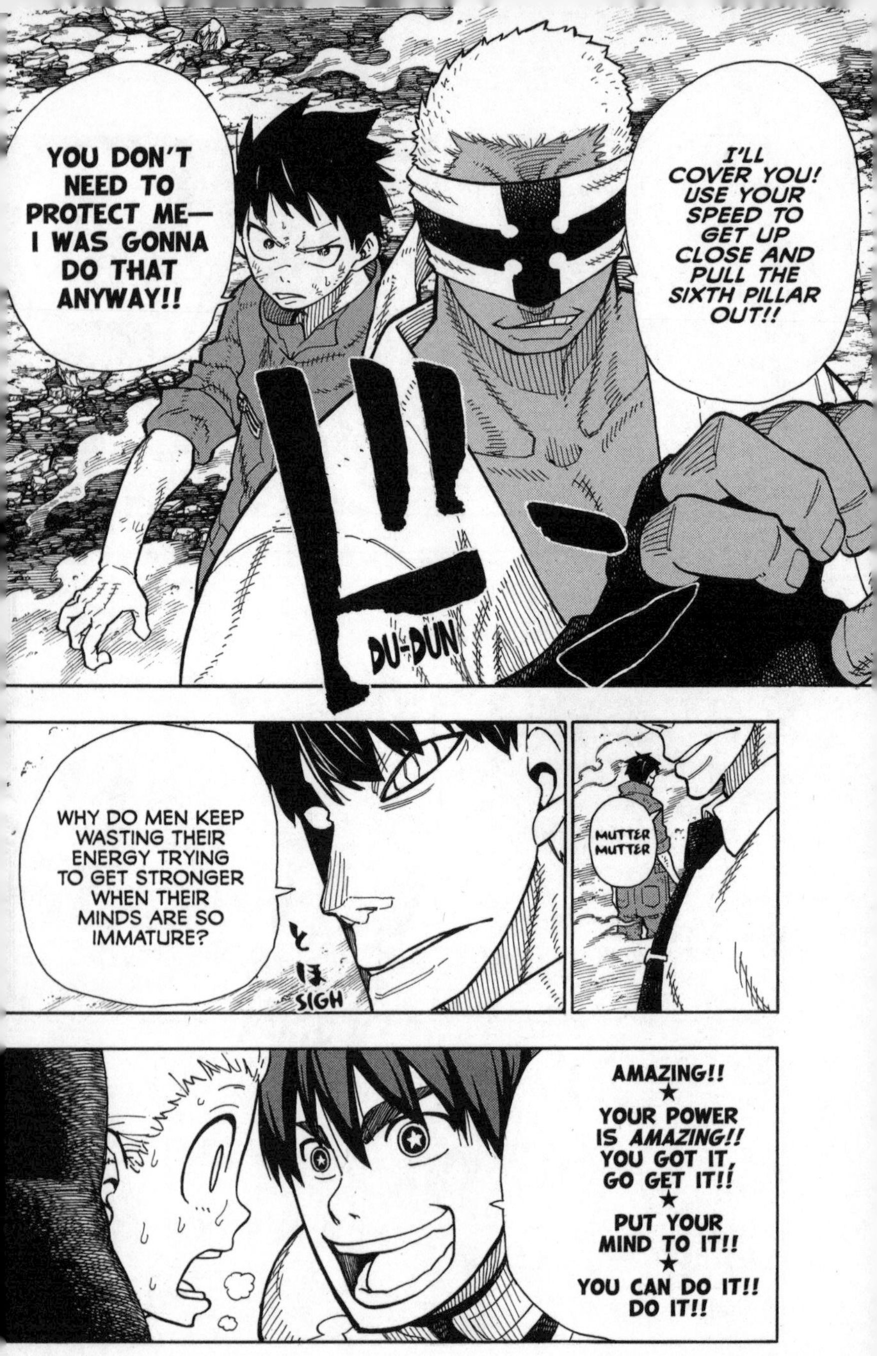
I'LL COVER YOU! USE YOUR SPEED TO GET UP CLOSE AND PULL THE SIXTH PILLAR OUT!!
YOU DON'T NEED TO PROTECT ME— I WAS GONNA DO THAT ANYWAY!!
DU-DUN
MUTTER MUTTER
WHY DO MEN KEEP WASTING THEIR ENERGY TRYING TO GET STRONGER WHEN THEIR MINDS ARE SO IMMATURE?
とほ
SIGH
AMAZING!! ★ YOUR POWER IS AMAZING!! YOU GOT IT, GO GET IT!! ★ PUT YOUR MIND TO IT!! ★ YOU CAN DO IT!! DO IT!!

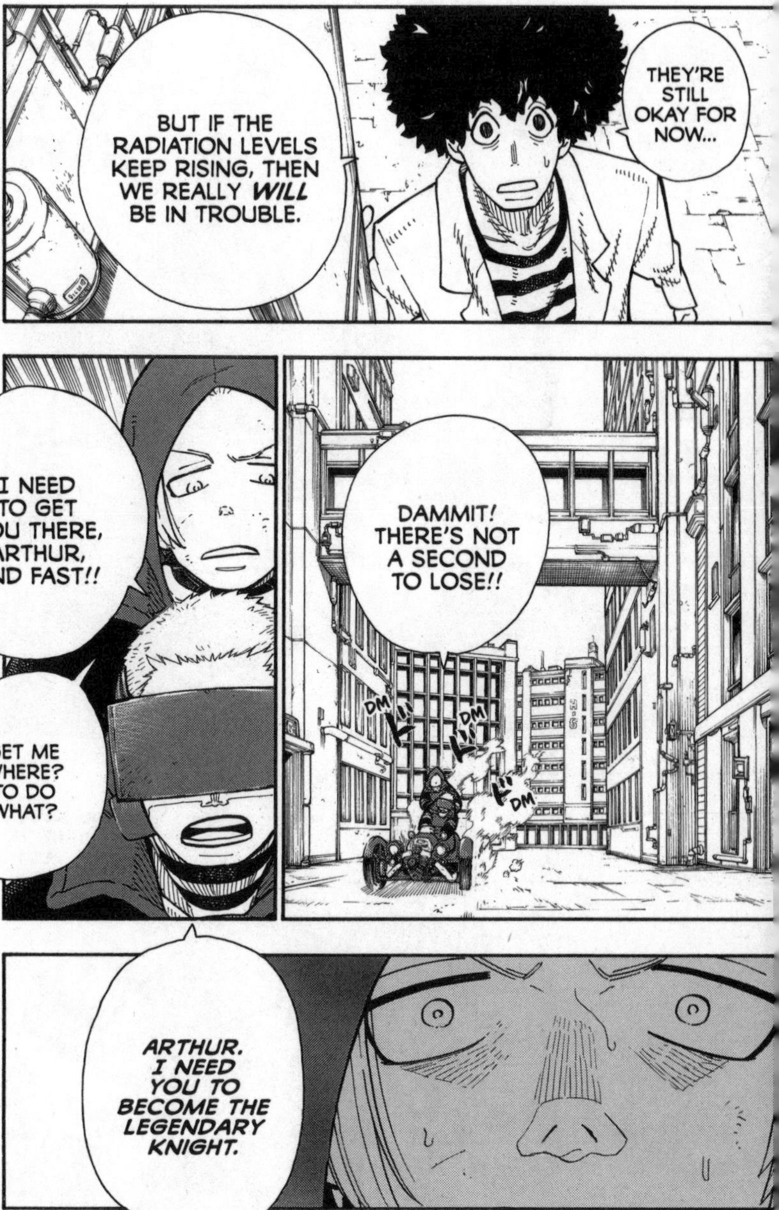
THEY'RE STILL OKAY FOR NOW...
BUT IF THE RADIATION LEVELS KEEP RISING, THEN WE REALLY **WILL** BE IN TROUBLE.
DAMMIT! THERE'S NOT A SECOND TO LOSE!!
DM
DM
DM
I NEED TO GET YOU THERE, ARTHUR, AND FAST!!
GET ME WHERE? TO DO WHAT?
ARTHUR. I NEED YOU TO BECOME THE LEGENDARY KNIGHT.

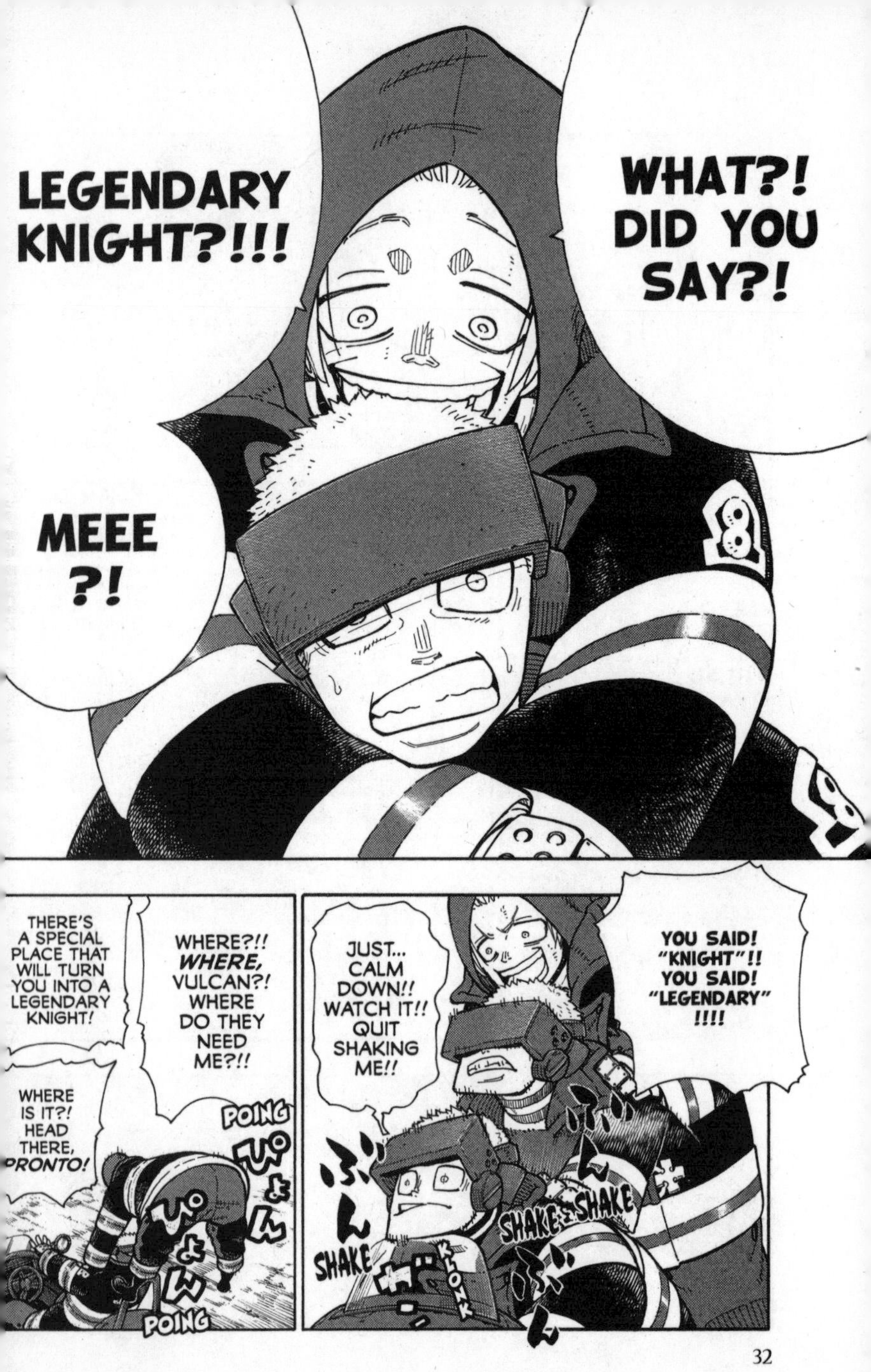
WHAT?! DID YOU SAY?!
LEGENDARY KNIGHT?!!!
MEEE ?!
YOU SAID! "KNIGHT"!! YOU SAID! "LEGENDARY" !!!!
JUST... CALM DOWN!! WATCH IT!! QUIT SHAKING ME!!
SHAKE SHAKE
SHAKE
KLONK
WHERE?!! *WHERE,* VULCAN?! WHERE DO THEY NEED ME?!!
THERE'S A SPECIAL PLACE THAT WILL TURN YOU INTO A LEGENDARY KNIGHT!
WHERE IS IT?! HEAD THERE, *PRONTO!*
POING
POING

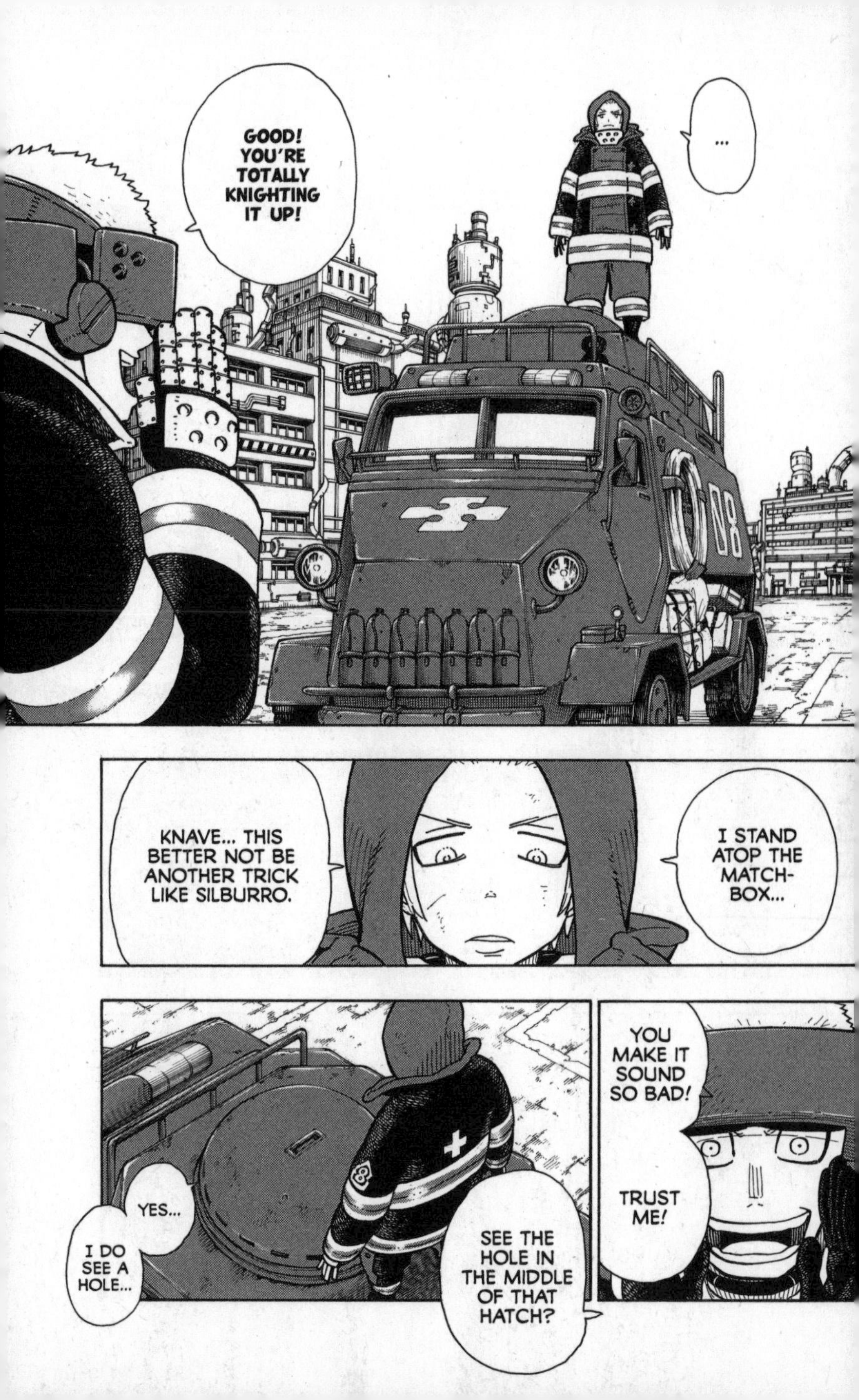
...
GOOD! YOU'RE TOTALLY KNIGHTING IT UP!
I STAND ATOP THE MATCH-BOX...
KNAVE... THIS BETTER NOT BE ANOTHER TRICK LIKE SILBURRO.
YOU MAKE IT SOUND SO BAD!
TRUST ME!
SEE THE HOLE IN THE MIDDLE OF THAT HATCH?
YES...
I DO SEE A HOLE...

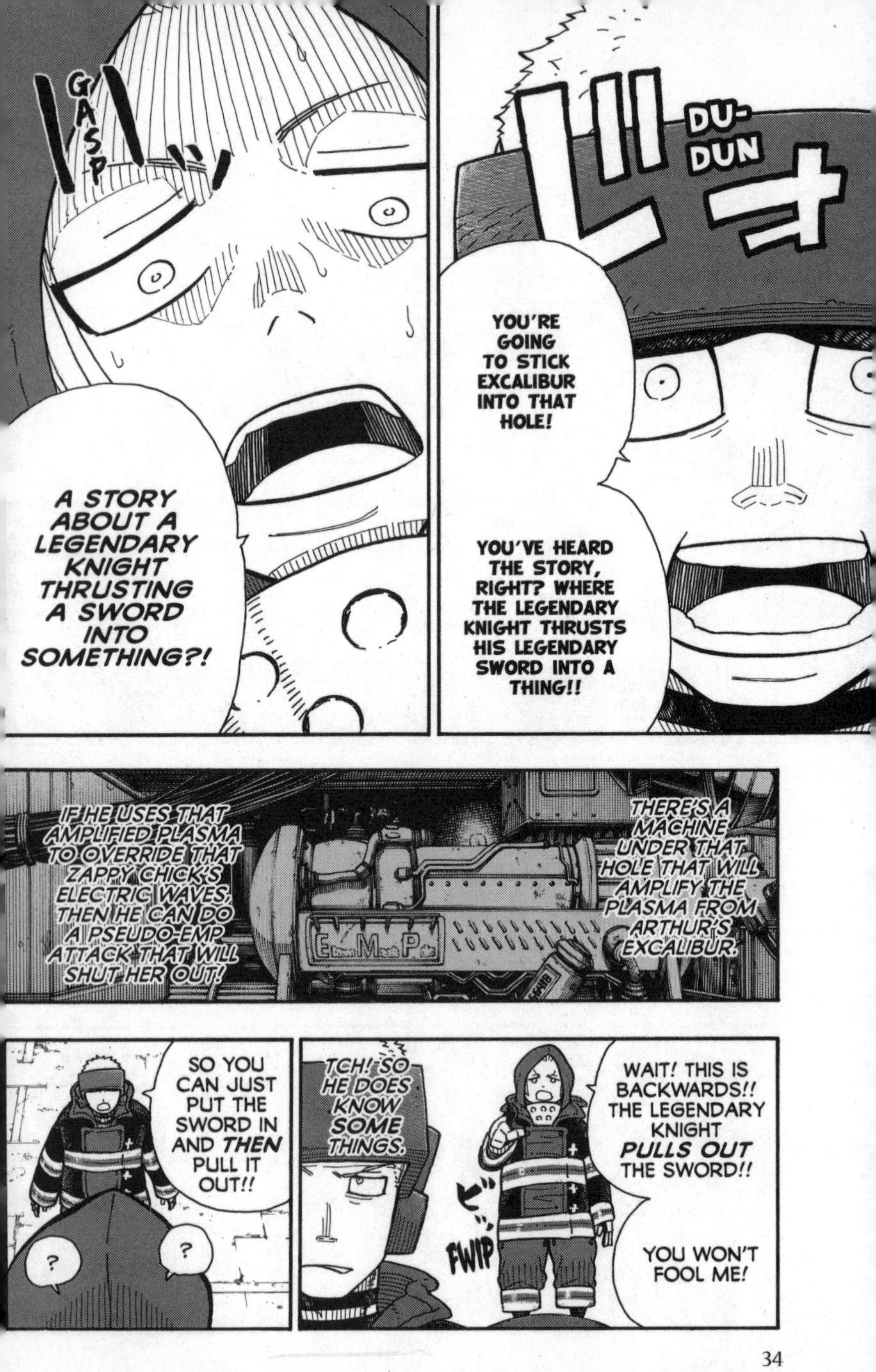
DU-DUN
YOU'RE GOING TO STICK EXCALIBUR INTO THAT HOLE!
YOU'VE HEARD THE STORY, RIGHT? WHERE THE LEGENDARY KNIGHT THRUSTS HIS LEGENDARY SWORD INTO A THING!!
GASP
A STORY ABOUT A LEGENDARY KNIGHT THRUSTING A SWORD INTO SOMETHING?!
THERE'S A MACHINE UNDER THAT HOLE THAT WILL AMPLIFY THE PLASMA FROM ARTHUR'S EXCALIBUR.
IF HE USES THAT AMPLIFIED PLASMA TO OVERRIDE THAT ZAPPY CHICK'S ELECTRIC WAVES, THEN HE CAN DO A PSEUDO-EMP ATTACK THAT WILL SHUT HER OUT!
E M P
WAIT! THIS IS BACKWARDS!! THE LEGENDARY KNIGHT *PULLS OUT* THE SWORD!!
TCH! SO HE DOES KNOW *SOME* THINGS.
YOU WON'T FOOL ME!
FWIP
SO YOU CAN JUST PUT THE SWORD IN AND *THEN* PULL IT OUT!!
?
?

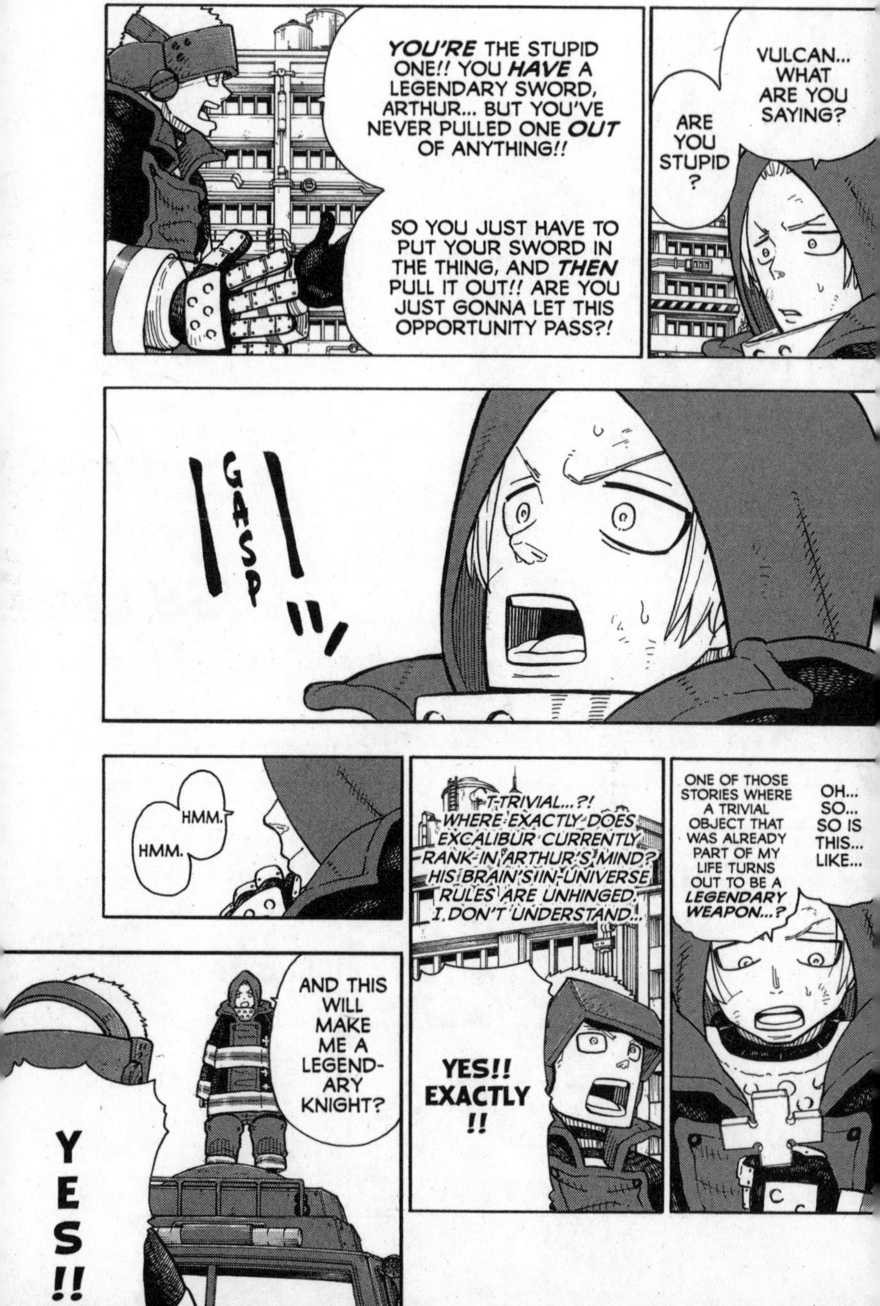
VULCAN... WHAT ARE YOU SAYING?
ARE YOU STUPID?
YOU'RE THE STUPID ONE!! YOU HAVE A LEGENDARY SWORD, ARTHUR... BUT YOU'VE NEVER PULLED ONE OUT OF ANYTHING!!
SO YOU JUST HAVE TO PUT YOUR SWORD IN THE THING, AND THEN PULL IT OUT!! ARE YOU JUST GONNA LET THIS OPPORTUNITY PASS?!
GASP!!
OH... SO... SO IS THIS... LIKE...
ONE OF THOSE STORIES WHERE A TRIVIAL OBJECT THAT WAS ALREADY PART OF MY LIFE TURNS OUT TO BE A LEGENDARY WEAPON...?
T-TRIVIAL...?! WHERE EXACTLY DOES EXCALIBUR CURRENTLY RANK IN ARTHUR'S MIND? HIS BRAIN'S IN-UNIVERSE RULES ARE UNHINGED. I DON'T UNDERSTAND...
YES!! EXACTLY!!
HMM.
HMM.
AND THIS WILL MAKE ME A LEGEND-ARY KNIGHT?
YES!!

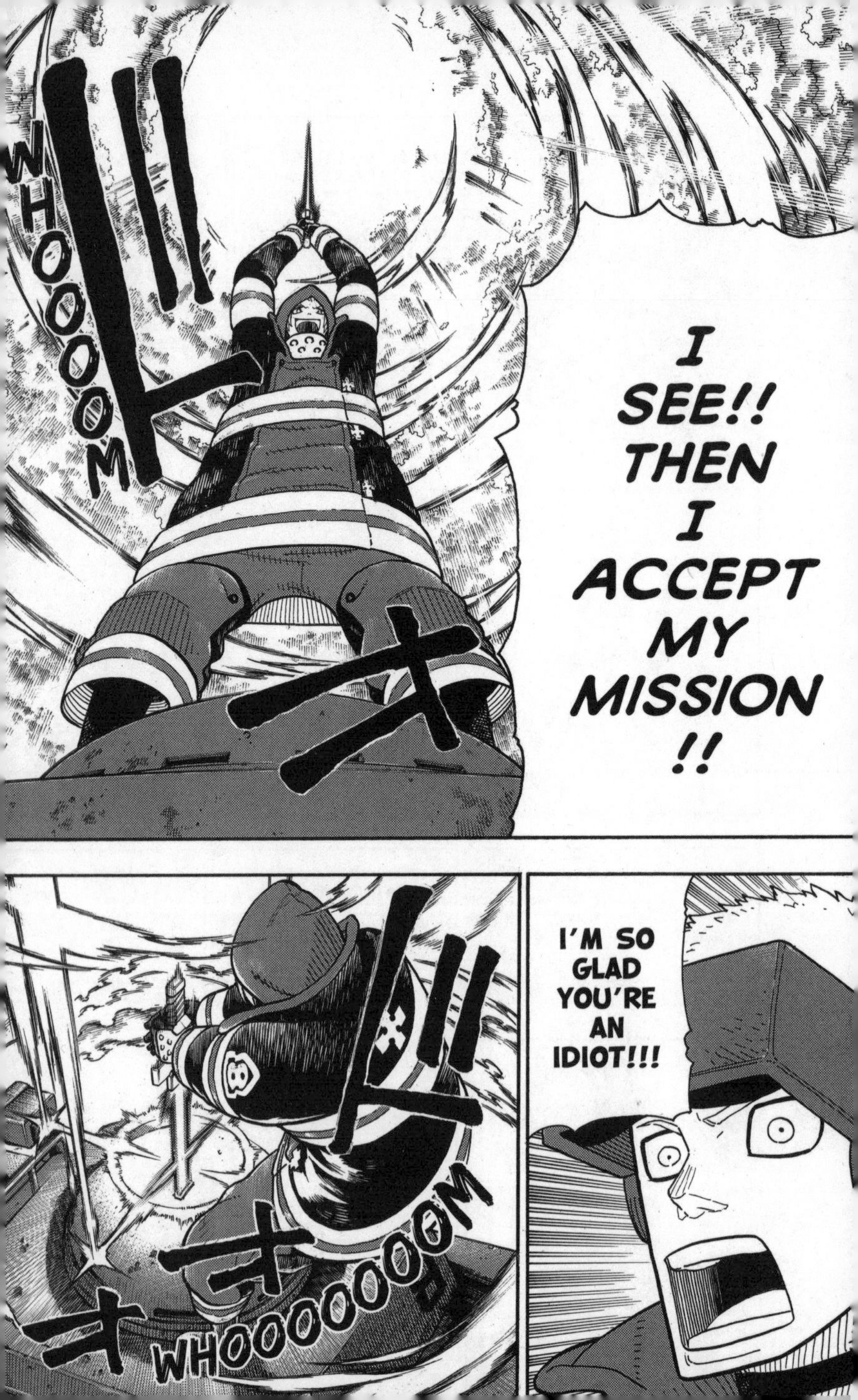
WHOOOOOM
I SEE!! THEN I ACCEPT MY MISSION!!
I'M SO GLAD YOU'RE AN IDIOT!!!
WHOOOOOOOM

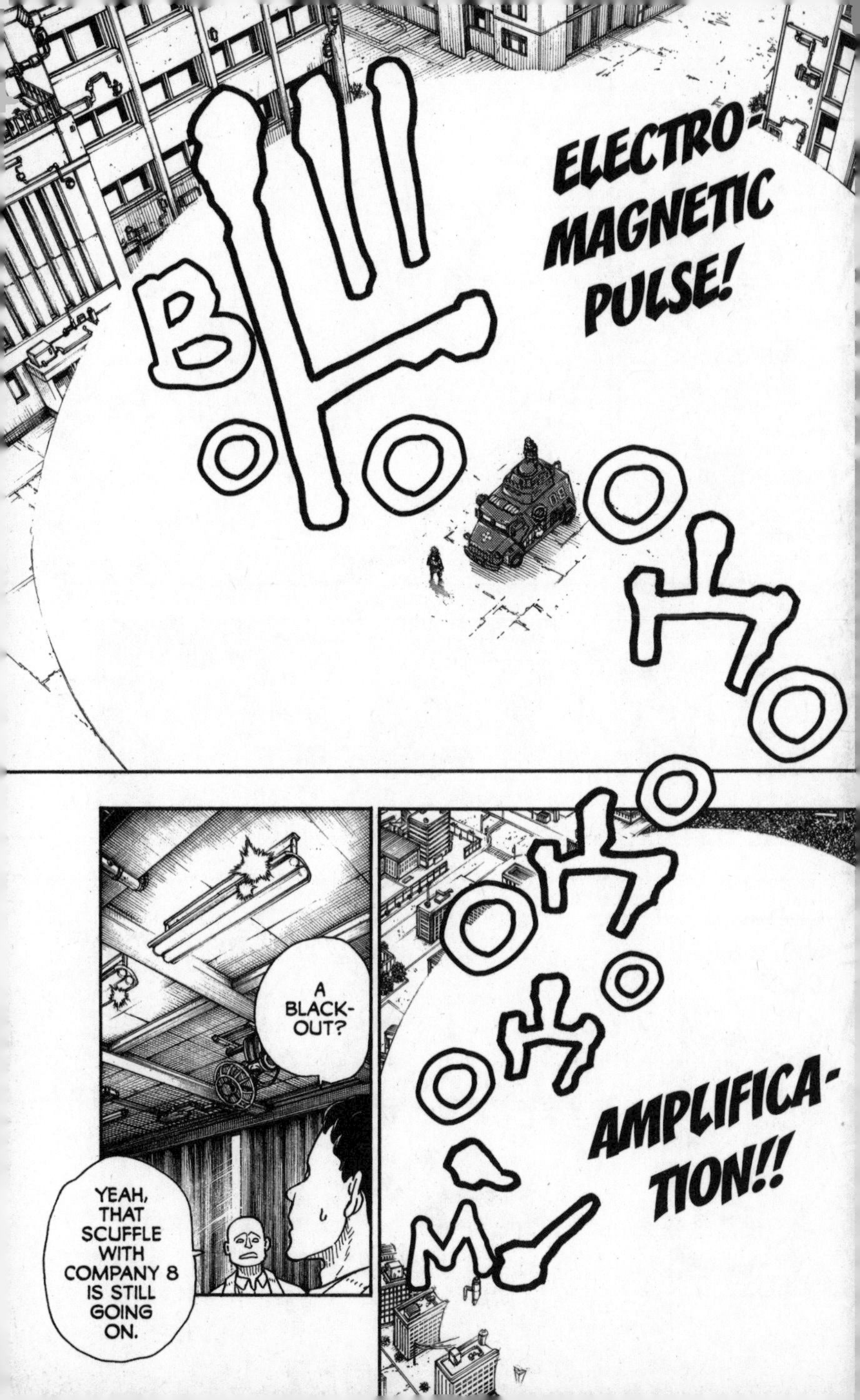
ELECTRO-MAGNETIC PULSE!
AMPLIFICA-TION!!
A BLACK-OUT?
YEAH, THAT SCUFFLE WITH COMPANY 8 IS STILL GOING ON.

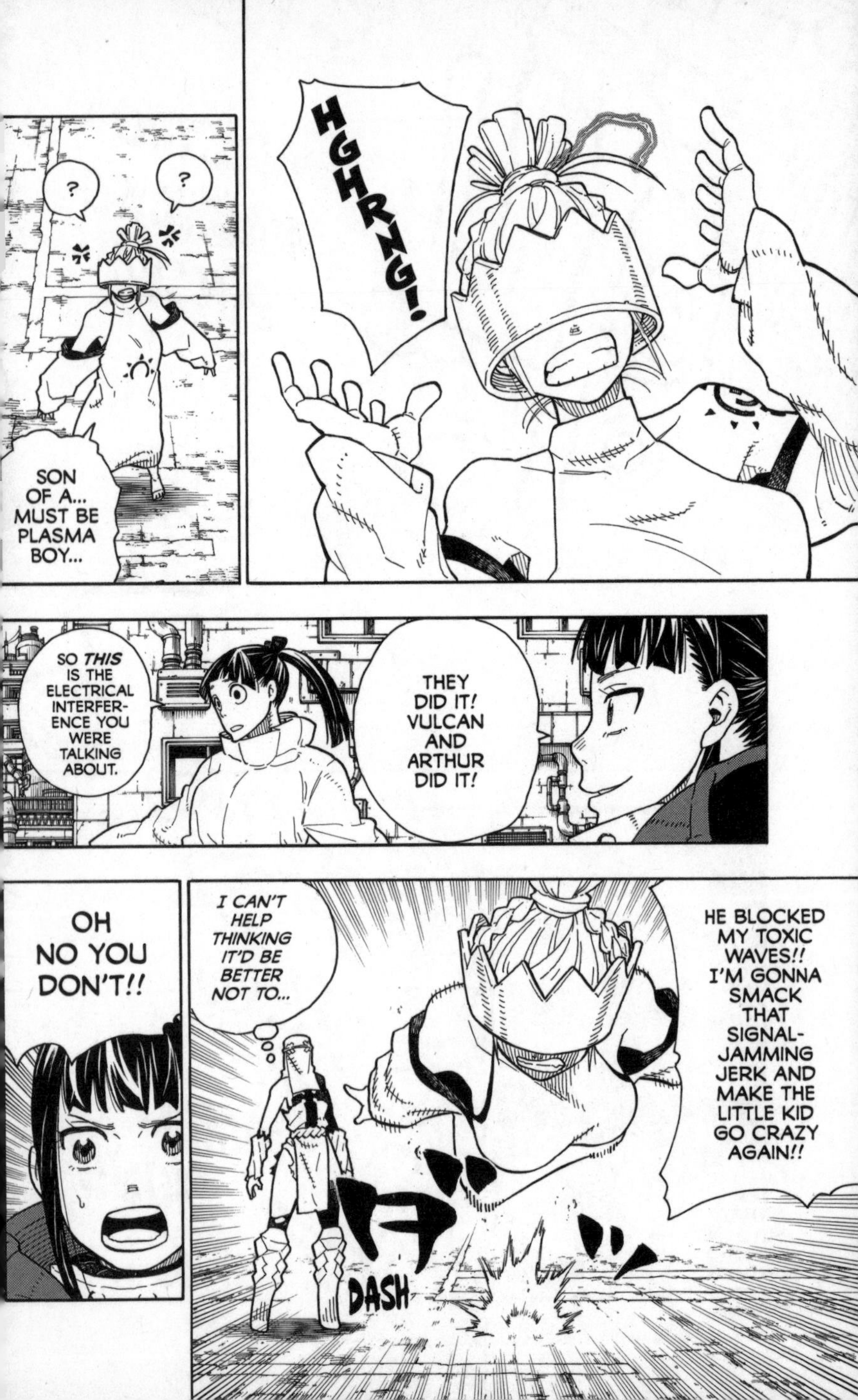
HGHRNG!
?
?
SON OF A... MUST BE PLASMA BOY...
THEY DID IT! VULCAN AND ARTHUR DID IT!
SO THIS IS THE ELECTRICAL INTERFERENCE YOU WERE TALKING ABOUT.
HE BLOCKED MY TOXIC WAVES!! I'M GONNA SMACK THAT SIGNAL-JAMMING JERK AND MAKE THE LITTLE KID GO CRAZY AGAIN!!
I CAN'T HELP THINKING IT'D BE BETTER NOT TO...
DASH
OH NO YOU DON'T!!

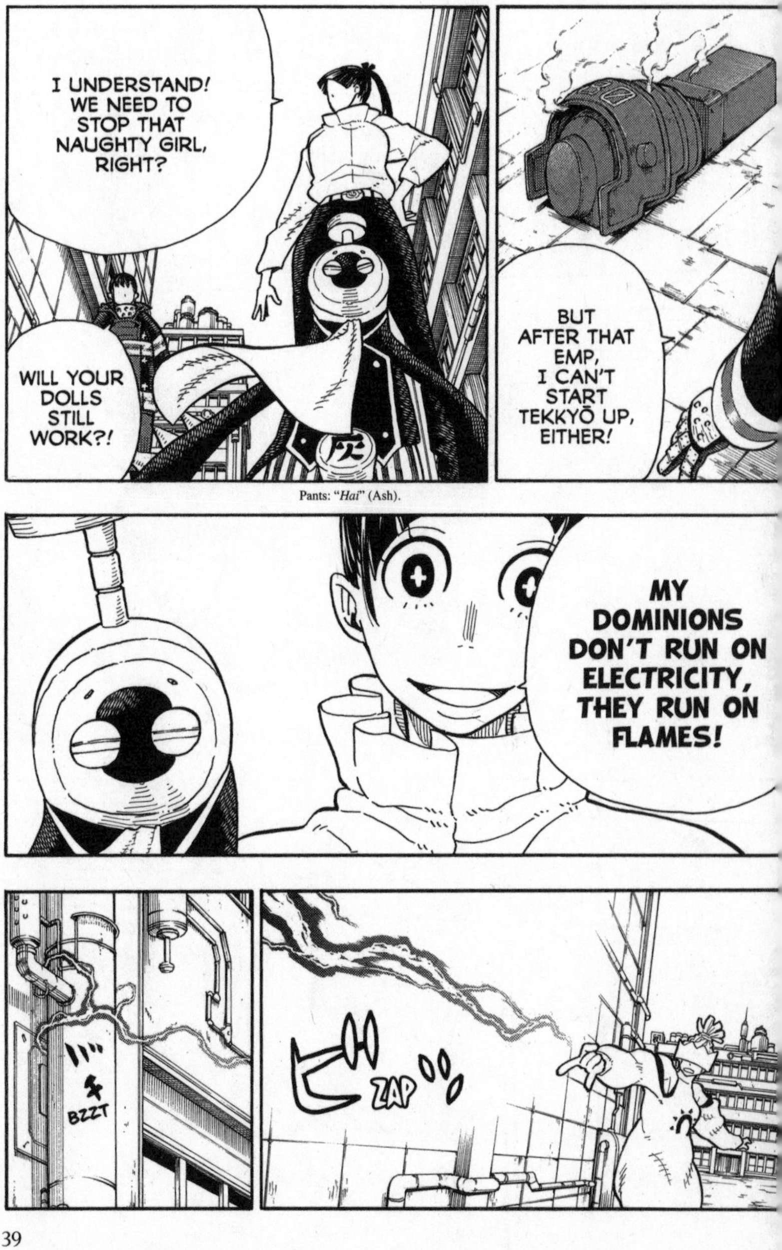

BUT AFTER THAT EMP, I CAN'T START TEKKYŌ UP, EITHER!
I UNDERSTAND! WE NEED TO STOP THAT NAUGHTY GIRL, RIGHT?
WILL YOUR DOLLS STILL WORK?!
MY DOMINIONS DON'T RUN ON ELECTRICITY, THEY RUN ON FLAMES!
ZAP
BZZT

Pants: "*Hai*" (Ash).

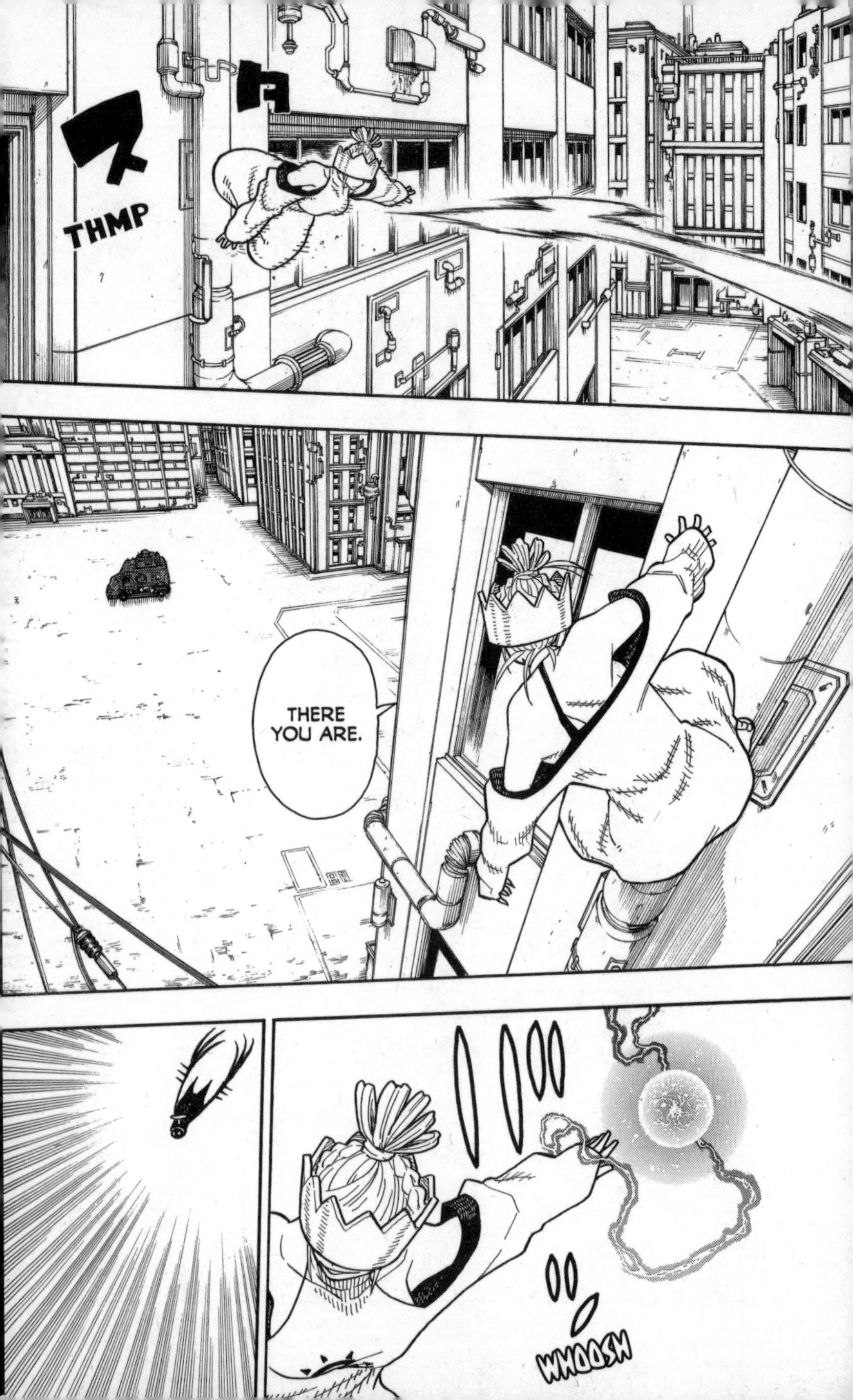
THMP
THERE YOU ARE.
WHOOSH

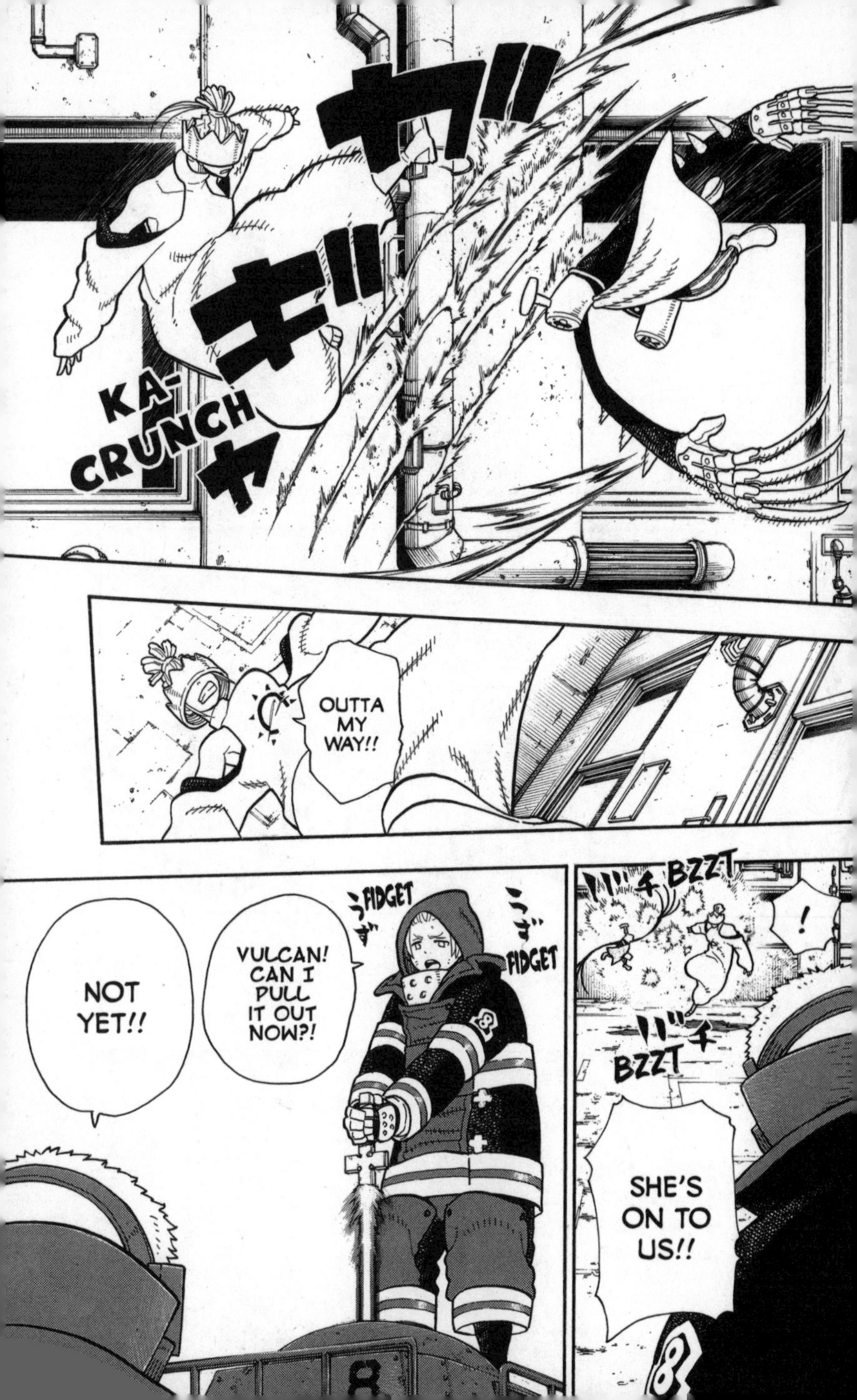
ガギ
KA-CRUNCH
OUTTA MY WAY!!
BZZT
!
BZZT
SHE'S ON TO US!!
FIDGET
FIDGET
VULCAN! CAN I PULL IT OUT NOW?!
NOT YET!!

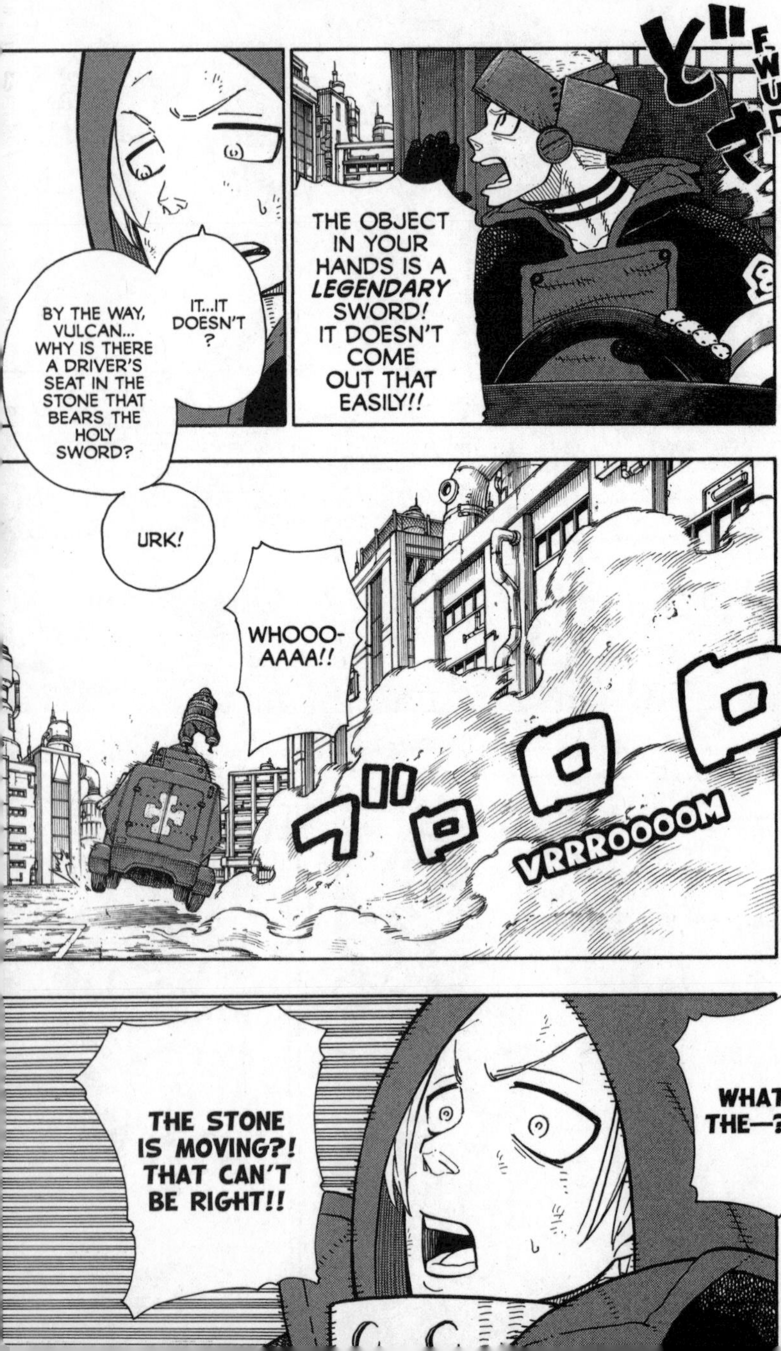
FWUD
THE OBJECT IN YOUR HANDS IS A *LEGENDARY* SWORD! IT DOESN'T COME OUT THAT EASILY!!
IT...IT DOESN'T ?
BY THE WAY, VULCAN... WHY IS THERE A DRIVER'S SEAT IN THE STONE THAT BEARS THE HOLY SWORD?
URK!
VRRROOOOM
WHOOO-AAAA!!
WHAT THE—?!
THE STONE IS MOVING?! THAT CAN'T BE RIGHT!!

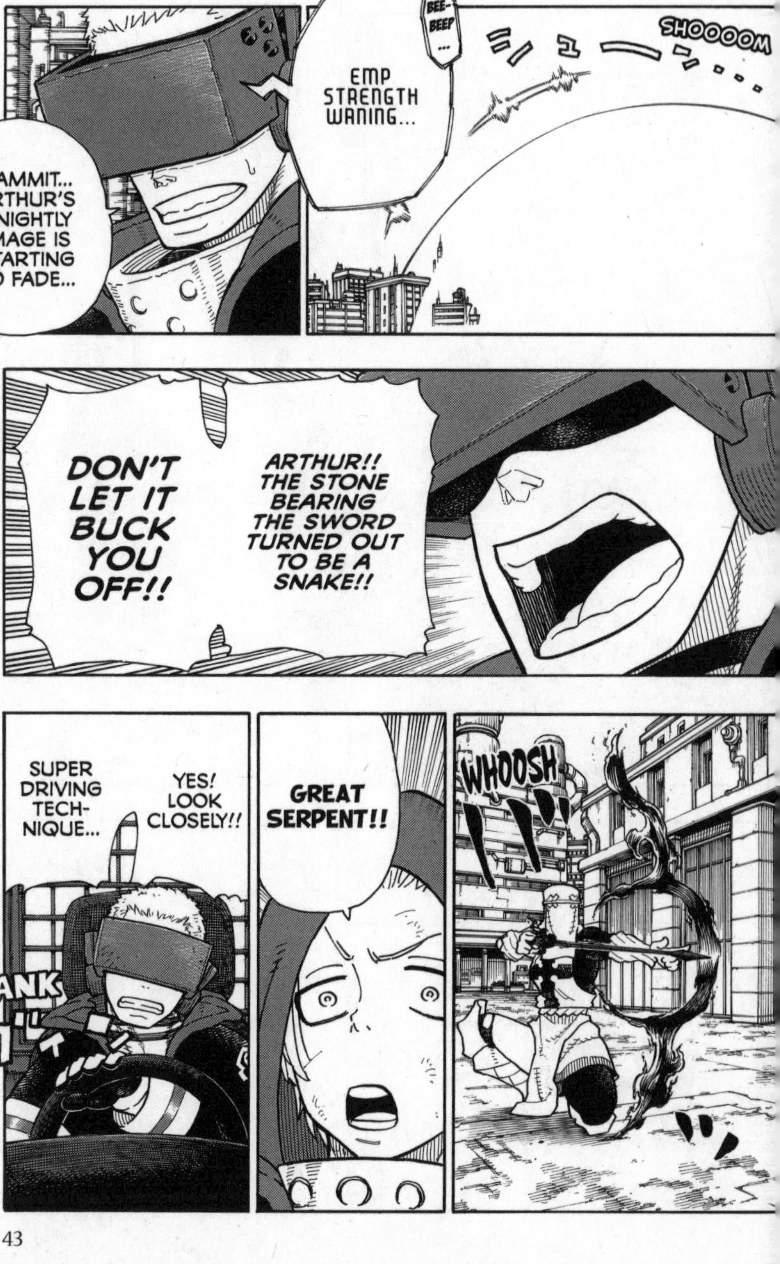
SHOOOOM
BEE-BEEP...
EMP STRENGTH WANING...
DAMMIT... ARTHUR'S KNIGHTLY IMAGE IS STARTING TO FADE...
ARTHUR!! THE STONE BEARING THE SWORD TURNED OUT TO BE A SNAKE!!
DON'T LET IT BUCK YOU OFF!!
WHOOSH
GREAT SERPENT!!
YES! LOOK CLOSELY!!
SUPER DRIVING TECH-NIQUE...
YANK

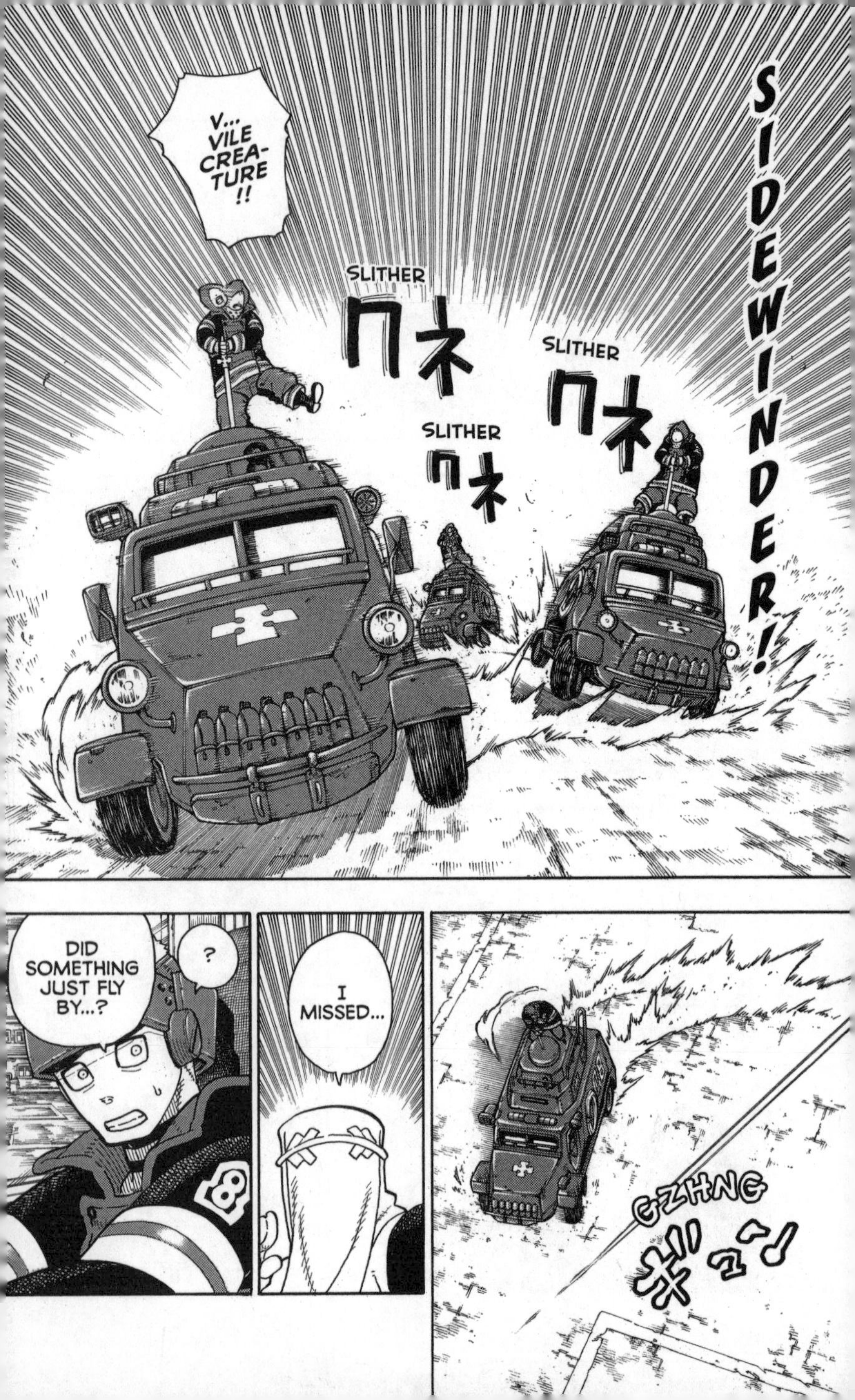

SIDEWINDER!
V... VILE CREA-TURE!!
SLITHER
クネ
SLITHER
クネ
SLITHER
クネ
GZHNG
ギュッ!
I MISSED...
?
DID SOMETHING JUST FLY BY...?

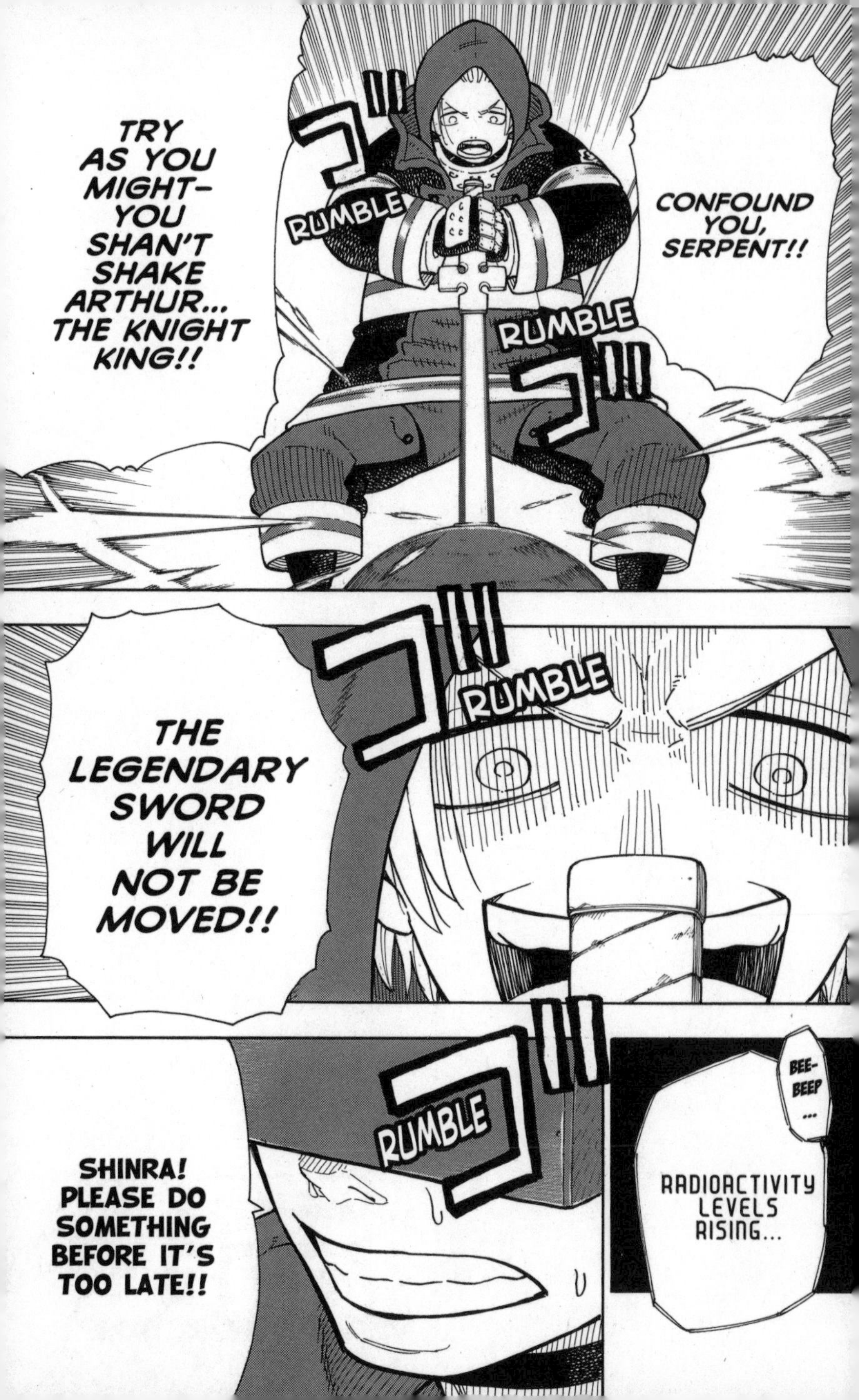
CONFOUND YOU, SERPENT!!
RUMBLE
RUMBLE
TRY AS YOU MIGHT— YOU SHAN'T SHAKE ARTHUR... THE KNIGHT KING!!
RUMBLE
THE LEGENDARY SWORD WILL NOT BE MOVED!!
BEE-BEEP...
RADIOACTIVITY LEVELS RISING...
RUMBLE
SHINRA! PLEASE DO SOMETHING BEFORE IT'S TOO LATE!!

FIRE FORCE

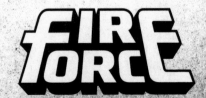

CHAPTER CXLIV:
PRESSURE

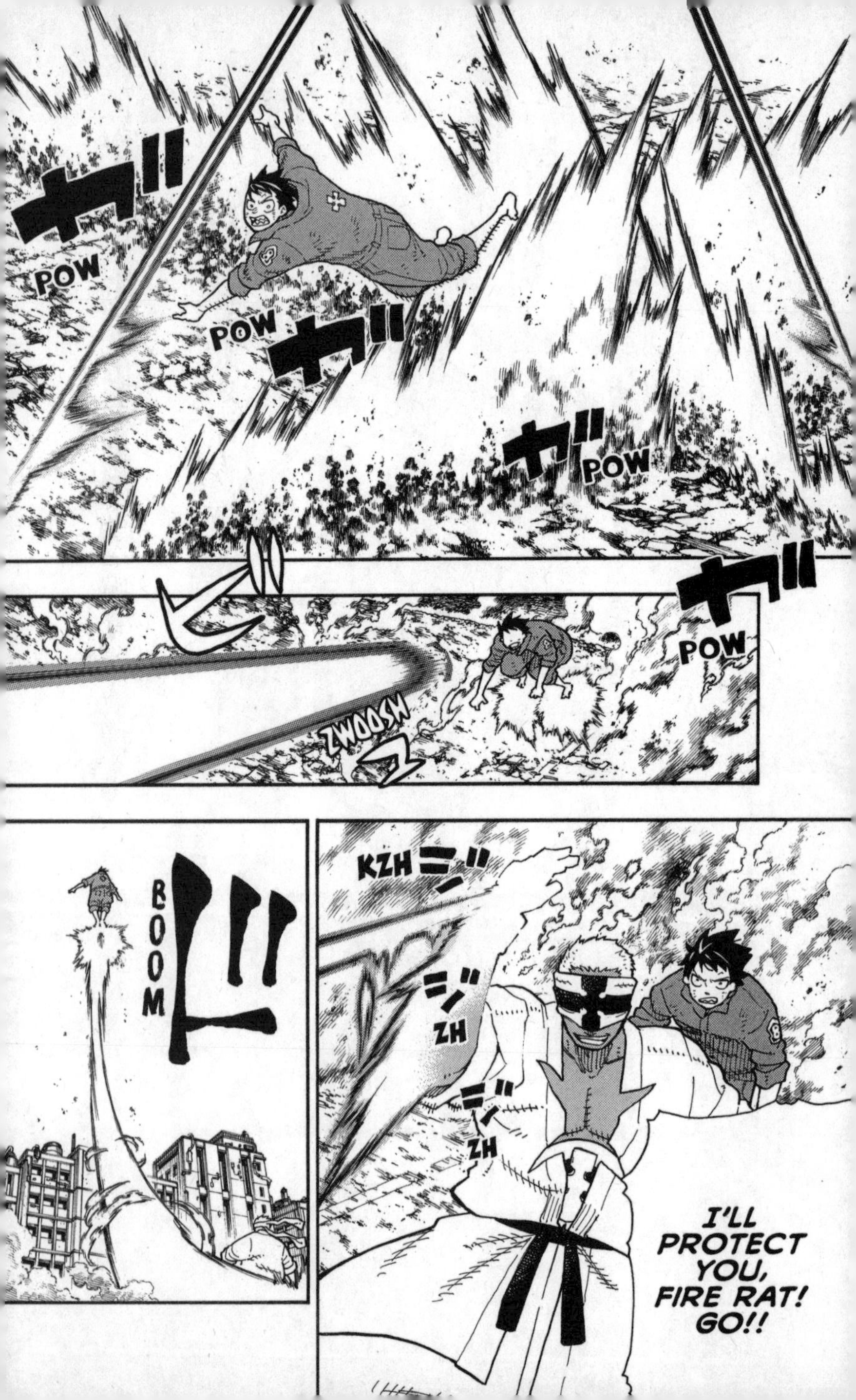
POW
POW
POW
POW
ZWOOSH
KZH
ZH
ZH
I'LL PROTECT YOU, FIRE RAT! GO!!
BOOM

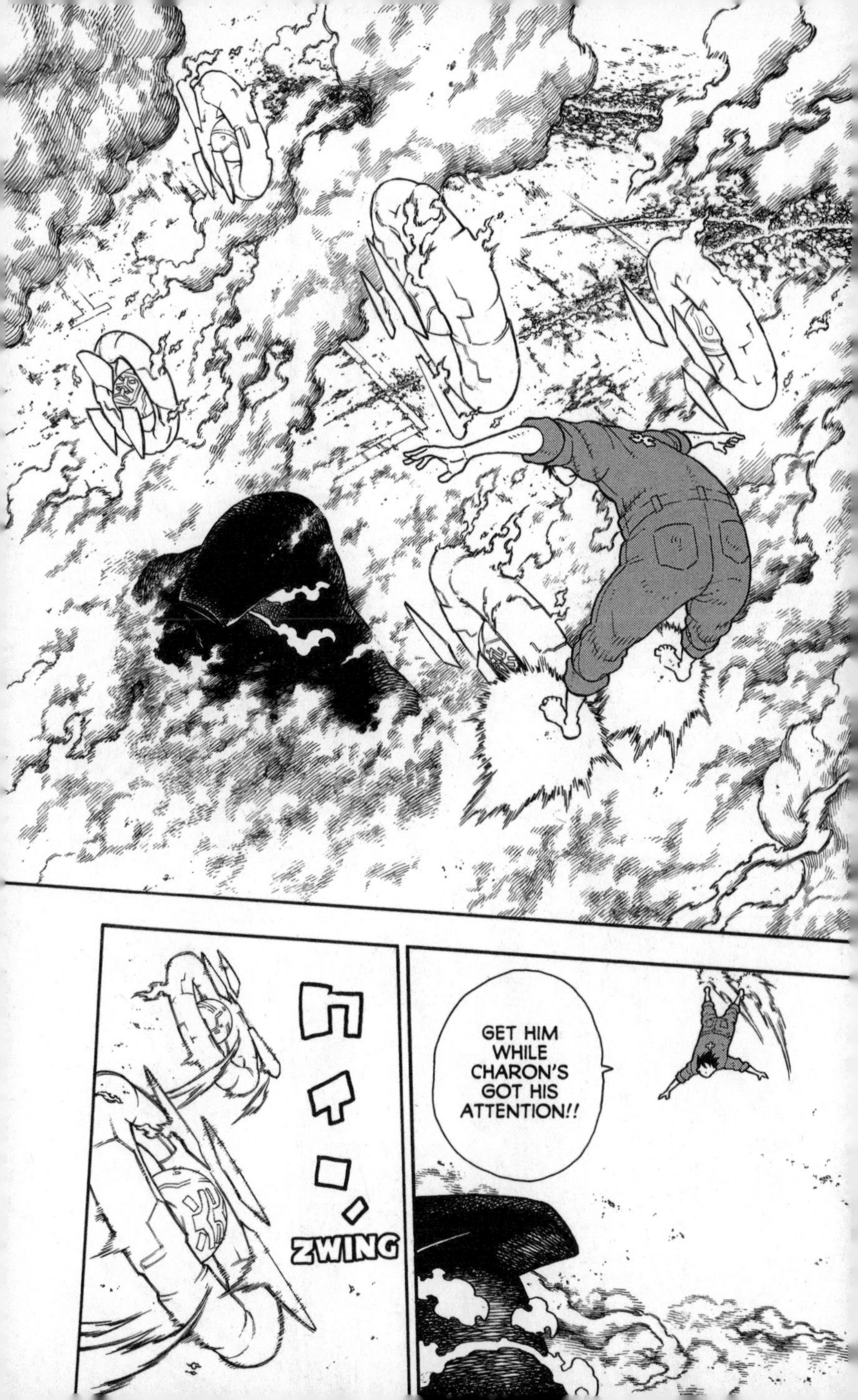
GET HIM WHILE CHARON'S GOT HIS ATTENTION!!
ZWING

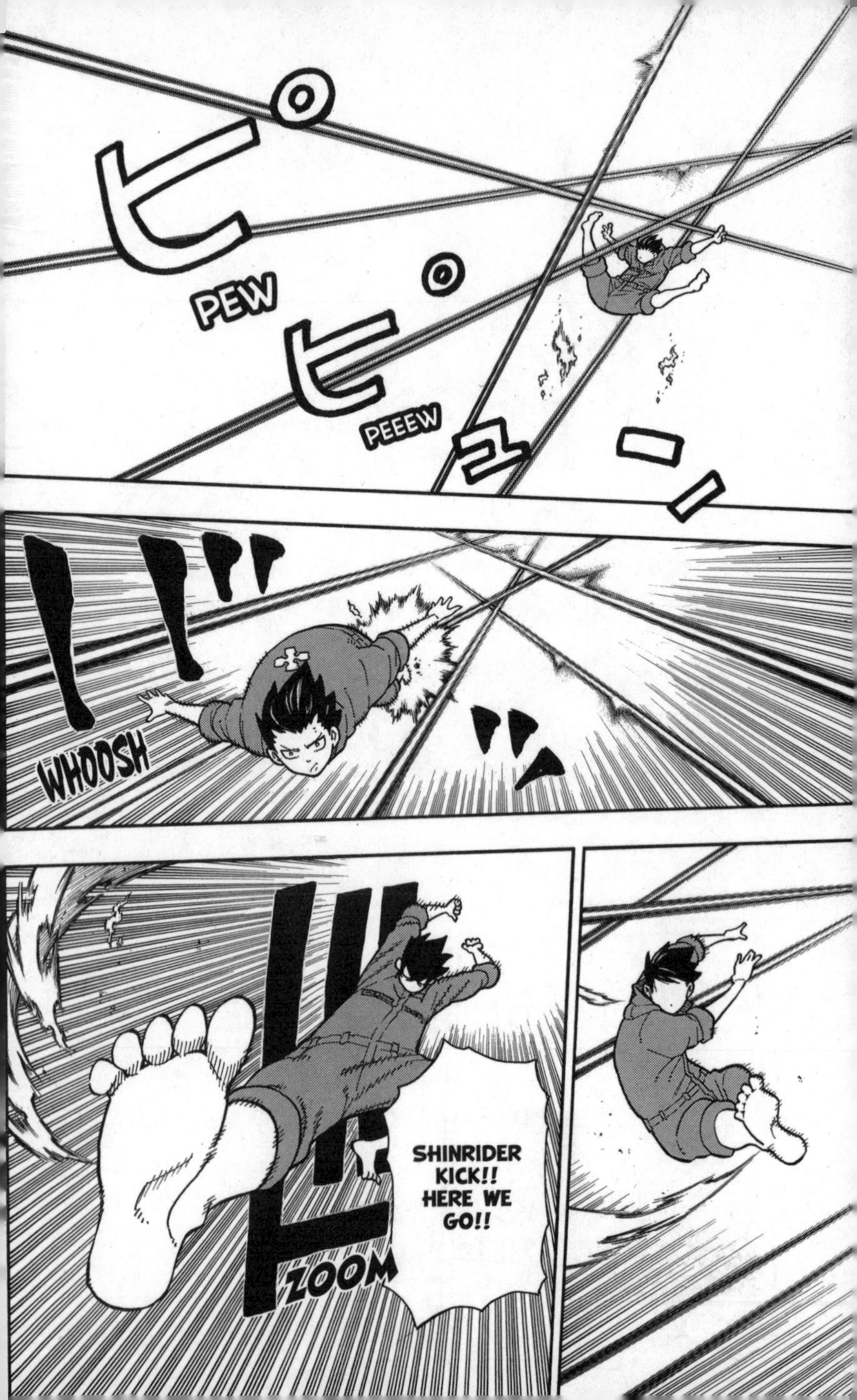
ピ
PEW
ピュー
PEEEW
WHOOSH
SHINRIDER KICK!! HERE WE GO!!
ZOOM

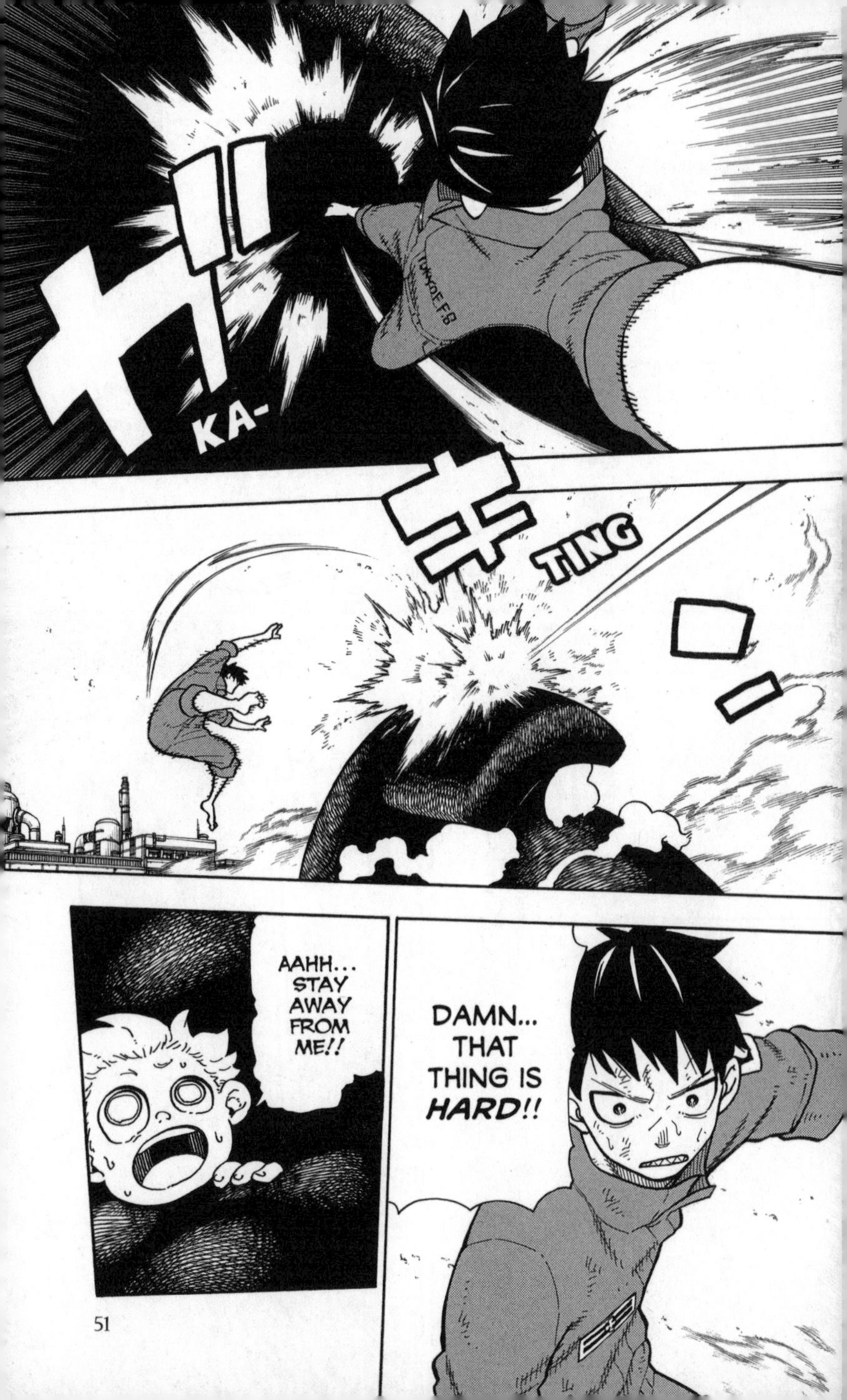
KA-
TING
DAMN... THAT THING IS ***HARD***!!
AAHH... STAY AWAY FROM ME!!

THE RADIOACTIVE DECAY ISN'T SLOWING DOWN... THE RADIOACTIVITY LEVELS ARE STILL RISING!

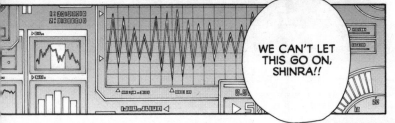

WE CAN'T LET THIS GO ON, SHINRA!!

AAHH! AAAAAA

TAK-KUN, CALM DOWN!!

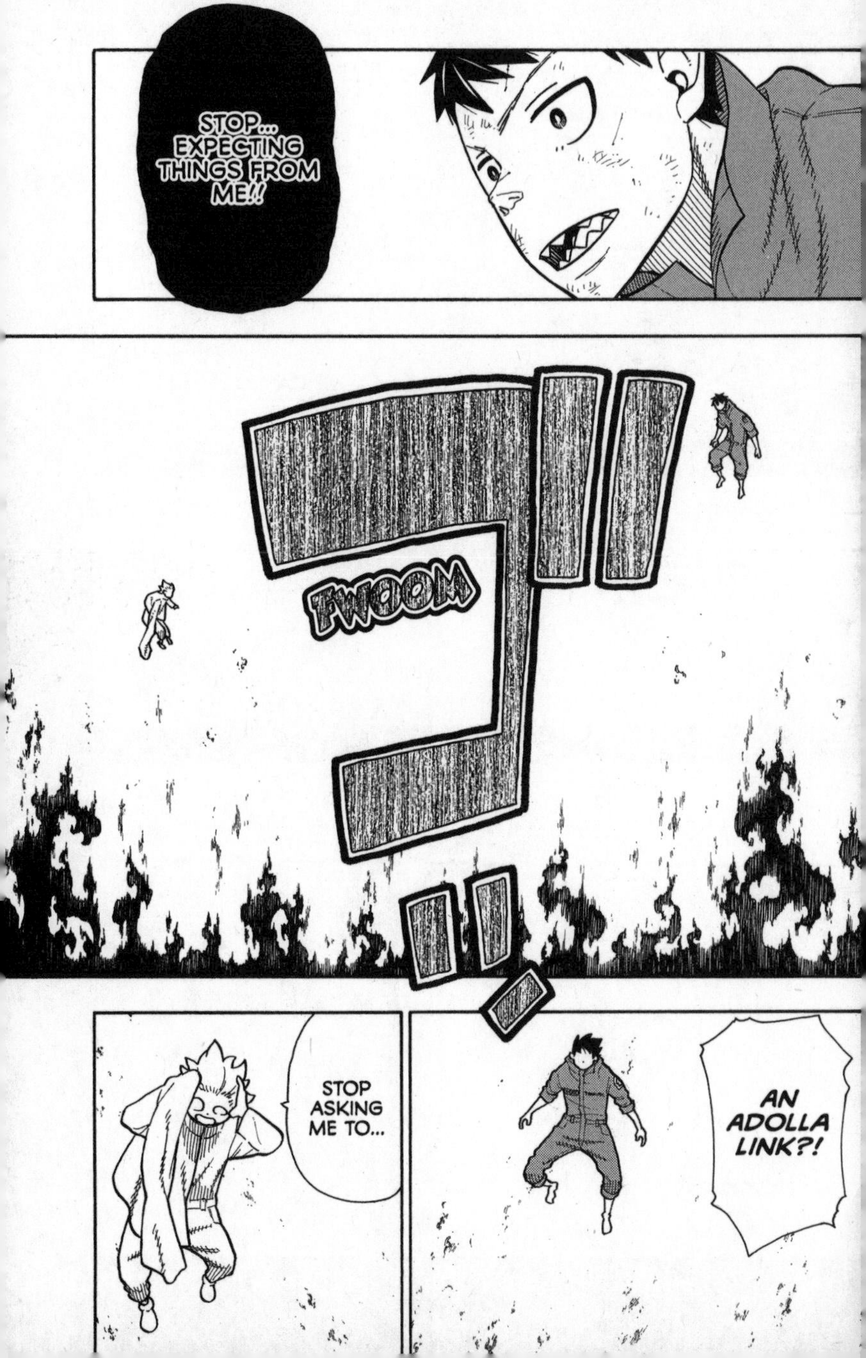
STOP... EXPECTING THINGS FROM ME!!
FWOOM
AN ADOLLA LINK?!
STOP ASKING ME TO...

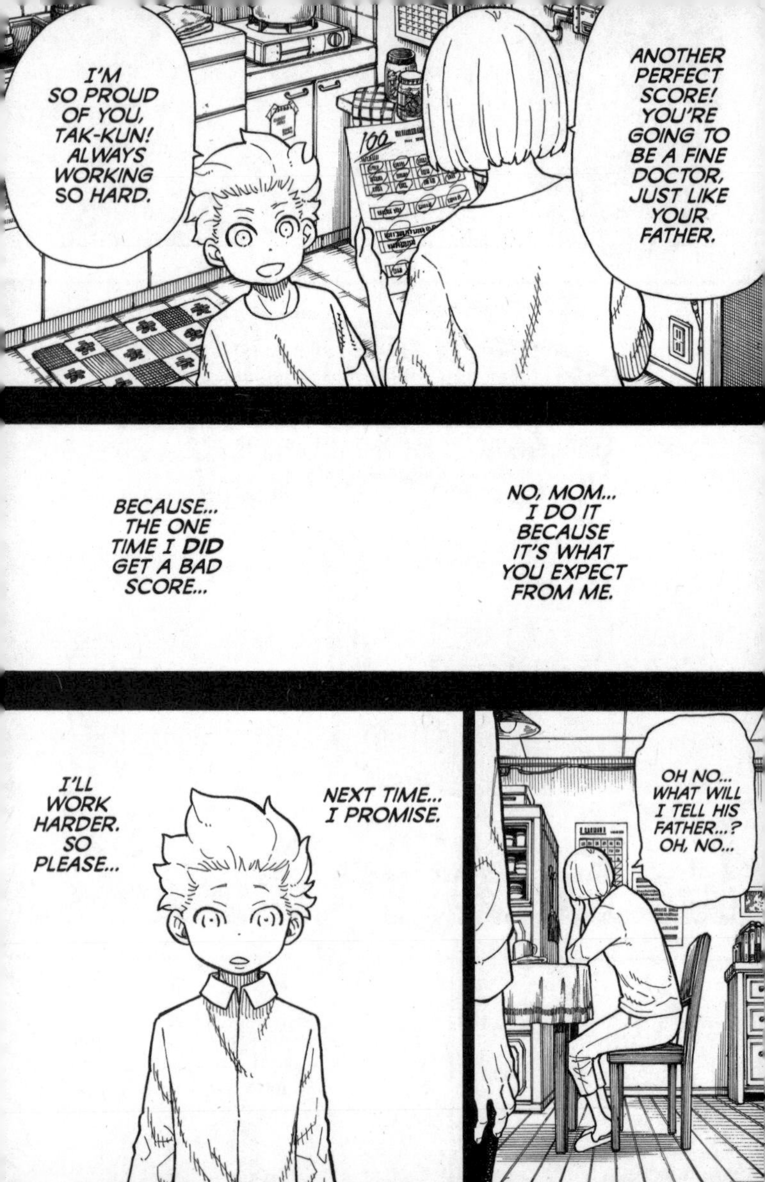
ANOTHER PERFECT SCORE! YOU'RE GOING TO BE A FINE DOCTOR, JUST LIKE YOUR FATHER.
I'M SO PROUD OF YOU, TAK-KUN! ALWAYS WORKING SO HARD.
NO, MOM... I DO IT BECAUSE IT'S WHAT YOU EXPECT FROM ME.
BECAUSE... THE ONE TIME I **DID** GET A BAD SCORE...
OH NO... WHAT WILL I TELL HIS FATHER...? OH, NO...
NEXT TIME... I PROMISE.
I'LL WORK HARDER. SO PLEASE...

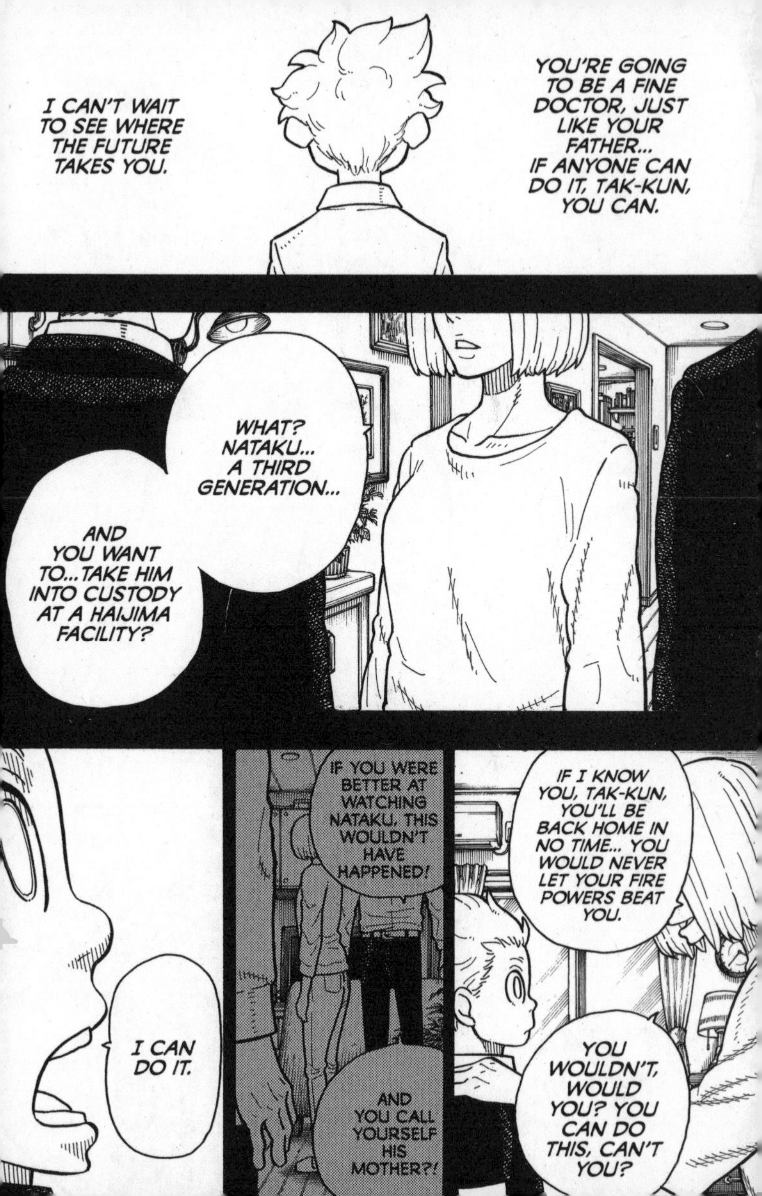
YOU'RE GOING TO BE A FINE DOCTOR, JUST LIKE YOUR FATHER... IF ANYONE CAN DO IT, TAK-KUN, YOU CAN.
I CAN'T WAIT TO SEE WHERE THE FUTURE TAKES YOU.
WHAT? NATAKU... A THIRD GENERATION...
AND YOU WANT TO...TAKE HIM INTO CUSTODY AT A HAIJIMA FACILITY?
IF I KNOW YOU, TAK-KUN, YOU'LL BE BACK HOME IN NO TIME... YOU WOULD NEVER LET YOUR FIRE POWERS BEAT YOU.
YOU WOULDN'T, WOULD YOU? YOU CAN DO THIS, CAN'T YOU?
IF YOU WERE BETTER AT WATCHING NATAKU, THIS WOULDN'T HAVE HAPPENED!
AND YOU CALL YOURSELF HIS MOTHER?!
I CAN DO IT.

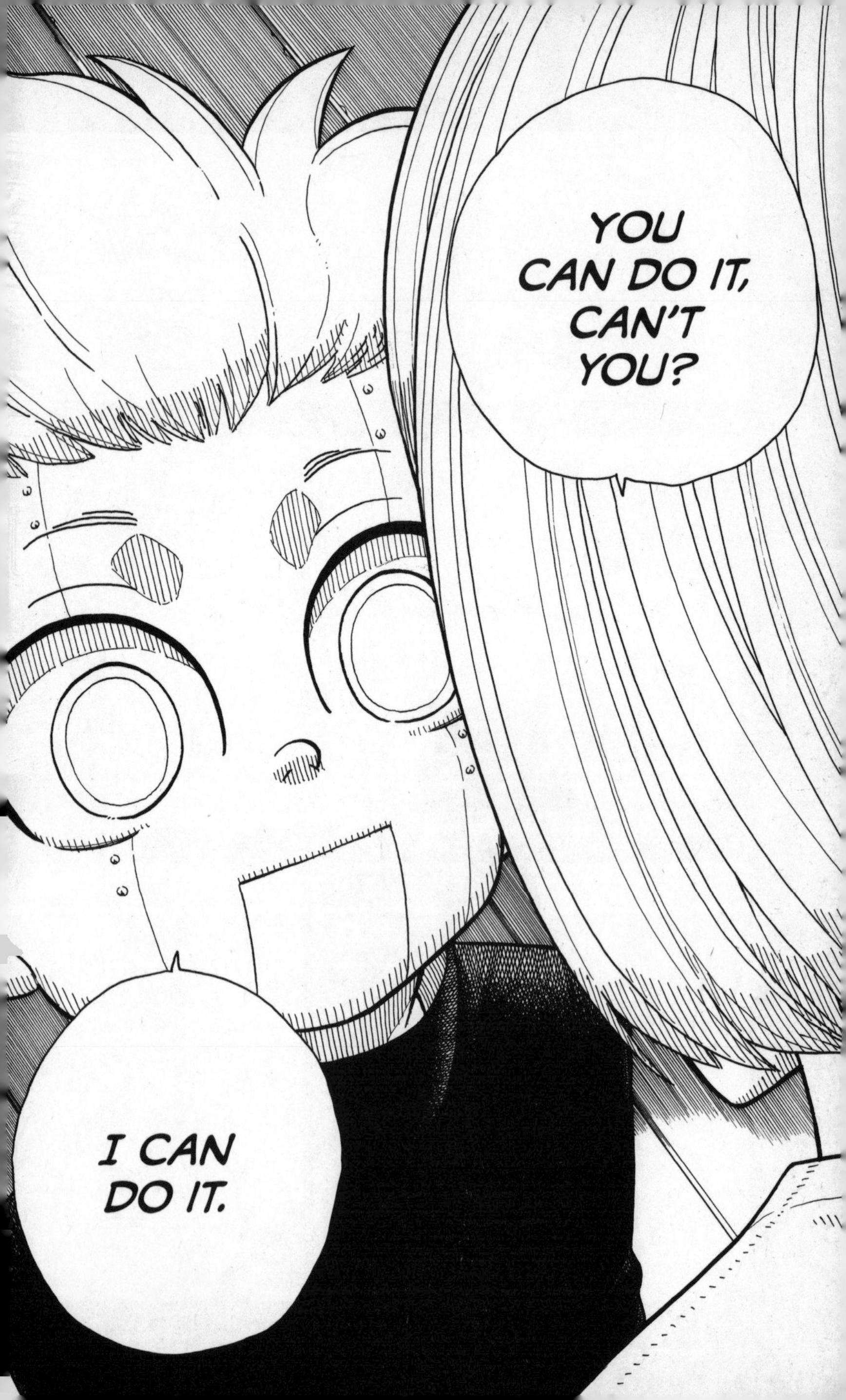
YOU CAN DO IT, CAN'T YOU?
I CAN DO IT.

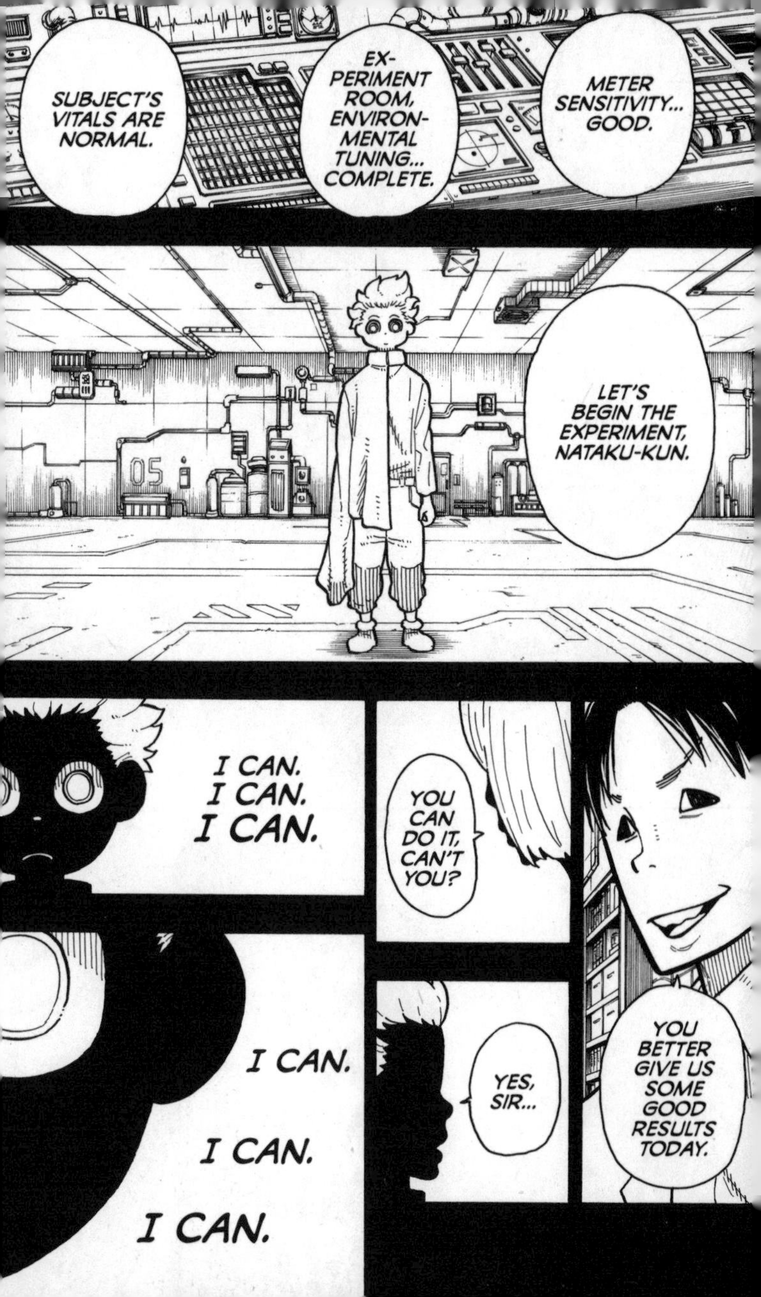
METER SENSITIVITY... GOOD.
EX-PERIMENT ROOM, ENVIRON-MENTAL TUNING... COMPLETE.
SUBJECT'S VITALS ARE NORMAL.
LET'S BEGIN THE EXPERIMENT, NATAKU-KUN.
YOU BETTER GIVE US SOME GOOD RESULTS TODAY.
YOU CAN DO IT, CAN'T YOU?
YES, SIR...
I CAN. I CAN. I CAN.
I CAN.
I CAN.
I CAN.

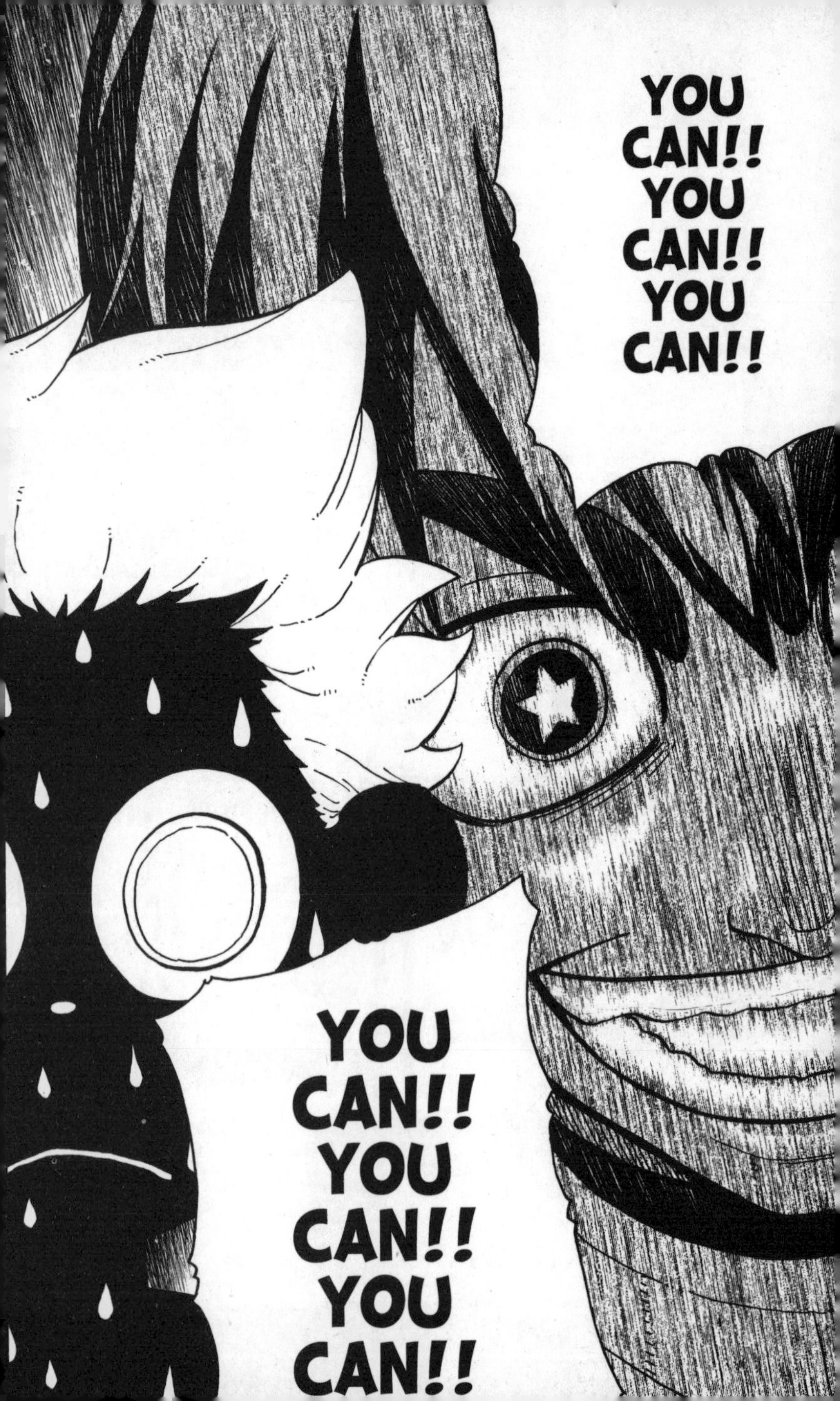
YOU CAN!! YOU CAN!! YOU CAN!!
YOU CAN!! YOU CAN!! YOU CAN!!

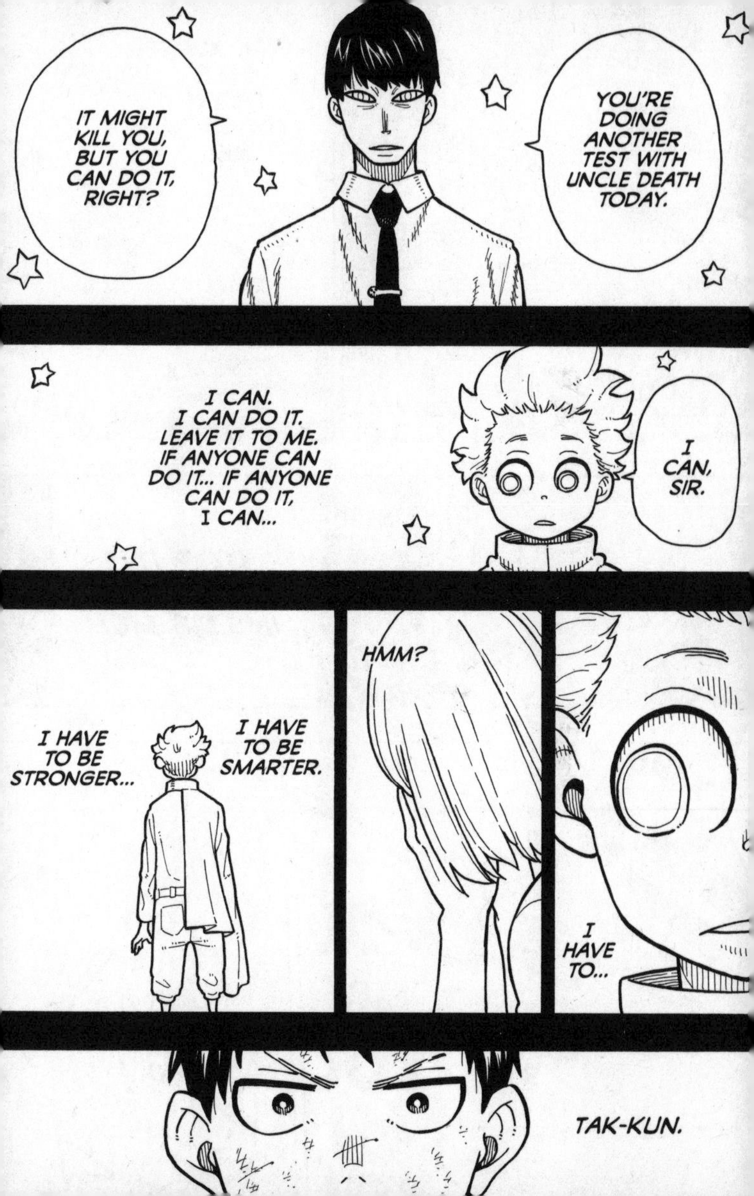
YOU'RE DOING ANOTHER TEST WITH UNCLE DEATH TODAY.
IT MIGHT KILL YOU, BUT YOU CAN DO IT, RIGHT?
I CAN, SIR.
I CAN. I CAN DO IT. LEAVE IT TO ME. IF ANYONE CAN DO IT... IF ANYONE CAN DO IT, I CAN...
I HAVE TO...
HMM?
I HAVE TO BE SMARTER.
I HAVE TO BE STRONGER...
TAK-KUN.

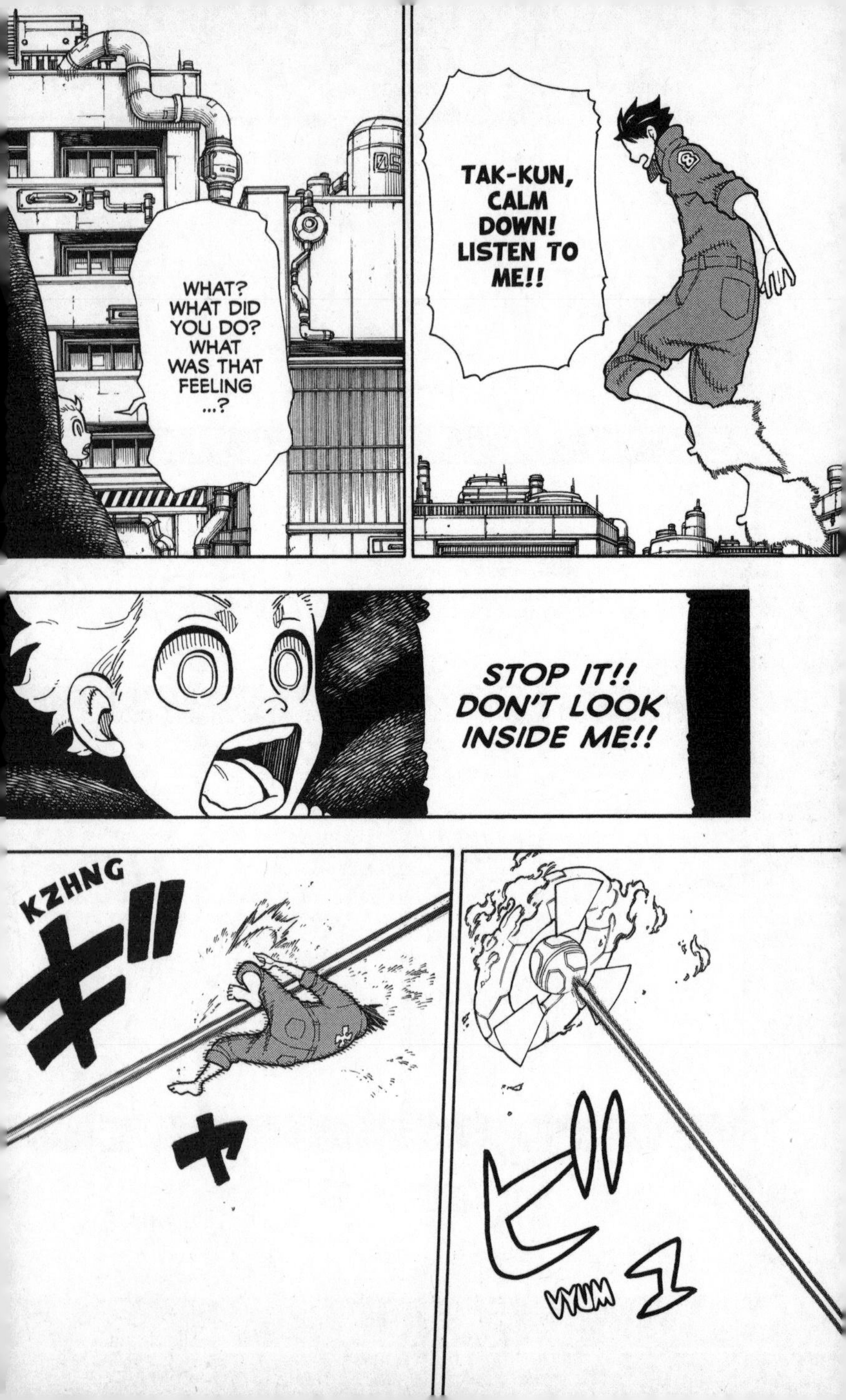
TAK-KUN, CALM DOWN! LISTEN TO ME!!
WHAT? WHAT DID YOU DO? WHAT WAS THAT FEELING ...?
STOP IT!! DON'T LOOK INSIDE ME!!
VYUM
KZHNG

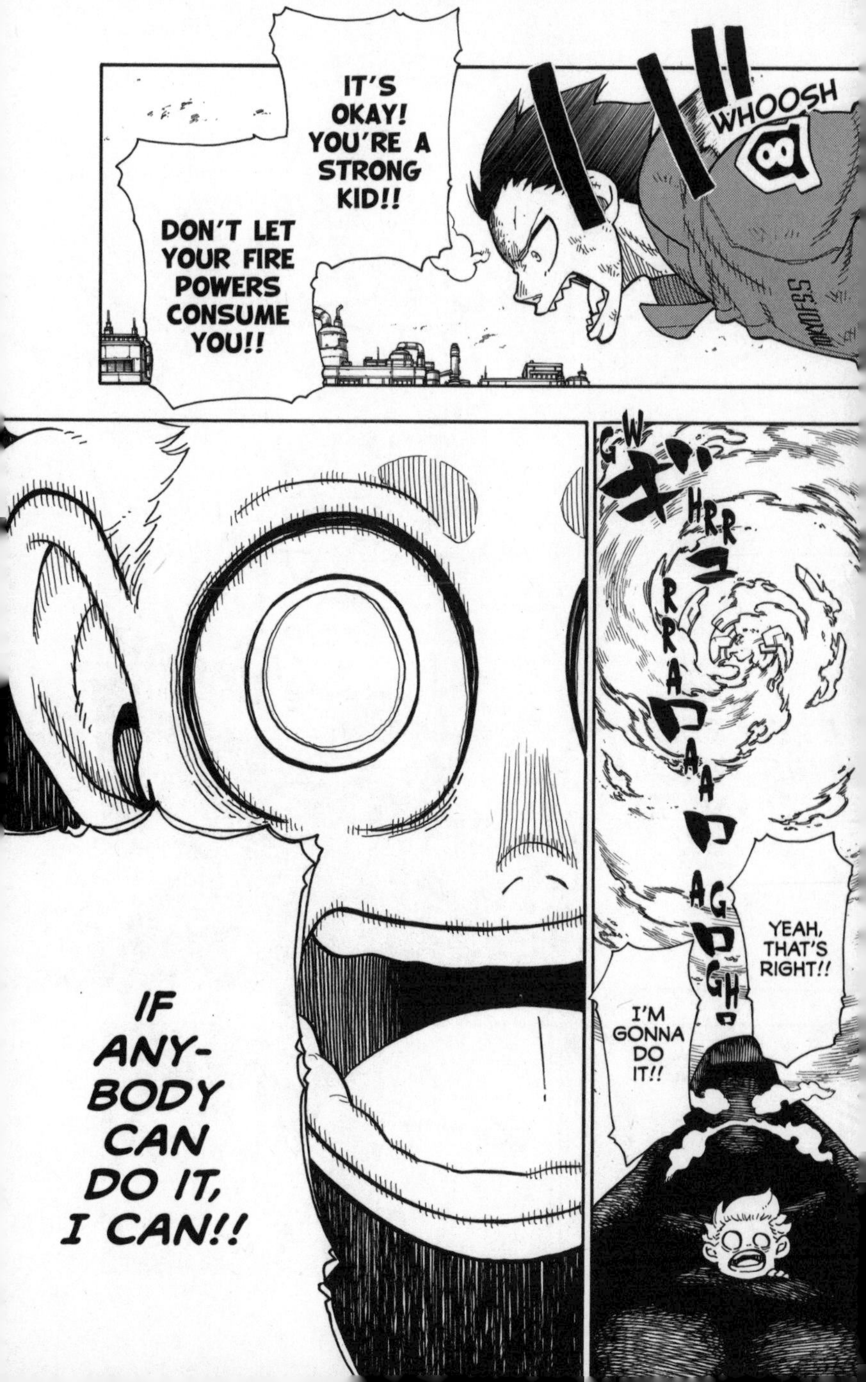
WHOOSH
IT'S OKAY! YOU'RE A STRONG KID!!
DON'T LET YOUR FIRE POWERS CONSUME YOU!!
GWHRRRRRAAAAGGH
YEAH, THAT'S RIGHT!!
I'M GONNA DO IT!!
IF ANY-BODY CAN DO IT, I CAN!!

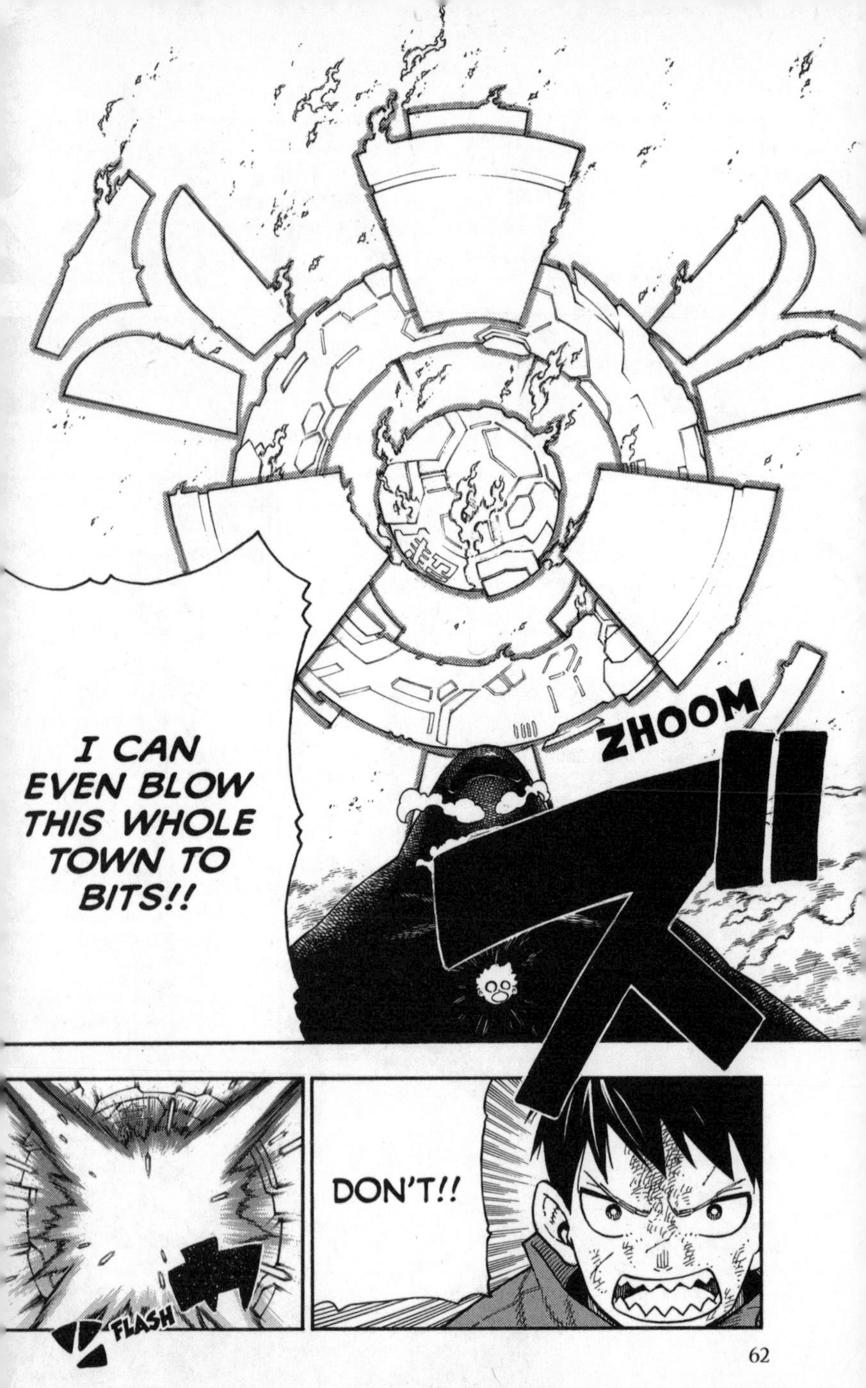
I CAN EVEN BLOW THIS WHOLE TOWN TO BITS!!
ZHOOM
DON'T!!
FLASH

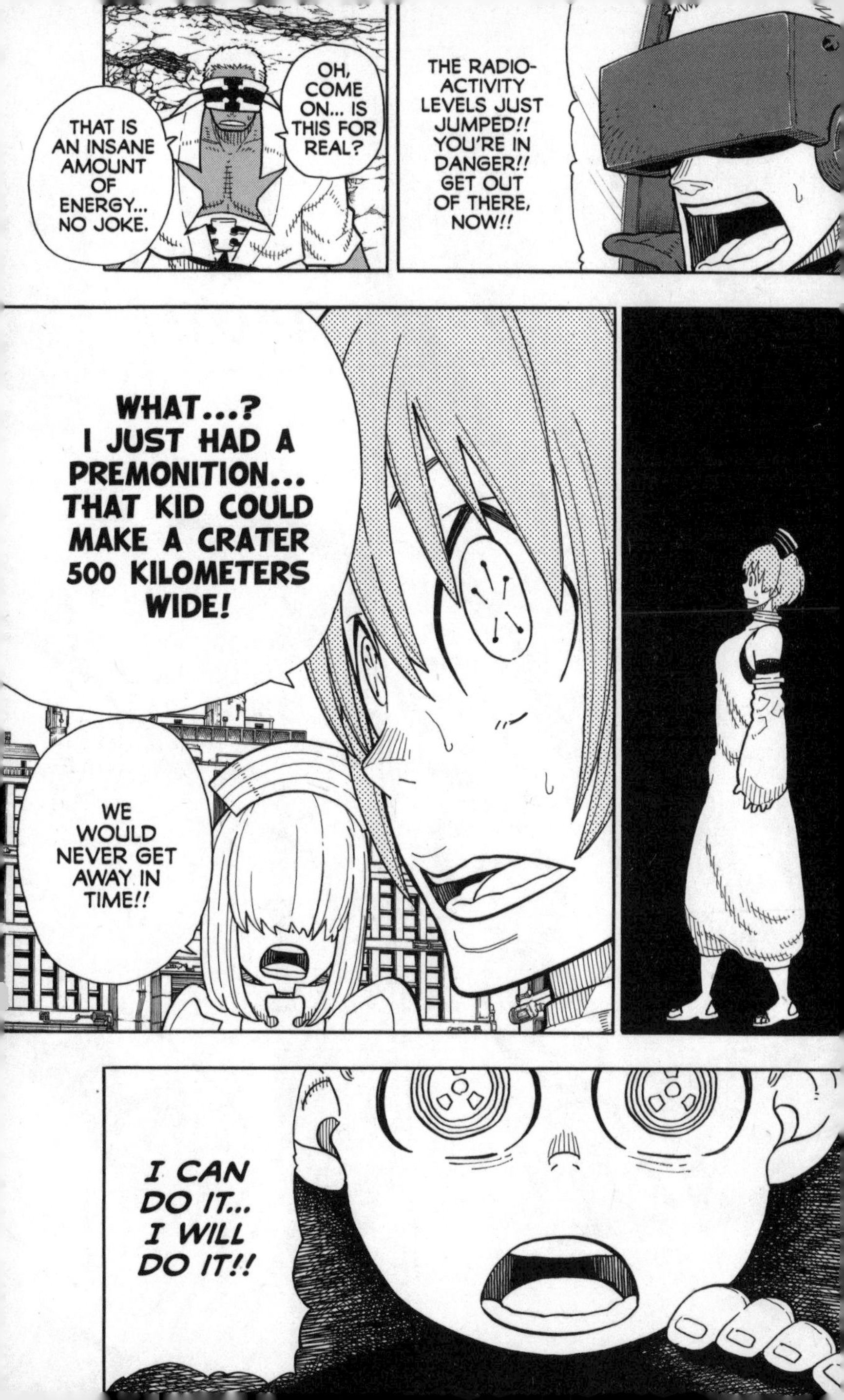
THE RADIO-ACTIVITY LEVELS JUST JUMPED!! YOU'RE IN DANGER!! GET OUT OF THERE, NOW!!
OH, COME ON... IS THIS FOR REAL?
THAT IS AN INSANE AMOUNT OF ENERGY... NO JOKE.
WHAT...? I JUST HAD A PREMONITION... THAT KID COULD MAKE A CRATER 500 KILOMETERS WIDE!
WE WOULD NEVER GET AWAY IN TIME!!
I CAN DO IT... I WILL DO IT!!

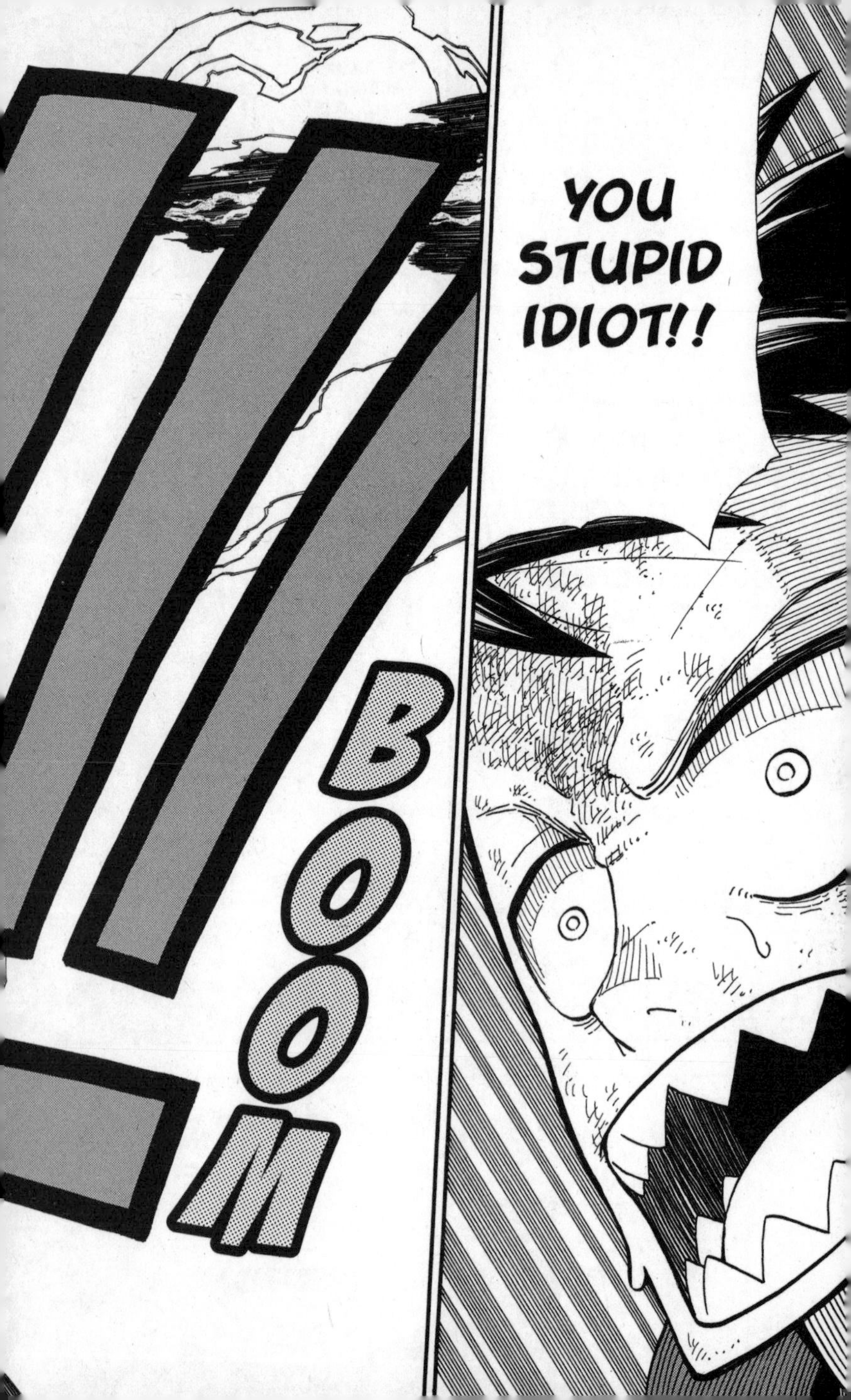
YOU STUPID IDIOT!!
BOOM

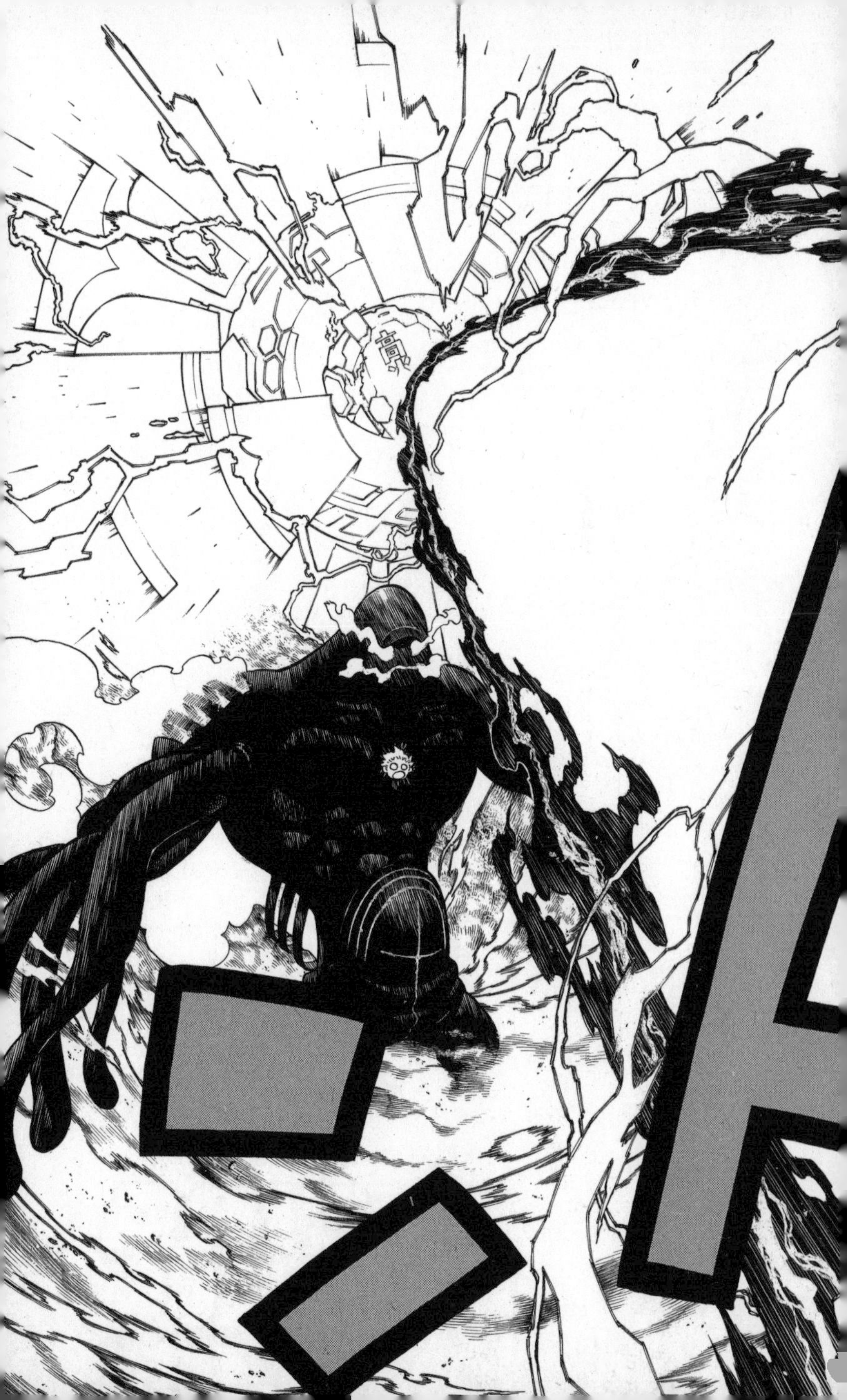

FIRE FORCE

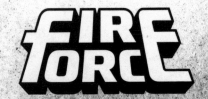

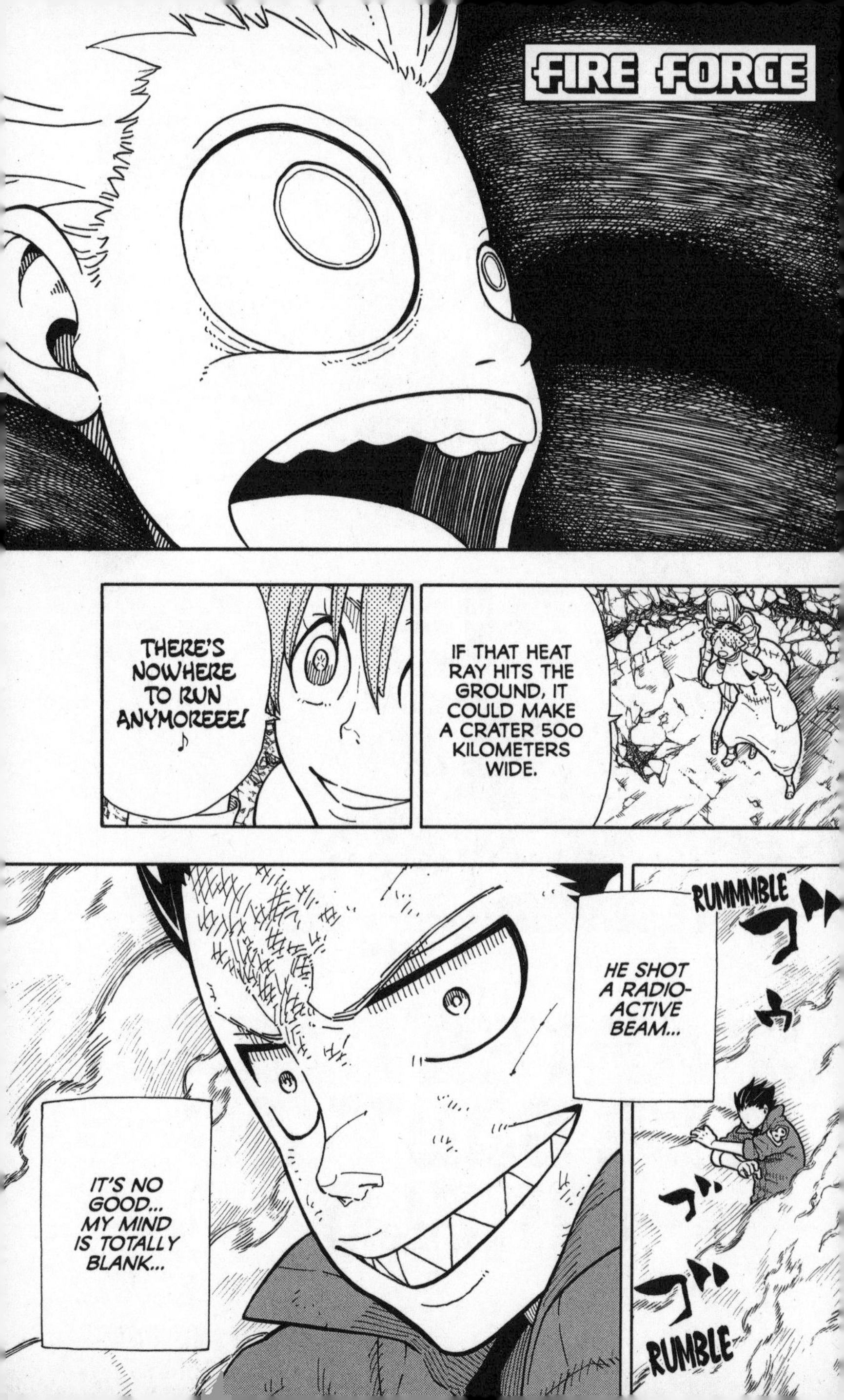
FIRE FORCE
IF THAT HEAT RAY HITS THE GROUND, IT COULD MAKE A CRATER 500 KILOMETERS WIDE.
THERE'S NOWHERE TO RUN ANYMOREEE! ♪
RUMMMBLE
HE SHOT A RADIO-ACTIVE BEAM...
RUMBLE
IT'S NO GOOD... MY MIND IS TOTALLY BLANK...

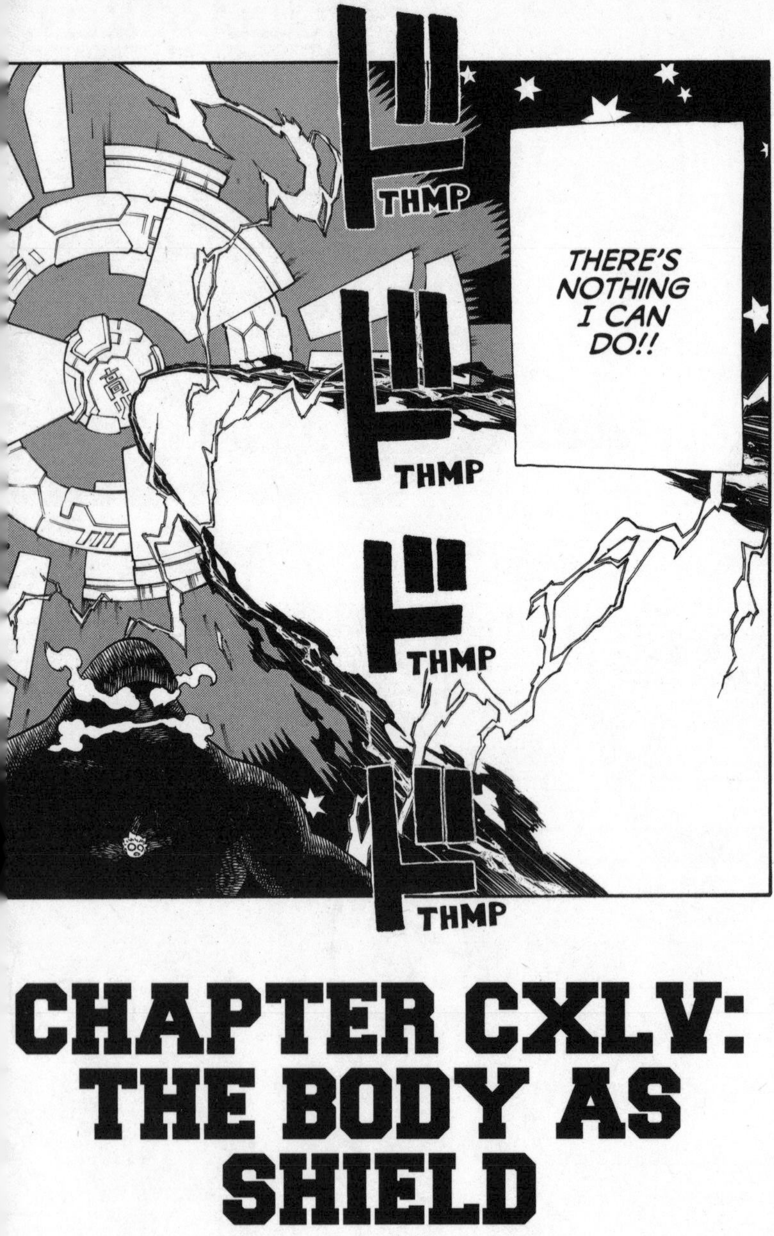
THERE'S NOTHING I CAN DO!!
ド THMP
ド THMP
ド THMP
ド THMP

CHAPTER CXLV: THE BODY AS SHIELD

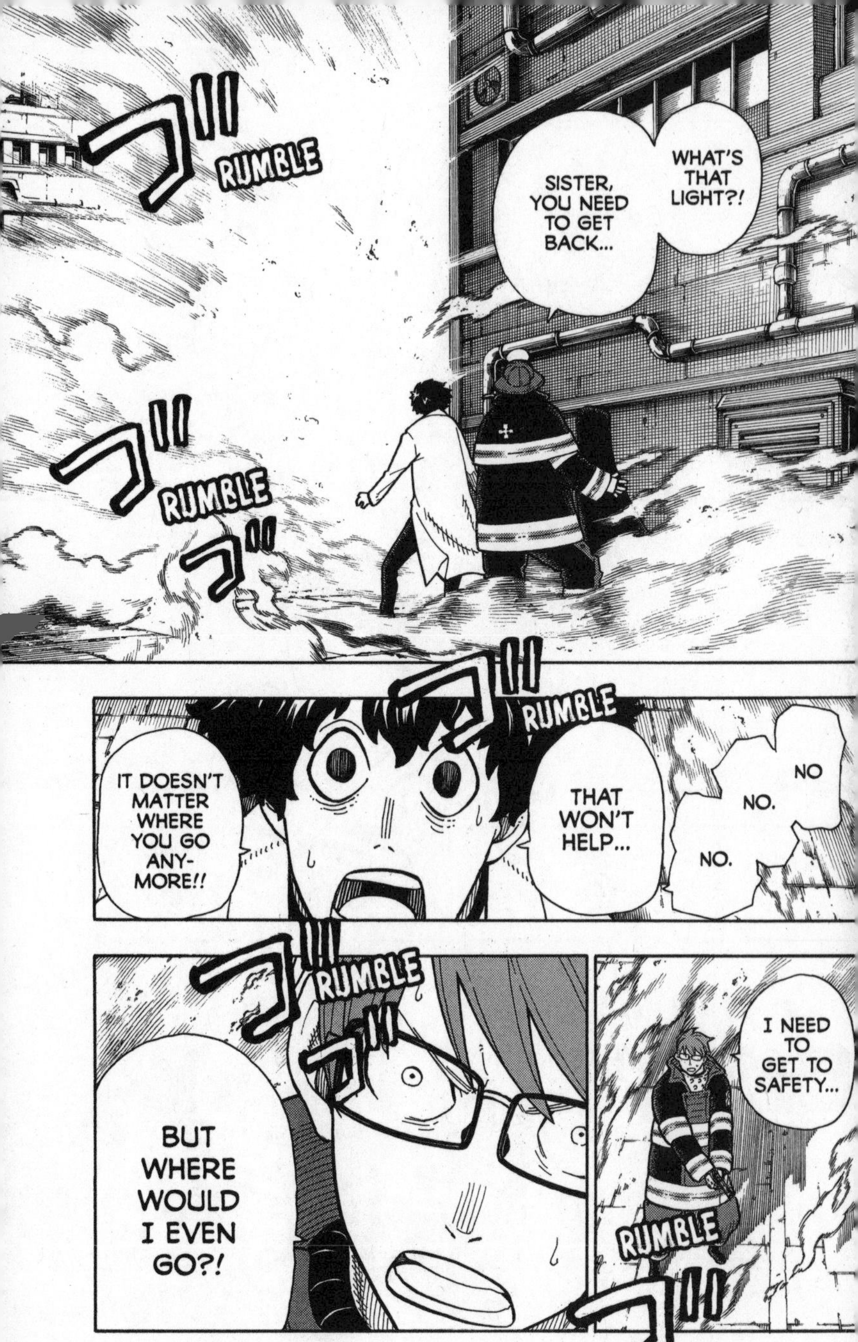
RUMBLE
WHAT'S THAT LIGHT?!
SISTER, YOU NEED TO GET BACK...
RUMBLE
RUMBLE
RUMBLE
NO NO. NO.
THAT WON'T HELP...
IT DOESN'T MATTER WHERE YOU GO ANY-MORE!!
I NEED TO GET TO SAFETY...
RUMBLE
RUMBLE
BUT WHERE WOULD I EVEN GO?!

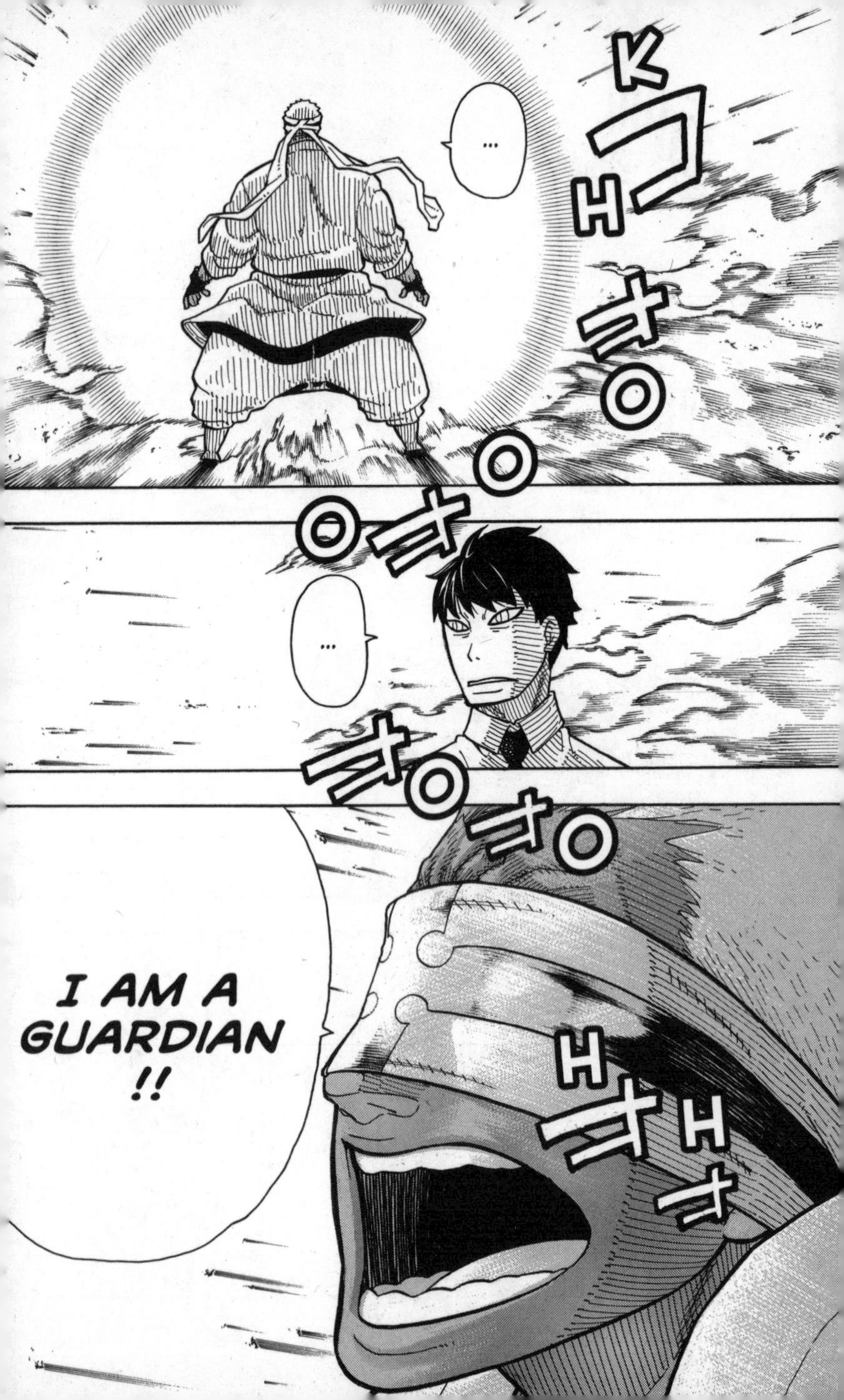
KH
...
...
I AM A GUARDIAN !!
HH

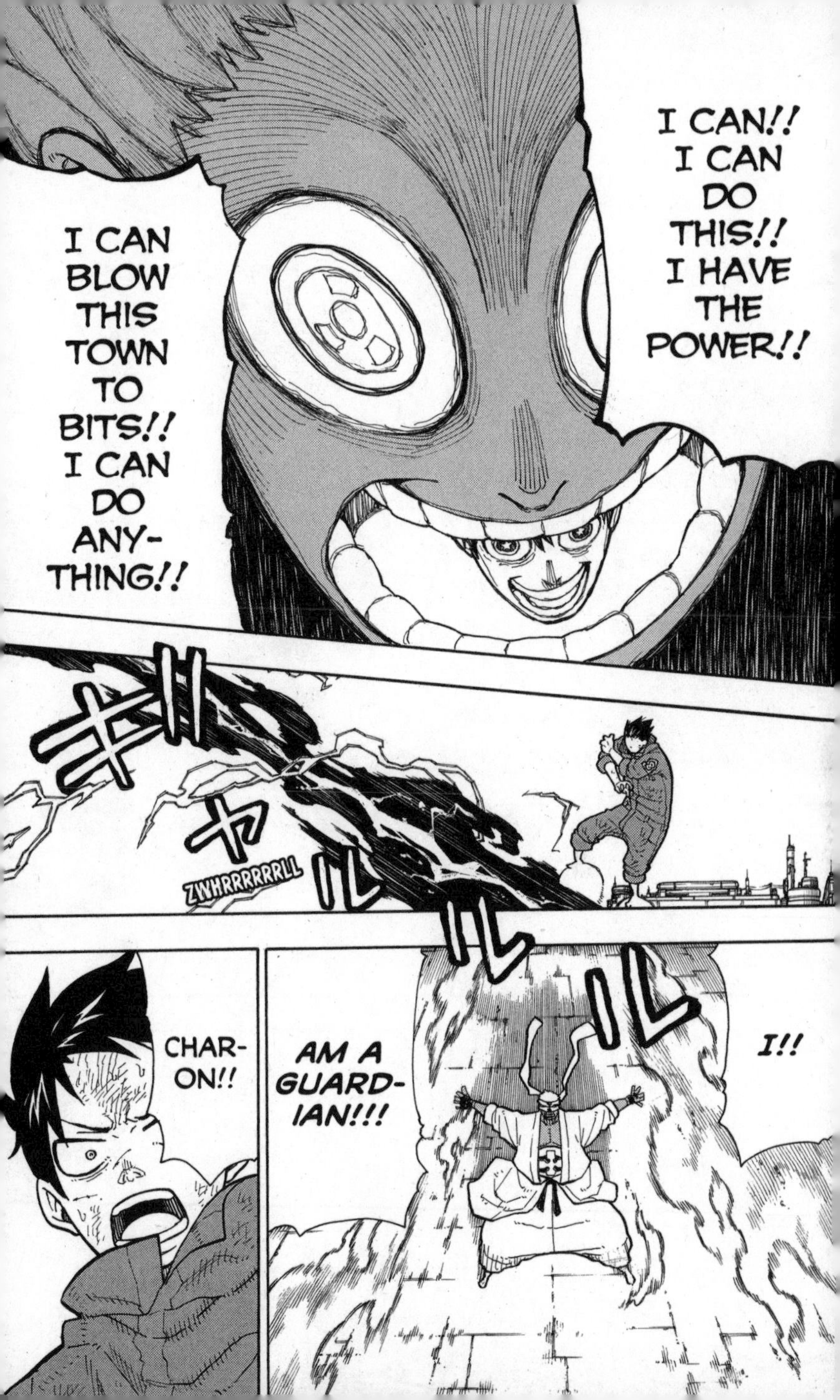
I CAN!! I CAN DO THIS!! I HAVE THE POWER!!
I CAN BLOW THIS TOWN TO BITS!! I CAN DO ANYTHING!!
ZWHRRRRRRLL
I!!
AM A GUARDIAN!!!
CHARON!!

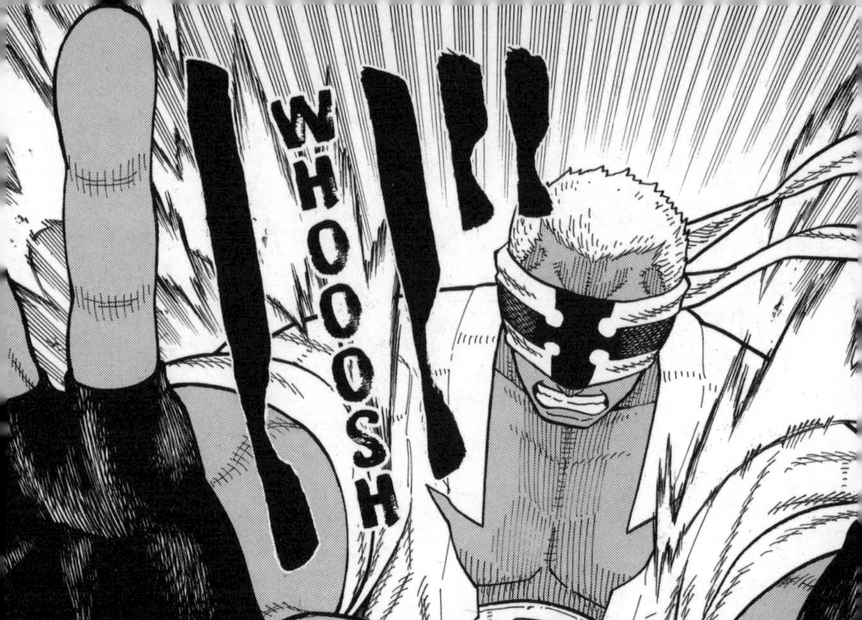
WHOOOOSH

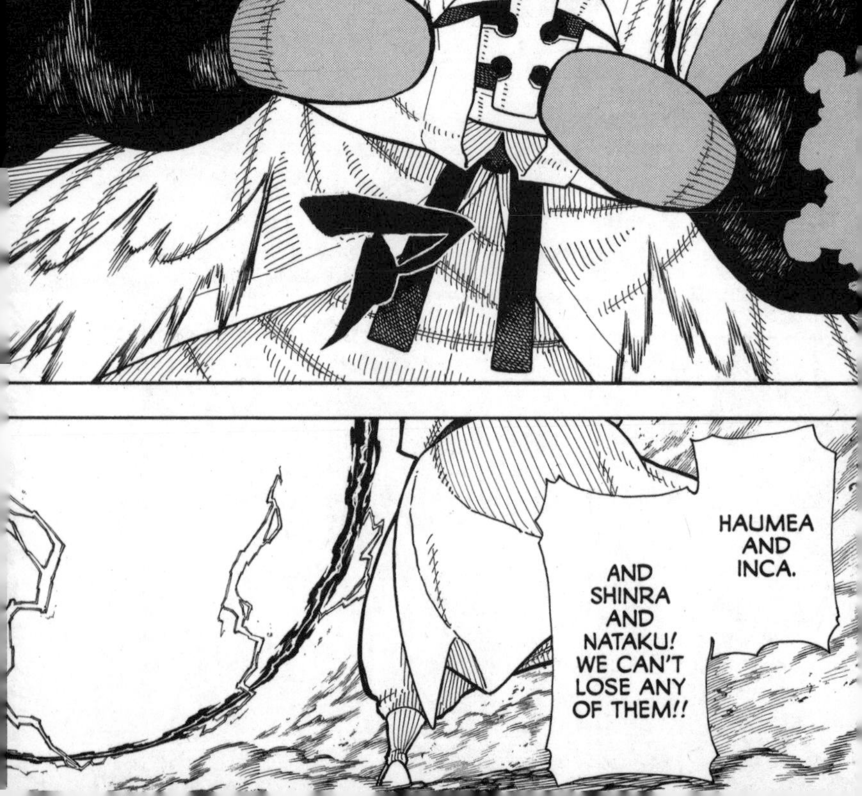
HAUMEA AND INCA.
AND SHINRA AND NATAKU! WE CAN'T LOSE ANY OF THEM!!

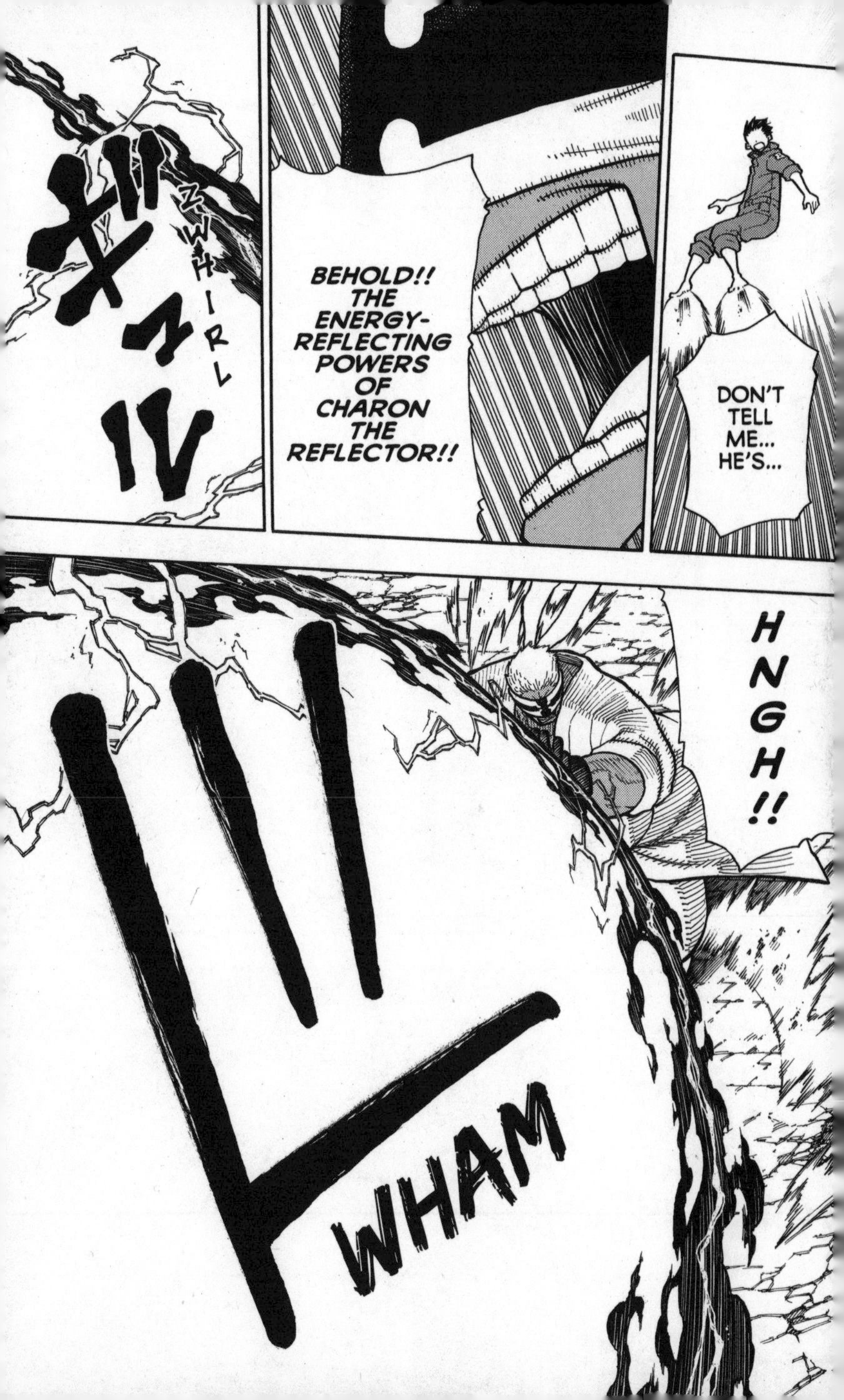
DON'T TELL ME... HE'S...
BEHOLD!! THE ENERGY-REFLECTING POWERS OF CHARON THE REFLECTOR!!
WHIRL
HNGH!!
WHAM

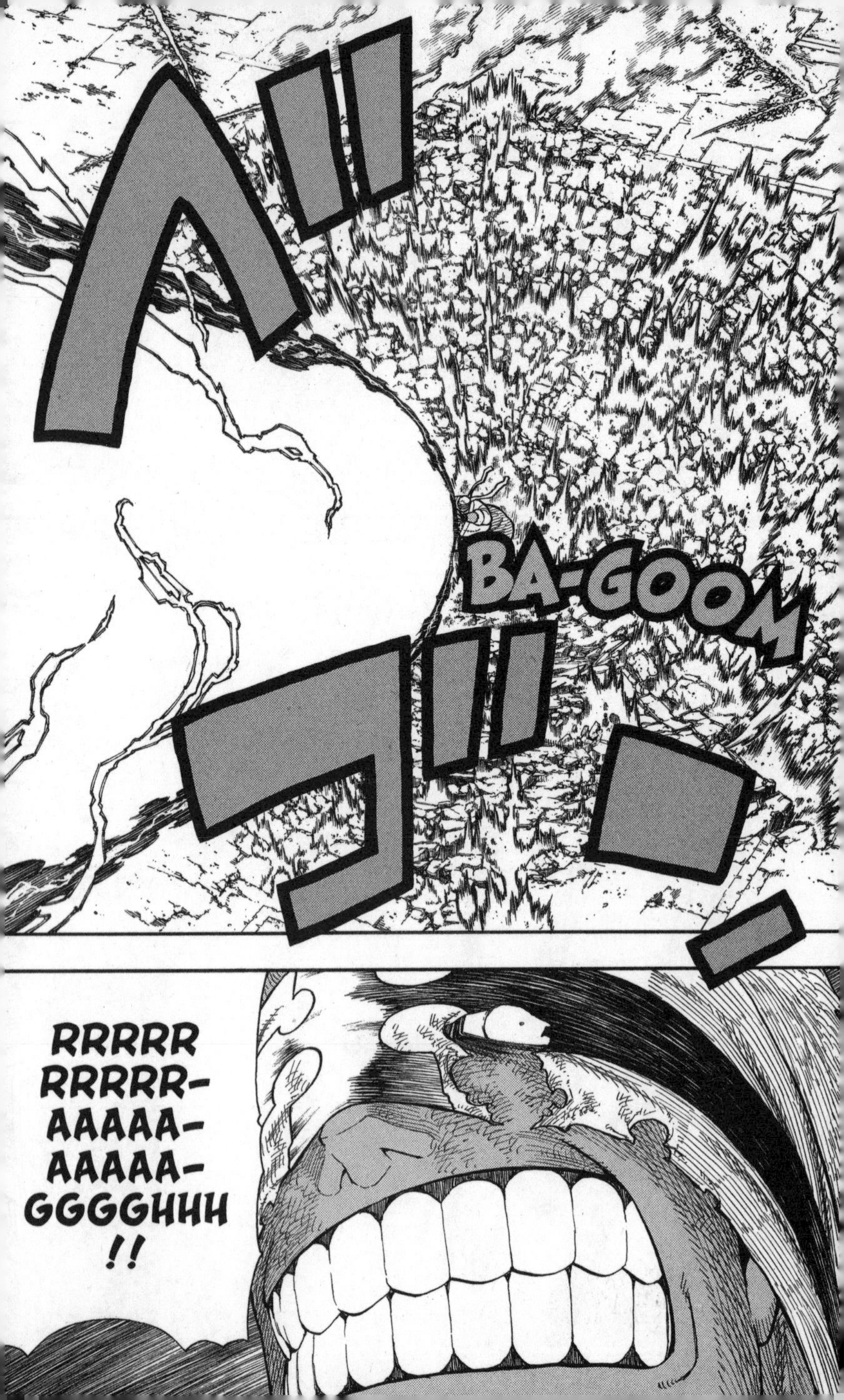
ベゴー
BA-GOOM
RRRRR RRRRR-AAAAA-AAAAA-GGGGHHH!!

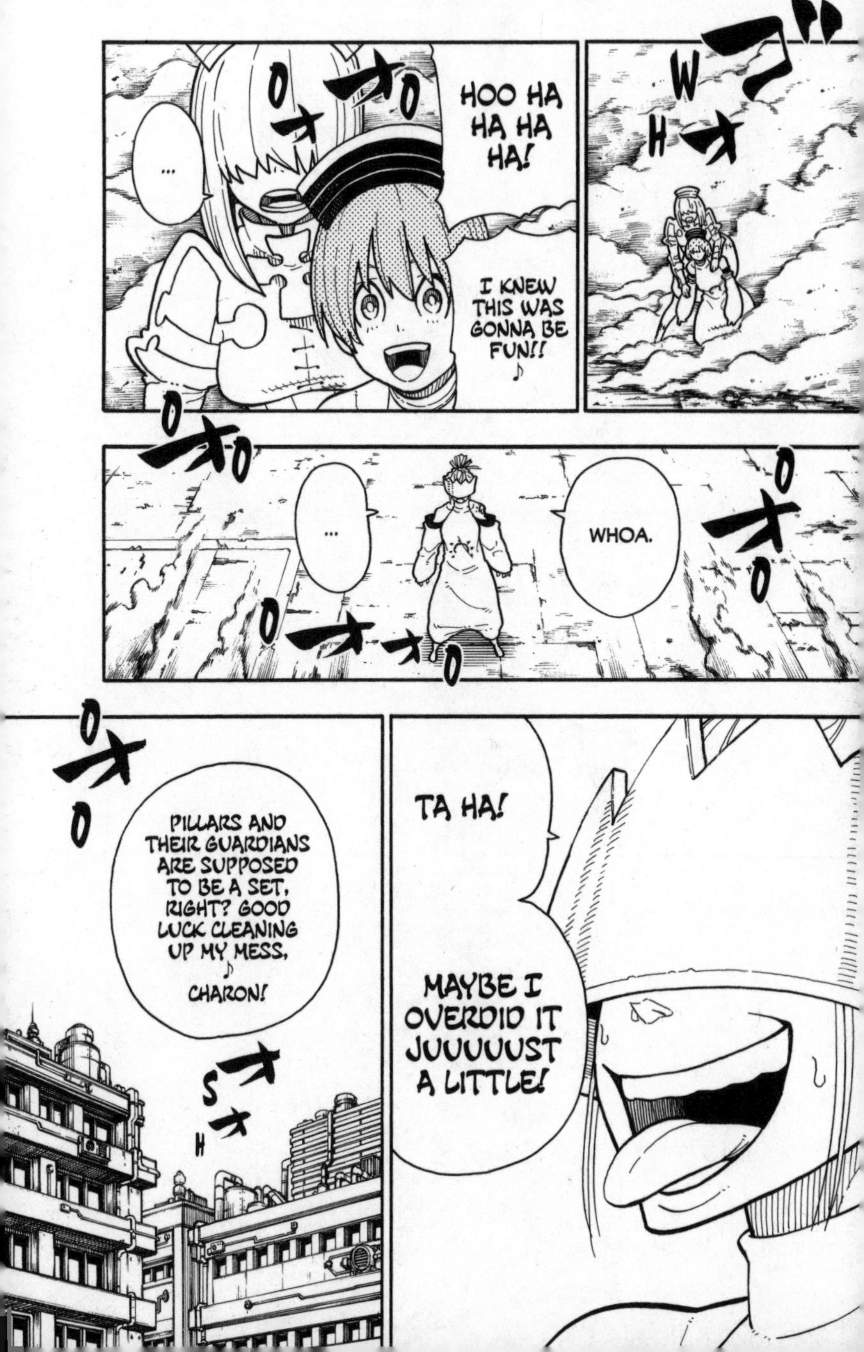
WH
HOO HA HA HA HA!
I KNEW THIS WAS GONNA BE FUN!! ♪
...
WHOA.
...
TA HA!
MAYBE I OVERDID IT JUUUUUST A LITTLE!
PILLARS AND THEIR GUARDIANS ARE SUPPOSED TO BE A SET, RIGHT? GOOD LUCK CLEANING UP MY MESS, ♪ CHARON!
SH

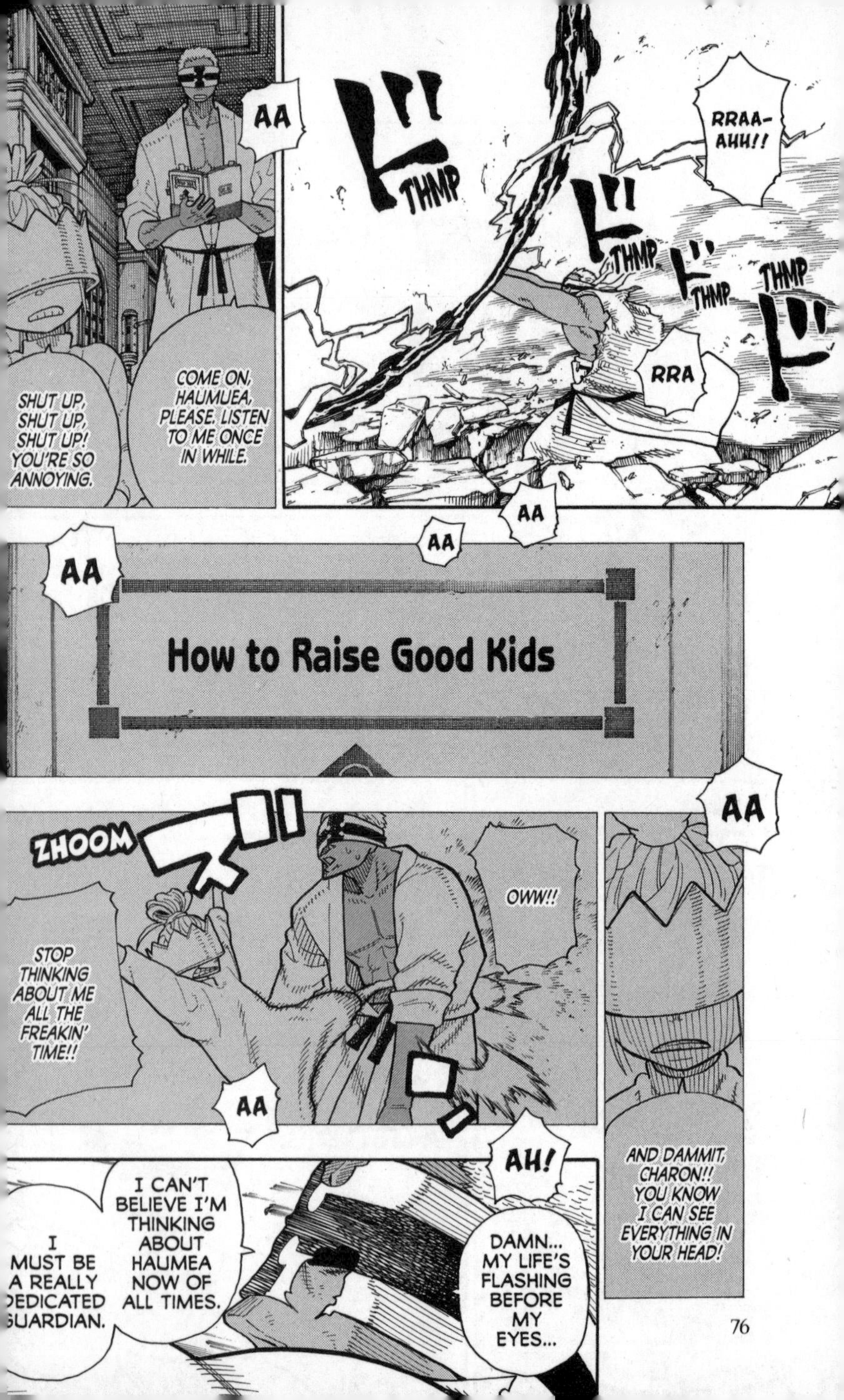

RRAA-AHH!!
ド THMP
ド THMP
ド THMP
ド THMP
RRA
AA
AA
COME ON, HAUMUEA, PLEASE. LISTEN TO ME ONCE IN WHILE.
SHUT UP, SHUT UP, SHUT UP! YOU'RE SO ANNOYING.
AA
AA
How to Raise Good Kids
AA
AND DAMMIT, CHARON!! YOU KNOW I CAN SEE EVERYTHING IN YOUR HEAD!
ZHOOM
OWW!!
STOP THINKING ABOUT ME ALL THE FREAKIN' TIME!!
AA
AH!
DAMN... MY LIFE'S FLASHING BEFORE MY EYES...
I CAN'T BELIEVE I'M THINKING ABOUT HAUMEA NOW OF ALL TIMES.
I MUST BE A REALLY DEDICATED GUARDIAN.

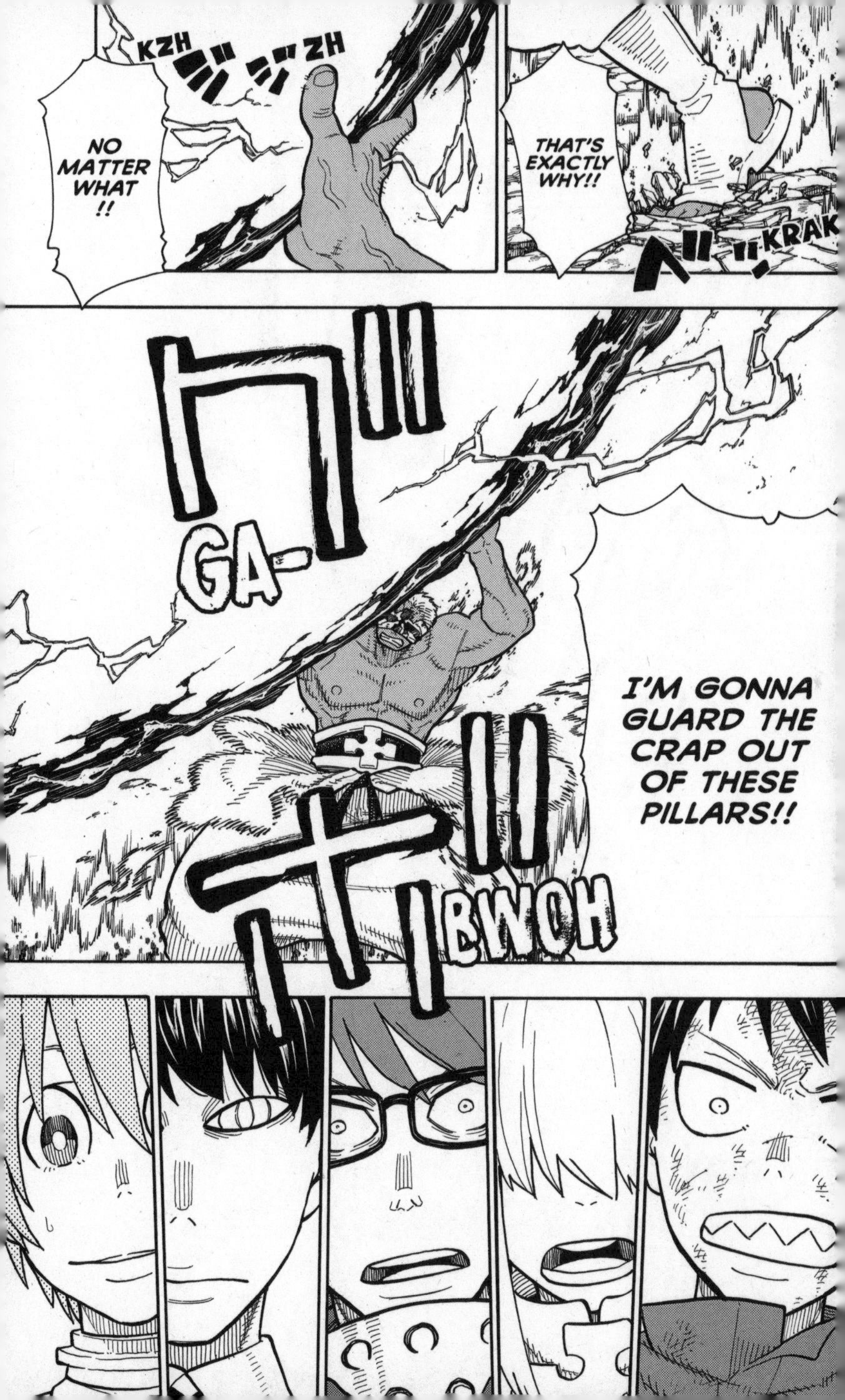
THAT'S EXACTLY WHY!!
KRAK
KZH ZH
NO MATTER WHAT!!
GA-
I'M GONNA GUARD THE CRAP OUT OF THESE PILLARS!!
BWOH

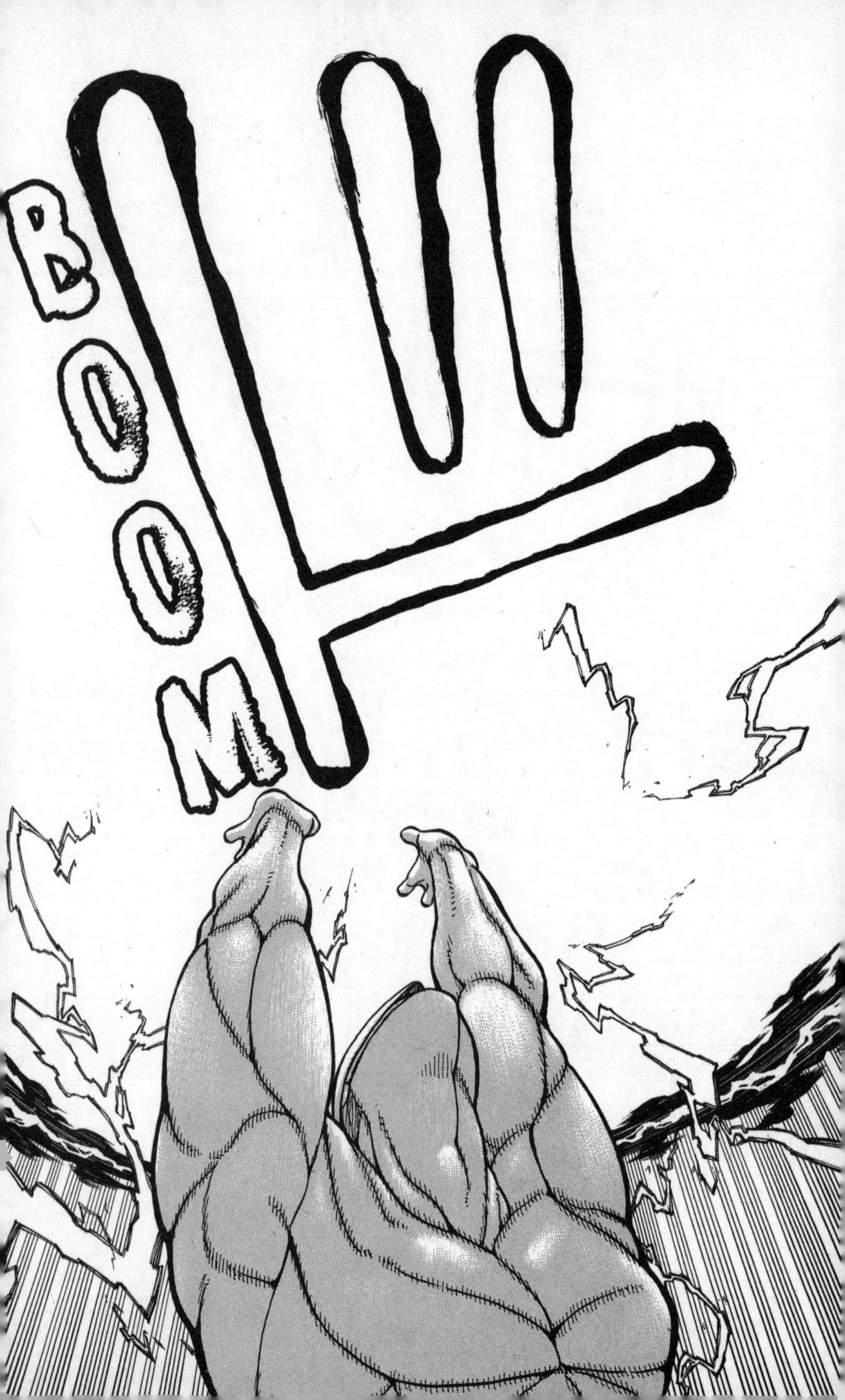
BOOM!!!

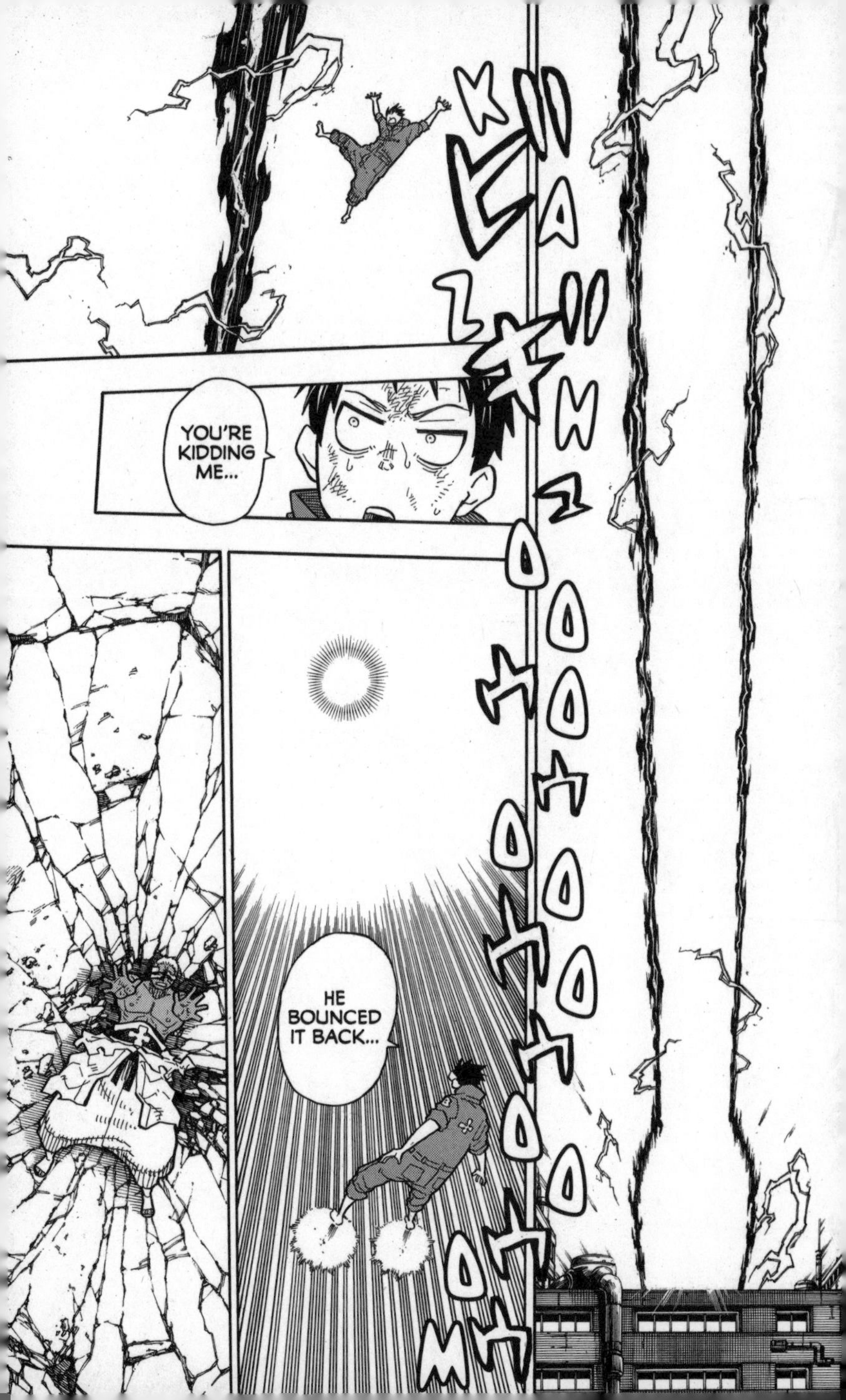
YOU'RE KIDDING ME...
HE BOUNCED IT BACK...

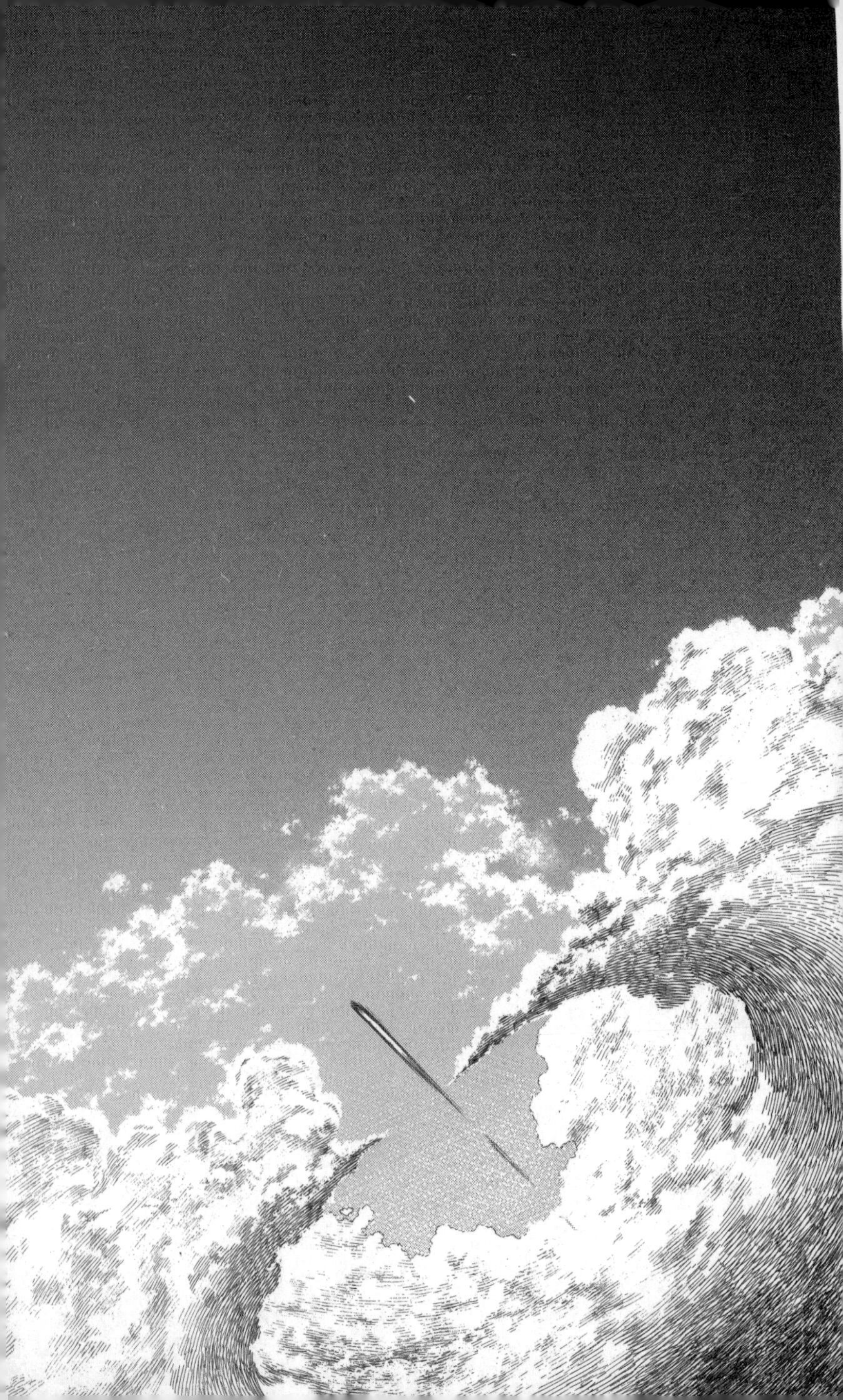

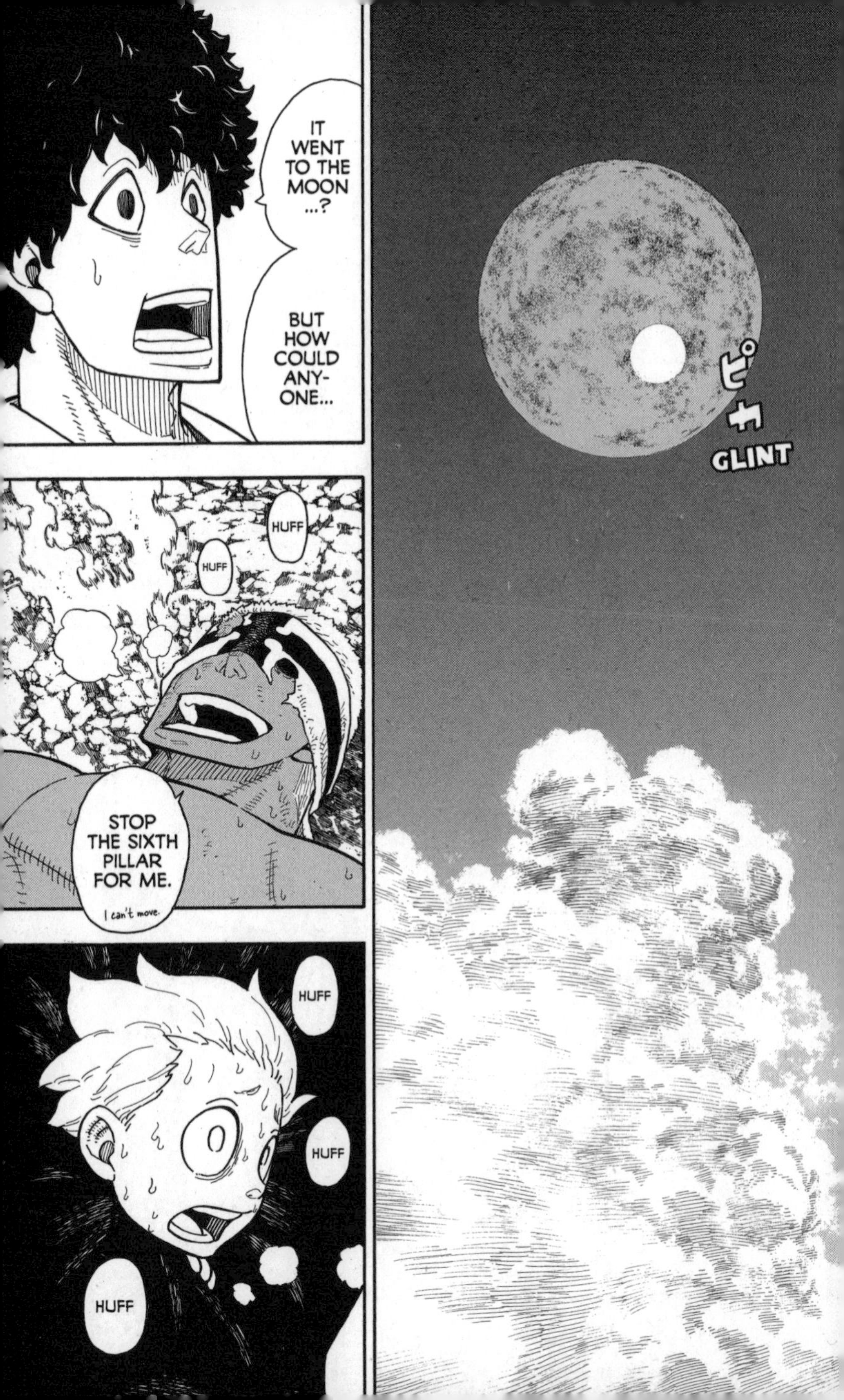
ピカ
GLINT
IT WENT TO THE MOON ...?
BUT HOW COULD ANY- ONE...
HUFF
HUFF
STOP THE SIXTH PILLAR FOR ME.
I can't move.
HUFF
HUFF
HUFF

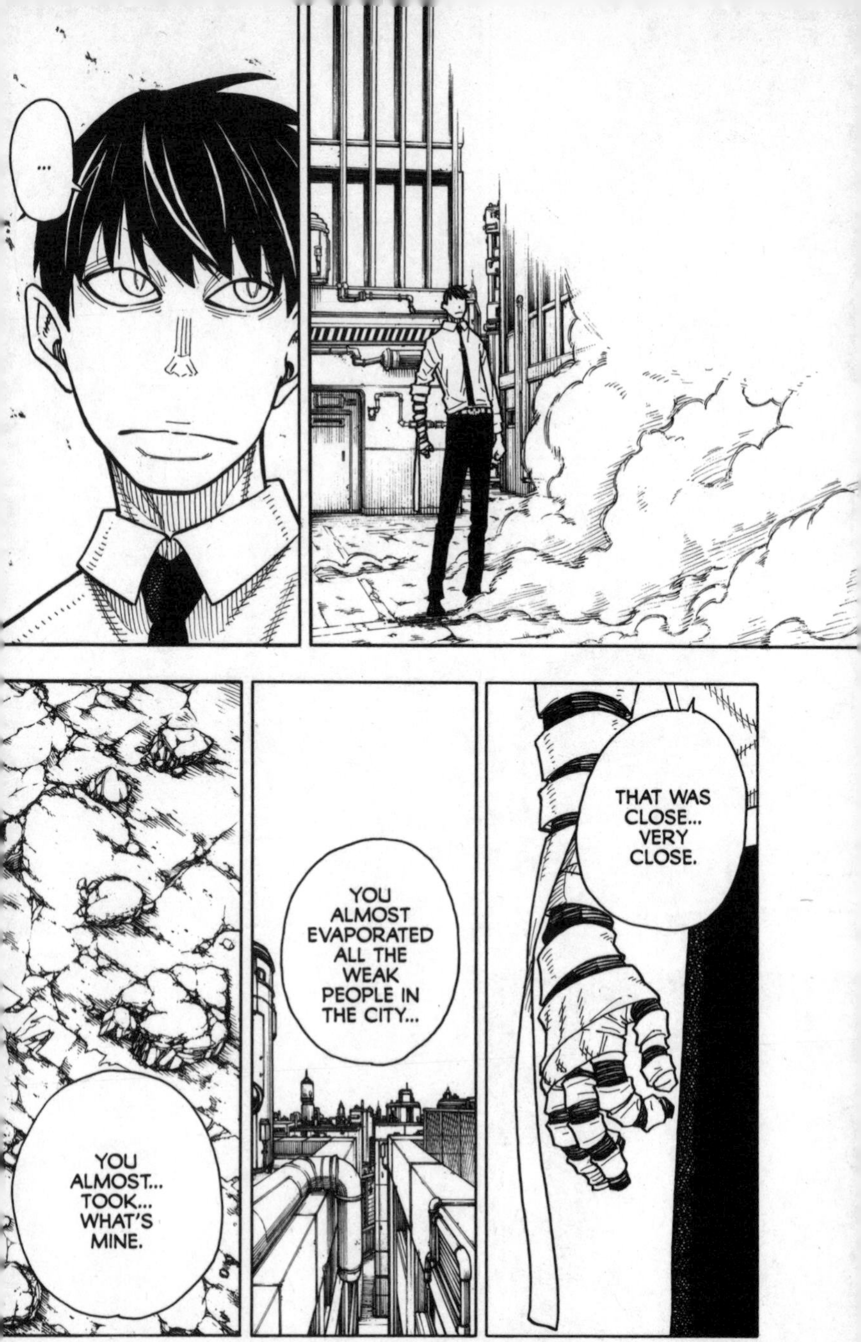
...
THAT WAS CLOSE... VERY CLOSE.
YOU ALMOST EVAPORATED ALL THE WEAK PEOPLE IN THE CITY...
YOU ALMOST... TOOK... WHAT'S MINE.

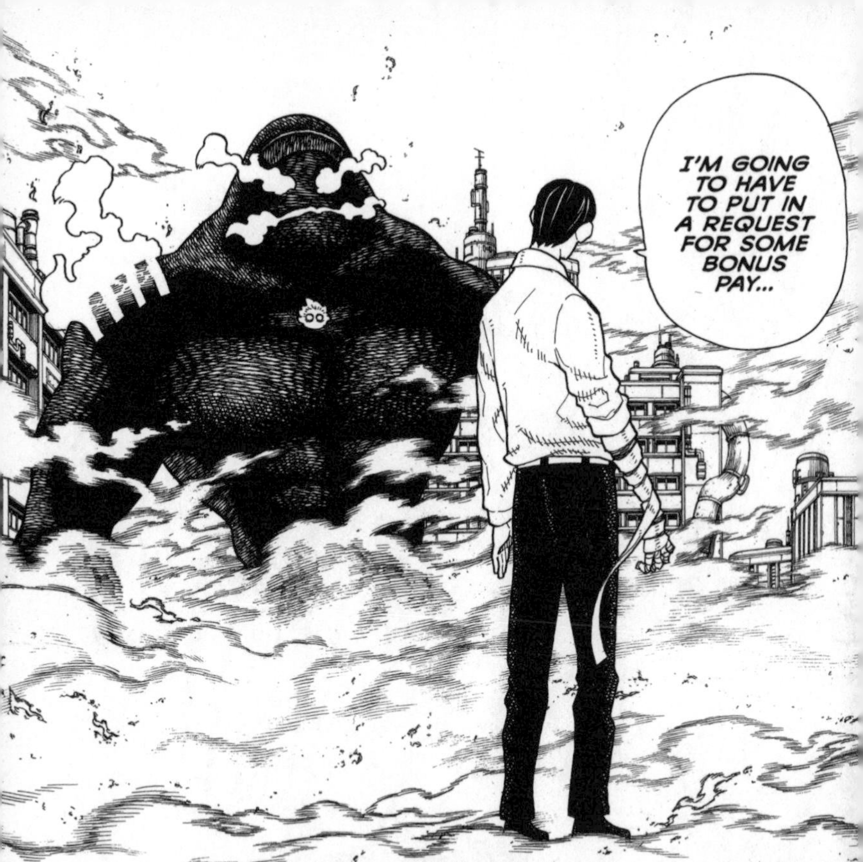
I'M GOING TO HAVE TO PUT IN A REQUEST FOR SOME BONUS PAY...
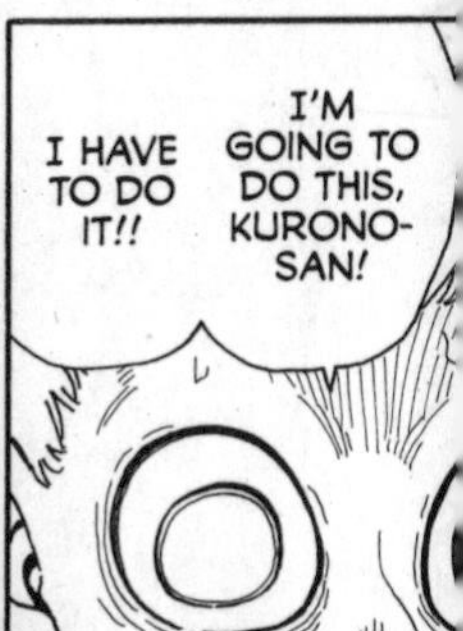
I'M GOING TO DO THIS, KURONO-SAN!
I HAVE TO DO IT!!
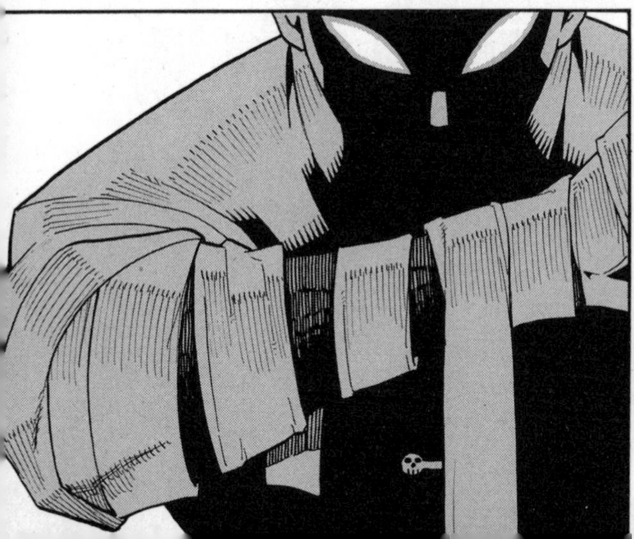

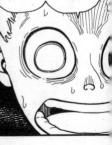

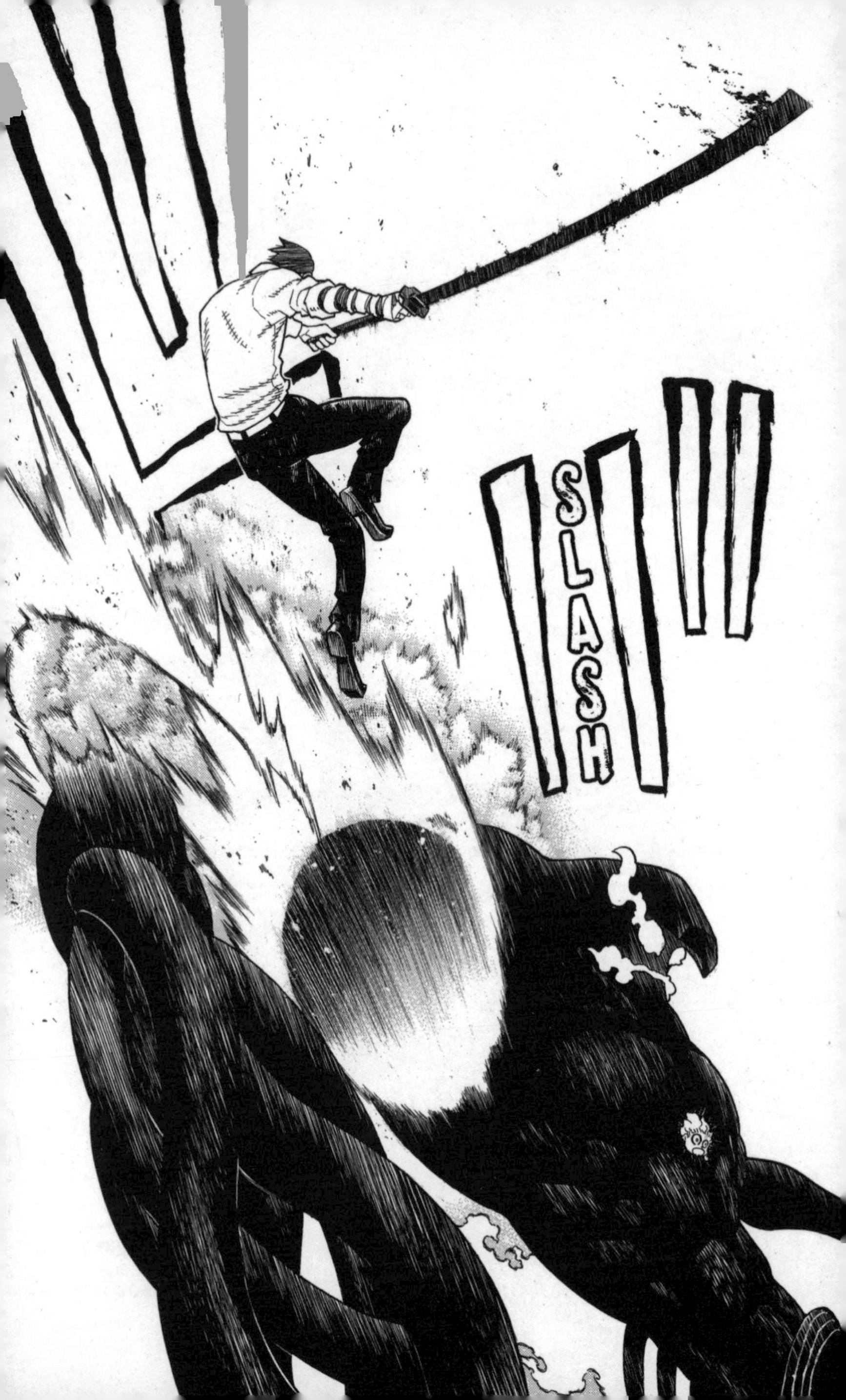
SLASH

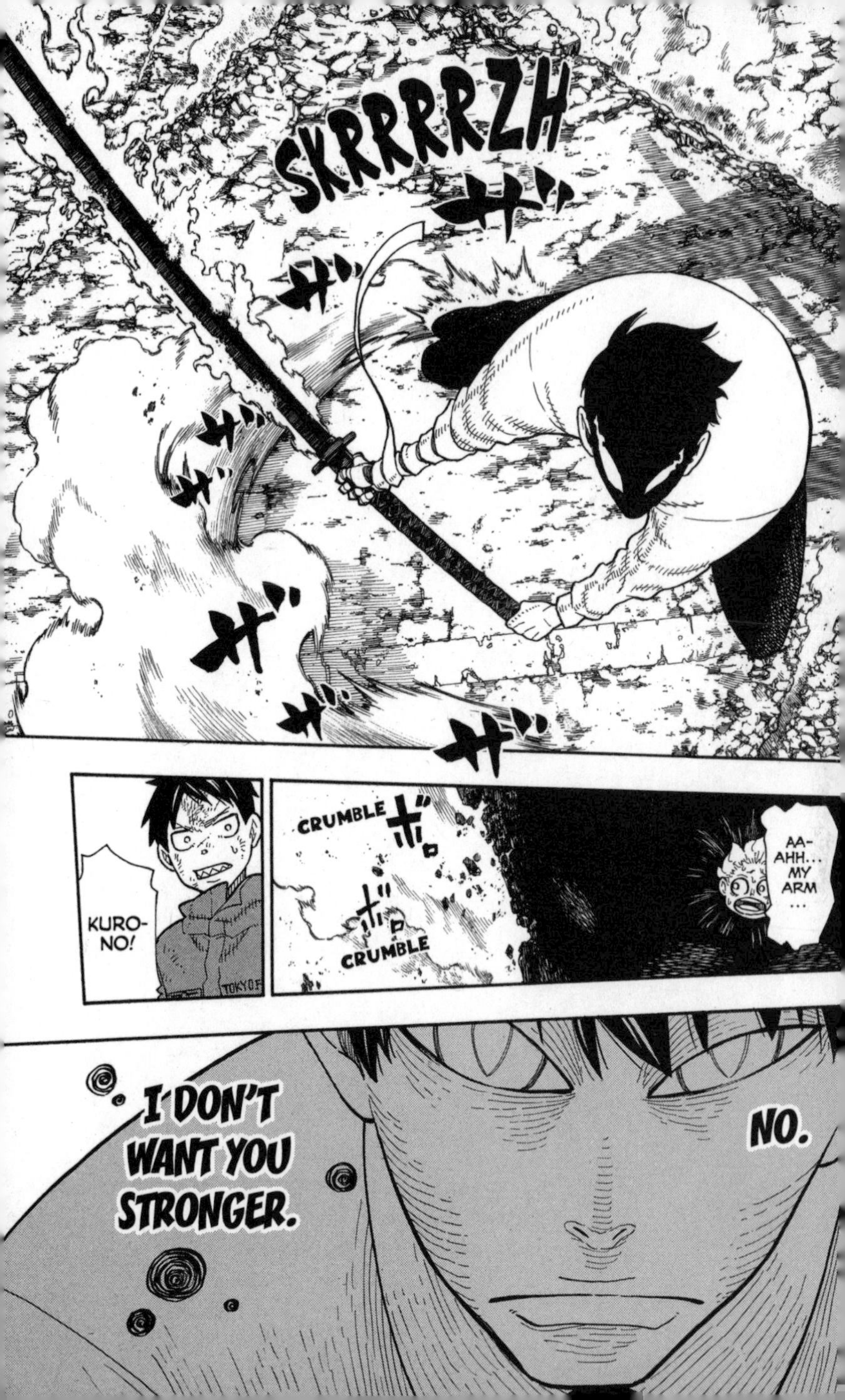
SKRRRRZH
AA-AHH... MY ARM...
CRUMBLE
CRUMBLE
KURO-NO!
NO.
I DON'T WANT YOU STRONGER.

FIRE FORCE

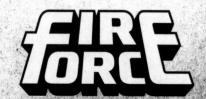

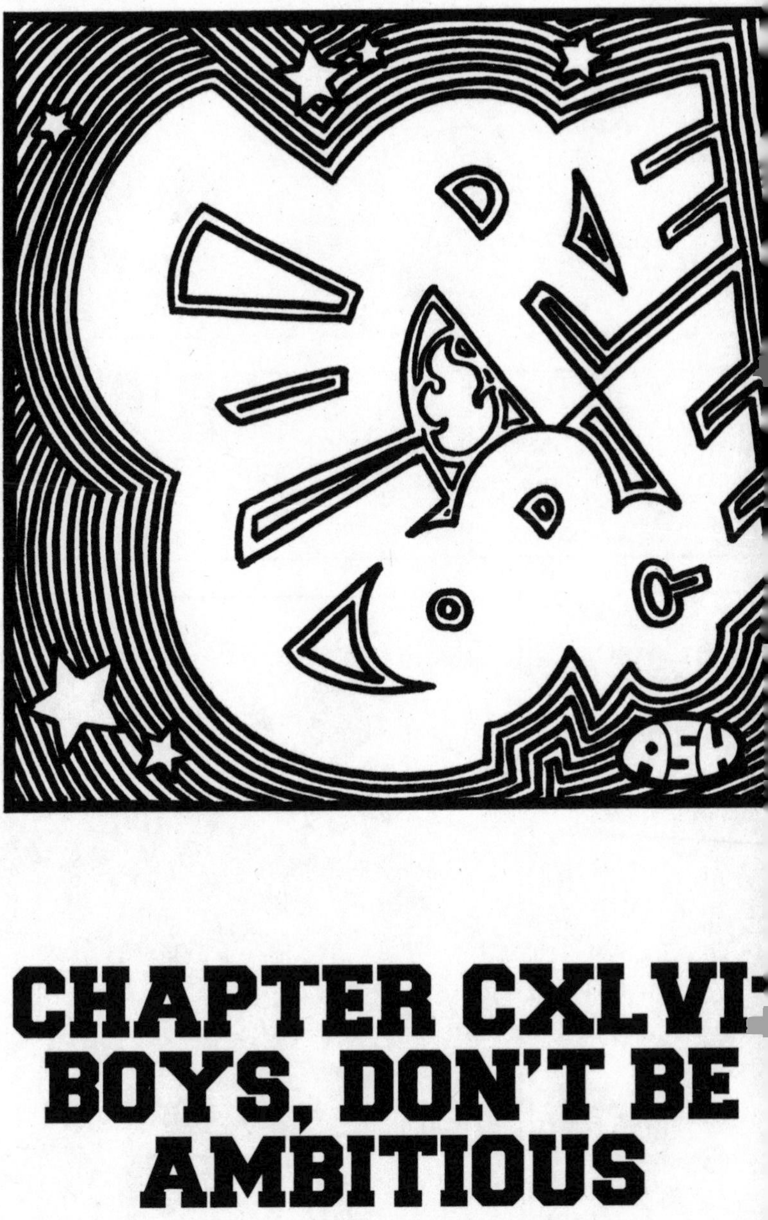
ASH

CHAPTER CXLVI: BOYS, DON'T BE AMBITIOUS

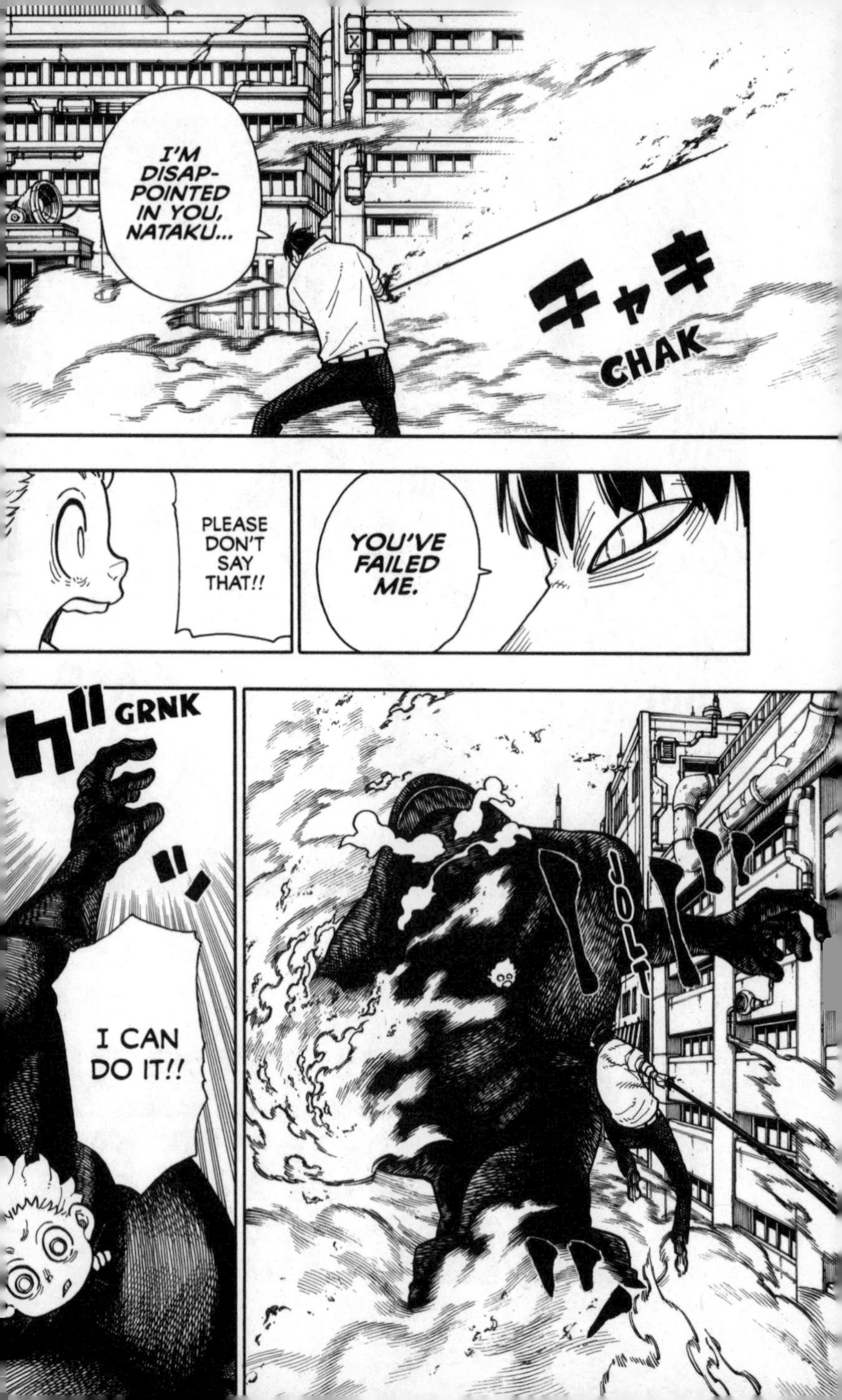
I'M DISAPPOINTED IN YOU, NATAKU...
チャキ
CHAK
YOU'VE FAILED ME.
PLEASE DON'T SAY THAT!!
JOLT
ガッ
GRNK
I CAN DO IT!!

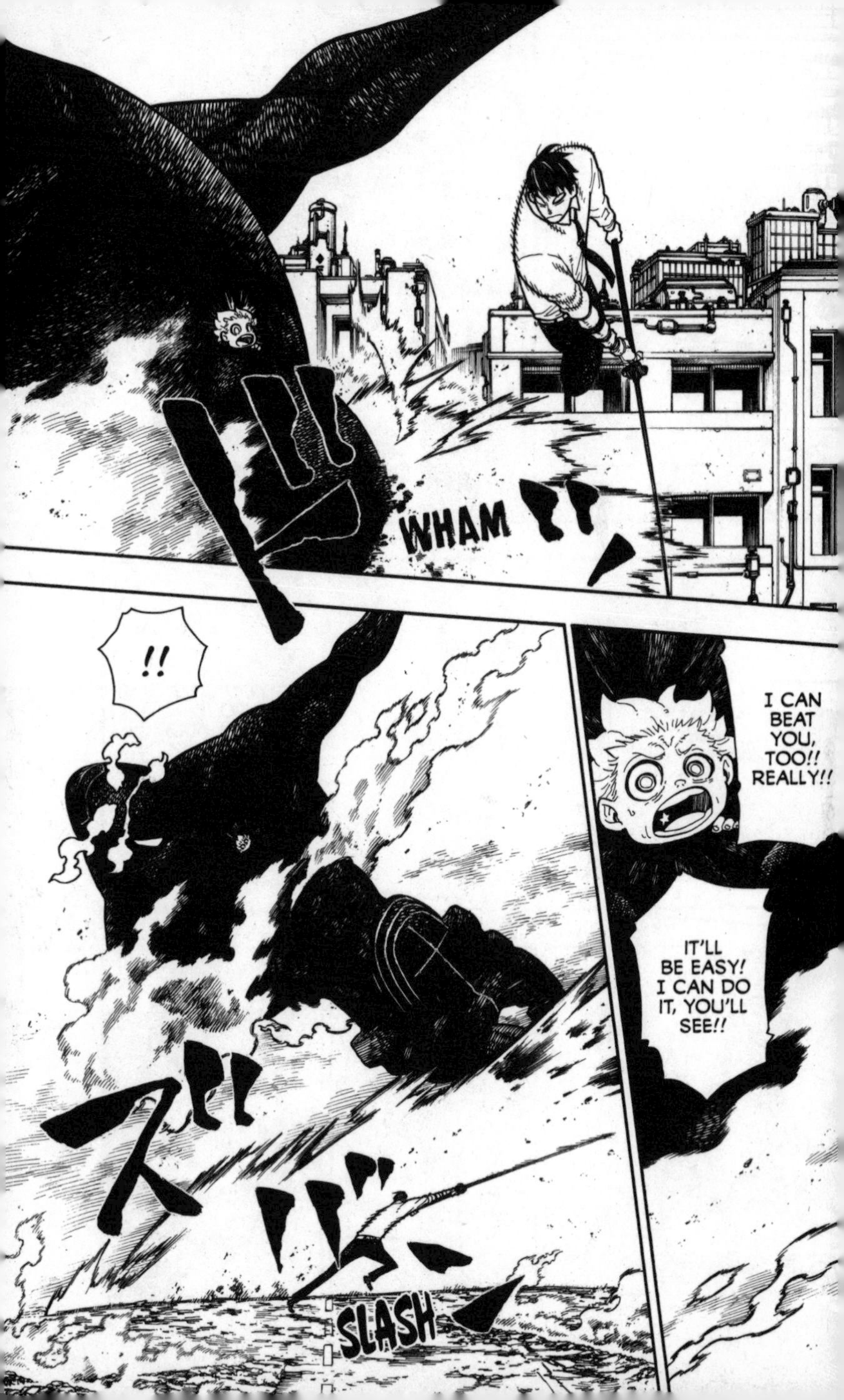
WHAM
I CAN BEAT YOU, TOO!! REALLY!!
IT'LL BE EASY! I CAN DO IT, YOU'LL SEE!!
!!
SLASH

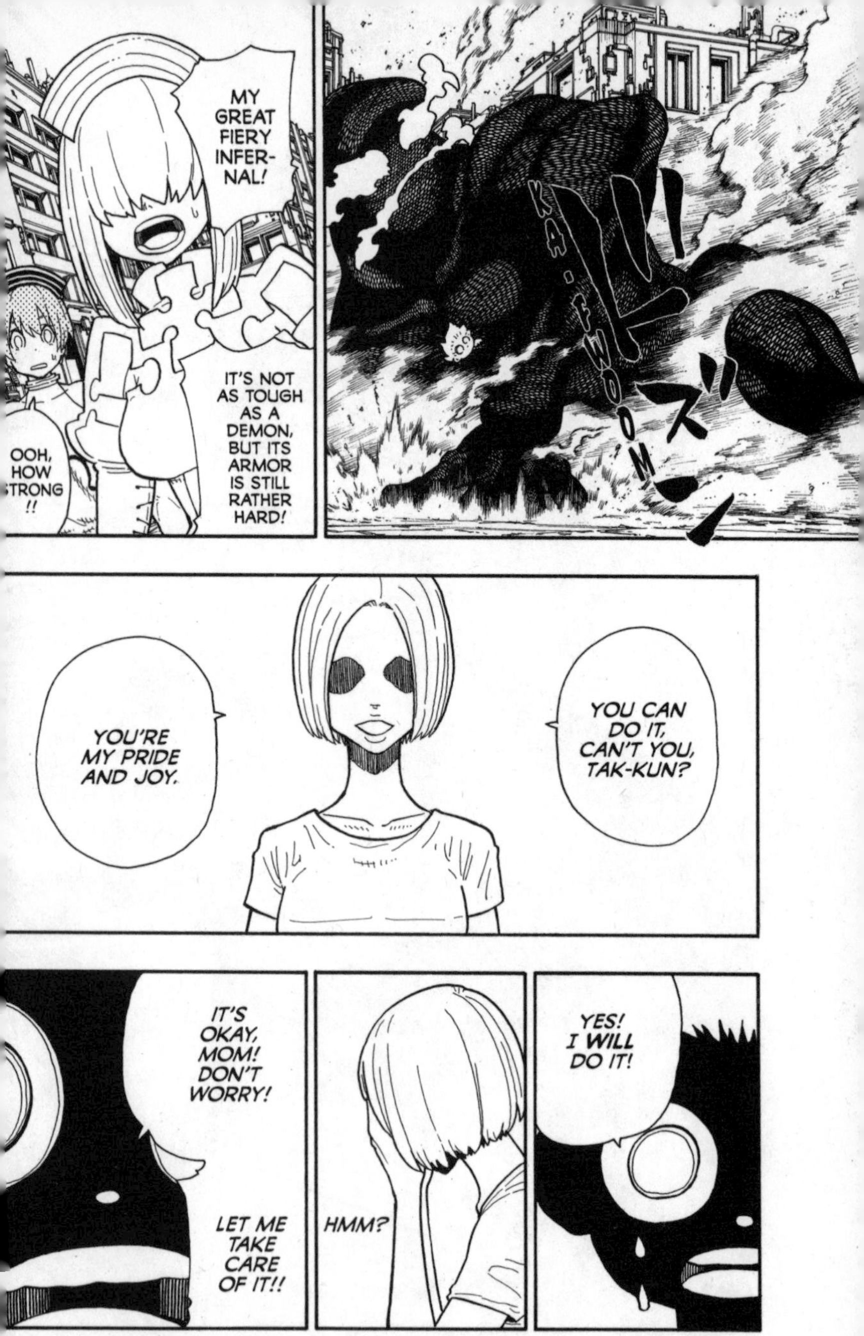
KA-FWOOM
MY GREAT FIERY INFERNAL!
IT'S NOT AS TOUGH AS A DEMON, BUT ITS ARMOR IS STILL RATHER HARD!
OOH, HOW STRONG!!
YOU CAN DO IT, CAN'T YOU, TAK-KUN?
YOU'RE MY PRIDE AND JOY.
YES! I WILL DO IT!
HMM?
IT'S OKAY, MOM! DON'T WORRY!
LET ME TAKE CARE OF IT!!

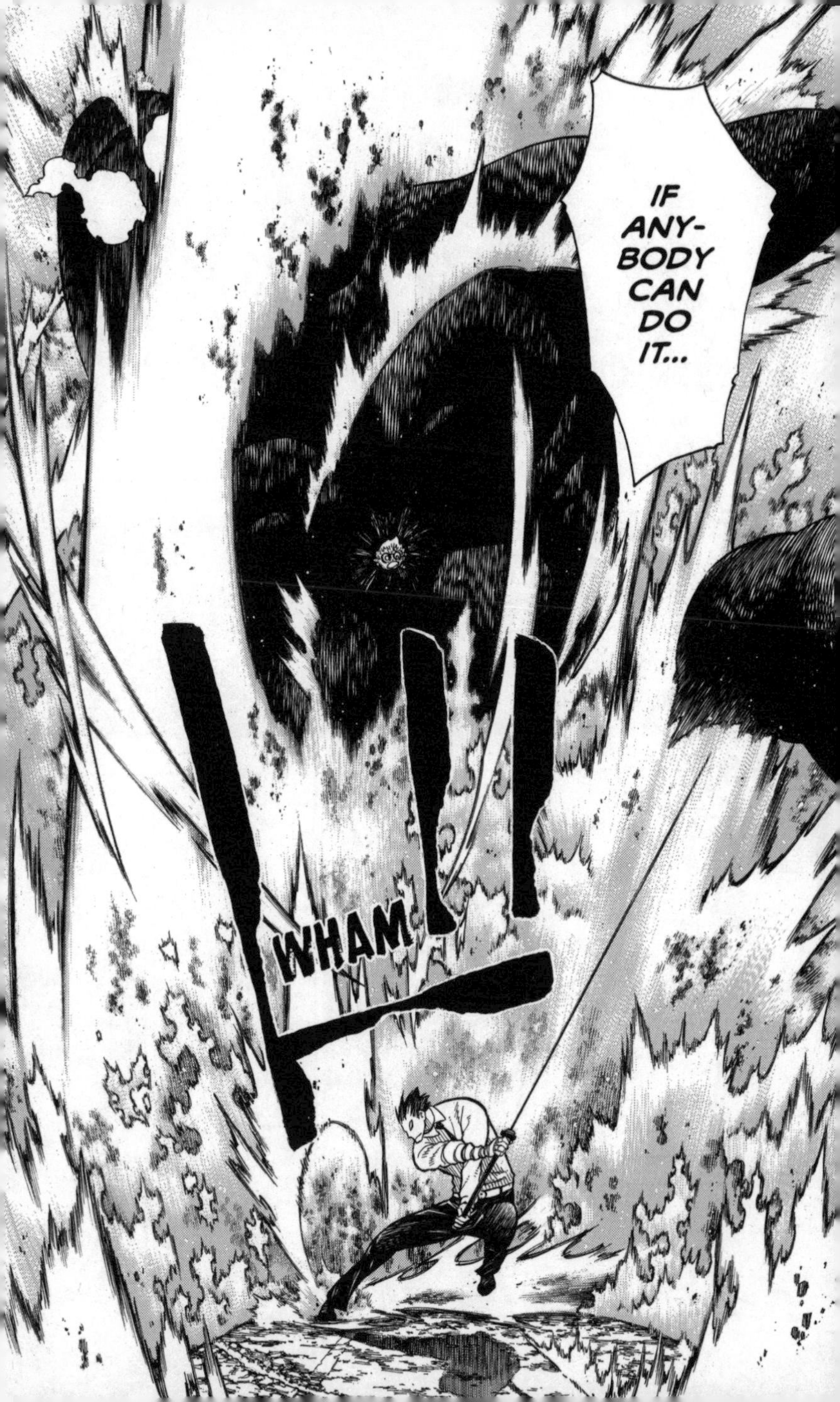
IF ANY-BODY CAN DO IT...
WHAM

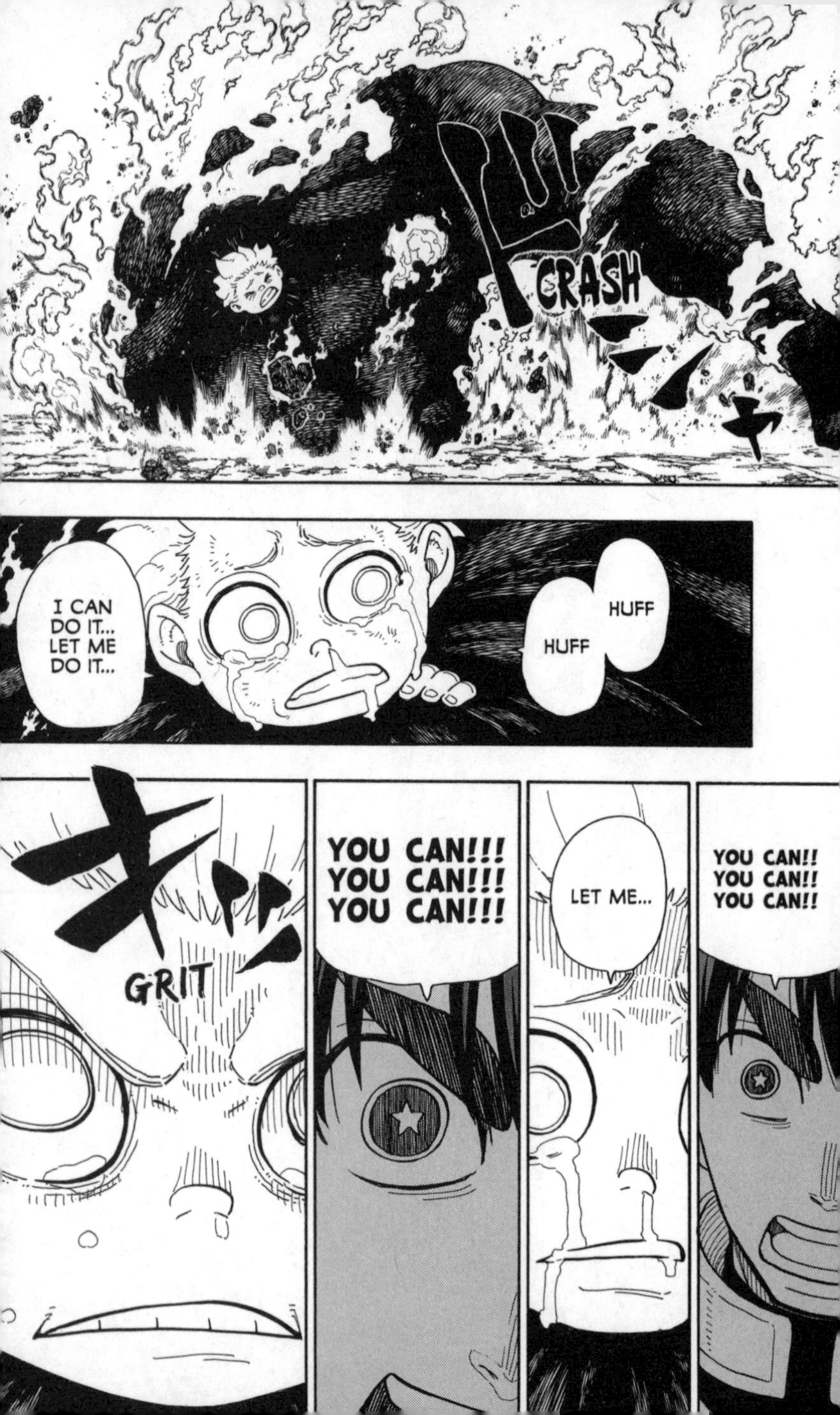
CRASH
HUFF
HUFF
I CAN DO IT... LET ME DO IT...
YOU CAN!! YOU CAN!! YOU CAN!!
LET ME...
YOU CAN!!! YOU CAN!!! YOU CAN!!!
GRIT

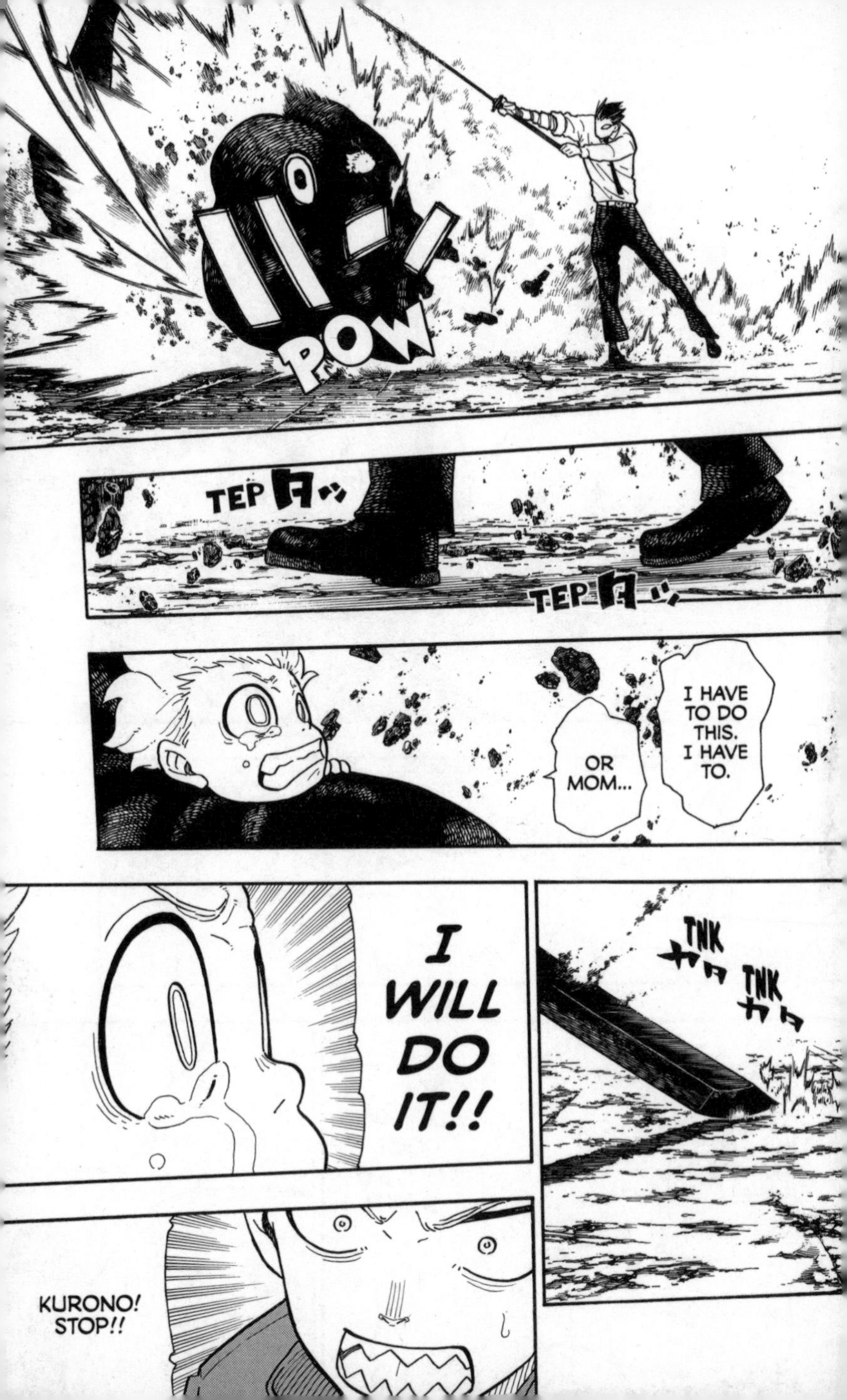
POW
TEP タッ
TEP タッ
I HAVE TO DO THIS. I HAVE TO.
OR MOM...
TNK
TNK
I WILL DO IT!!
KURONO! STOP!!

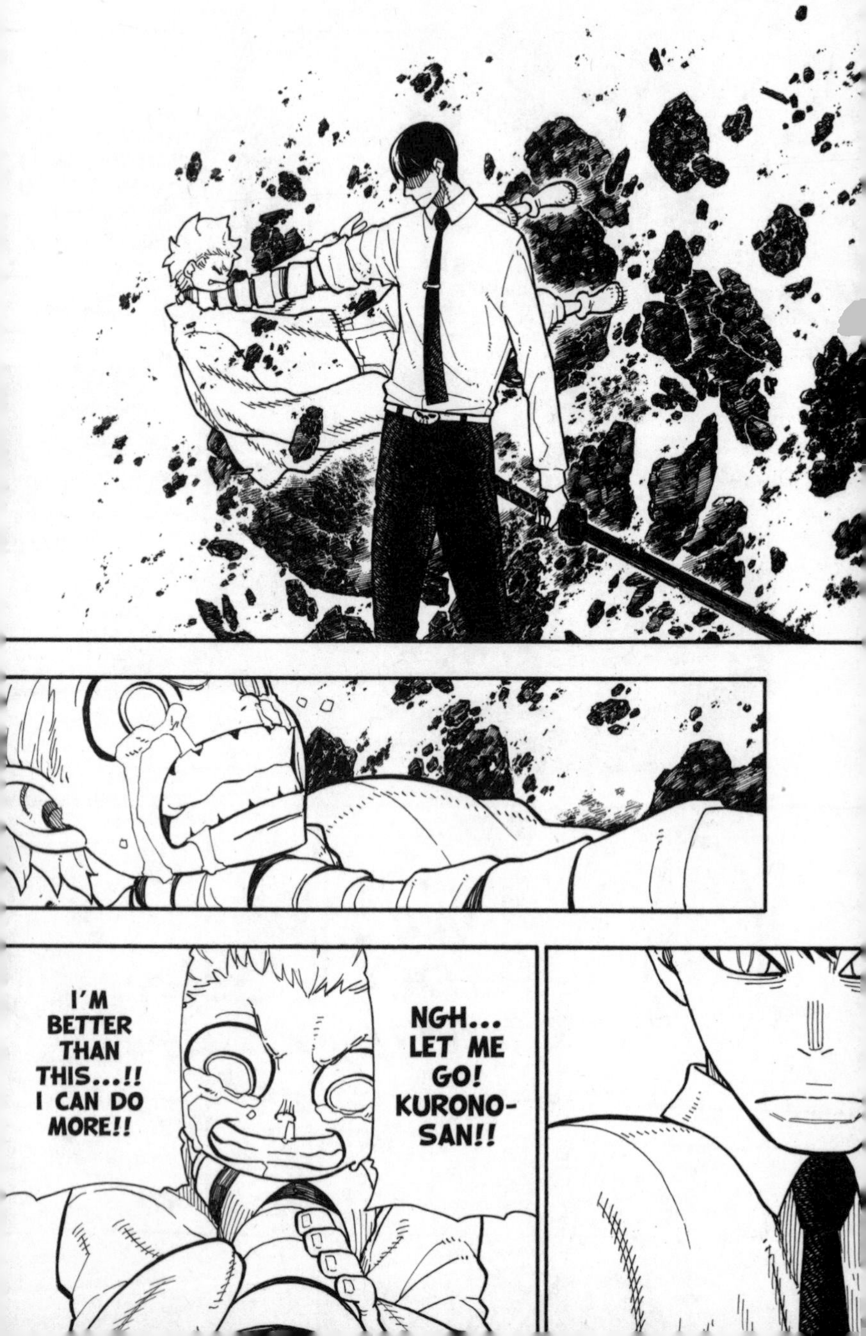
NGH... LET ME GO! KURONO-SAN!!
I'M BETTER THAN THIS...!! I CAN DO MORE!!

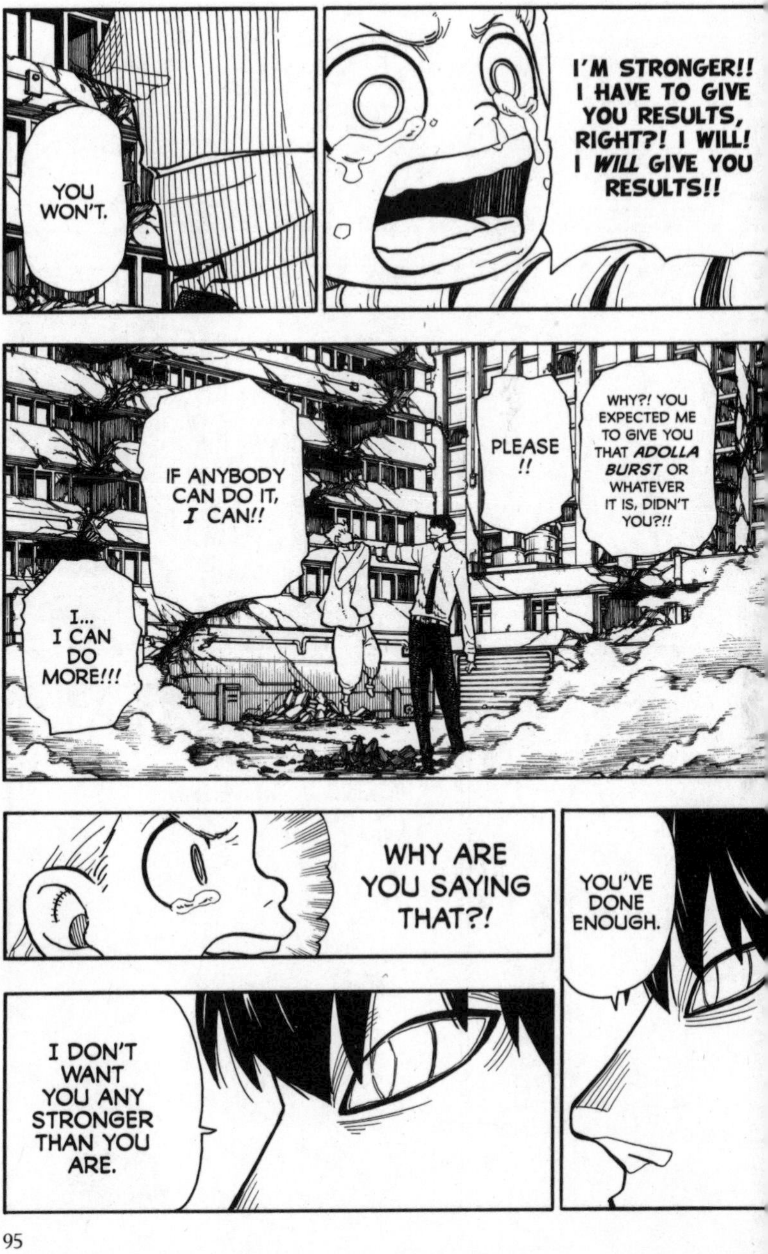
I'M STRONGER!! I HAVE TO GIVE YOU RESULTS, RIGHT?! I WILL! I *WILL* GIVE YOU RESULTS!!
YOU WON'T.
WHY?! YOU EXPECTED ME TO GIVE YOU THAT *ADOLLA BURST* OR WHATEVER IT IS, DIDN'T YOU?!!
PLEASE !!
IF ANYBODY CAN DO IT, *I* CAN!!
I... I CAN DO MORE!!!
YOU'VE DONE ENOUGH.
WHY ARE YOU SAYING THAT?!
I DON'T WANT YOU ANY STRONGER THAN YOU ARE.

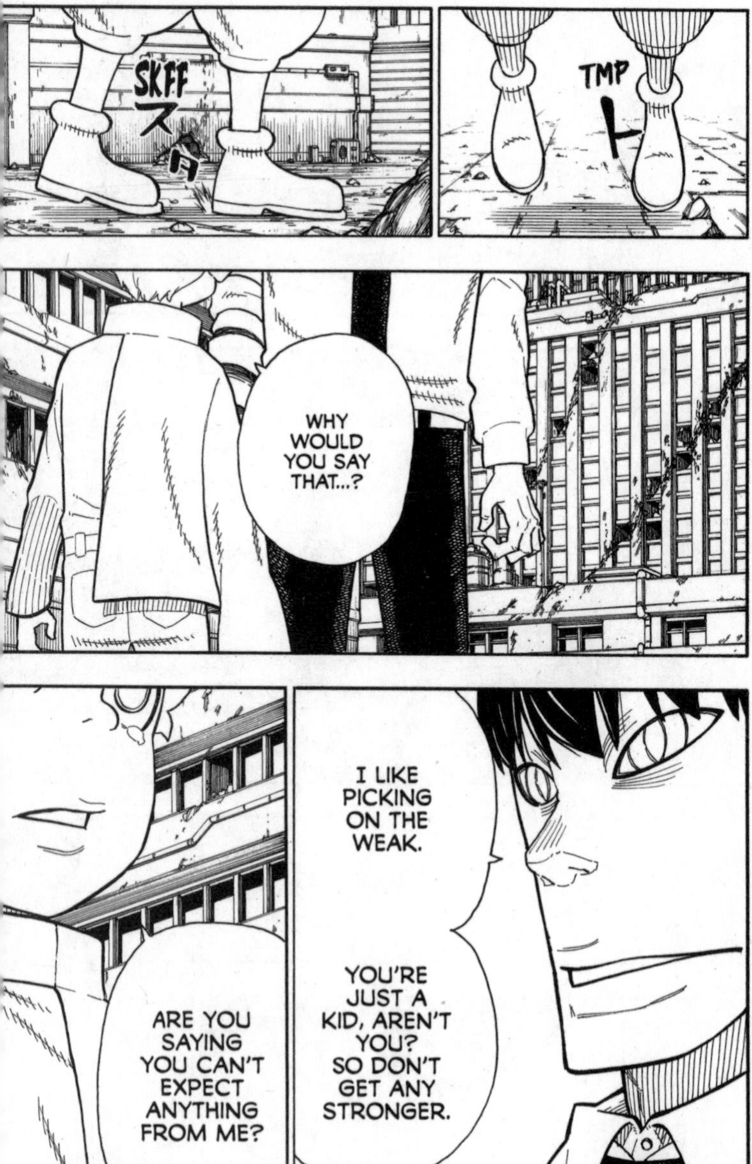
TMP
ト
SKFF
ス
WHY WOULD YOU SAY THAT...?
I LIKE PICKING ON THE WEAK.
YOU'RE JUST A KID, AREN'T YOU? SO DON'T GET ANY STRONGER.
ARE YOU SAYING YOU CAN'T EXPECT ANYTHING FROM ME?

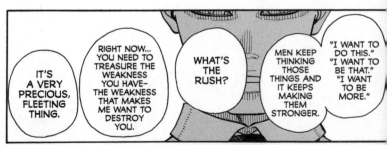

"I WANT TO DO THIS." "I WANT TO BE THAT." "I WANT TO BE MORE."
MEN KEEP THINKING THOSE THINGS AND IT KEEPS MAKING THEM STRONGER.
WHAT'S THE RUSH?
RIGHT NOW... YOU NEED TO TREASURE THE WEAKNESS YOU HAVE– THE WEAKNESS THAT MAKES ME WANT TO DESTROY YOU.
IT'S A VERY PRECIOUS, FLEETING THING.
SO DO ME A FAVOR AND STAY WEAK.
...
NOBODY... HAS EVER SAID ANYTHING LIKE THAT TO ME BEFORE...
MY MOM AND MY DAD BOTH EXPECT WAY TOO MUCH FROM ME...
THEY SAY, "IF ANYBODY CAN DO IT, YOU CAN."
AND IF I CAN'T... THEY LOOK SO DISAP-POINTED...
I'M SO SCARED OF LETTING THEM DOWN...
THERE'S A CRAZY MAN INSIDE ME, EGGING ME ON.
IGNORING HOW I FEEL.
YOU'RE STILL A KID.

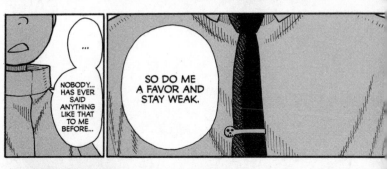

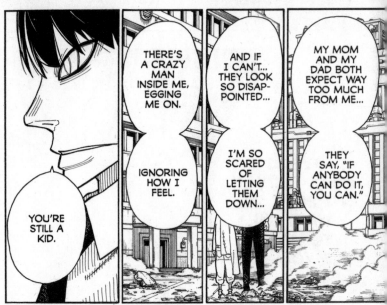

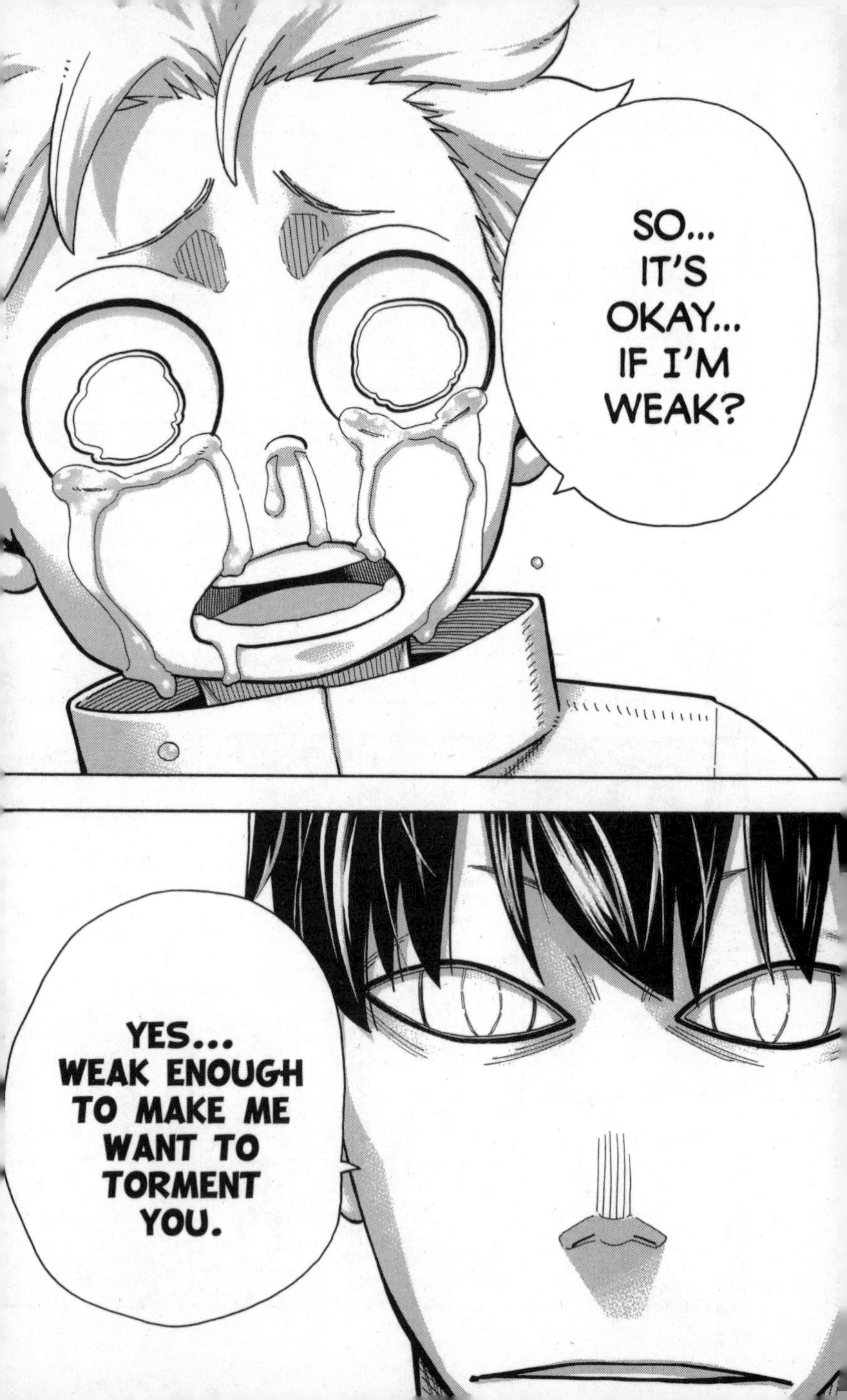
SO... IT'S OKAY... IF I'M WEAK?
YES... WEAK ENOUGH TO MAKE ME WANT TO TORMENT YOU.

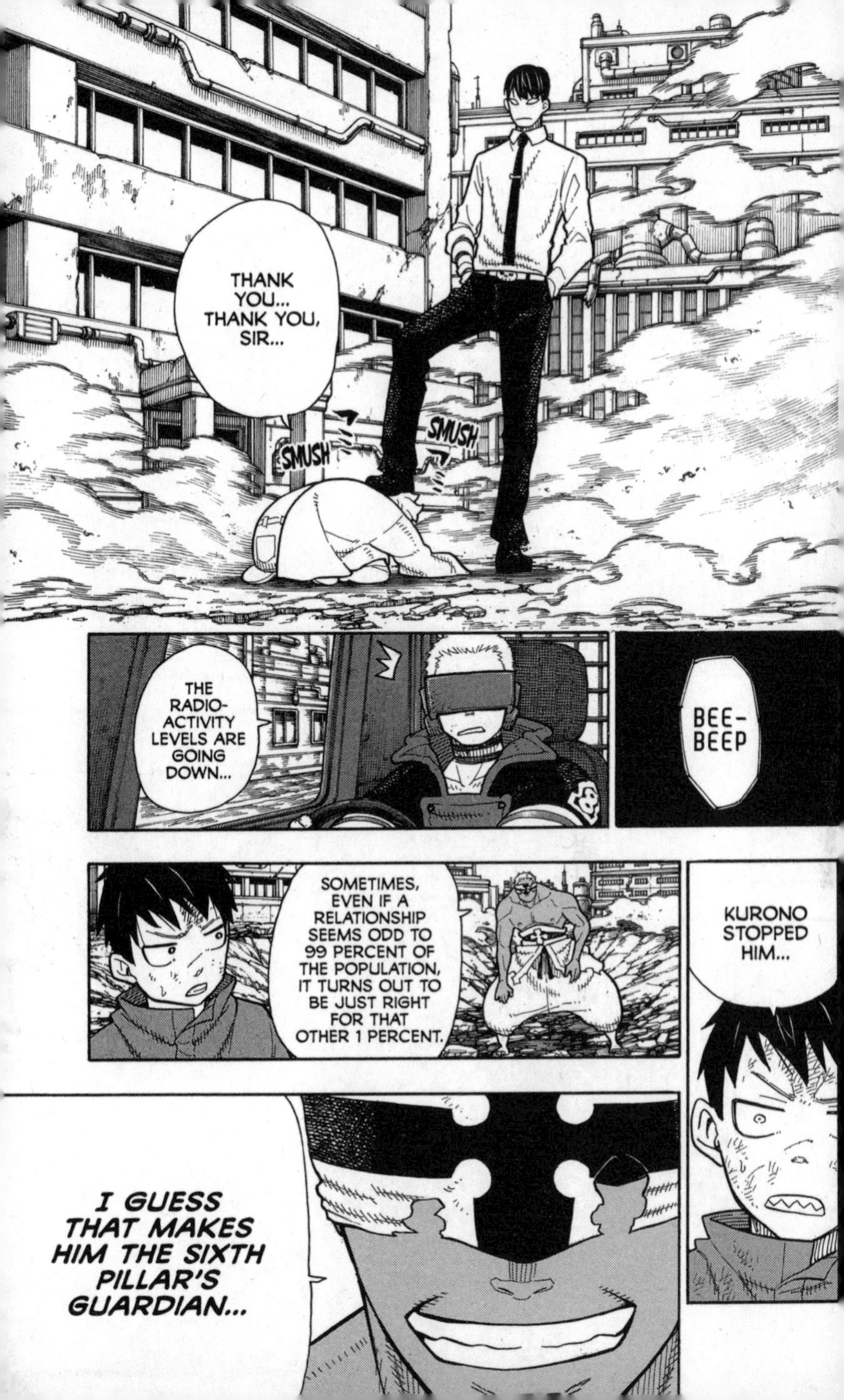
THANK YOU... THANK YOU, SIR...
SMUSH
SMUSH
BEE-BEEP
THE RADIO-ACTIVITY LEVELS ARE GOING DOWN...
KURONO STOPPED HIM...
SOMETIMES, EVEN IF A RELATIONSHIP SEEMS ODD TO 99 PERCENT OF THE POPULATION, IT TURNS OUT TO BE JUST RIGHT FOR THAT OTHER 1 PERCENT.
I GUESS THAT MAKES HIM THE SIXTH PILLAR'S GUARDIAN...

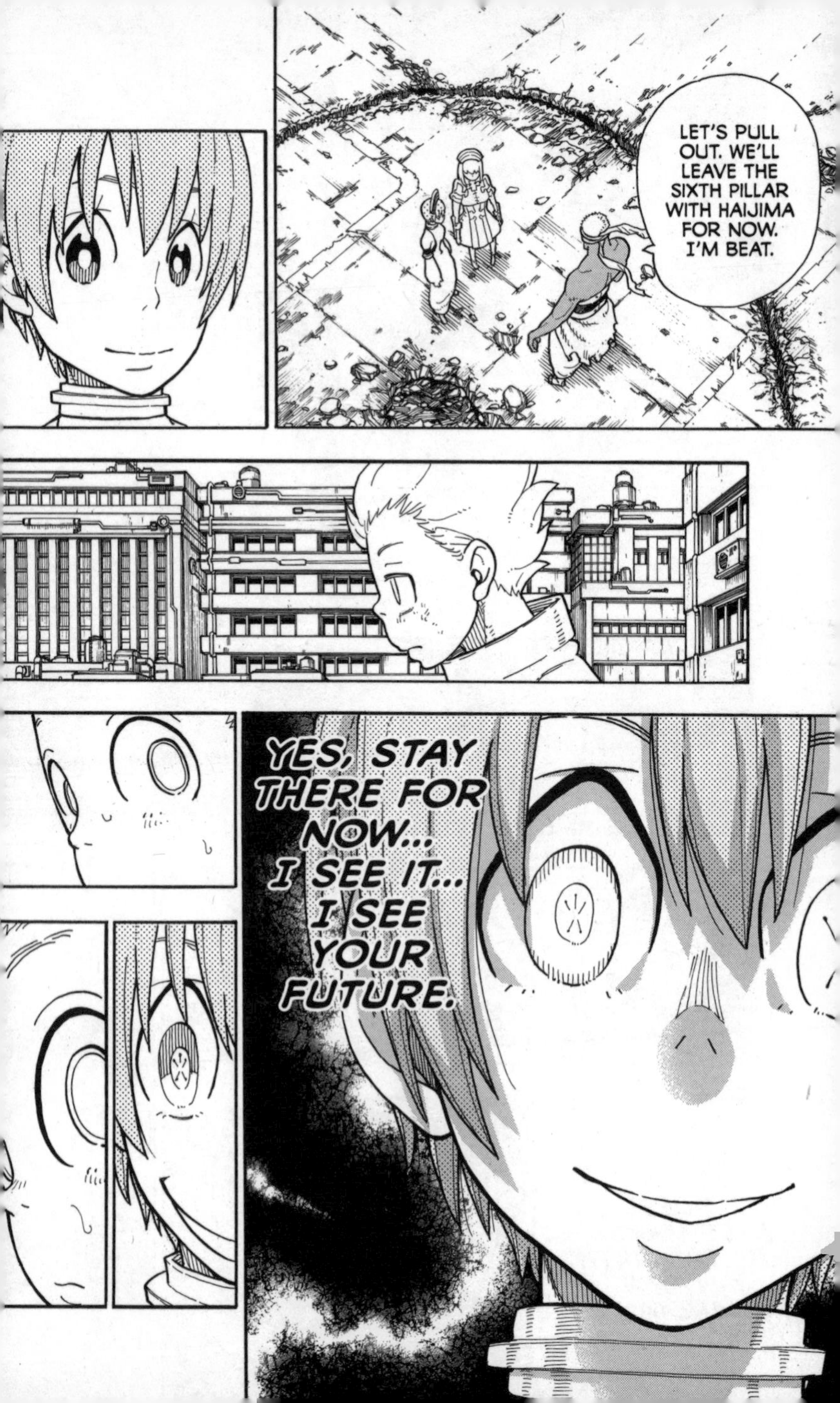
LET'S PULL OUT. WE'LL LEAVE THE SIXTH PILLAR WITH HAIJIMA FOR NOW. I'M BEAT.
YES, STAY THERE FOR NOW... I SEE IT... I SEE YOUR FUTURE.

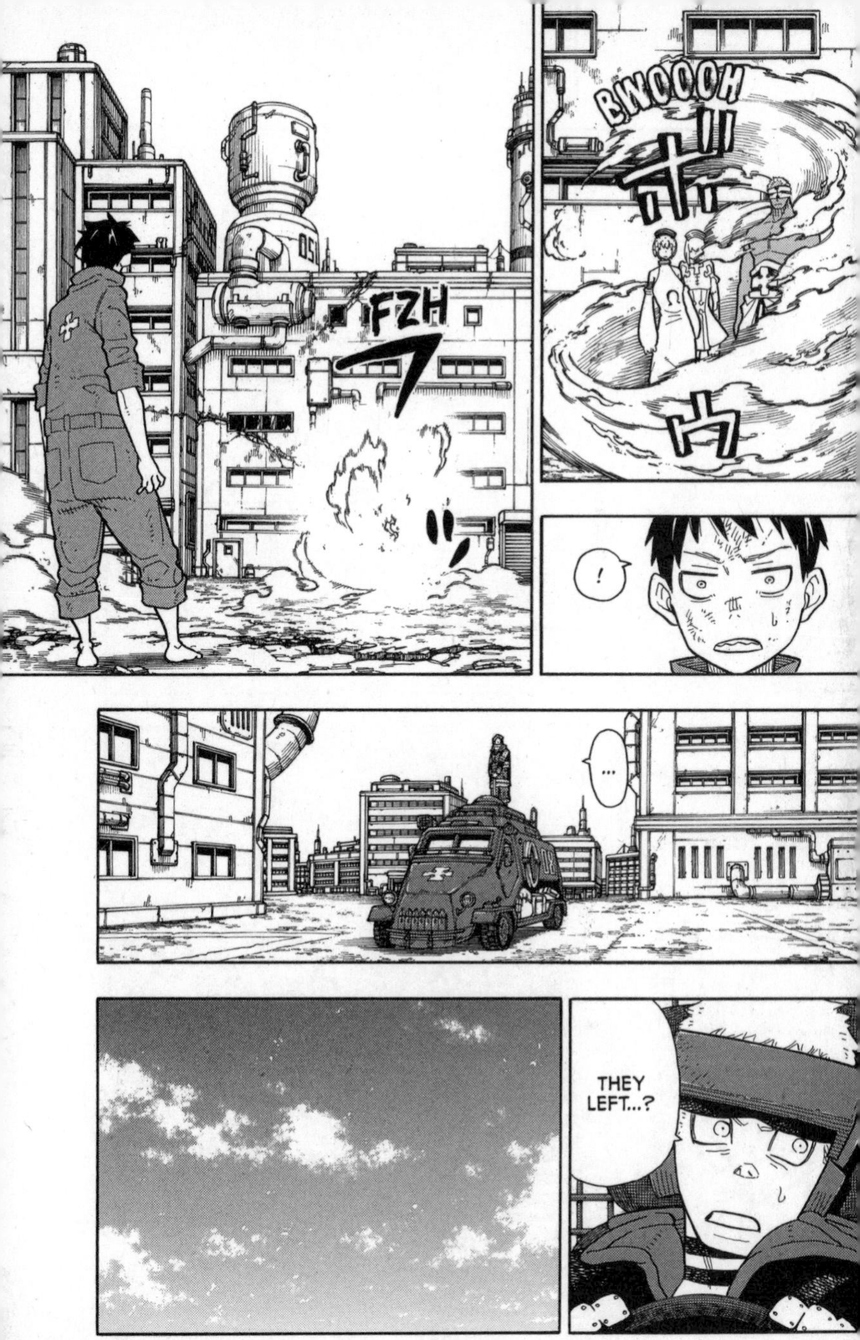
BWOOOH
!
FZH
...
THEY
LEFT...?

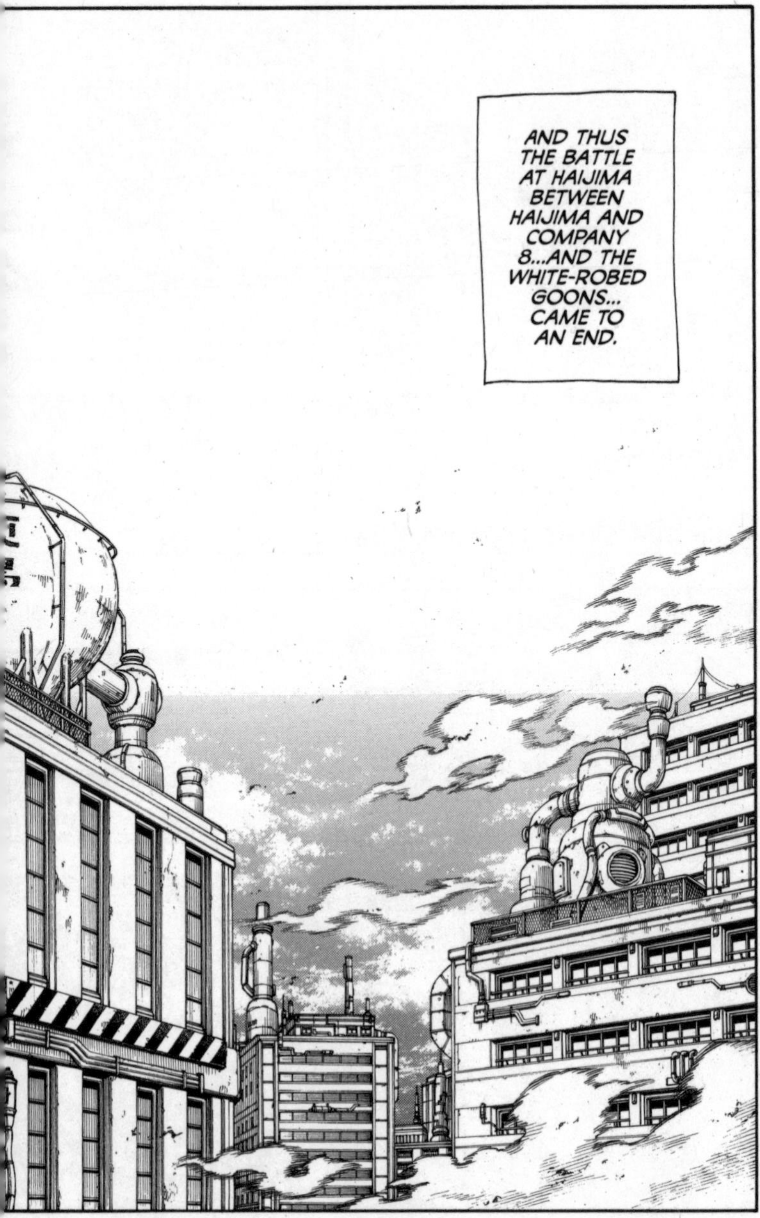
AND THUS THE BATTLE AT HAIJIMA BETWEEN HAIJIMA AND COMPANY 8...AND THE WHITE-ROBED GOONS... CAME TO AN END.

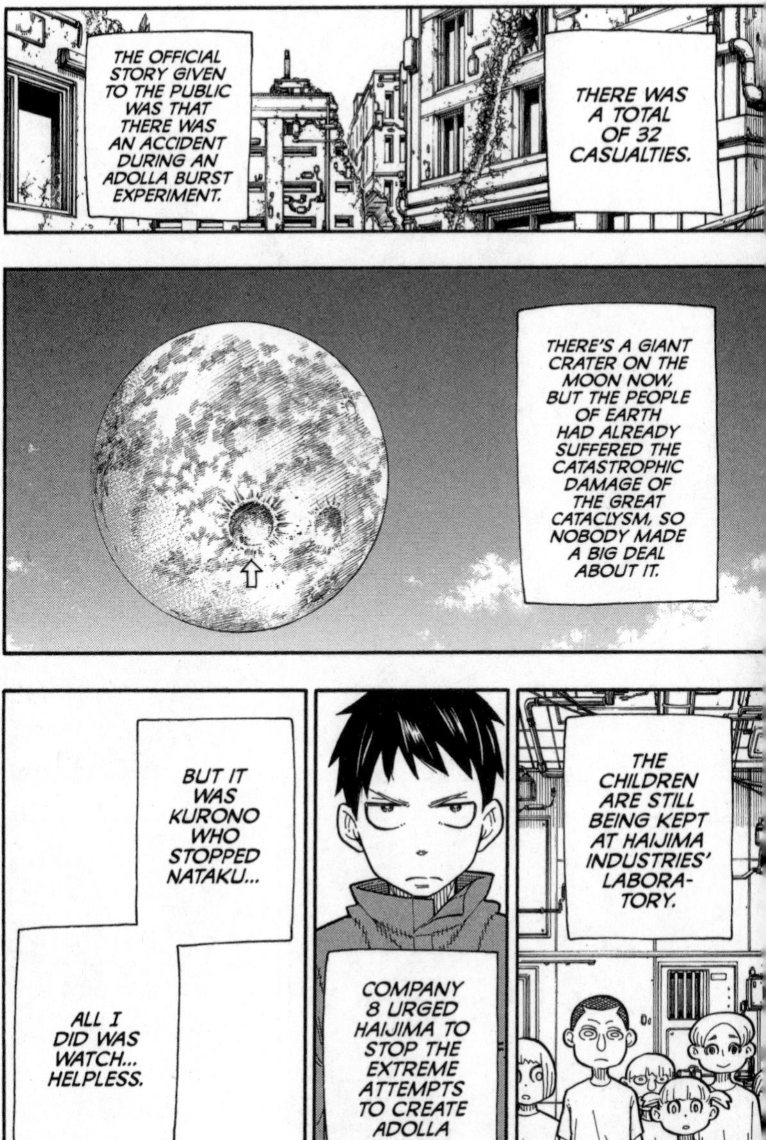
THERE WAS A TOTAL OF 32 CASUALTIES.
THE OFFICIAL STORY GIVEN TO THE PUBLIC WAS THAT THERE WAS AN ACCIDENT DURING AN ADOLLA BURST EXPERIMENT.
THERE'S A GIANT CRATER ON THE MOON NOW, BUT THE PEOPLE OF EARTH HAD ALREADY SUFFERED THE CATASTROPHIC DAMAGE OF THE GREAT CATACLYSM, SO NOBODY MADE A BIG DEAL ABOUT IT.
THE CHILDREN ARE STILL BEING KEPT AT HAIJIMA INDUSTRIES' LABORA-TORY.
COMPANY 8 URGED HAIJIMA TO STOP THE EXTREME ATTEMPTS TO CREATE ADOLLA BURSTS.
BUT IT WAS KURONO WHO STOPPED NATAKU...
ALL I DID WAS WATCH... HELPLESS.

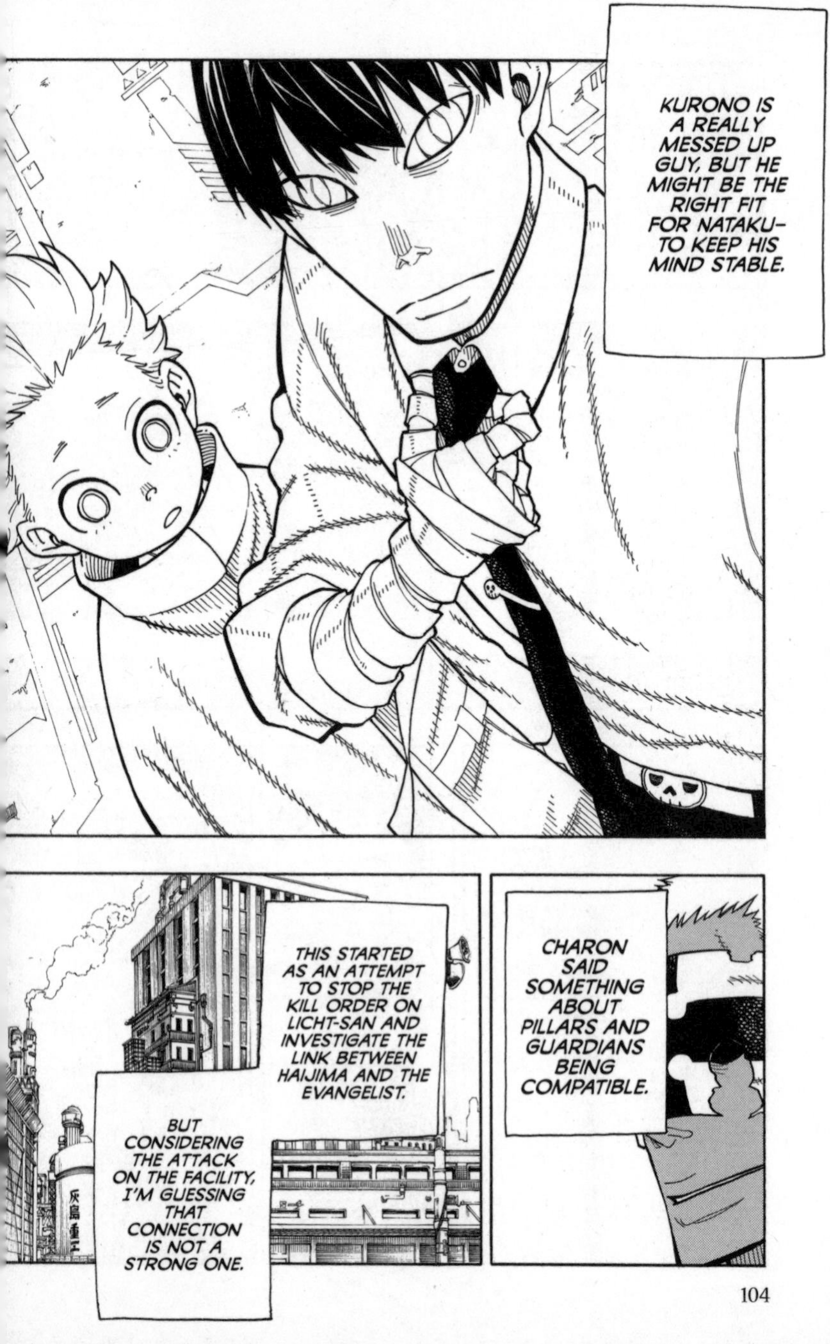
KURONO IS A REALLY MESSED UP GUY, BUT HE MIGHT BE THE RIGHT FIT FOR NATAKU— TO KEEP HIS MIND STABLE.
CHARON SAID SOMETHING ABOUT PILLARS AND GUARDIANS BEING COMPATIBLE.
THIS STARTED AS AN ATTEMPT TO STOP THE KILL ORDER ON LICHT-SAN AND INVESTIGATE THE LINK BETWEEN HAIJIMA AND THE EVANGELIST.
BUT CONSIDERING THE ATTACK ON THE FACILITY, I'M GUESSING THAT CONNECTION IS NOT A STRONG ONE.
灰島重工

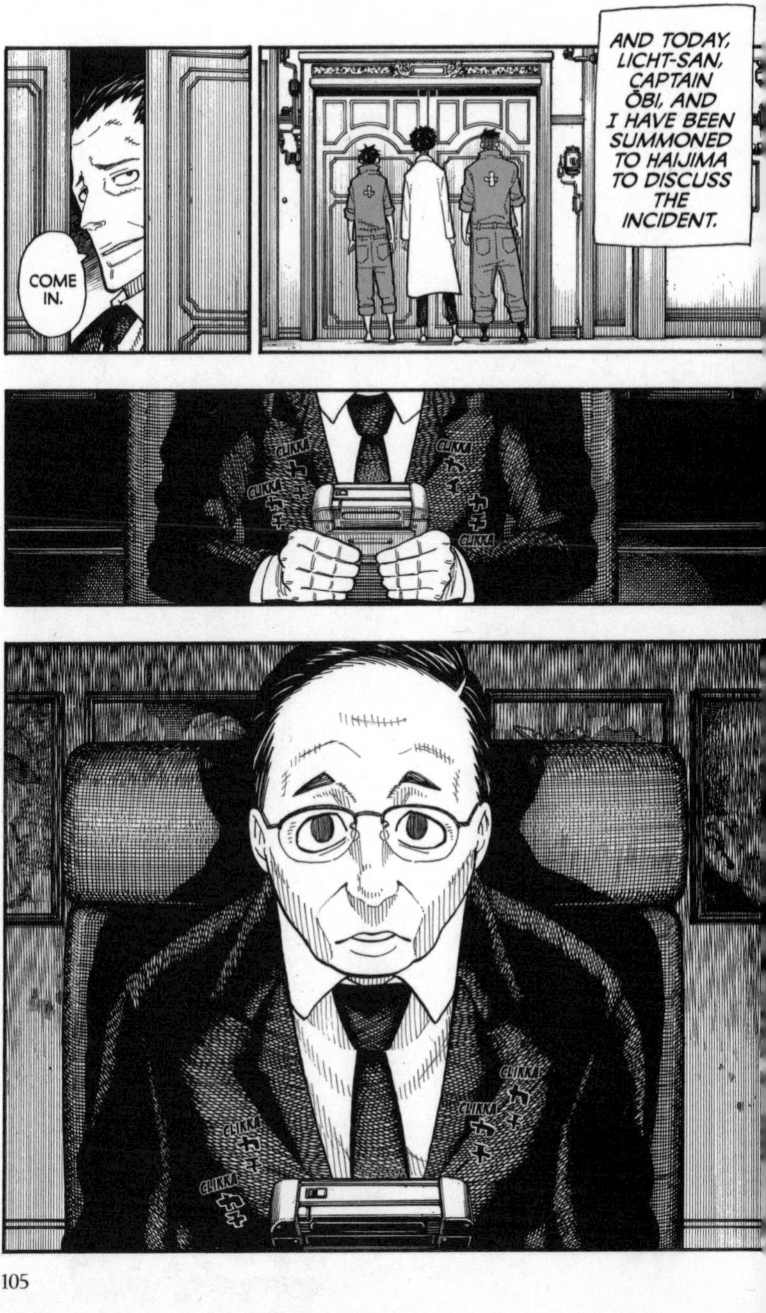
AND TODAY, LICHT-SAN, CAPTAIN ŌBI, AND I HAVE BEEN SUMMONED TO HAIJIMA TO DISCUSS THE INCIDENT.
COME IN.
CLIKKA
CLIKKA
CLIKKA
CLIKKA
CLIKKA
CLIKKA
CLIKKA
CLIKKA

FIRE FORCE

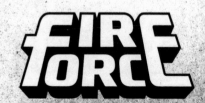

CHAPTER CXLVII: OATH

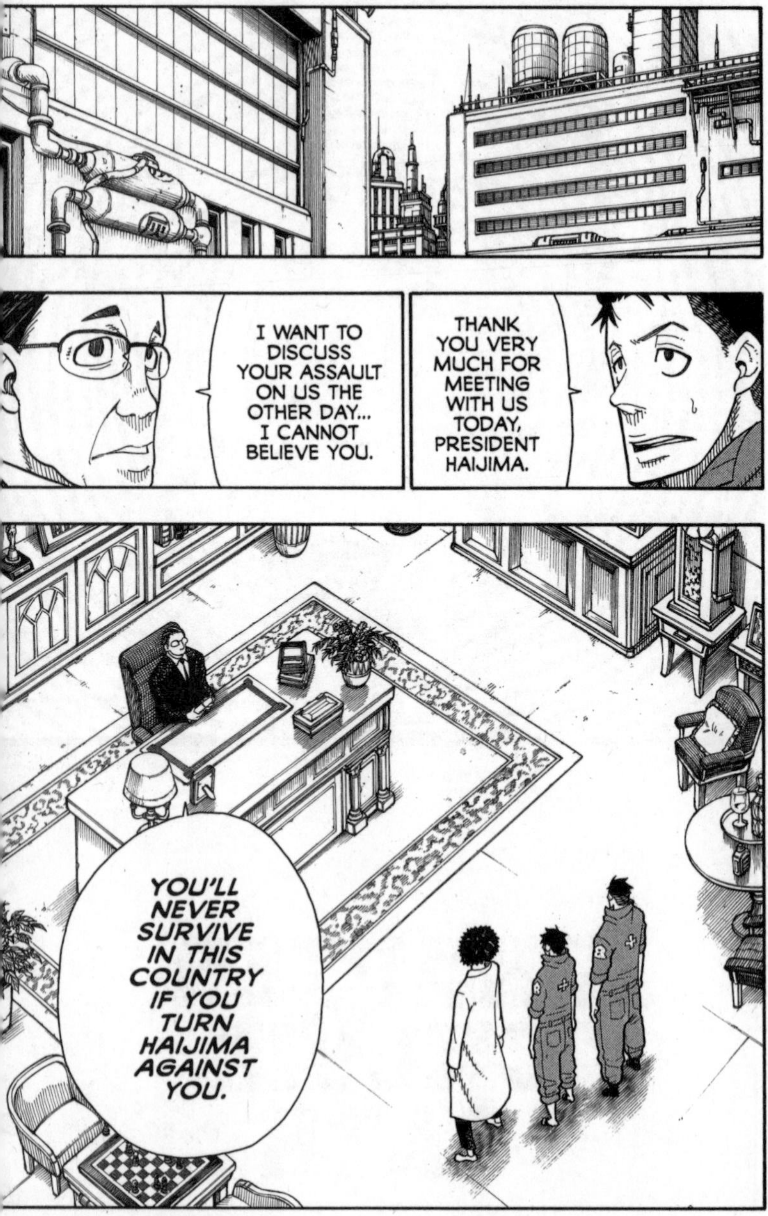
THANK YOU VERY MUCH FOR MEETING WITH US TODAY, PRESIDENT HAIJIMA.
I WANT TO DISCUSS YOUR ASSAULT ON US THE OTHER DAY... I CANNOT BELIEVE YOU.
YOU'LL NEVER SURVIVE IN THIS COUNTRY IF YOU TURN HAIJIMA AGAINST YOU.

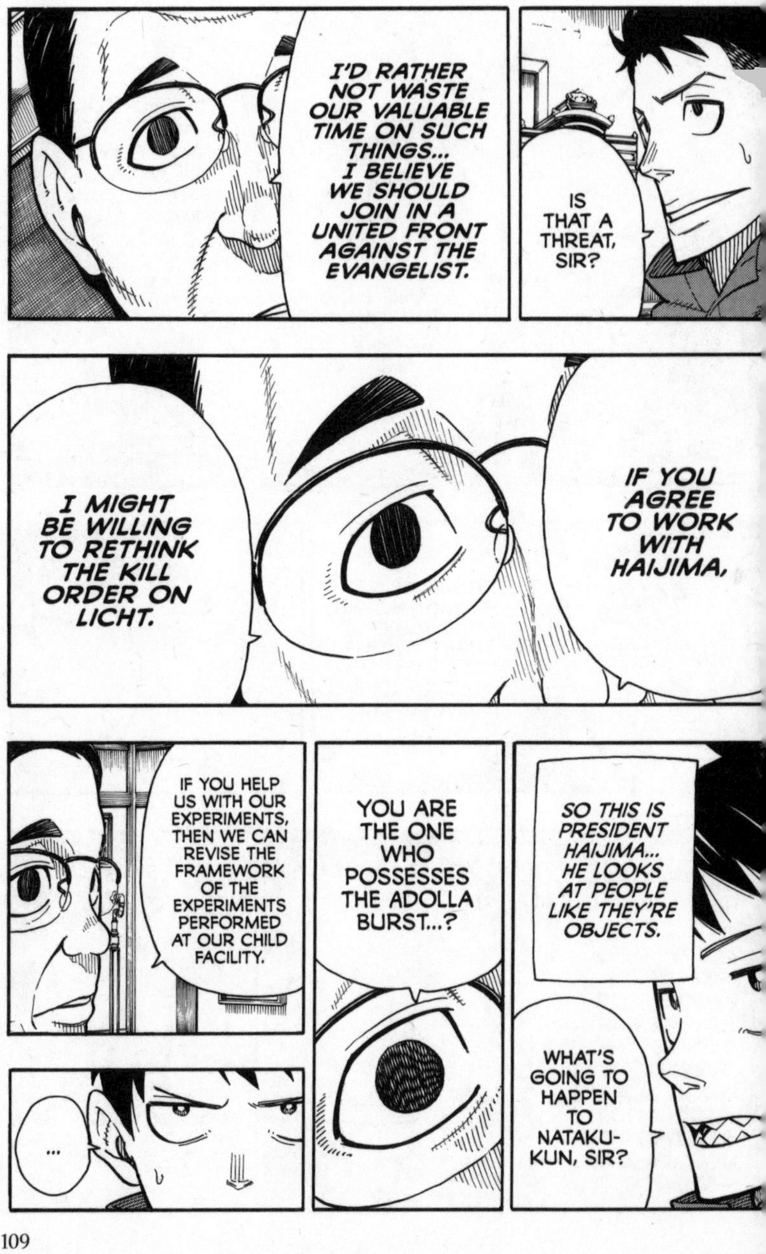
IS THAT A THREAT, SIR?
I'D RATHER NOT WASTE OUR VALUABLE TIME ON SUCH THINGS... I BELIEVE WE SHOULD JOIN IN A UNITED FRONT AGAINST THE EVANGELIST.
IF YOU AGREE TO WORK WITH HAIJIMA,
I MIGHT BE WILLING TO RETHINK THE KILL ORDER ON LICHT.
SO THIS IS PRESIDENT HAIJIMA... HE LOOKS AT PEOPLE LIKE THEY'RE OBJECTS.
WHAT'S GOING TO HAPPEN TO NATAKU-KUN, SIR?
YOU ARE THE ONE WHO POSSESSES THE ADOLLA BURST...?
IF YOU HELP US WITH OUR EXPERIMENTS, THEN WE CAN REVISE THE FRAMEWORK OF THE EXPERIMENTS PERFORMED AT OUR CHILD FACILITY.
...

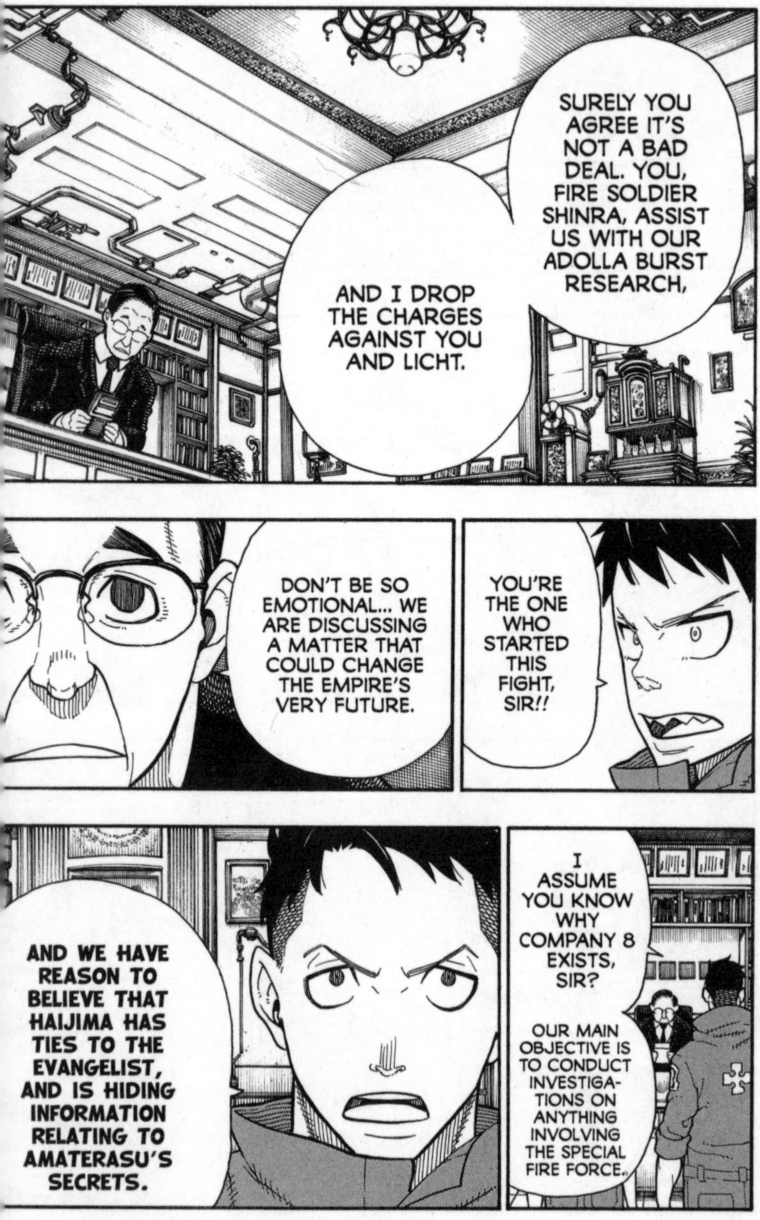
SURELY YOU AGREE IT'S NOT A BAD DEAL. YOU, FIRE SOLDIER SHINRA, ASSIST US WITH OUR ADOLLA BURST RESEARCH,
AND I DROP THE CHARGES AGAINST YOU AND LICHT.
YOU'RE THE ONE WHO STARTED THIS FIGHT, SIR!!
DON'T BE SO EMOTIONAL... WE ARE DISCUSSING A MATTER THAT COULD CHANGE THE EMPIRE'S VERY FUTURE.
I ASSUME YOU KNOW WHY COMPANY 8 EXISTS, SIR?
OUR MAIN OBJECTIVE IS TO CONDUCT INVESTIGA-TIONS ON ANYTHING INVOLVING THE SPECIAL FIRE FORCE.
AND WE HAVE REASON TO BELIEVE THAT HAIJIMA HAS TIES TO THE EVANGELIST, AND IS HIDING INFORMATION RELATING TO AMATERASU'S SECRETS.

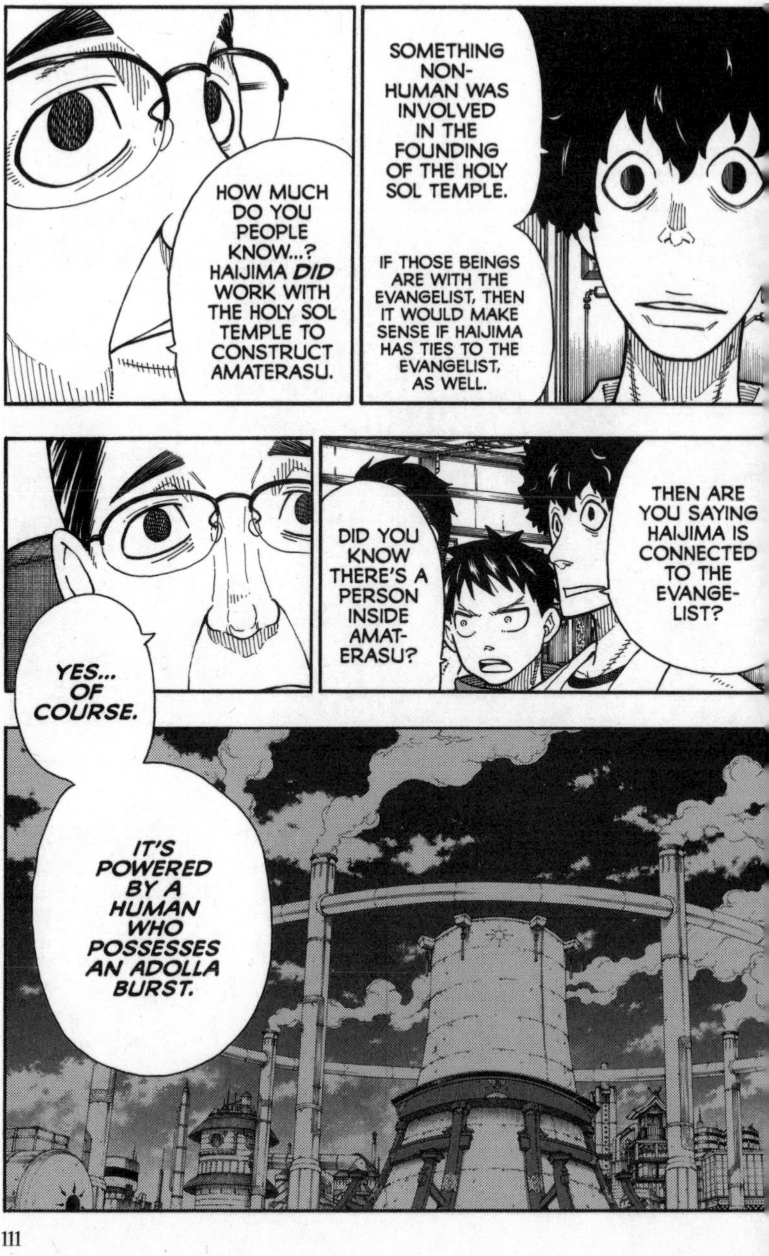
SOMETHING NON-HUMAN WAS INVOLVED IN THE FOUNDING OF THE HOLY SOL TEMPLE.
IF THOSE BEINGS ARE WITH THE EVANGELIST, THEN IT WOULD MAKE SENSE IF HAIJIMA HAS TIES TO THE EVANGELIST, AS WELL.
HOW MUCH DO YOU PEOPLE KNOW...? HAIJIMA *DID* WORK WITH THE HOLY SOL TEMPLE TO CONSTRUCT AMATERASU.
THEN ARE YOU SAYING HAIJIMA IS CONNECTED TO THE EVANGE-LIST?
DID YOU KNOW THERE'S A PERSON INSIDE AMAT-ERASU?
YES... OF COURSE.
IT'S POWERED BY A HUMAN WHO POSSESSES AN ADOLLA BURST.

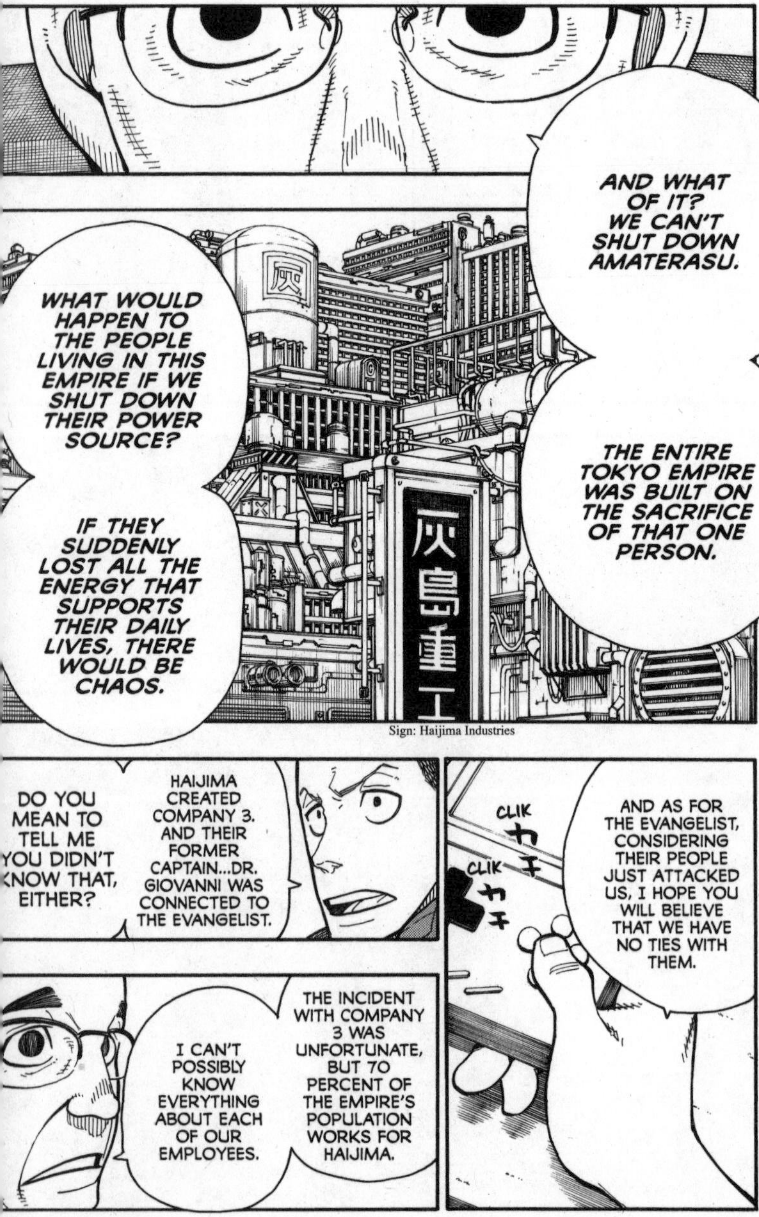
AND WHAT OF IT? WE CAN'T SHUT DOWN AMATERASU.
THE ENTIRE TOKYO EMPIRE WAS BUILT ON THE SACRIFICE OF THAT ONE PERSON.
WHAT WOULD HAPPEN TO THE PEOPLE LIVING IN THIS EMPIRE IF WE SHUT DOWN THEIR POWER SOURCE?
IF THEY SUDDENLY LOST ALL THE ENERGY THAT SUPPORTS THEIR DAILY LIVES, THERE WOULD BE CHAOS.
灰
灰島重工
Sign: Haijima Industries
AND AS FOR THE EVANGELIST, CONSIDERING THEIR PEOPLE JUST ATTACKED US, I HOPE YOU WILL BELIEVE THAT WE HAVE NO TIES WITH THEM.
CLIK カチ
CLIK カチ
HAIJIMA CREATED COMPANY 3. AND THEIR FORMER CAPTAIN...DR. GIOVANNI WAS CONNECTED TO THE EVANGELIST.
DO YOU MEAN TO TELL ME YOU DIDN'T KNOW THAT, EITHER?
THE INCIDENT WITH COMPANY 3 WAS UNFORTUNATE, BUT 70 PERCENT OF THE EMPIRE'S POPULATION WORKS FOR HAIJIMA.
I CAN'T POSSIBLY KNOW EVERYTHING ABOUT EACH OF OUR EMPLOYEES.

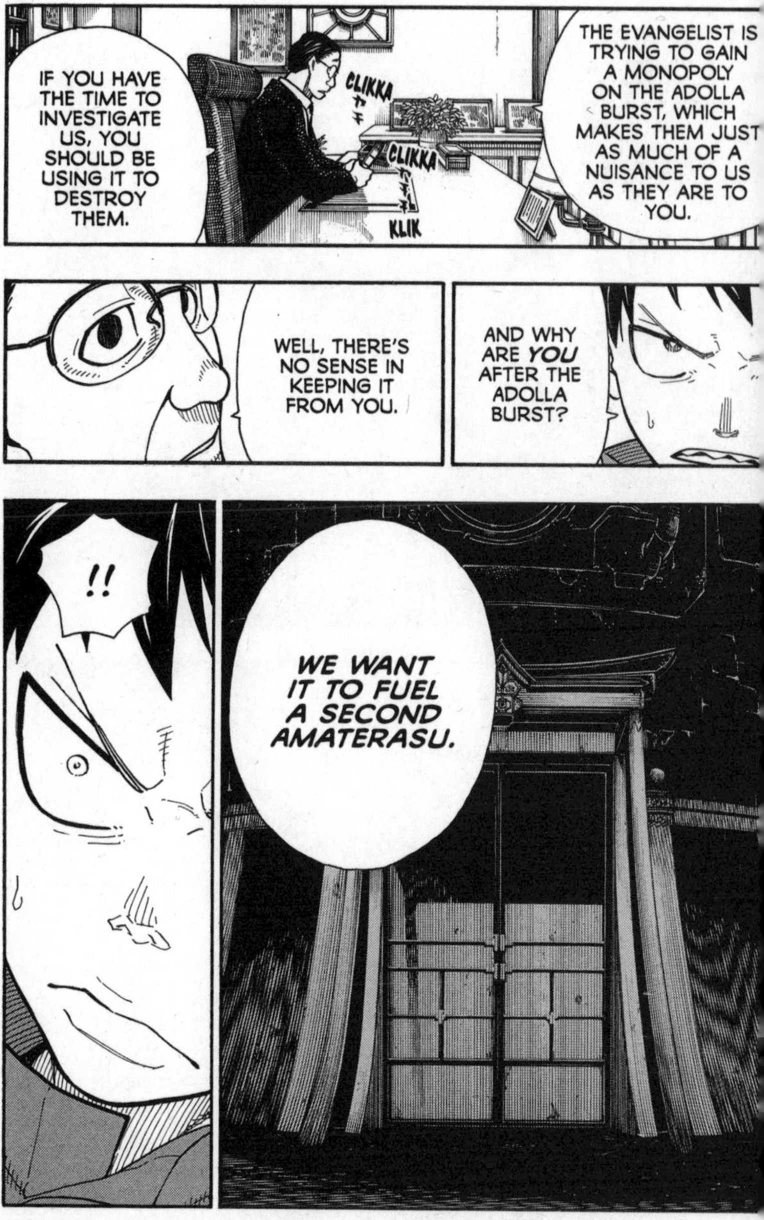
THE EVANGELIST IS TRYING TO GAIN A MONOPOLY ON THE ADOLLA BURST, WHICH MAKES THEM JUST AS MUCH OF A NUISANCE TO US AS THEY ARE TO YOU.
CLIKKA
CLIKKA
KLIK
IF YOU HAVE THE TIME TO INVESTIGATE US, YOU SHOULD BE USING IT TO DESTROY THEM.
AND WHY ARE YOU AFTER THE ADOLLA BURST?
WELL, THERE'S NO SENSE IN KEEPING IT FROM YOU.
WE WANT IT TO FUEL A SECOND AMATERASU.
!!

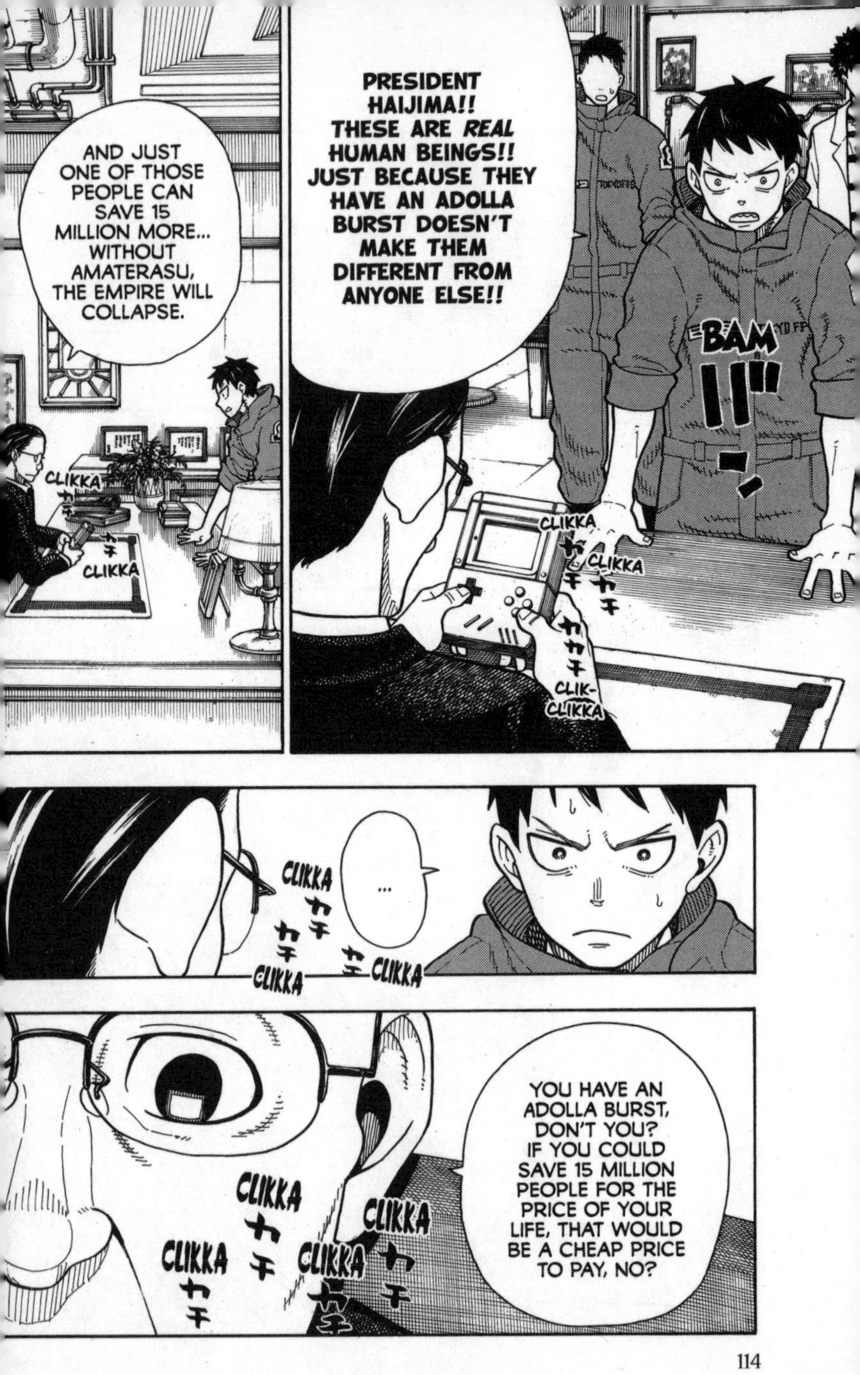
PRESIDENT HAIJIMA!! THESE ARE *REAL* HUMAN BEINGS!! JUST BECAUSE THEY HAVE AN ADOLLA BURST DOESN'T MAKE THEM DIFFERENT FROM ANYONE ELSE!!
BAM
CLIKKA
CLIKKA
CLIK-CLIKKA
AND JUST ONE OF THOSE PEOPLE CAN SAVE 15 MILLION MORE... WITHOUT AMATERASU, THE EMPIRE WILL COLLAPSE.
CLIKKA
CLIKKA
...
CLIKKA
CLIKKA
CLIKKA
YOU HAVE AN ADOLLA BURST, DON'T YOU? IF YOU COULD SAVE 15 MILLION PEOPLE FOR THE PRICE OF YOUR LIFE, THAT WOULD BE A CHEAP PRICE TO PAY, NO?
CLIKKA
CLIKKA
CLIKKA
CLIKKA

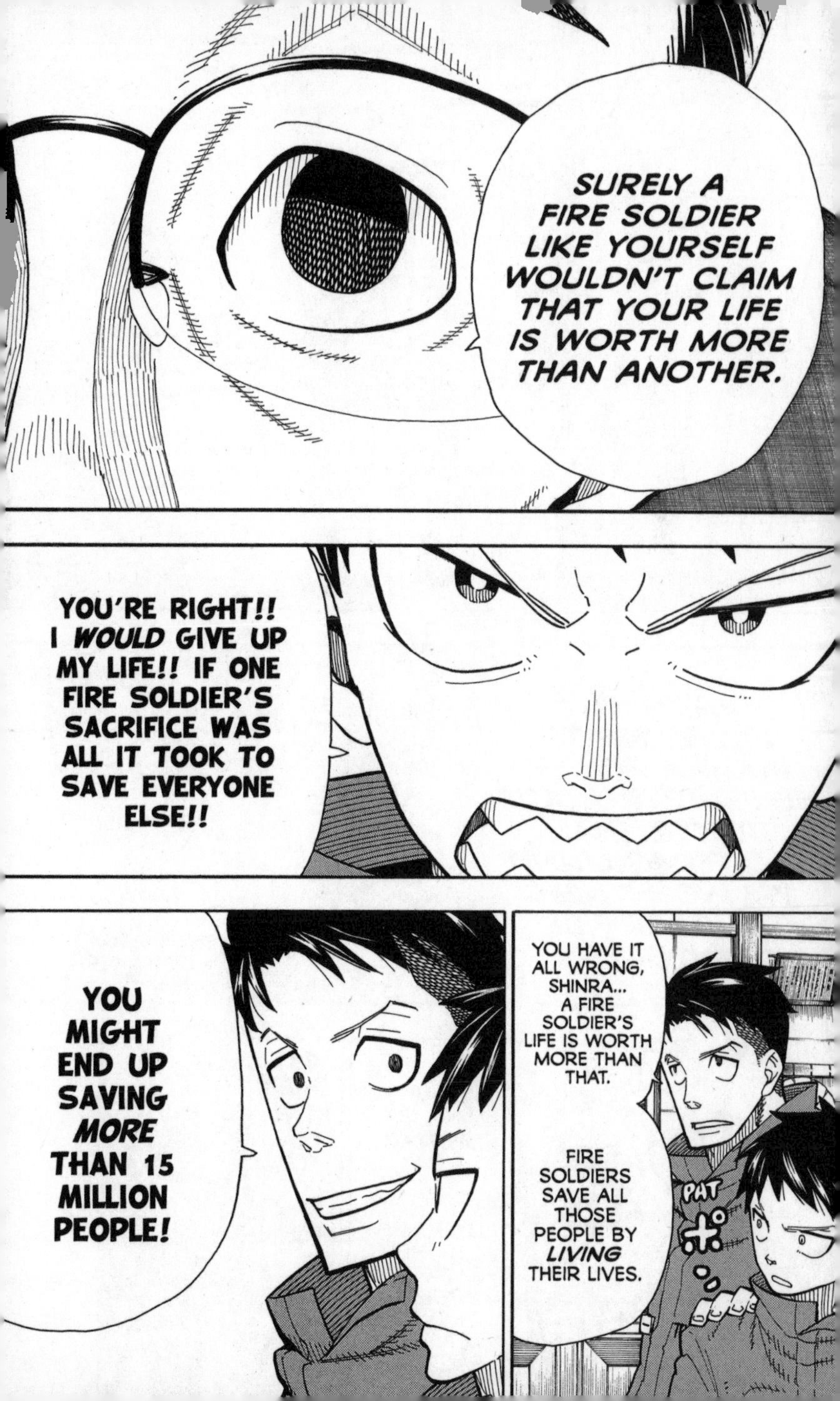
SURELY A FIRE SOLDIER LIKE YOURSELF WOULDN'T CLAIM THAT YOUR LIFE IS WORTH MORE THAN ANOTHER.
YOU'RE RIGHT!! I *WOULD* GIVE UP MY LIFE!! IF ONE FIRE SOLDIER'S SACRIFICE WAS ALL IT TOOK TO SAVE EVERYONE ELSE!!
YOU HAVE IT ALL WRONG, SHINRA... A FIRE SOLDIER'S LIFE IS WORTH MORE THAN THAT.
FIRE SOLDIERS SAVE ALL THOSE PEOPLE BY *LIVING* THEIR LIVES.
PAT
YOU MIGHT END UP SAVING *MORE* THAN 15 MILLION PEOPLE!

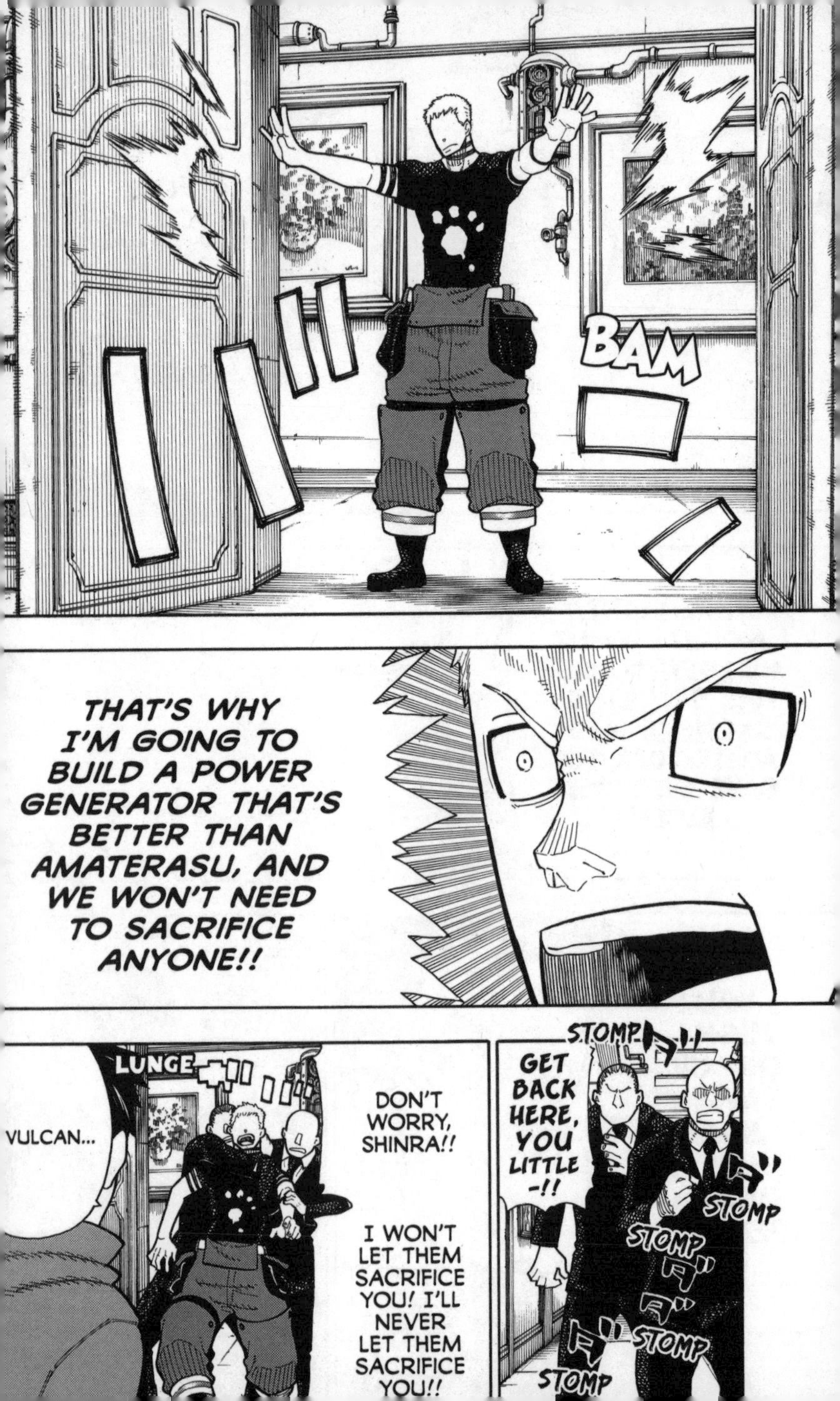
BAM
THAT'S WHY I'M GOING TO BUILD A POWER GENERATOR THAT'S BETTER THAN AMATERASU, AND WE WON'T NEED TO SACRIFICE ANYONE!!
STOMP
GET BACK HERE, YOU LITTLE -!!
STOMP
STOMP
STOMP
STOMP
DON'T WORRY, SHINRA!!
LUNGE
VULCAN...
I WON'T LET THEM SACRIFICE YOU! I'LL NEVER LET THEM SACRIFICE YOU!!

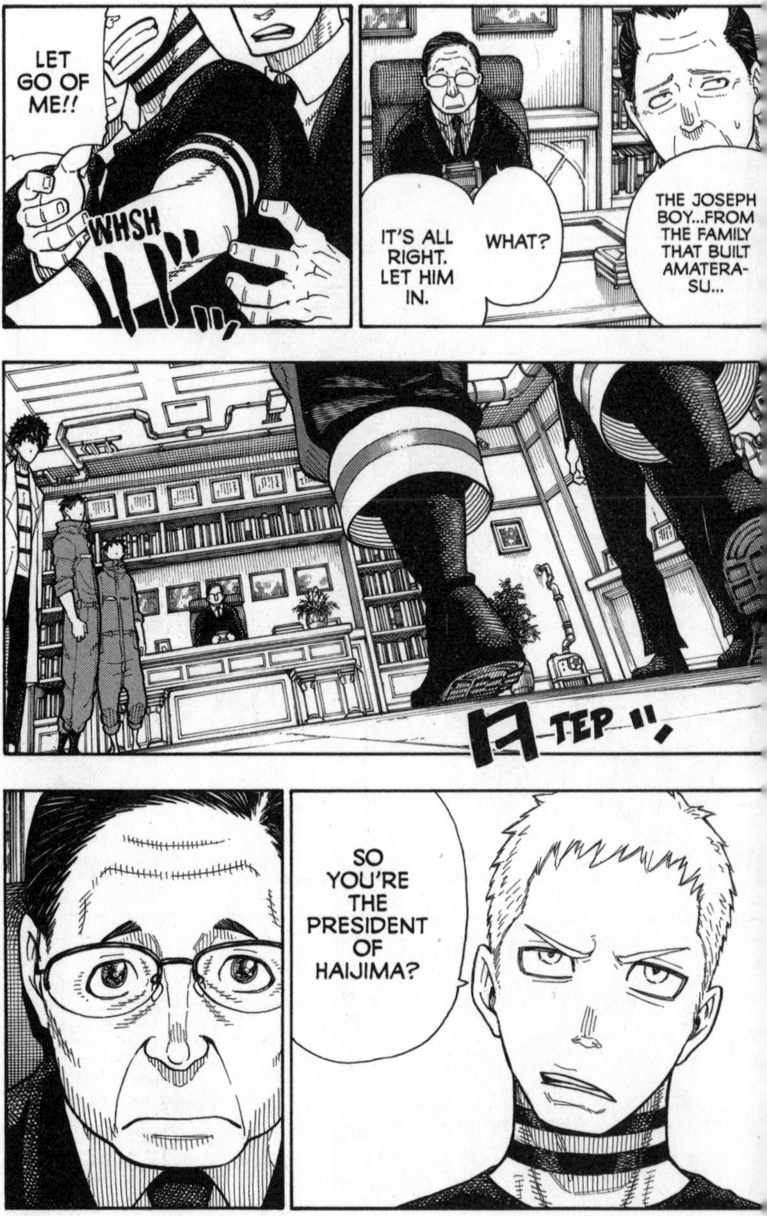
THE JOSEPH BOY...FROM THE FAMILY THAT BUILT AMATERA-SU...
WHAT?
IT'S ALL RIGHT. LET HIM IN.
LET GO OF ME!!
WHSH
STEP
SO YOU'RE THE PRESIDENT OF HAIJIMA?

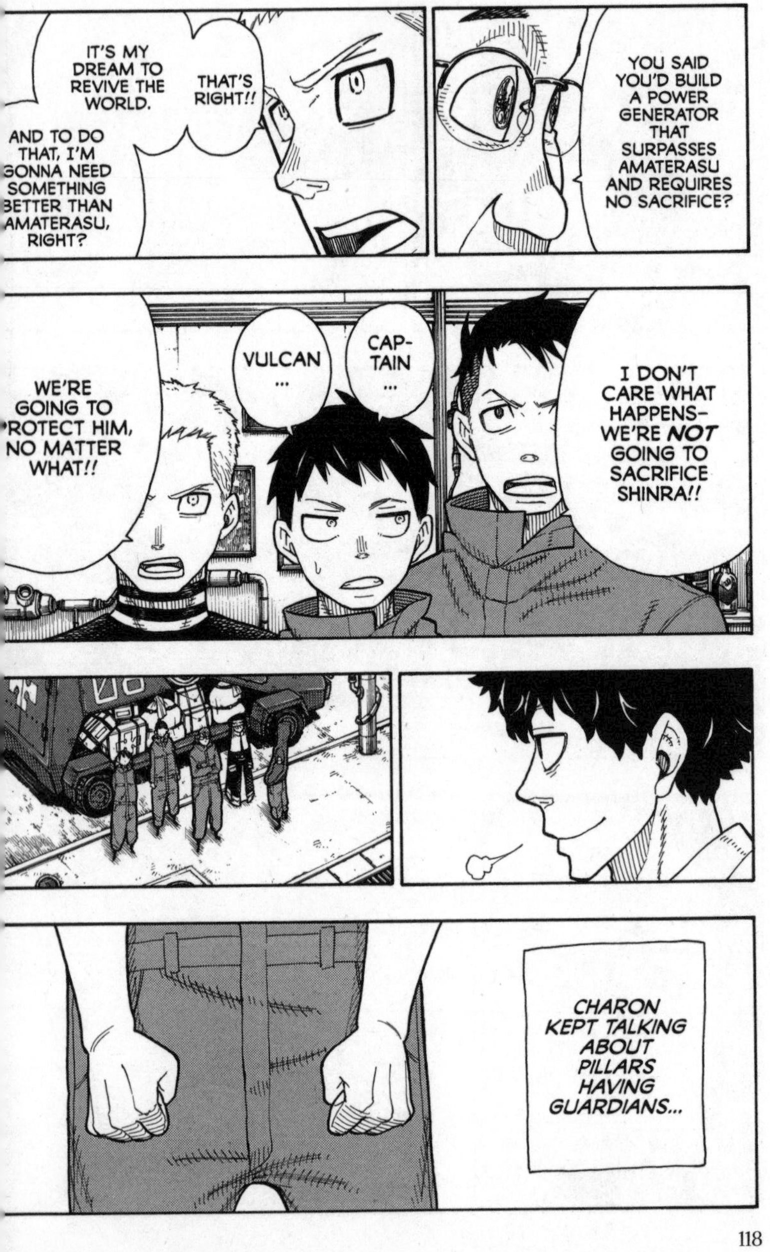
YOU SAID YOU'D BUILD A POWER GENERATOR THAT SURPASSES AMATERASU AND REQUIRES NO SACRIFICE?
THAT'S RIGHT!!
IT'S MY DREAM TO REVIVE THE WORLD.
AND TO DO THAT, I'M GONNA NEED SOMETHING BETTER THAN AMATERASU, RIGHT?
I DON'T CARE WHAT HAPPENS— WE'RE *NOT* GOING TO SACRIFICE SHINRA!!
CAP-TAIN ...
VULCAN ...
WE'RE GOING TO PROTECT HIM, NO MATTER WHAT!!
CHARON KEPT TALKING ABOUT PILLARS HAVING GUARDIANS...

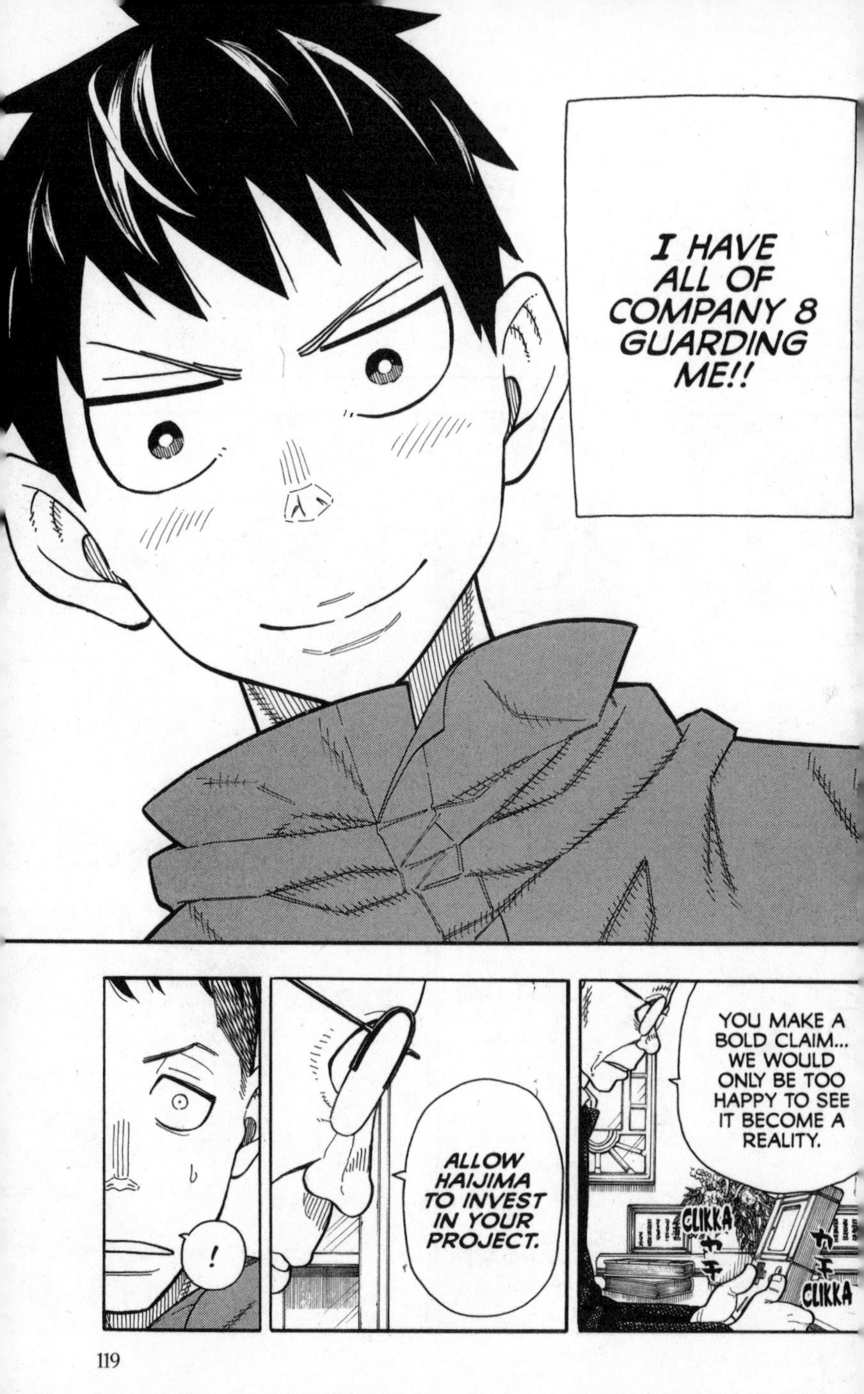
I HAVE ALL OF COMPANY 8 GUARDING ME!!
YOU MAKE A BOLD CLAIM... WE WOULD ONLY BE TOO HAPPY TO SEE IT BECOME A REALITY.
CLIKKA
CLIKKA
ALLOW HAIJIMA TO INVEST IN YOUR PROJECT.
!

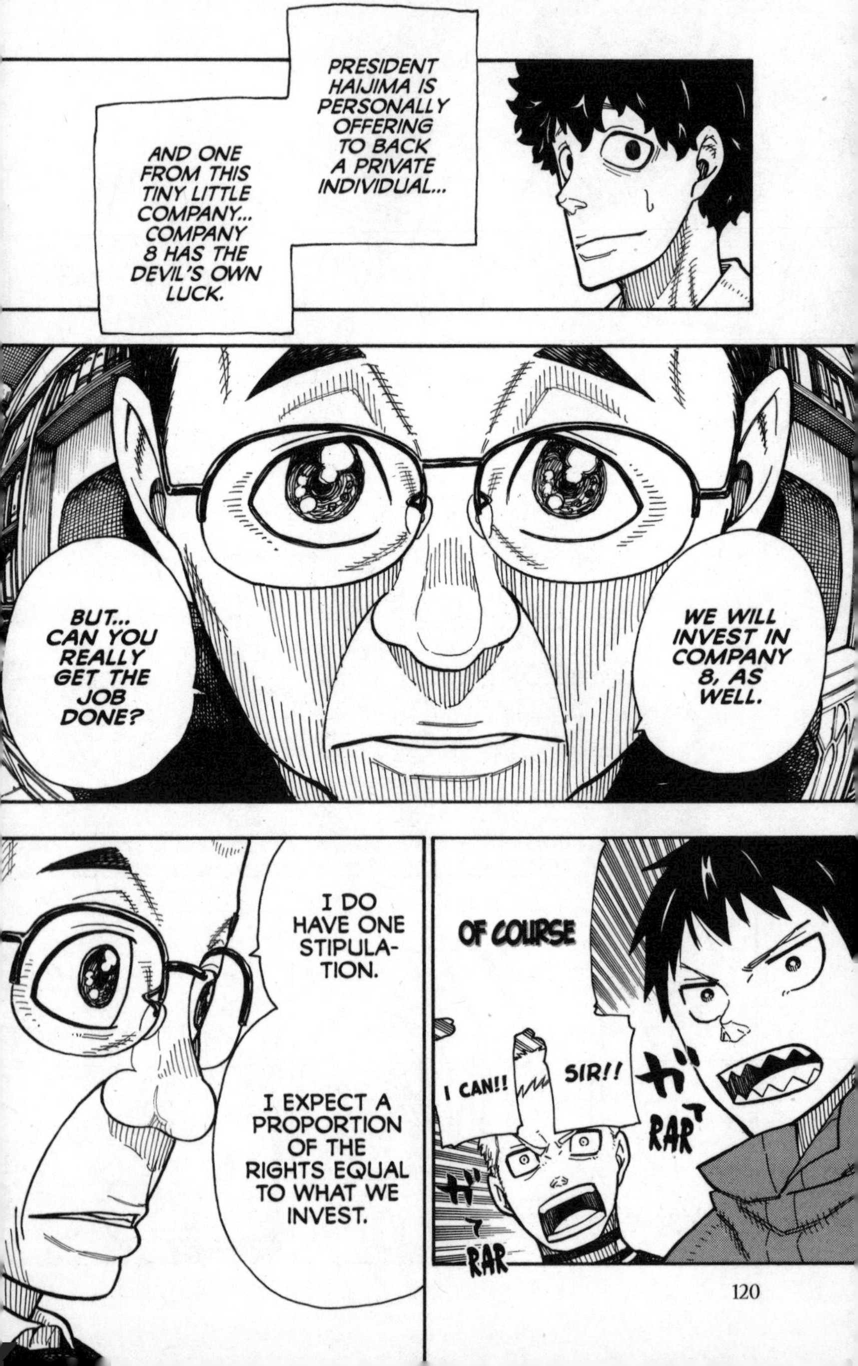
PRESIDENT HAIJIMA IS PERSONALLY OFFERING TO BACK A PRIVATE INDIVIDUAL...
AND ONE FROM THIS TINY LITTLE COMPANY... COMPANY 8 HAS THE DEVIL'S OWN LUCK.
WE WILL INVEST IN COMPANY 8, AS WELL.
BUT... CAN YOU REALLY GET THE JOB DONE?
OF COURSE
SIR!!
I CAN!!
RAR
RAR
I DO HAVE ONE STIPULATION.
I EXPECT A PROPORTION OF THE RIGHTS EQUAL TO WHAT WE INVEST.

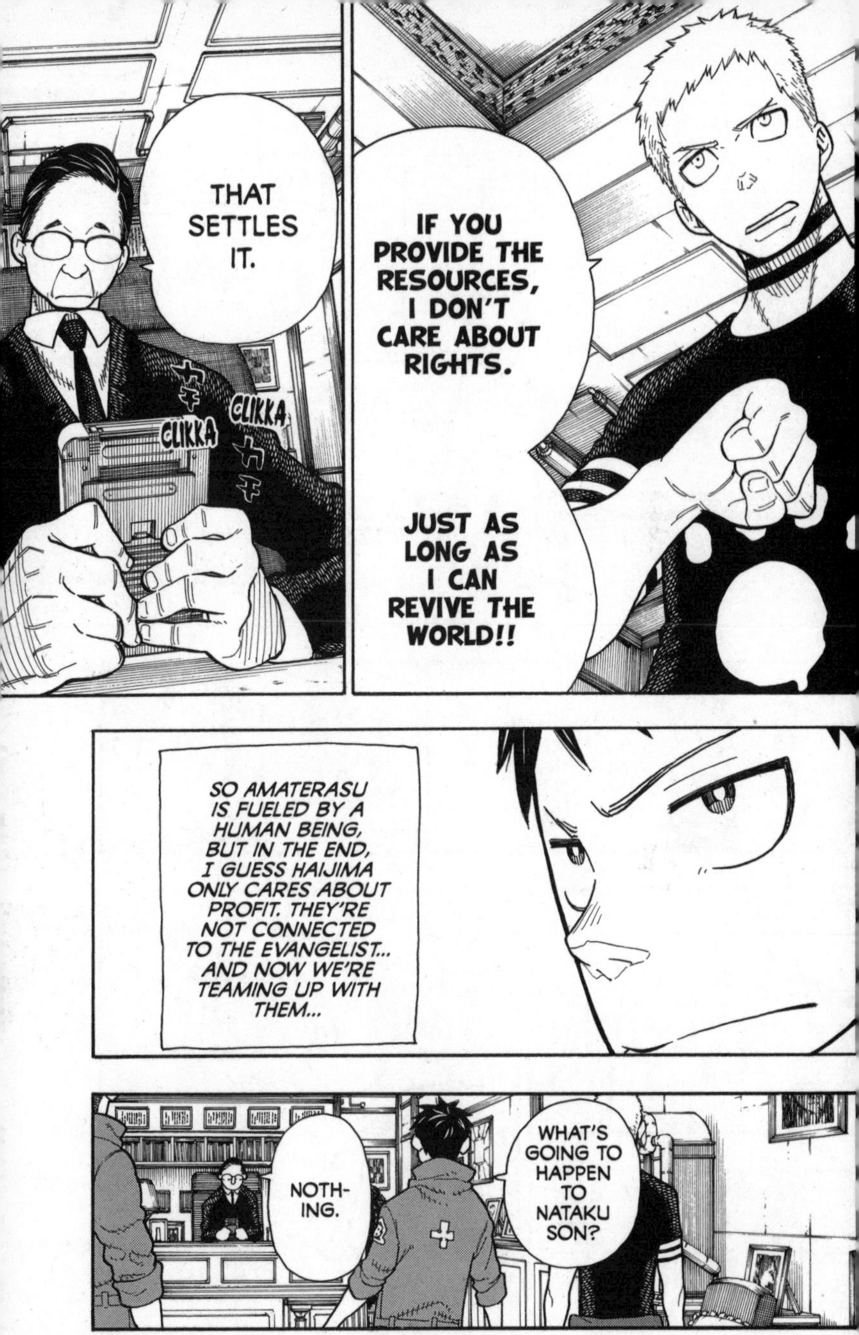
IF YOU PROVIDE THE RESOURCES, I DON'T CARE ABOUT RIGHTS.
JUST AS LONG AS I CAN REVIVE THE WORLD!!
THAT SETTLES IT.
CLIKKA
CLIKKA
SO AMATERASU IS FUELED BY A HUMAN BEING, BUT IN THE END, I GUESS HAIJIMA ONLY CARES ABOUT PROFIT. THEY'RE NOT CONNECTED TO THE EVANGELIST... AND NOW WE'RE TEAMING UP WITH THEM...
WHAT'S GOING TO HAPPEN TO NATAKU SON?
NOTH-ING.

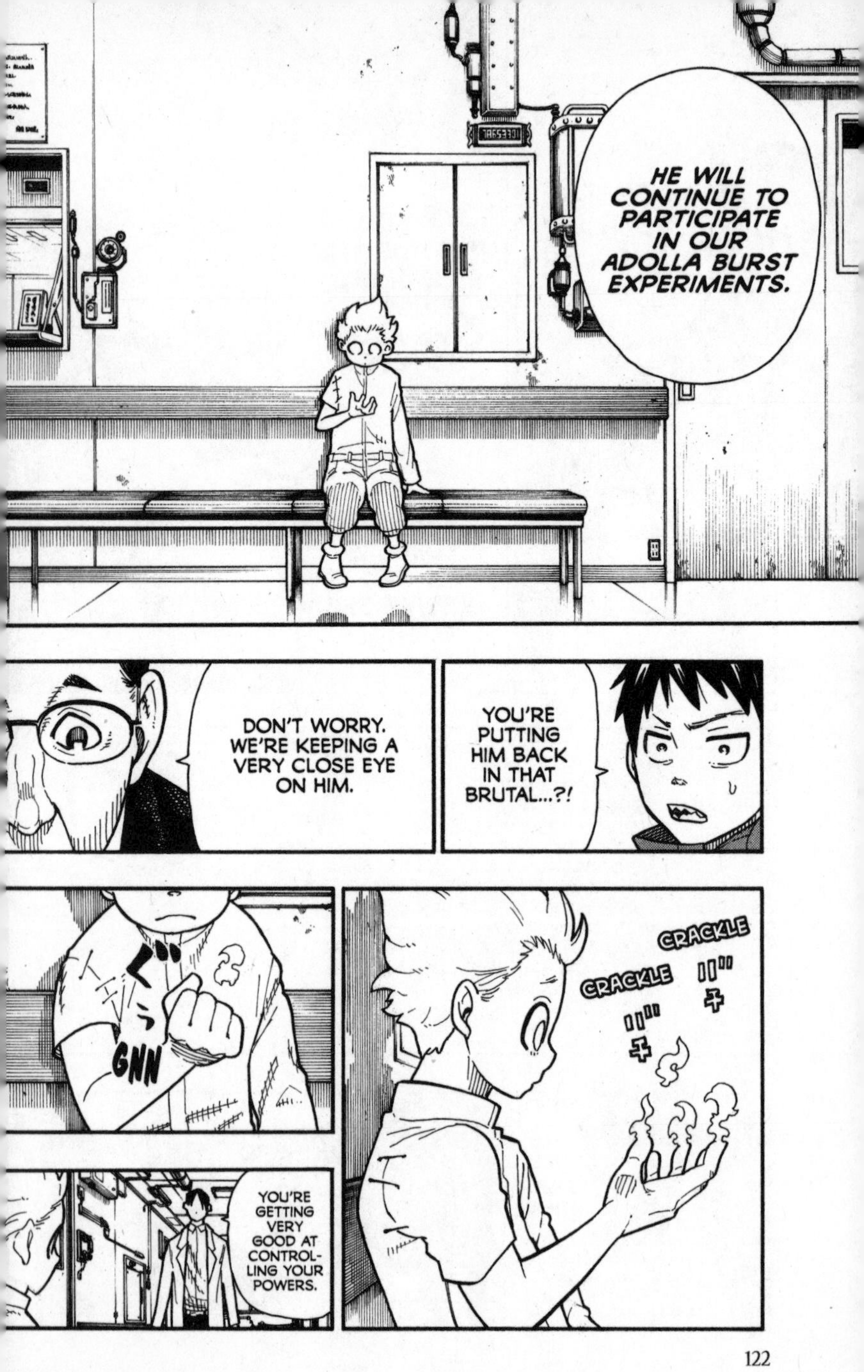

HE WILL CONTINUE TO PARTICIPATE IN OUR ADOLLA BURST EXPERIMENTS.
YOU'RE PUTTING HIM BACK IN THAT BRUTAL...?!
DON'T WORRY. WE'RE KEEPING A VERY CLOSE EYE ON HIM.
CRACKLE
CRACKLE
GNN
YOU'RE GETTING VERY GOOD AT CONTROL-LING YOUR POWERS.

FWOOSH

NOT REALLY... I STILL GET NERVOUS WITHOUT MY FIREPROOF MANTLE.

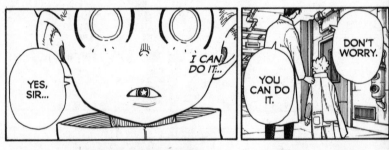

I CAN DO IT...

YES, SIR...

DON'T WORRY.

YOU CAN DO IT.

COME ON. IT'S TIME TO PLAY WITH UNCLE DEATH.

KURONO-SAN...

BEEEEP

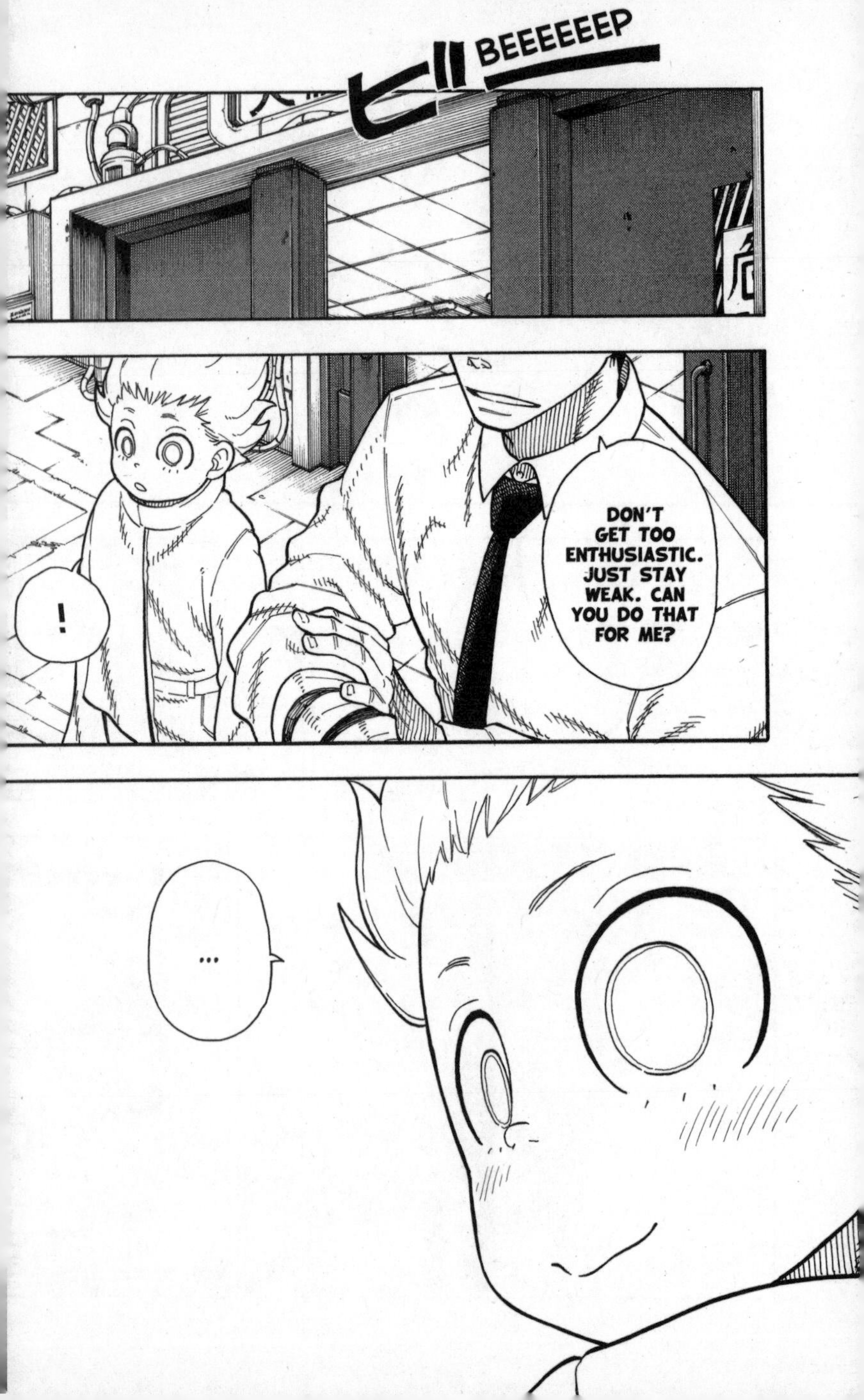
BEEEEEEP
DON'T GET TOO ENTHUSIASTIC. JUST STAY WEAK. CAN YOU DO THAT FOR ME?
!
...

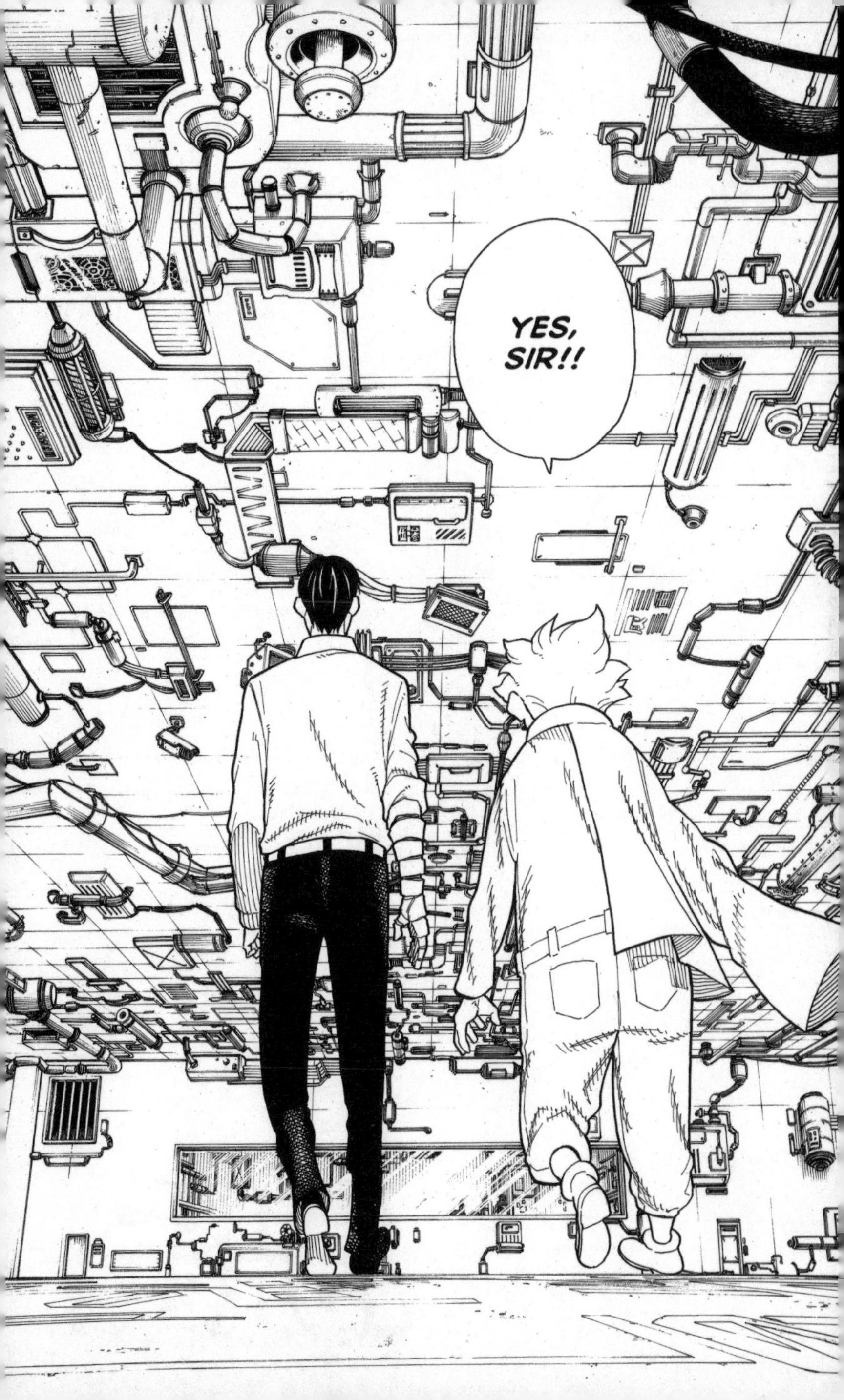
YES, SIR!!

FIRE FORCE

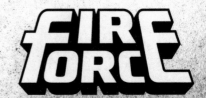

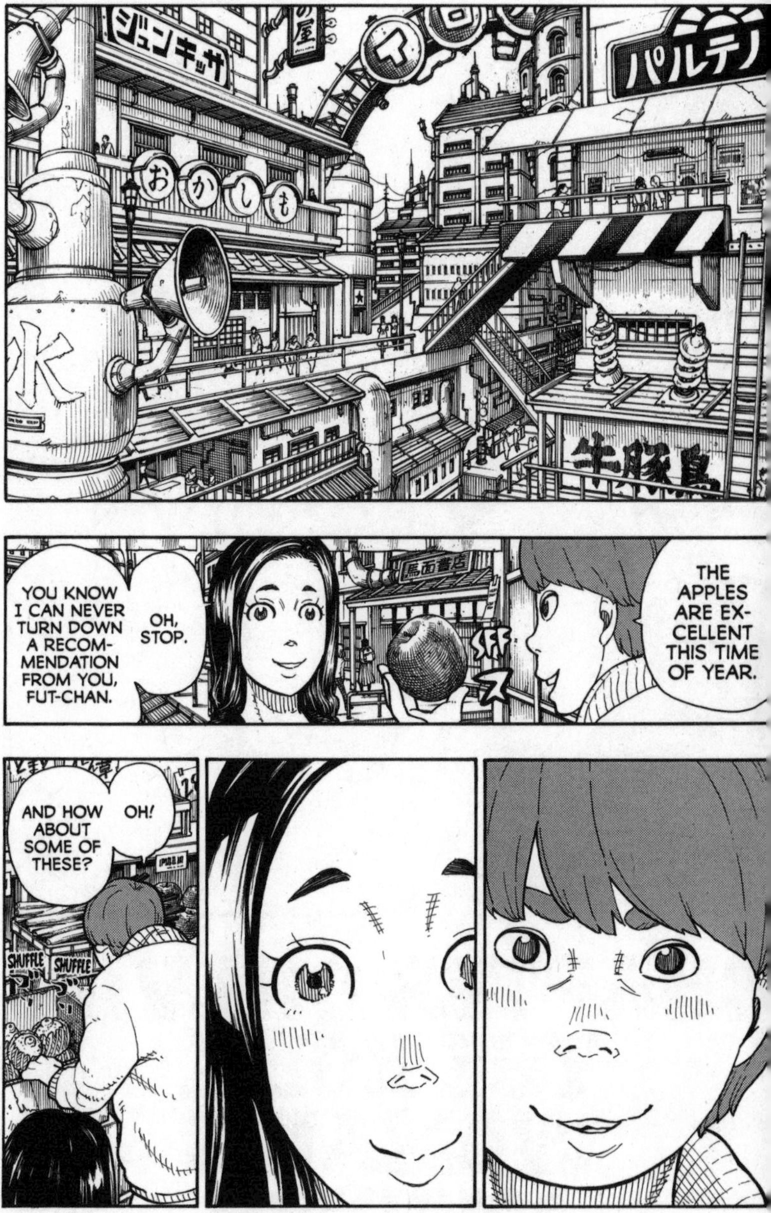
ジュンキッサ
おかしも
パルテノ
牛豚鳥
THE APPLES ARE EXCELLENT THIS TIME OF YEAR.
馬面書店
SFF
OH, STOP.
YOU KNOW I CAN NEVER TURN DOWN A RECOMMENDATION FROM YOU, FUT-CHAN.
OH!
AND HOW ABOUT SOME OF THESE?
SHUFFLE
SHUFFLE

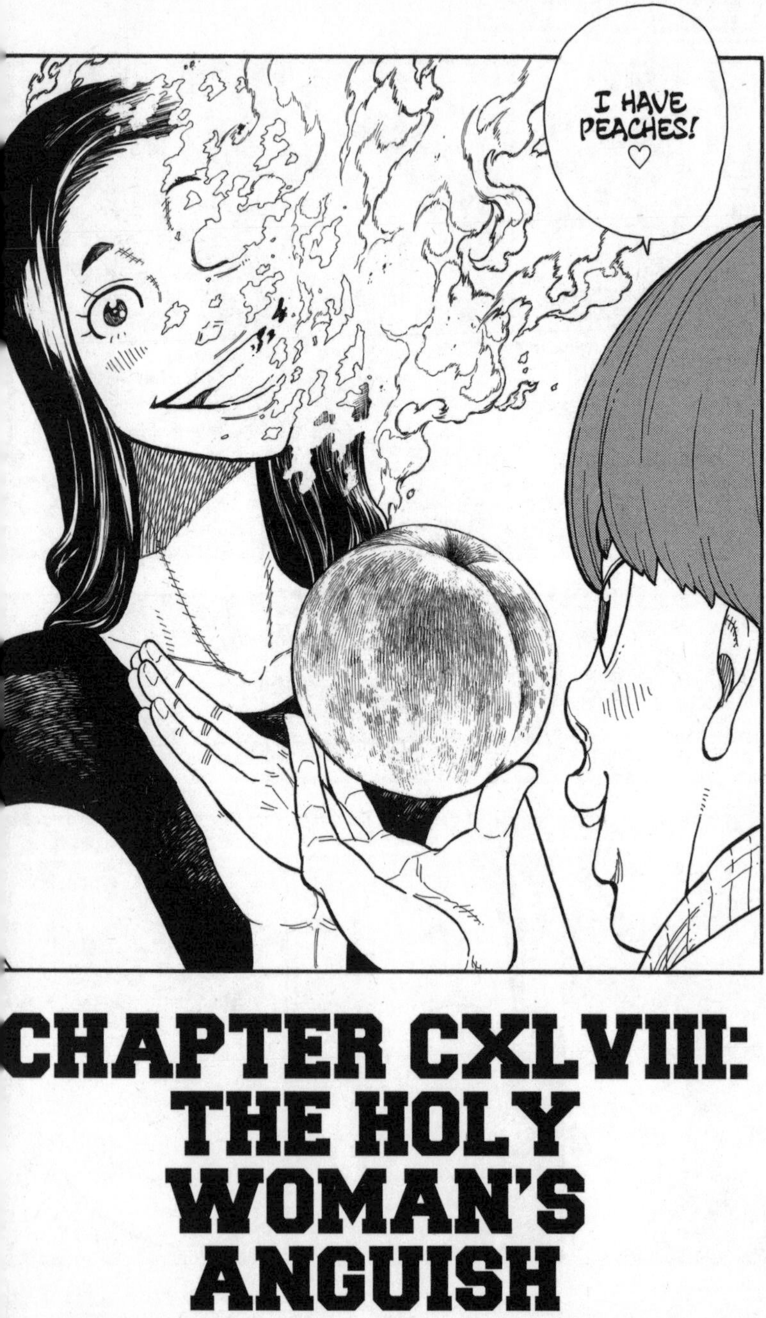
I HAVE PEACHES! ♡

CHAPTER CXLVIII: THE HOLY WOMAN'S ANGUISH

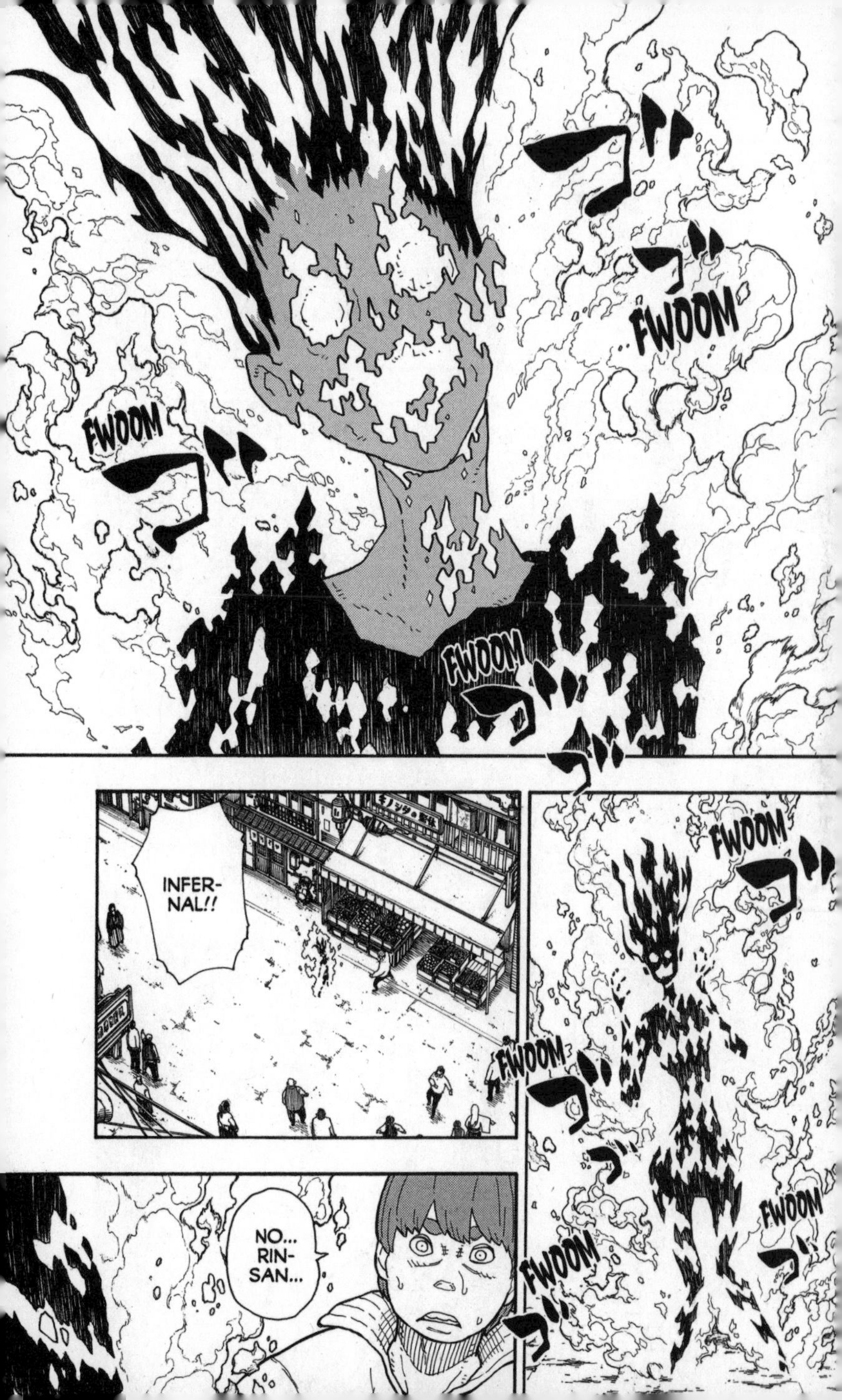
FWOOM
FWOOM
FWOOM
FWOOM
FWOOM
FWOOM
FWOOM
FWOOM
INFER-
NAL!!
NO...
RIN-
SAN...

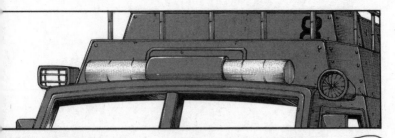

ONE CASUALTY...

ROGER THAT.

THE FIRE IS IN THE ARAKAWA SHOPPING DISTRICT BAZAAR! IT WAS STARTED BY A SINGLE INFERNAL... THERE'S ALSO ONE CASUALTY— AN EMPLOYEE AT THE FRUIT STAND.

Extinguisher: Tokyo Empire ✠

SISTER IRIS, BE READY.

ZHOOM

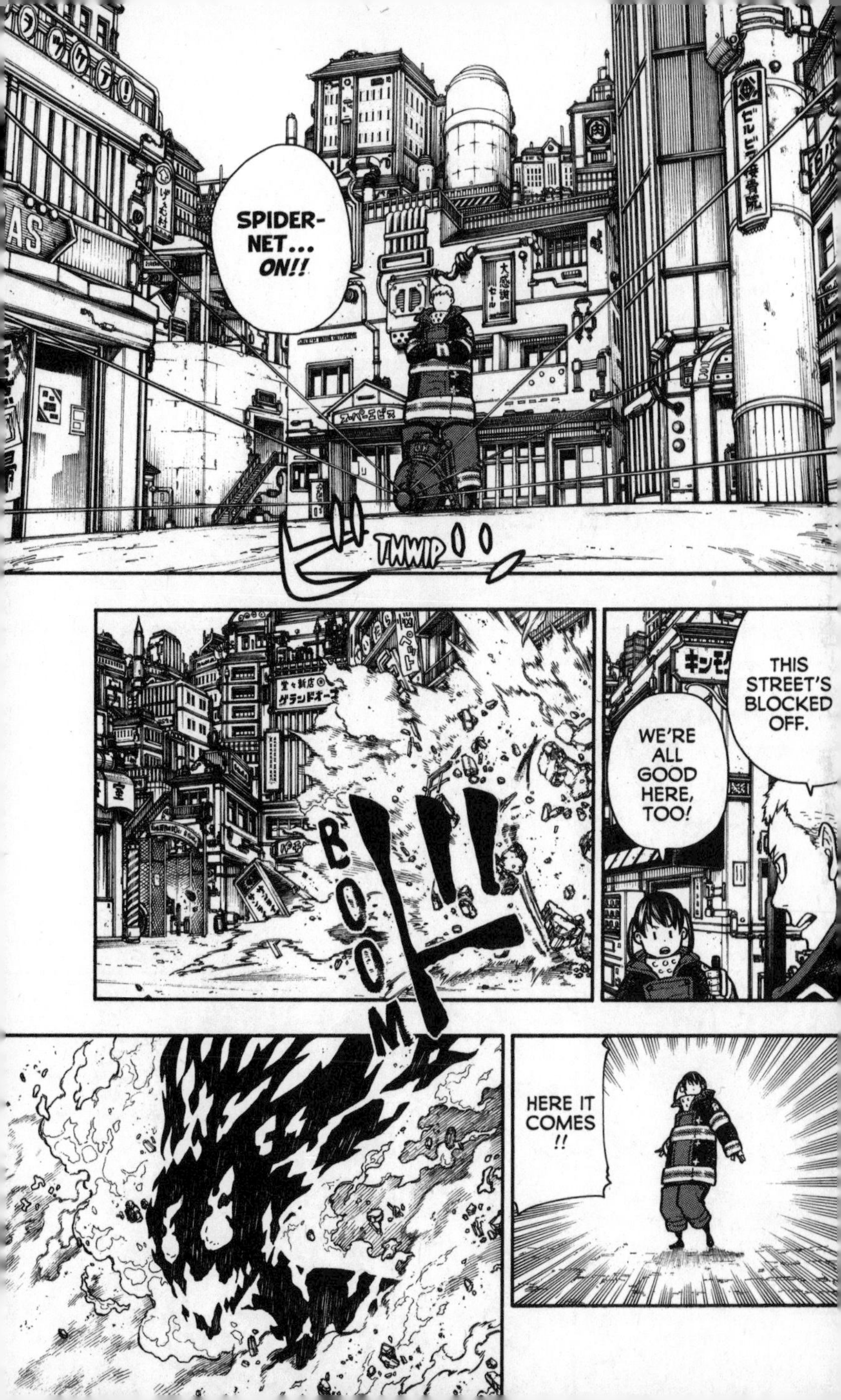
SPIDER-NET... ON!!
THWIP
THIS STREET'S BLOCKED OFF.
WE'RE ALL GOOD HERE, TOO!
BOOOM
HERE IT COMES!!

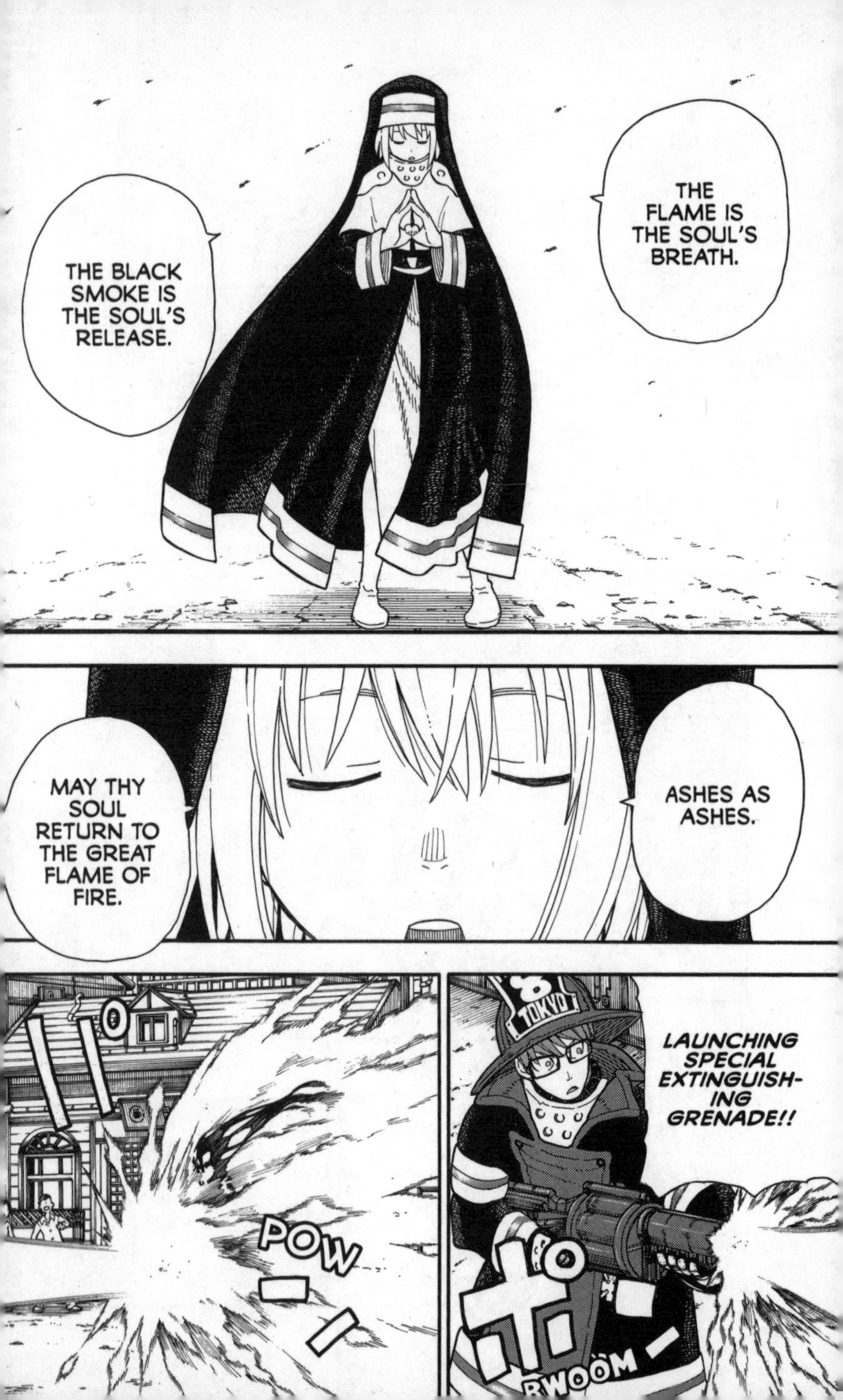

THE FLAME IS THE SOUL'S BREATH.
THE BLACK SMOKE IS THE SOUL'S RELEASE.
ASHES AS ASHES.
MAY THY SOUL RETURN TO THE GREAT FLAME OF FIRE.
8 TOKYO
LAUNCHING SPECIAL EXTINGUISH-ING GRENADE!!
BWOOM
POW

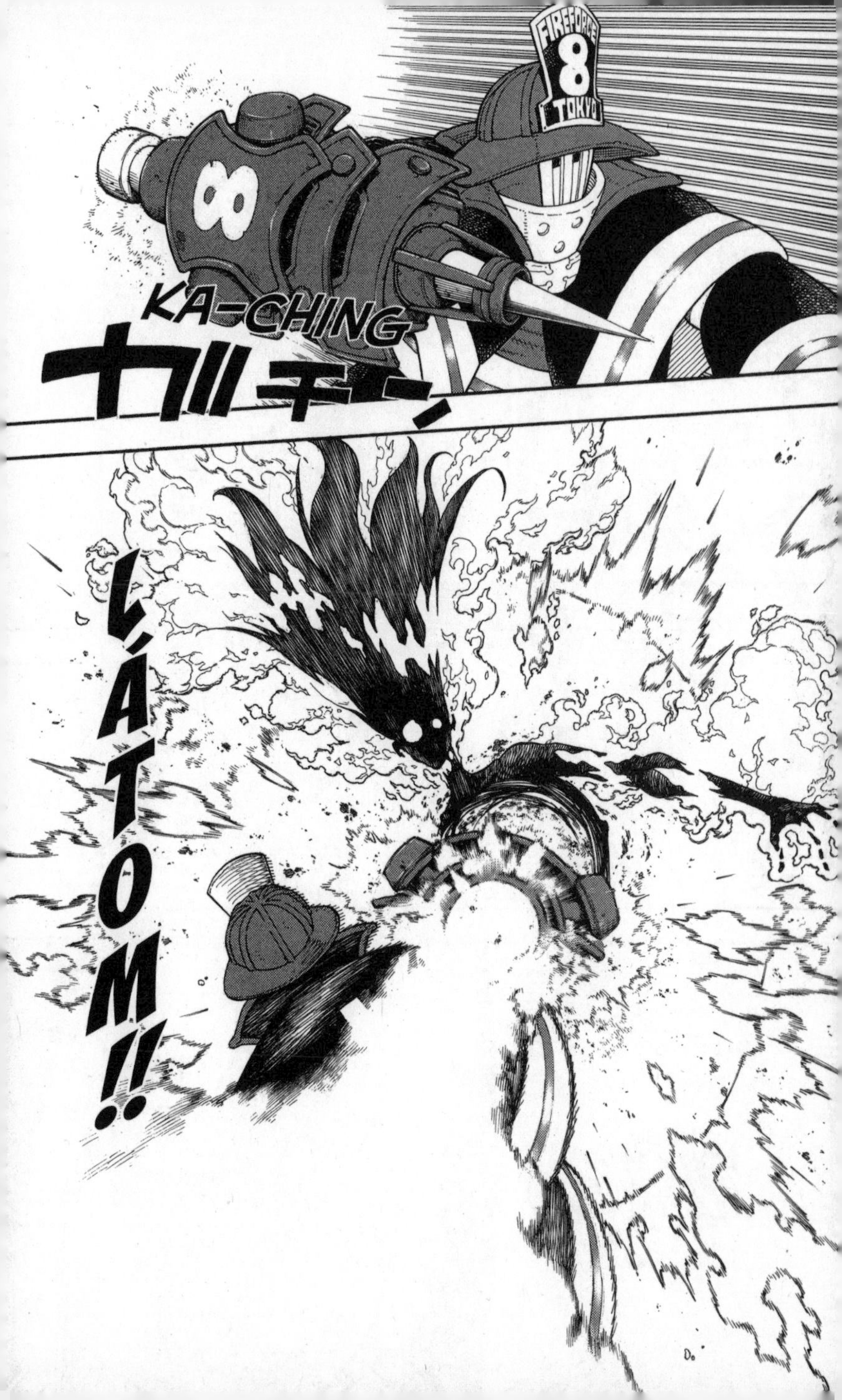
KA-CHING
LÁTOM!!

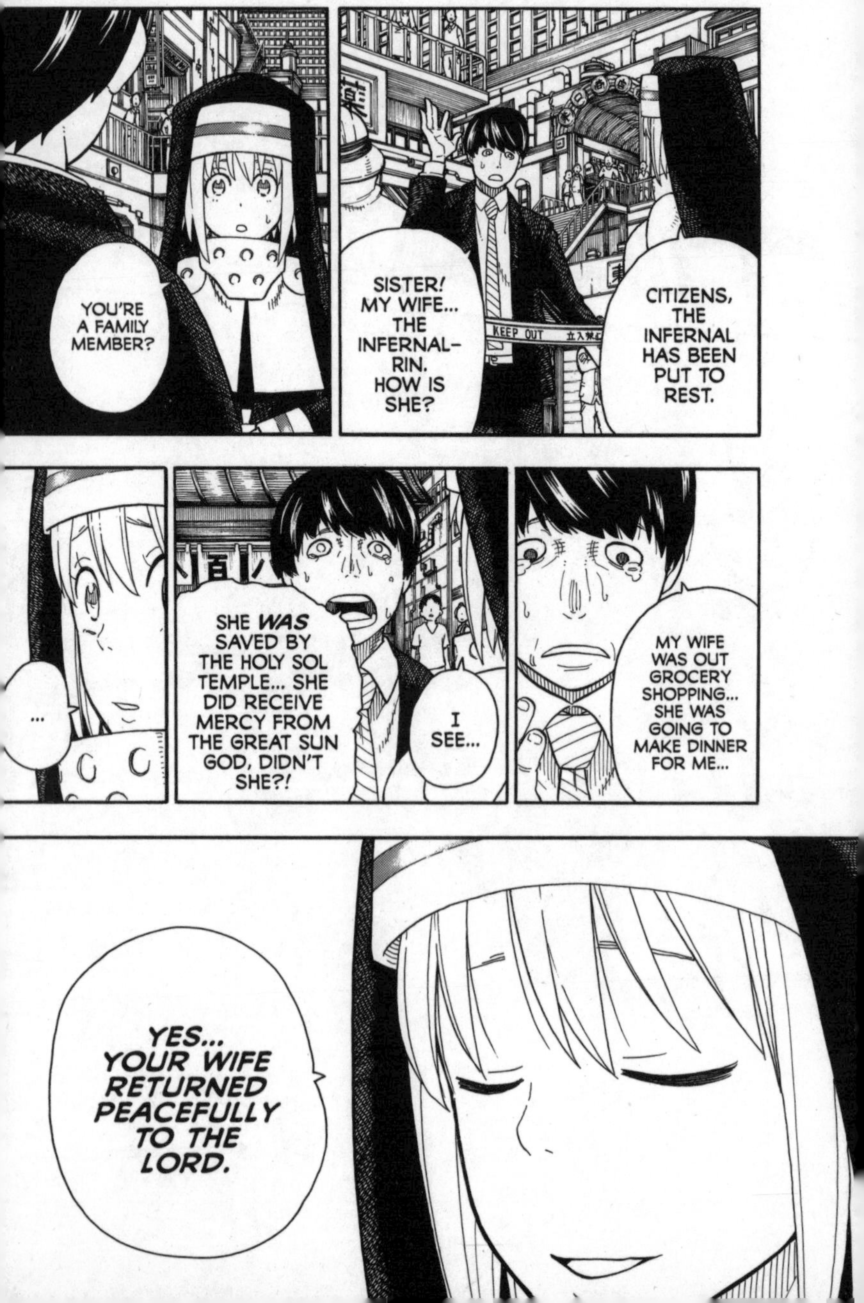
CITIZENS, THE INFERNAL HAS BEEN PUT TO REST.
SISTER! MY WIFE... THE INFERNAL— RIN. HOW IS SHE?
KEEP OUT
YOU'RE A FAMILY MEMBER?
MY WIFE WAS OUT GROCERY SHOPPING... SHE WAS GOING TO MAKE DINNER FOR ME...
I SEE...
SHE *WAS* SAVED BY THE HOLY SOL TEMPLE... SHE DID RECEIVE MERCY FROM THE GREAT SUN GOD, DIDN'T SHE?!
...
YES... YOUR WIFE RETURNED PEACEFULLY TO THE LORD.

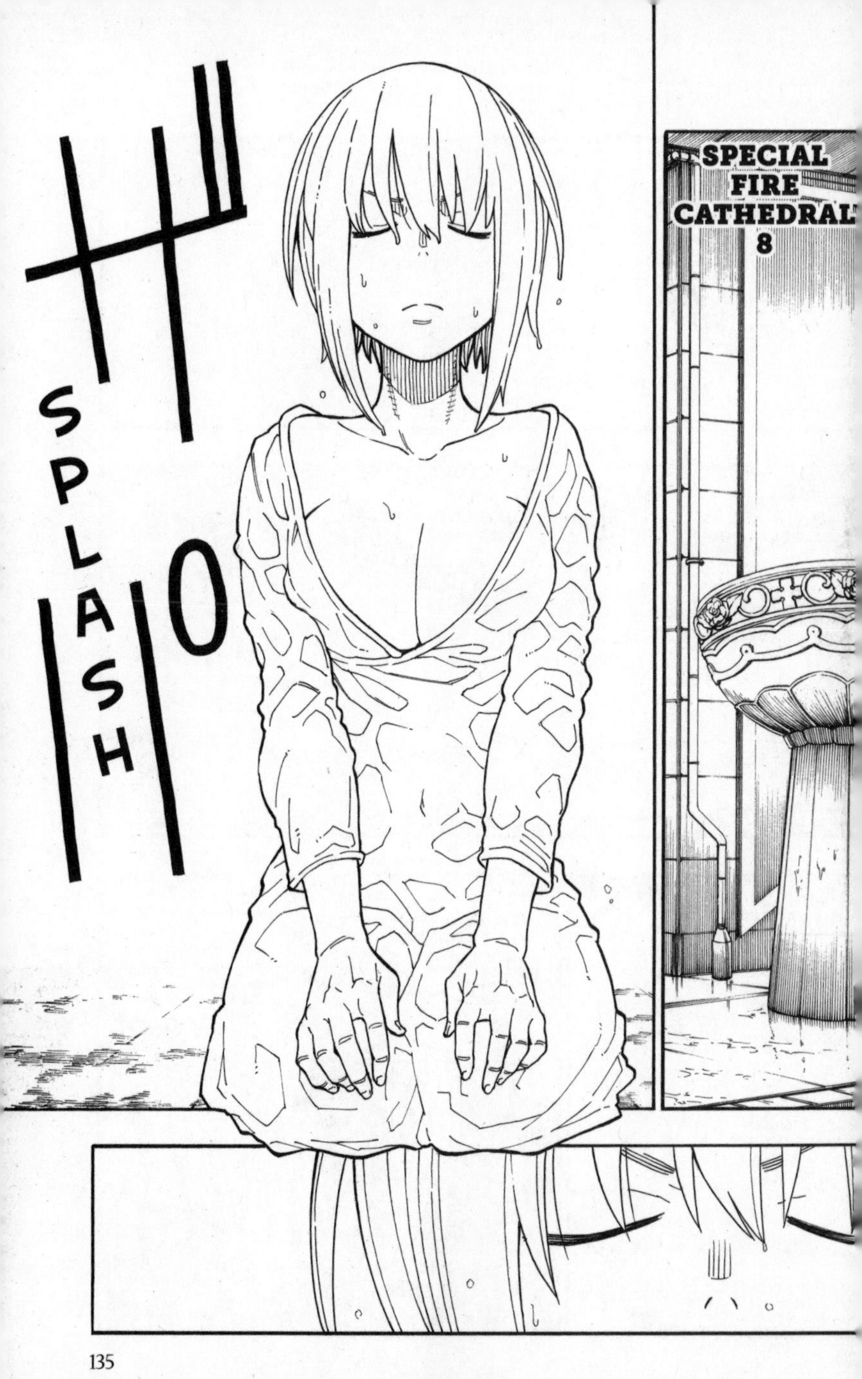
SPECIAL FIRE CATHEDRAL 8
SPLASH

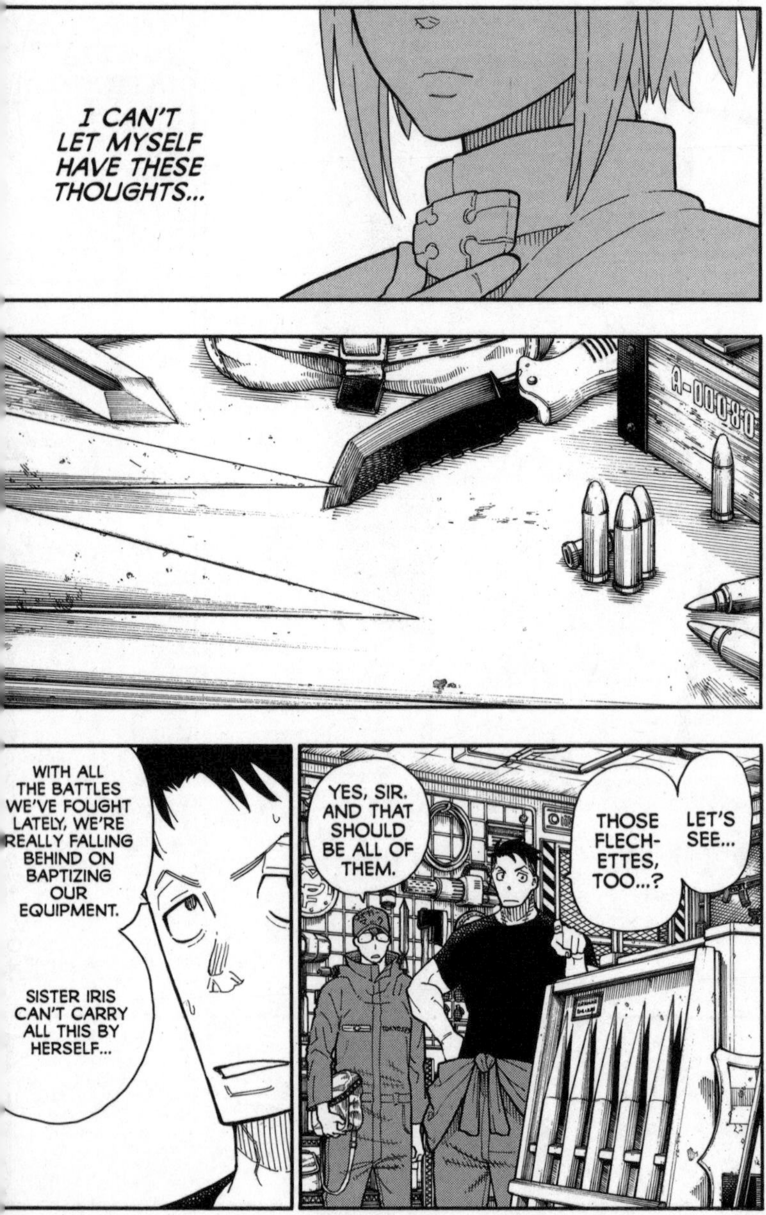
I CAN'T LET MYSELF HAVE THESE THOUGHTS...
LET'S SEE...
THOSE FLECH-ETTES, TOO...?
YES, SIR. AND THAT SHOULD BE ALL OF THEM.
WITH ALL THE BATTLES WE'VE FOUGHT LATELY, WE'RE REALLY FALLING BEHIND ON BAPTIZING OUR EQUIPMENT.
SISTER IRIS CAN'T CARRY ALL THIS BY HERSELF...

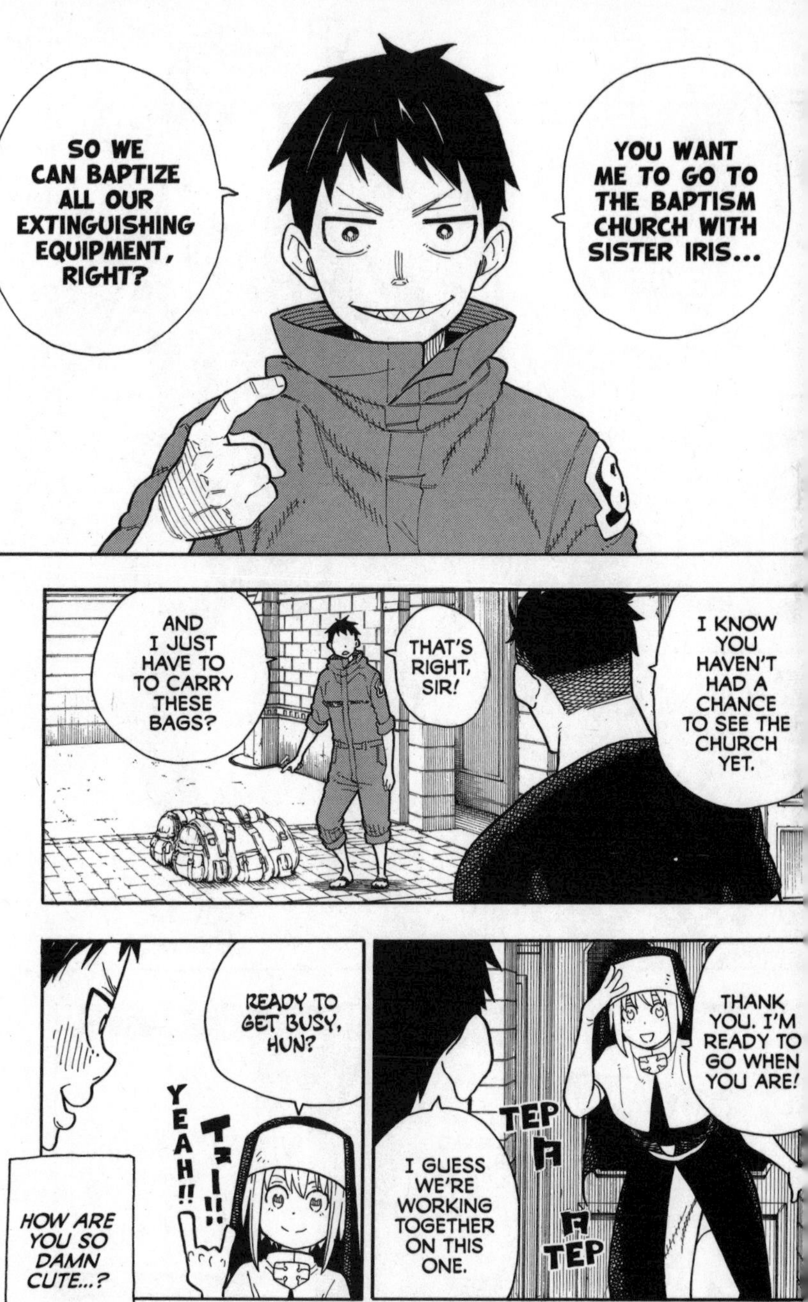

YOU WANT ME TO GO TO THE BAPTISM CHURCH WITH SISTER IRIS...
SO WE CAN BAPTIZE ALL OUR EXTINGUISHING EQUIPMENT, RIGHT?
I KNOW YOU HAVEN'T HAD A CHANCE TO SEE THE CHURCH YET.
THAT'S RIGHT, SIR!
AND I JUST HAVE TO TO CARRY THESE BAGS?
THANK YOU. I'M READY TO GO WHEN YOU ARE!
TEP
TEP
I GUESS WE'RE WORKING TOGETHER ON THIS ONE.
READY TO GET BUSY, HUN?
YEAH!!
HOW ARE YOU SO DAMN CUTE...?

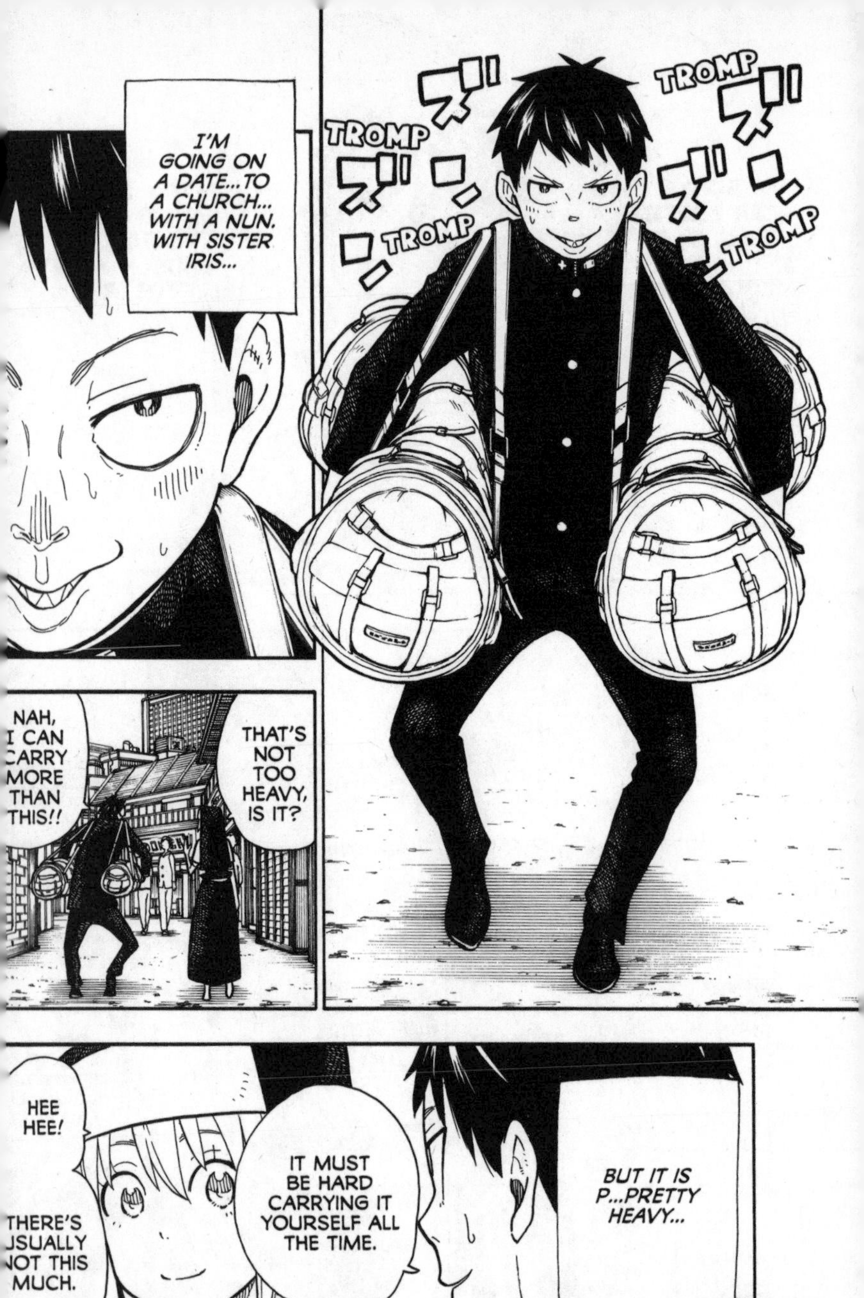
TROMP
TROMP
TROMP
TROMP
I'M GOING ON A DATE...TO A CHURCH... WITH A NUN. WITH SISTER IRIS...
THAT'S NOT TOO HEAVY, IS IT?
NAH, I CAN CARRY MORE THAN THIS!!
BUT IT IS P...PRETTY HEAVY...
IT MUST BE HARD CARRYING IT YOURSELF ALL THE TIME.
HEE HEE!
THERE'S USUALLY NOT THIS MUCH.

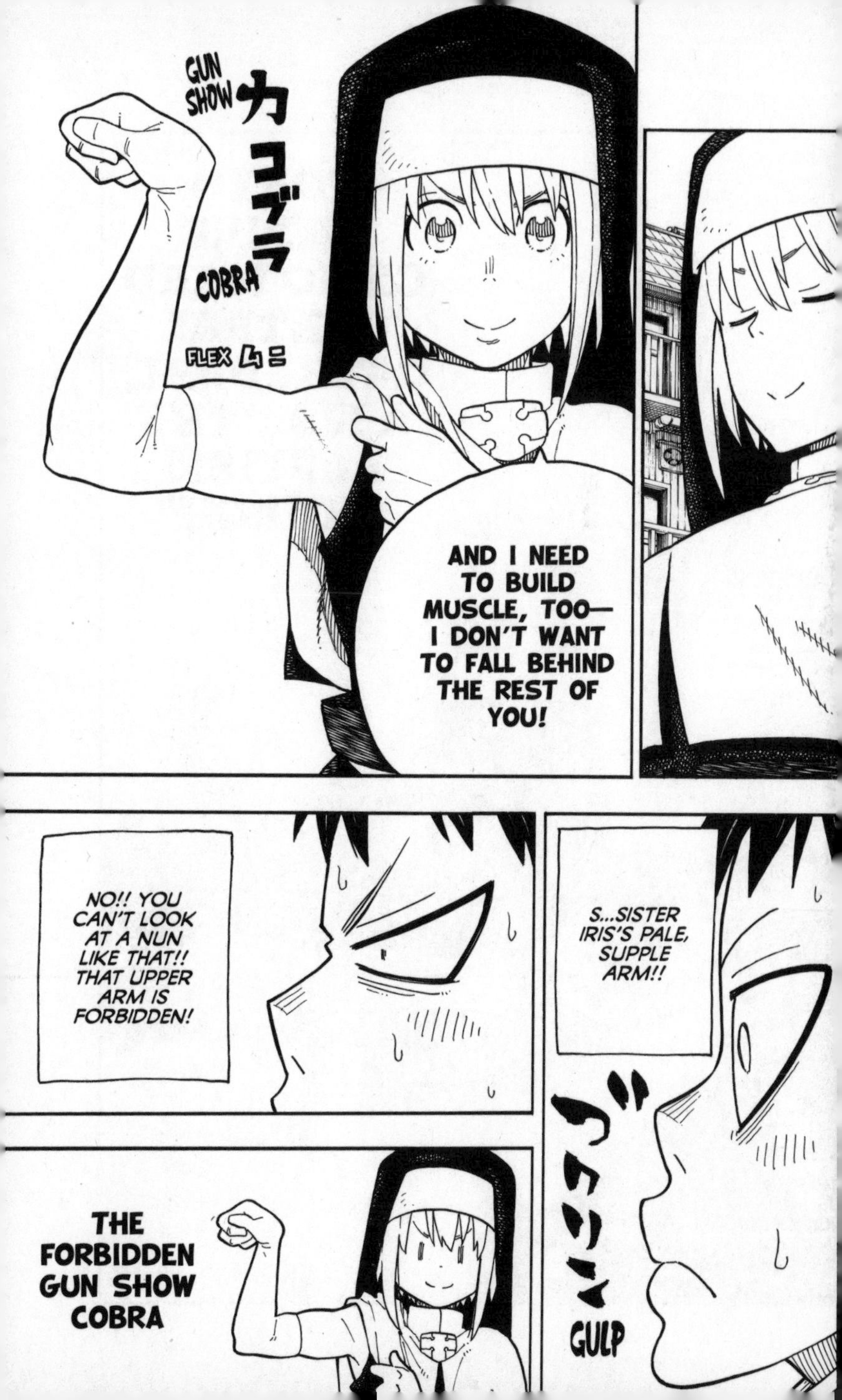
GUN SHOW
力コブラ
COBRA
FLEX
AND I NEED TO BUILD MUSCLE, TOO— I DON'T WANT TO FALL BEHIND THE REST OF YOU!
S...SISTER IRIS'S PALE, SUPPLE ARM!!
ゴクリ
GULP
NO!! YOU CAN'T LOOK AT A NUN LIKE THAT!! THAT UPPER ARM IS FORBIDDEN!
THE FORBIDDEN GUN SHOW COBRA

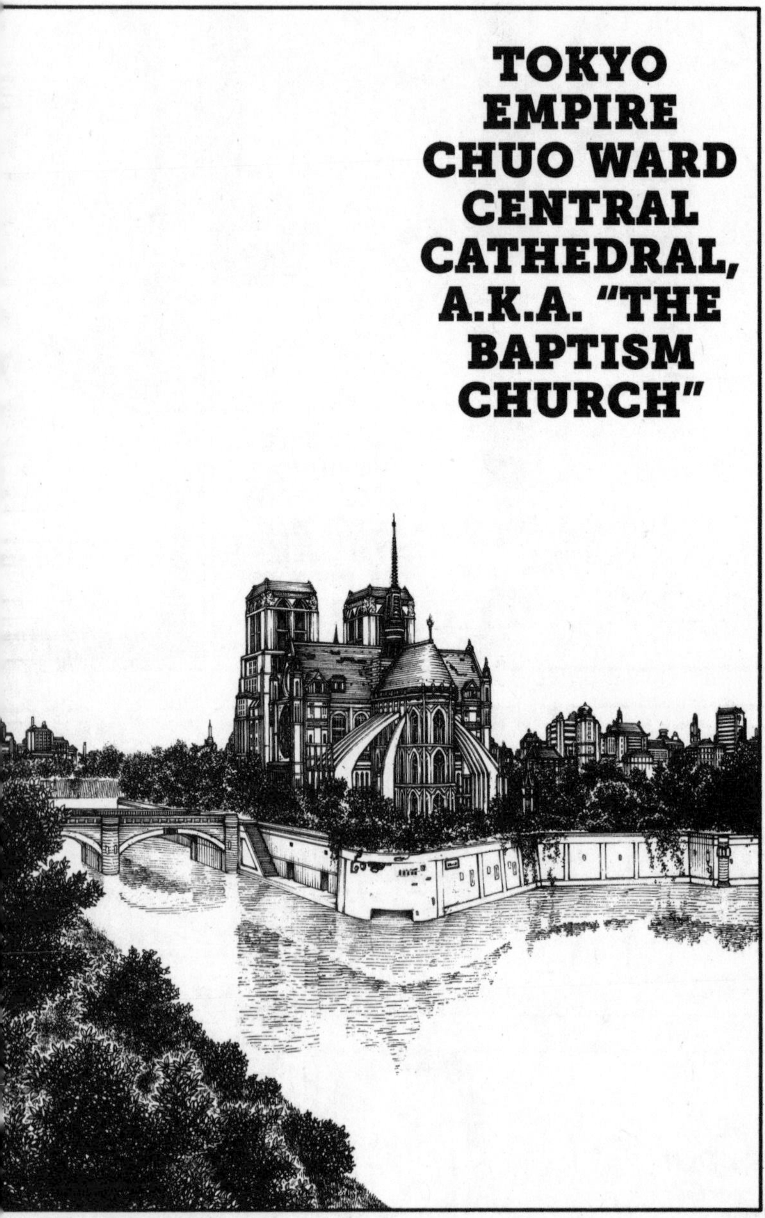
TOKYO EMPIRE CHUO WARD CENTRAL CATHEDRAL, A.K.A. "THE BAPTISM CHURCH"

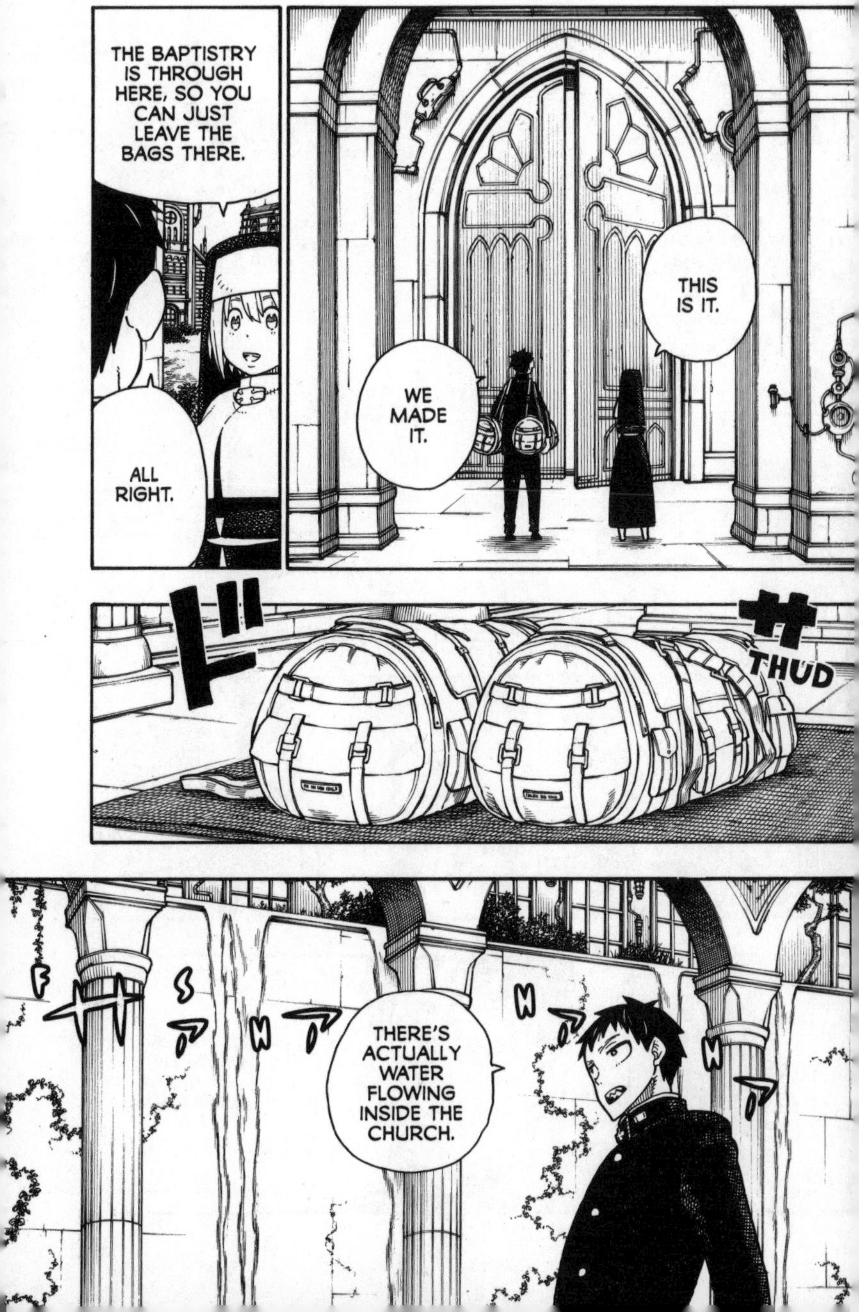
THIS IS IT.
WE MADE IT.
THE BAPTISTRY IS THROUGH HERE, SO YOU CAN JUST LEAVE THE BAGS THERE.
ALL RIGHT.
THUD
THERE'S ACTUALLY WATER FLOWING INSIDE THE CHURCH.

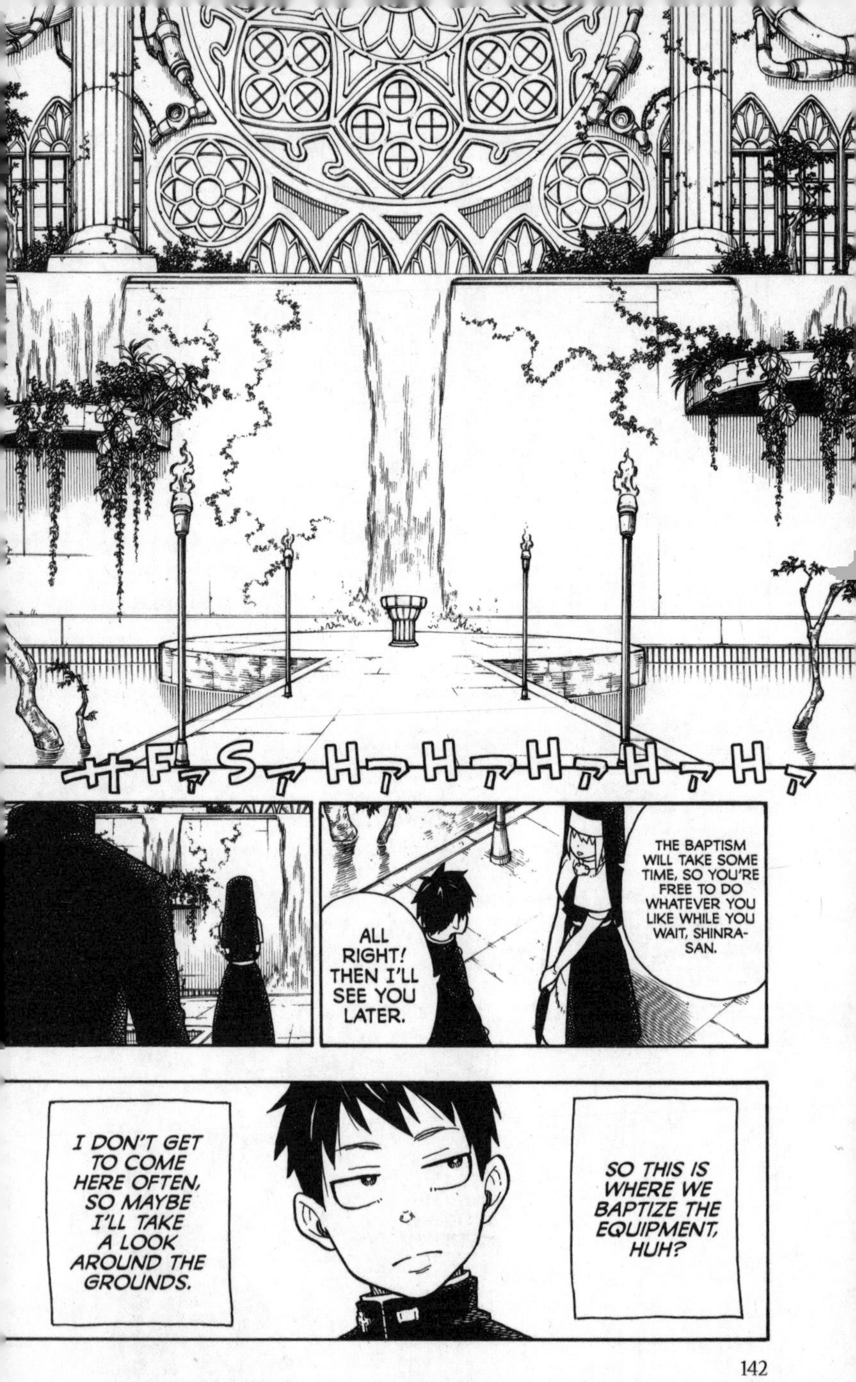
FSHHHHH
THE BAPTISM WILL TAKE SOME TIME, SO YOU'RE FREE TO DO WHATEVER YOU LIKE WHILE YOU WAIT, SHINRA-SAN.
ALL RIGHT! THEN I'LL SEE YOU LATER.
SO THIS IS WHERE WE BAPTIZE THE EQUIPMENT, HUH?
I DON'T GET TO COME HERE OFTEN, SO MAYBE I'LL TAKE A LOOK AROUND THE GROUNDS.

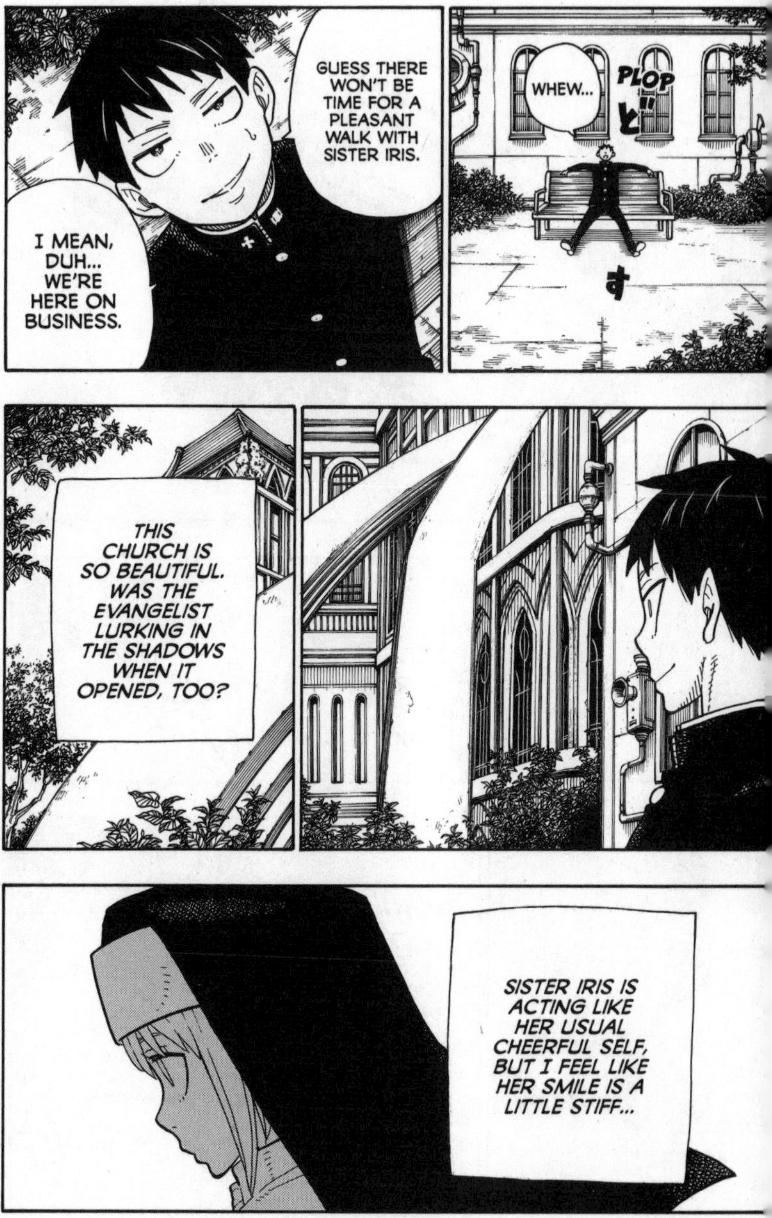
WHEW...
PLOP
と
す
GUESS THERE WON'T BE TIME FOR A PLEASANT WALK WITH SISTER IRIS.
I MEAN, DUH... WE'RE HERE ON BUSINESS.
THIS CHURCH IS SO BEAUTIFUL. WAS THE EVANGELIST LURKING IN THE SHADOWS WHEN IT OPENED, TOO?
SISTER IRIS IS ACTING LIKE HER USUAL CHEERFUL SELF, BUT I FEEL LIKE HER SMILE IS A LITTLE STIFF...

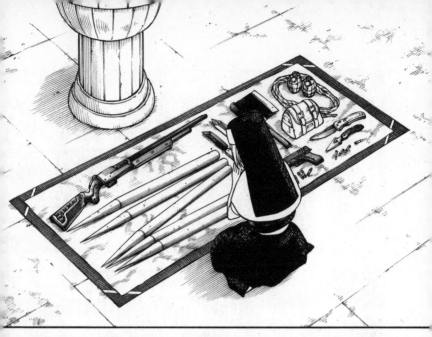

THE HOLY SOL TEMPLE WAS STARTED BY THE EVANGELIST... WHAT HAVE I BEEN BELIEVING IN...? WHAT HAVE I BEEN DEVOTING MYSELF TO?

SISTER IRIS, I CAN TELL YOU ARE DISTRACTED.

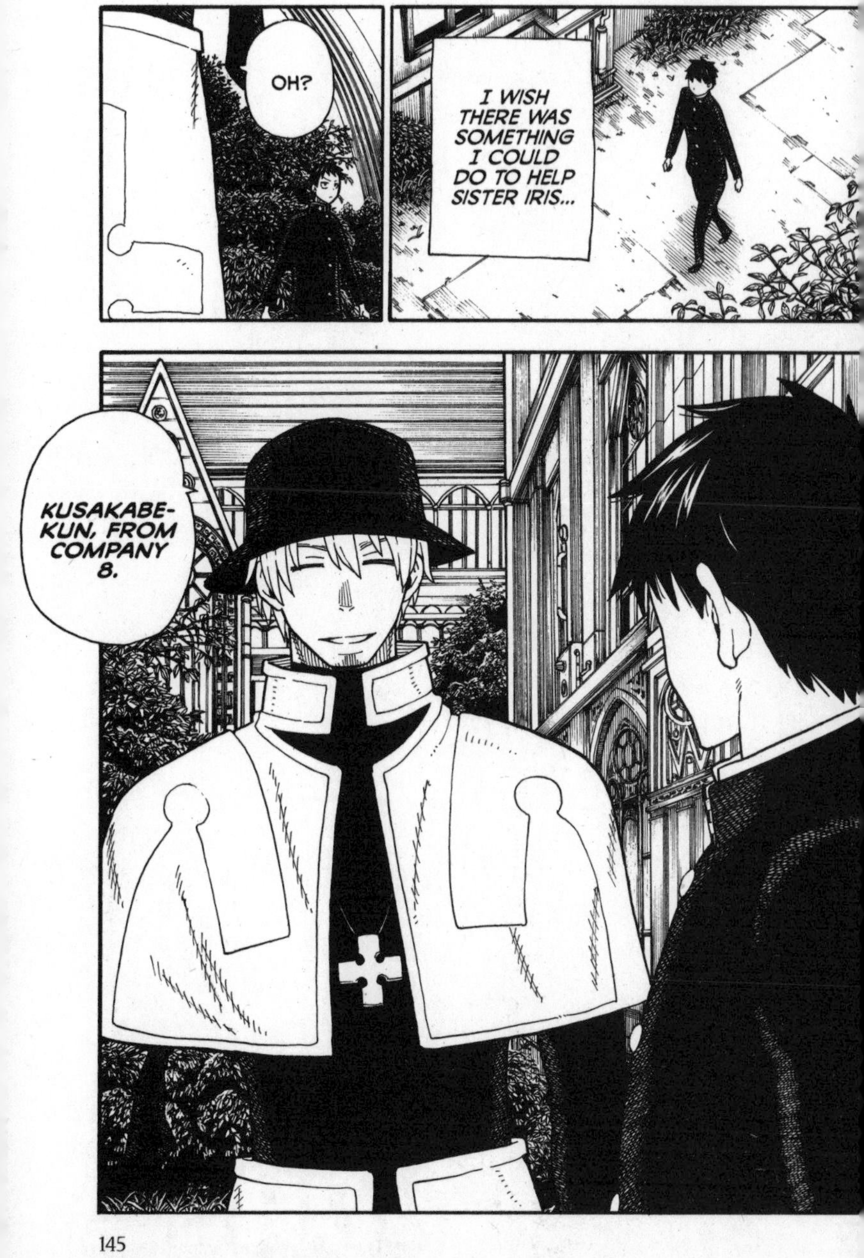
I WISH THERE WAS SOMETHING I COULD DO TO HELP SISTER IRIS...
OH?
KUSAKABE-KUN, FROM COMPANY 8.

FIRE FORCE

CHAPTER CXLIX: THE REWARDS OF DEVOTION

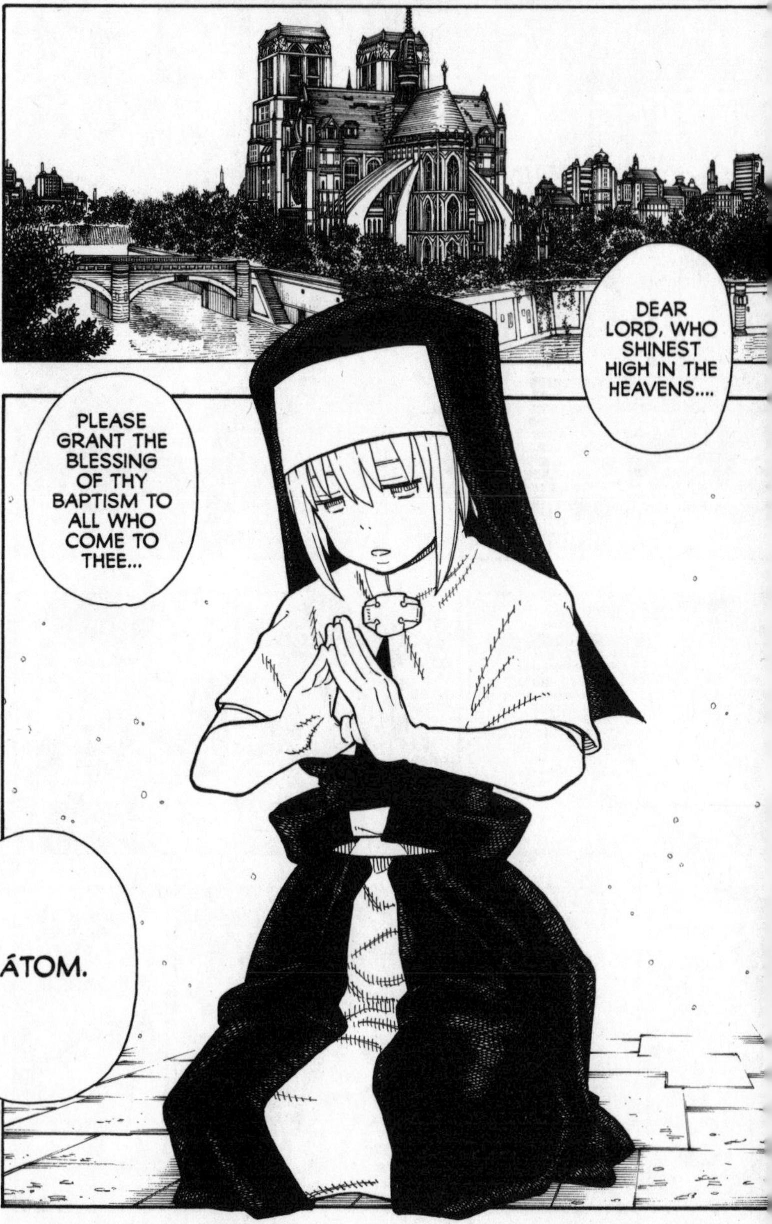
DEAR LORD, WHO SHINEST HIGH IN THE HEAVENS....
PLEASE GRANT THE BLESSING OF THY BAPTISM TO ALL WHO COME TO THEE...
LÁTOM.

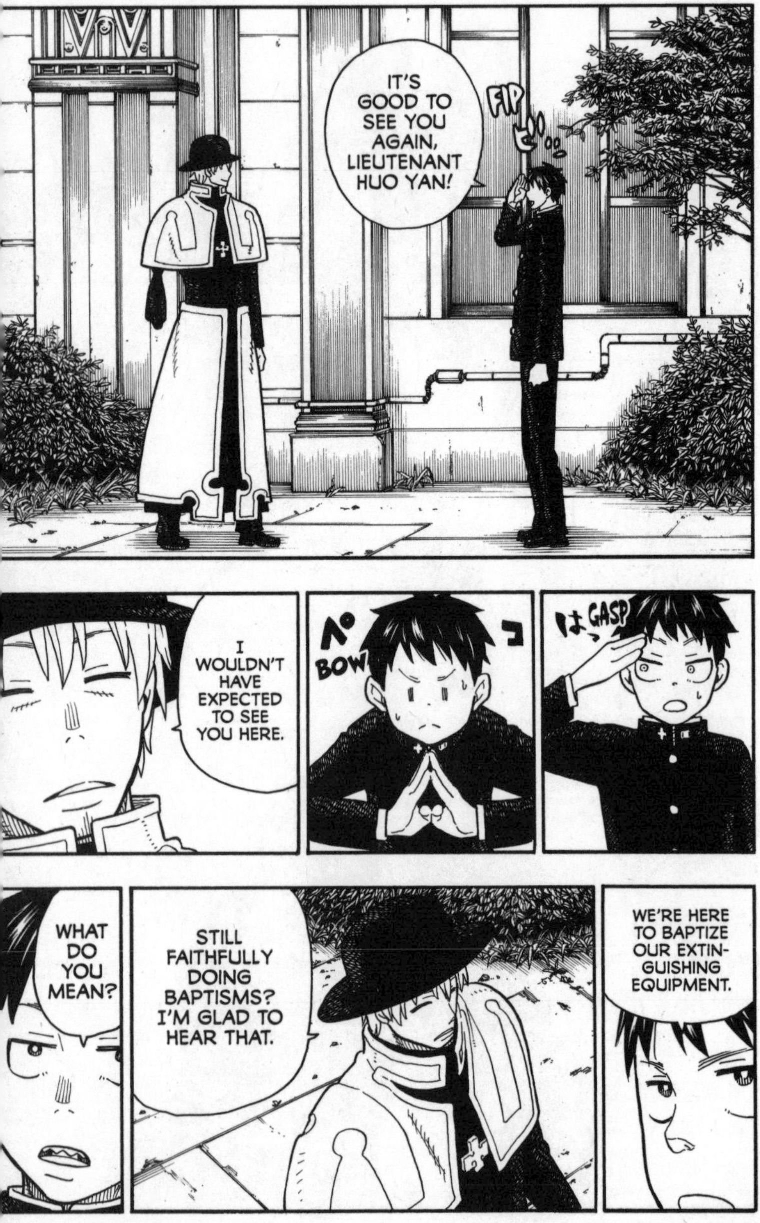
IT'S GOOD TO SEE YOU AGAIN, LIEUTENANT HUO YAN!
FIP
は GASP
ペ BOW コ
I WOULDN'T HAVE EXPECTED TO SEE YOU HERE.
WE'RE HERE TO BAPTIZE OUR EXTIN-GUISHING EQUIPMENT.
STILL FAITHFULLY DOING BAPTISMS? I'M GLAD TO HEAR THAT.
WHAT DO YOU MEAN?

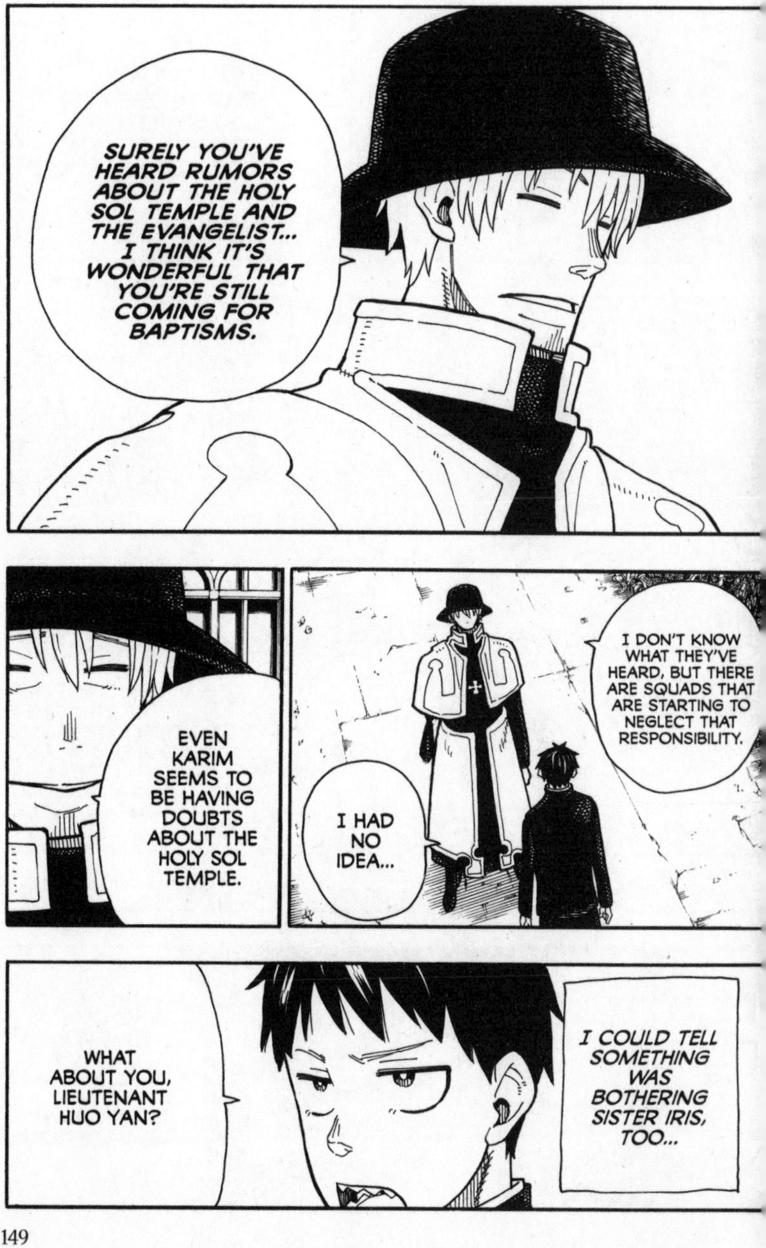
SURELY YOU'VE HEARD RUMORS ABOUT THE HOLY SOL TEMPLE AND THE EVANGELIST... I THINK IT'S WONDERFUL THAT YOU'RE STILL COMING FOR BAPTISMS.
I DON'T KNOW WHAT THEY'VE HEARD, BUT THERE ARE SQUADS THAT ARE STARTING TO NEGLECT THAT RESPONSIBILITY.
I HAD NO IDEA...
EVEN KARIM SEEMS TO BE HAVING DOUBTS ABOUT THE HOLY SOL TEMPLE.
I COULD TELL SOMETHING WAS BOTHERING SISTER IRIS, TOO...
WHAT ABOUT YOU, LIEUTENANT HUO YAN?

I WAS STUNNED TO HEAR THAT IT MIGHT HAVE BEEN THE EVANGELIST WHO CREATED THE HOLY SOL TEMPLE.

BUT THE HOLY SOL TEMPLE DOESN'T WORSHIP THE EVANGELIST— WE WORSHIP FIRE AND THE SUN.

AS LONG AS THE SUN I'VE REVERED ALL THESE YEARS IS STILL THERE, MY FAITH WILL NOT BE SHAKEN.

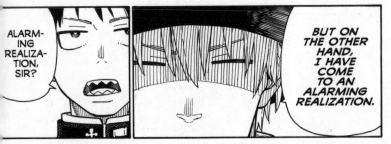

ALARM- ING REALIZA- TION, SIR?

BUT ON THE OTHER HAND, I HAVE COME TO AN ALARMING REALIZATION.

150

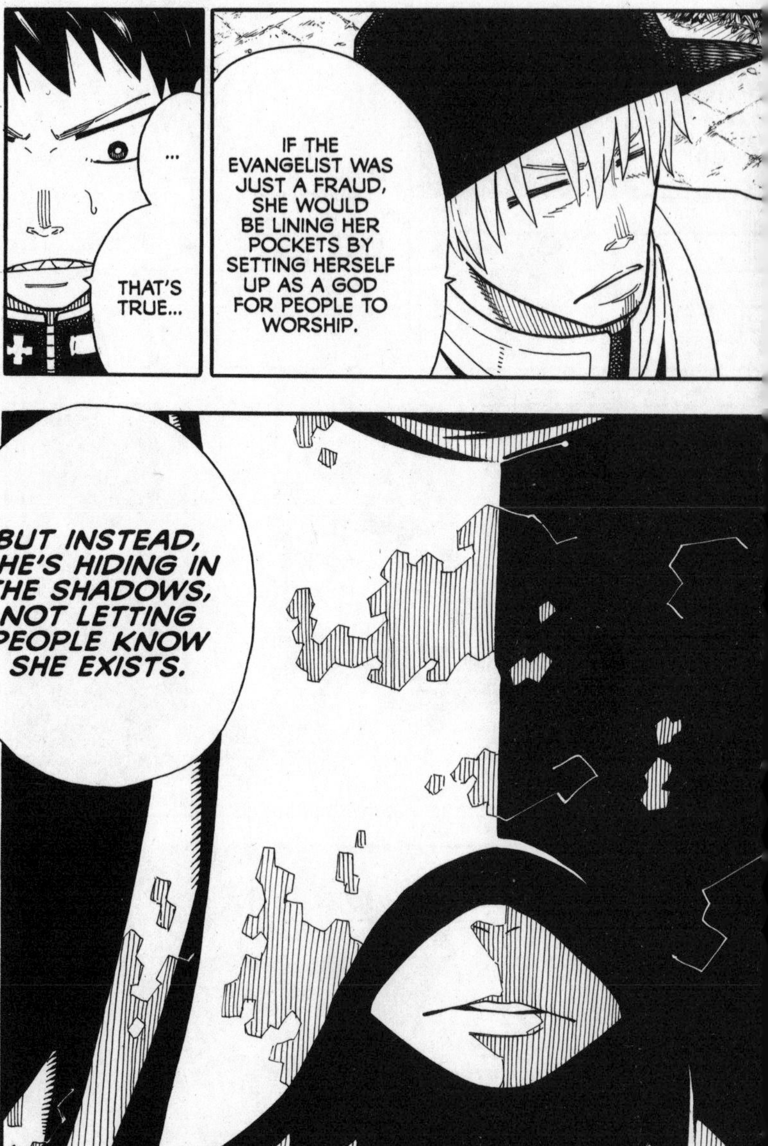
IF THE EVANGELIST WAS JUST A FRAUD, SHE WOULD BE LINING HER POCKETS BY SETTING HERSELF UP AS A GOD FOR PEOPLE TO WORSHIP.
...
THAT'S TRUE...
BUT INSTEAD, SHE'S HIDING IN THE SHADOWS, NOT LETTING PEOPLE KNOW SHE EXISTS.

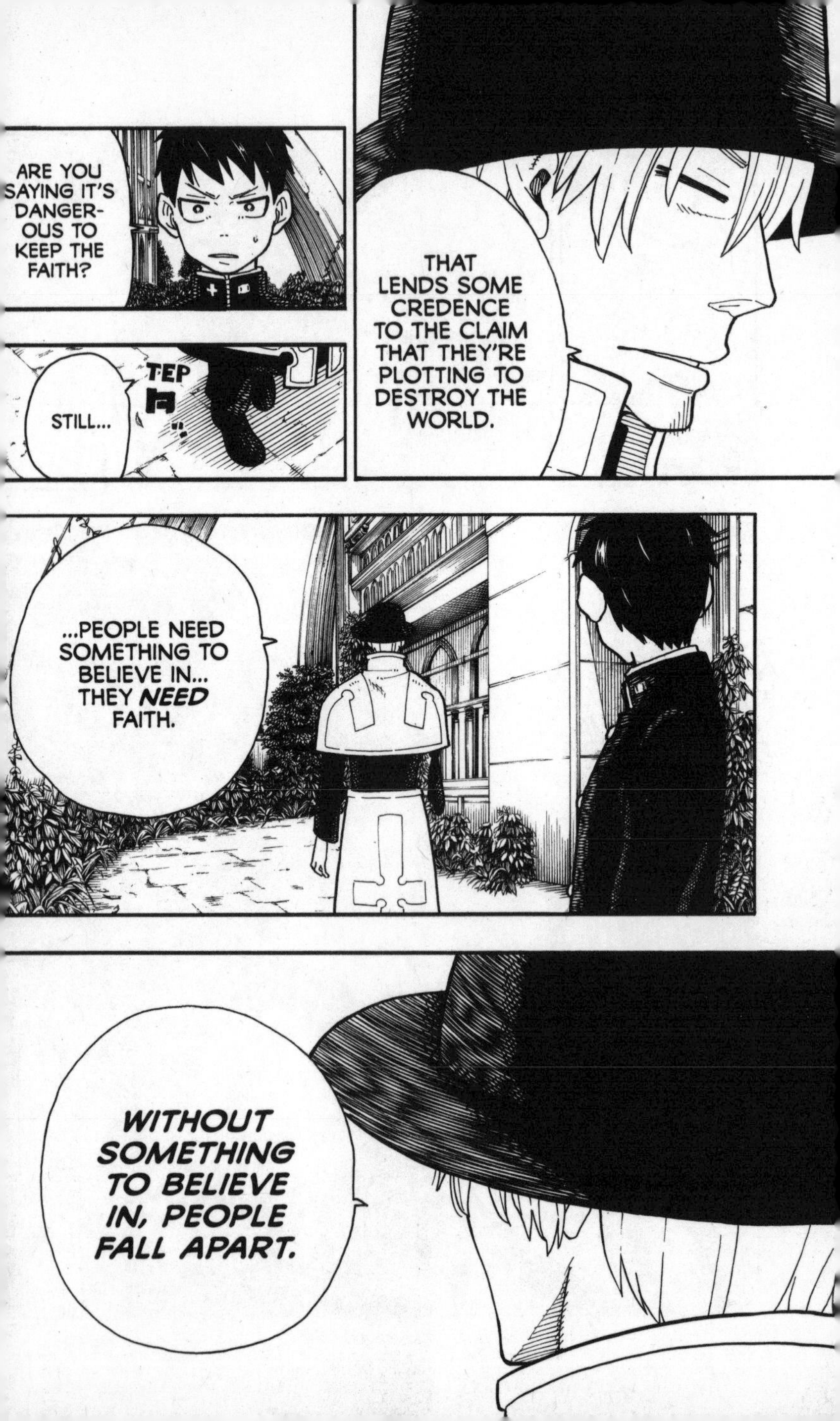
THAT LENDS SOME CREDENCE TO THE CLAIM THAT THEY'RE PLOTTING TO DESTROY THE WORLD.
ARE YOU SAYING IT'S DANGER-OUS TO KEEP THE FAITH?
TEP
STILL...
...PEOPLE NEED SOMETHING TO BELIEVE IN... THEY *NEED* FAITH.
WITHOUT SOMETHING TO BELIEVE IN, PEOPLE FALL APART.

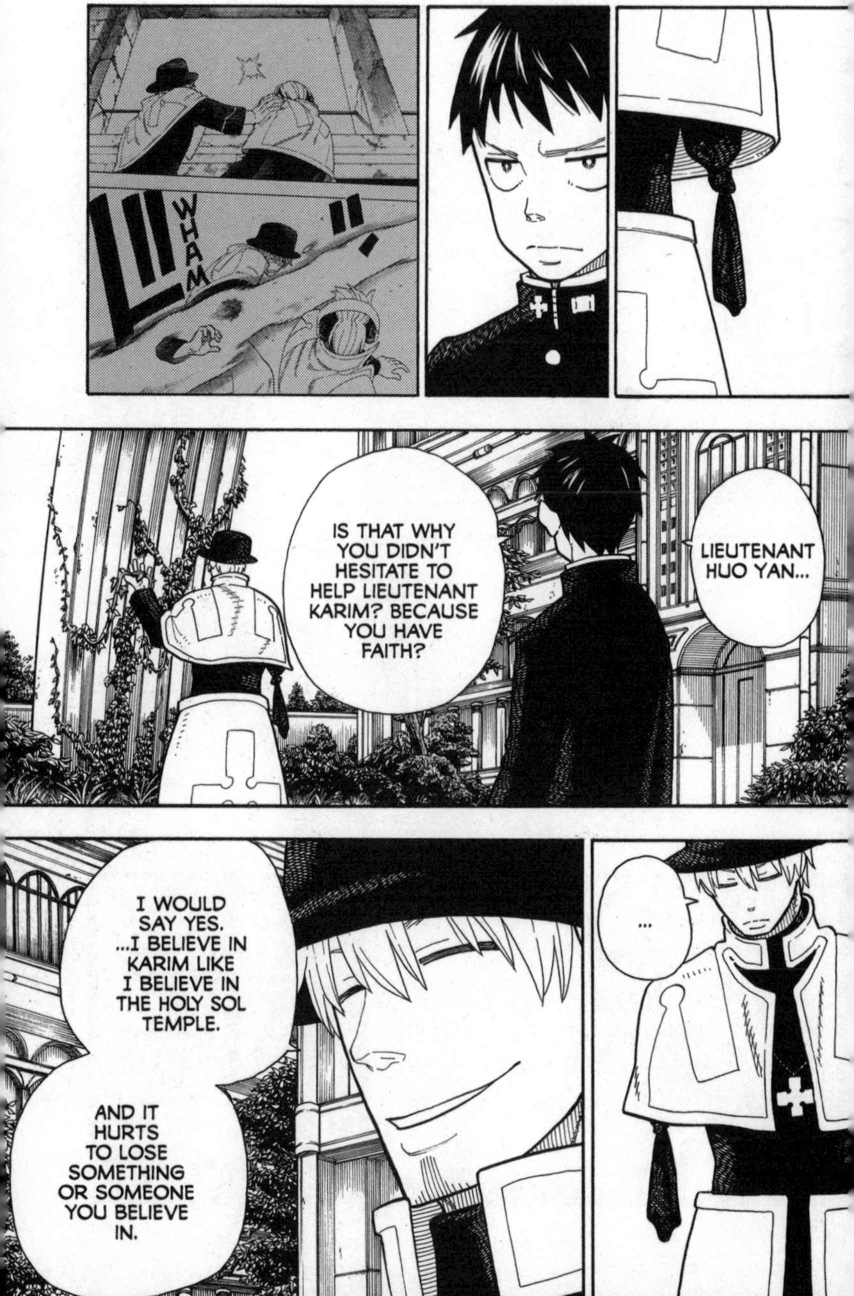
WHAM
LIEUTENANT HUO YAN...
IS THAT WHY YOU DIDN'T HESITATE TO HELP LIEUTENANT KARIM? BECAUSE YOU HAVE FAITH?
...
I WOULD SAY YES. ...I BELIEVE IN KARIM LIKE I BELIEVE IN THE HOLY SOL TEMPLE.
AND IT HURTS TO LOSE SOMETHING OR SOMEONE YOU BELIEVE IN.

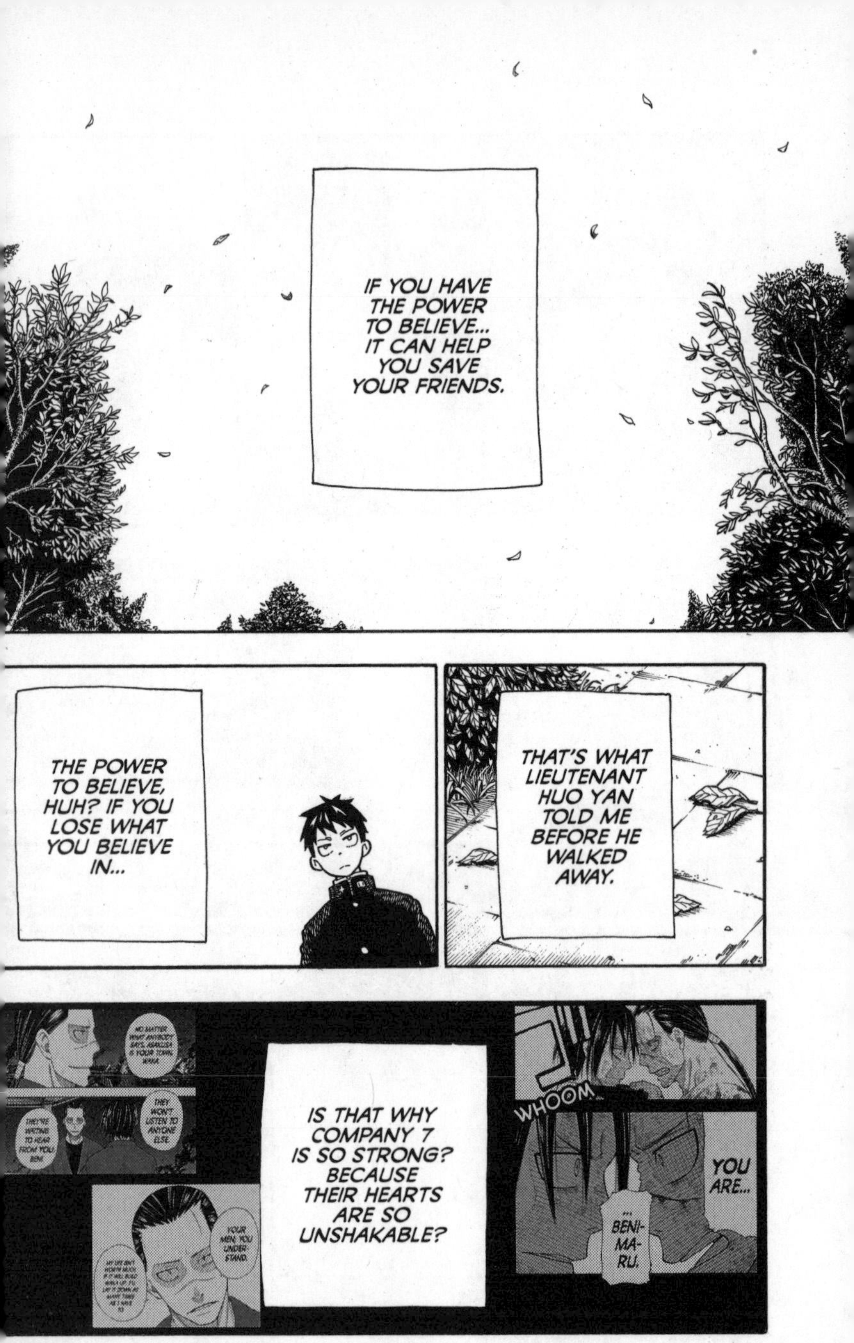
IF YOU HAVE THE POWER TO BELIEVE... IT CAN HELP YOU SAVE YOUR FRIENDS.
THAT'S WHAT LIEUTENANT HUO YAN TOLD ME BEFORE HE WALKED AWAY.
THE POWER TO BELIEVE, HUH? IF YOU LOSE WHAT YOU BELIEVE IN...
WHOOM
YOU ARE...
...BENIMARU.
IS THAT WHY COMPANY 7 IS SO STRONG? BECAUSE THEIR HEARTS ARE SO UNSHAKABLE?
NO MATTER WHAT ANYBODY SAYS, ASAKUSA IS YOUR TOWN, WAKA.
THEY WON'T LISTEN TO ANYONE ELSE.
THEY'RE WAITING TO HEAR FROM YOU, BENI.
YOUR MEN, YOU UNDERSTAND.

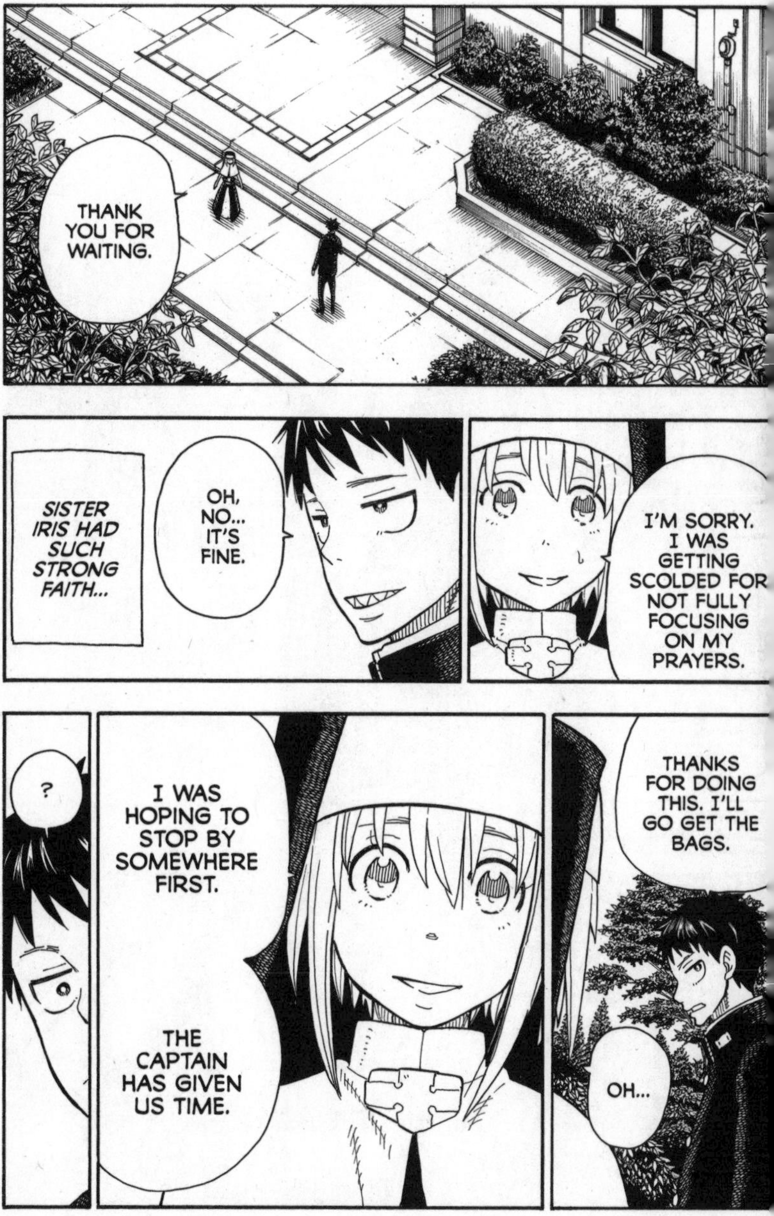
THANK YOU FOR WAITING.
I'M SORRY. I WAS GETTING SCOLDED FOR NOT FULLY FOCUSING ON MY PRAYERS.
OH, NO... IT'S FINE.
SISTER IRIS HAD SUCH STRONG FAITH...
THANKS FOR DOING THIS. I'LL GO GET THE BAGS.
OH...
I WAS HOPING TO STOP BY SOMEWHERE FIRST.
THE CAPTAIN HAS GIVEN US TIME.
?

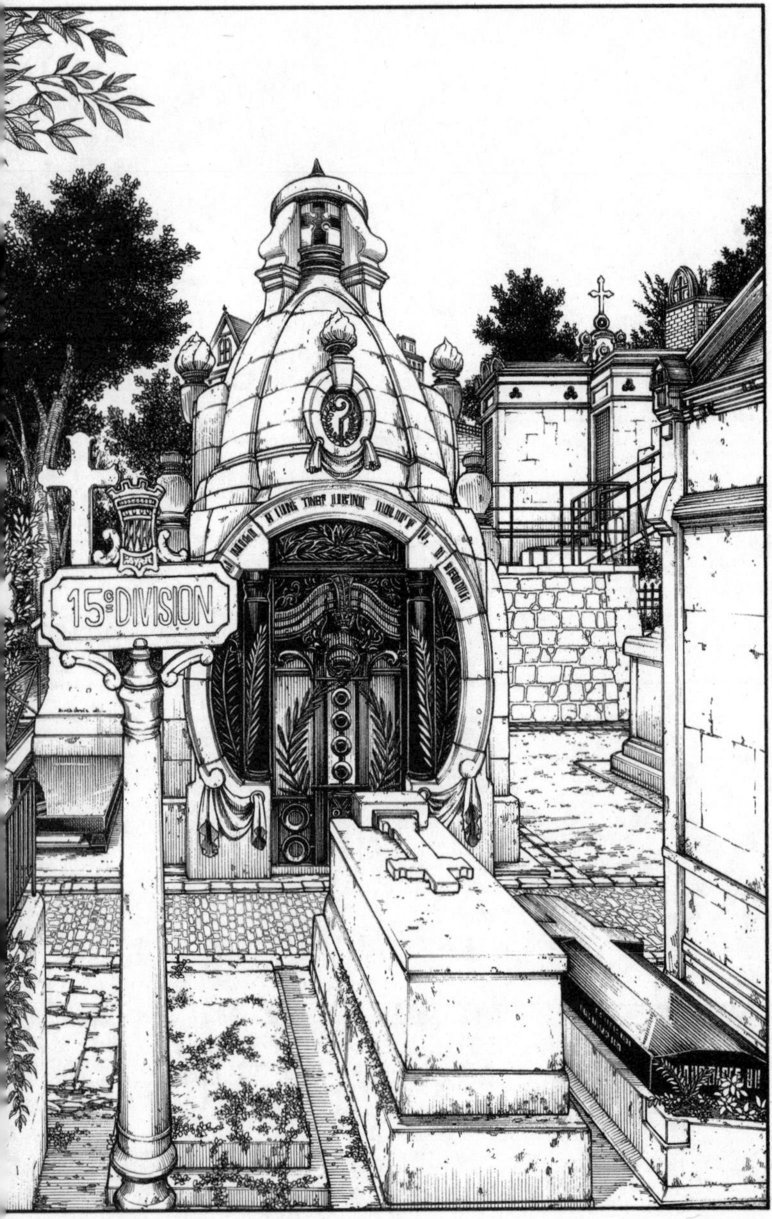
15e DIVISION

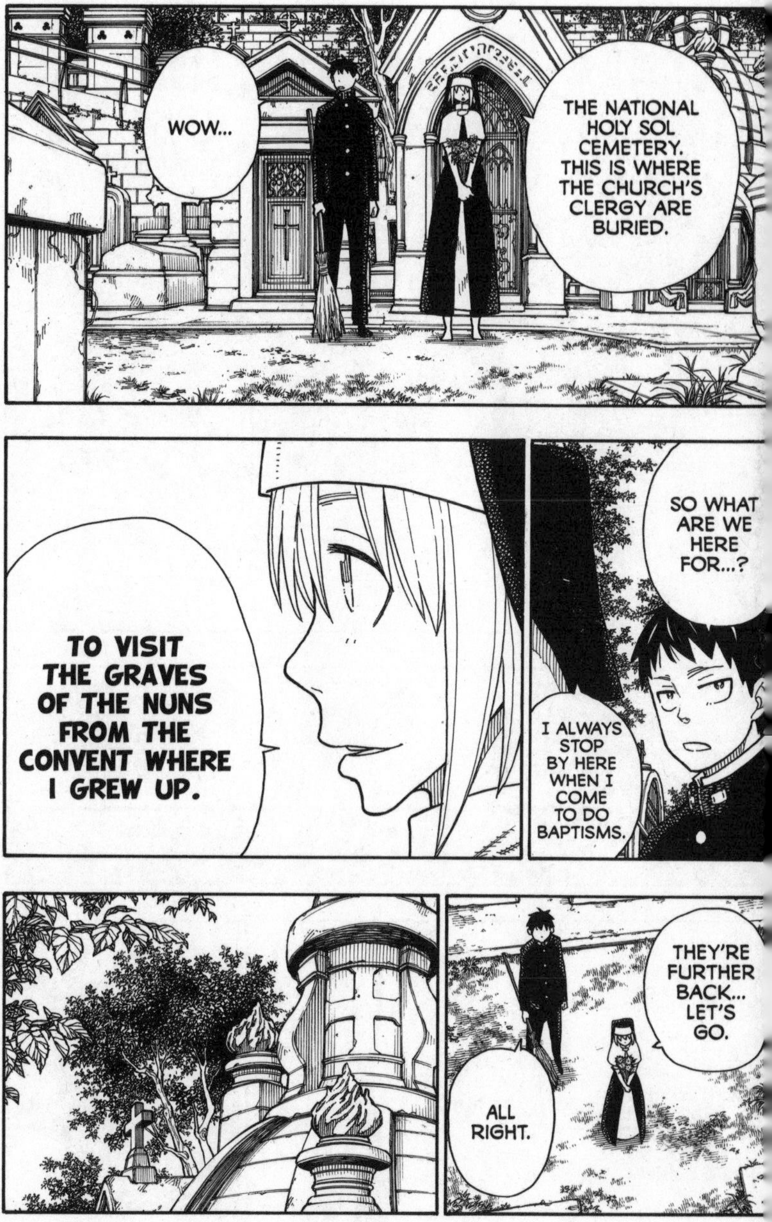
THE NATIONAL HOLY SOL CEMETERY. THIS IS WHERE THE CHURCH'S CLERGY ARE BURIED.
WOW...
SO WHAT ARE WE HERE FOR...?
I ALWAYS STOP BY HERE WHEN I COME TO DO BAPTISMS.
TO VISIT THE GRAVES OF THE NUNS FROM THE CONVENT WHERE I GREW UP.
THEY'RE FURTHER BACK... LET'S GO.
ALL RIGHT.

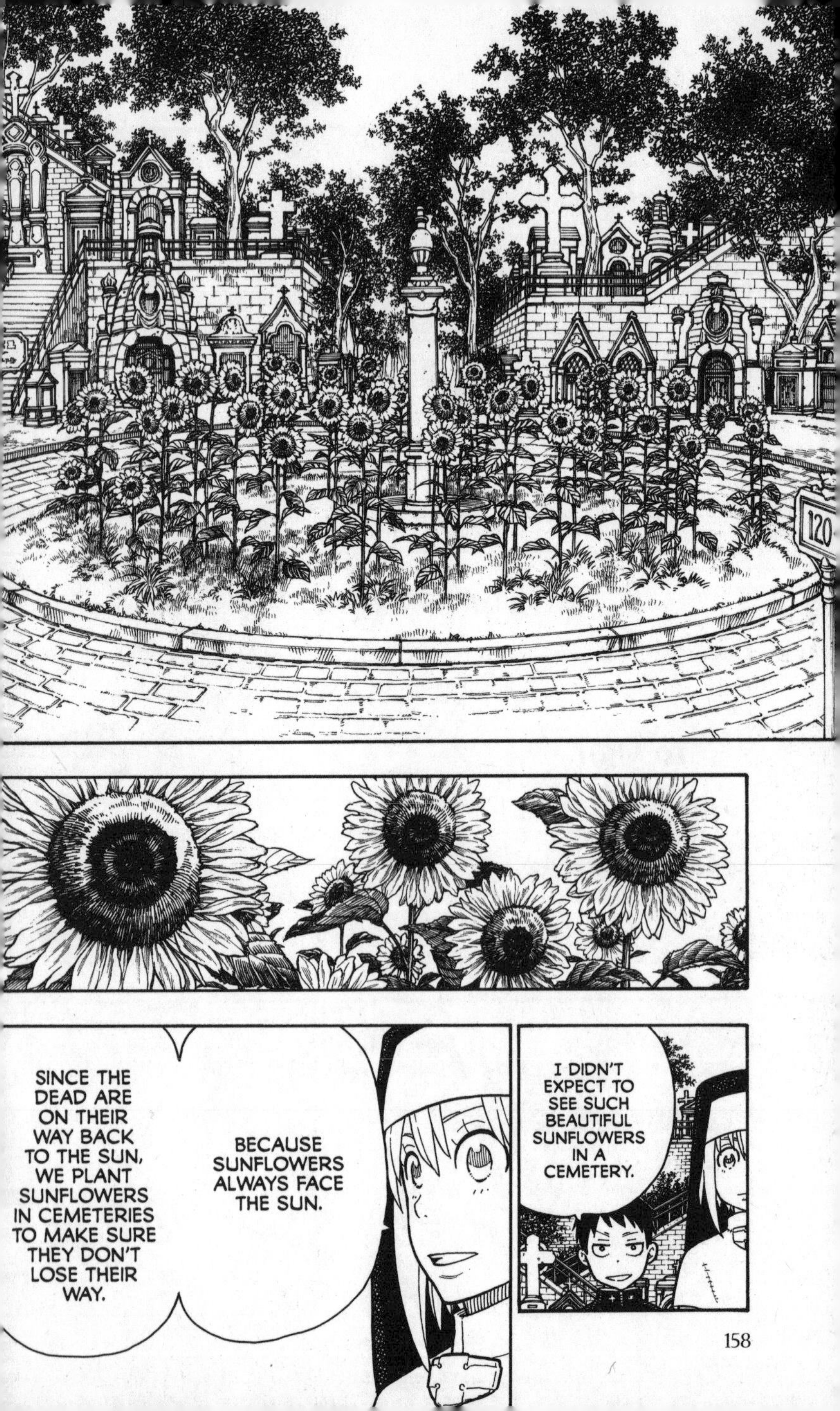
120
I DIDN'T EXPECT TO SEE SUCH BEAUTIFUL SUNFLOWERS IN A CEMETERY.
BECAUSE SUNFLOWERS ALWAYS FACE THE SUN.
SINCE THE DEAD ARE ON THEIR WAY BACK TO THE SUN, WE PLANT SUNFLOWERS IN CEMETERIES TO MAKE SURE THEY DON'T LOSE THEIR WAY.

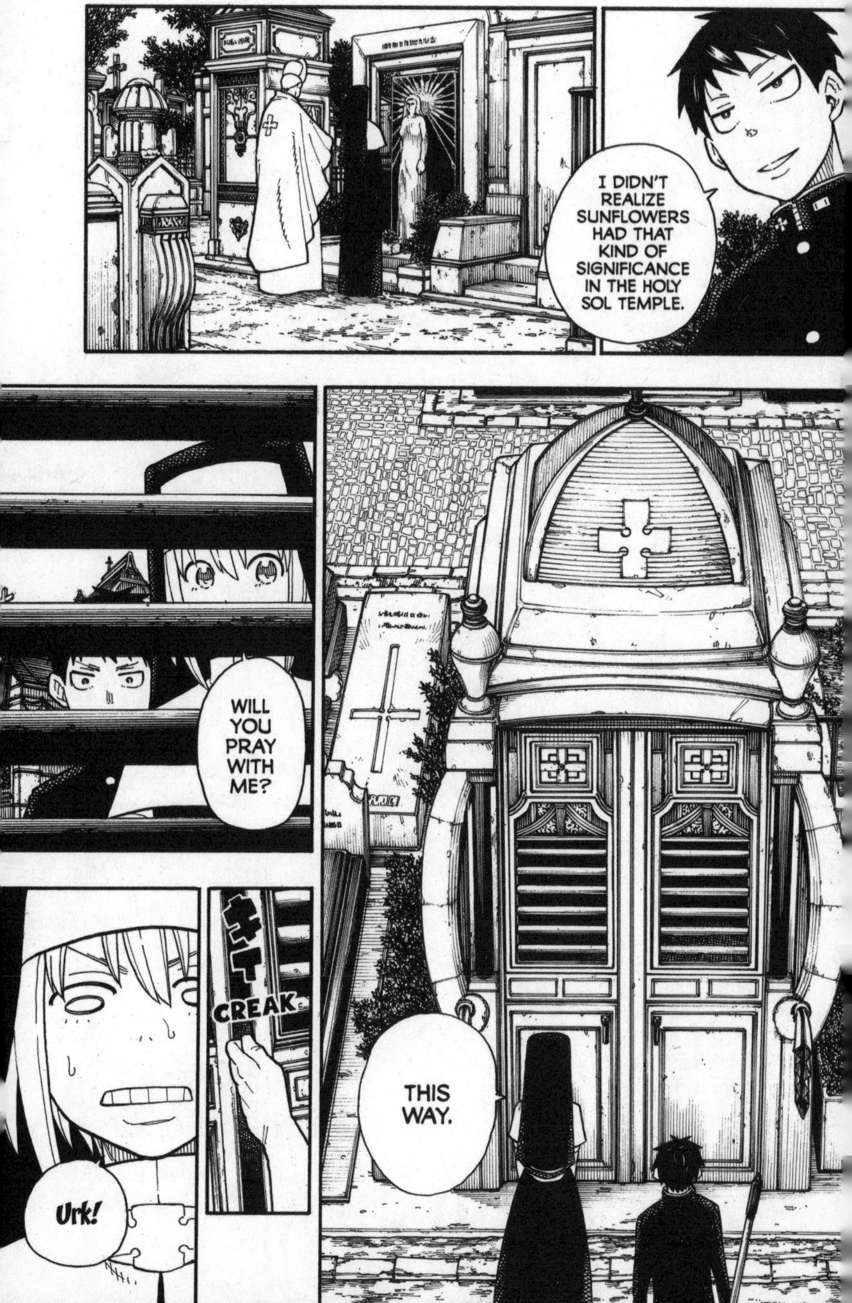
I DIDN'T REALIZE SUNFLOWERS HAD THAT KIND OF SIGNIFICANCE IN THE HOLY SOL TEMPLE.
THIS WAY.
WILL YOU PRAY WITH ME?
CREAK
Urk!

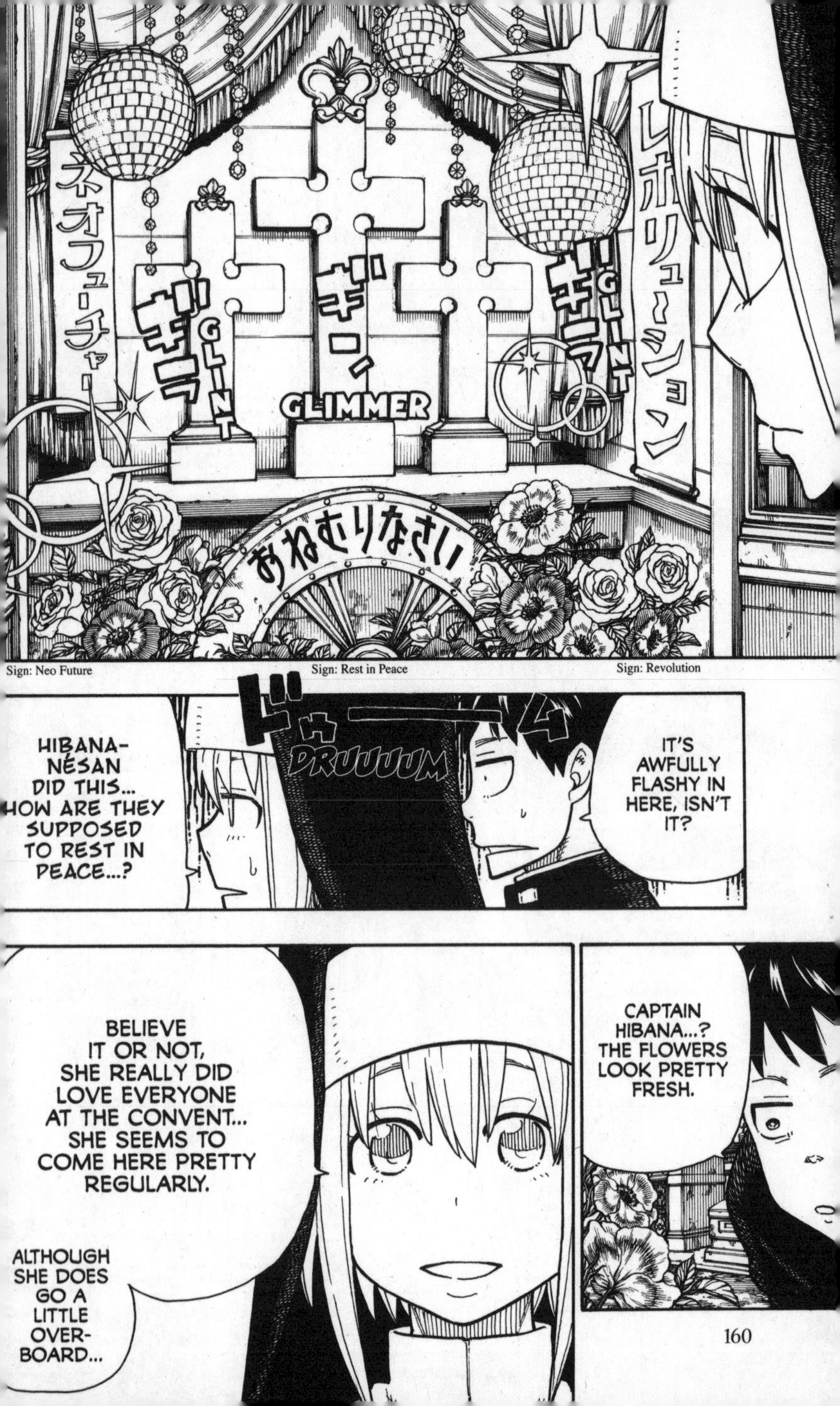
レボリューション
ギラ
GLINT
ギロ
GLIMMER
ギラ
GLINT
ネオフューチャー
おねむりなさい
Sign: Neo Future
Sign: Rest in Peace
Sign: Revolution
ドゥーーーム
DRUUUUM
IT'S AWFULLY FLASHY IN HERE, ISN'T IT?
HIBANA-NÉSAN DID THIS... HOW ARE THEY SUPPOSED TO REST IN PEACE...?
CAPTAIN HIBANA...? THE FLOWERS LOOK PRETTY FRESH.
BELIEVE IT OR NOT, SHE REALLY DID LOVE EVERYONE AT THE CONVENT... SHE SEEMS TO COME HERE PRETTY REGULARLY.
ALTHOUGH SHE DOES GO A LITTLE OVER-BOARD...

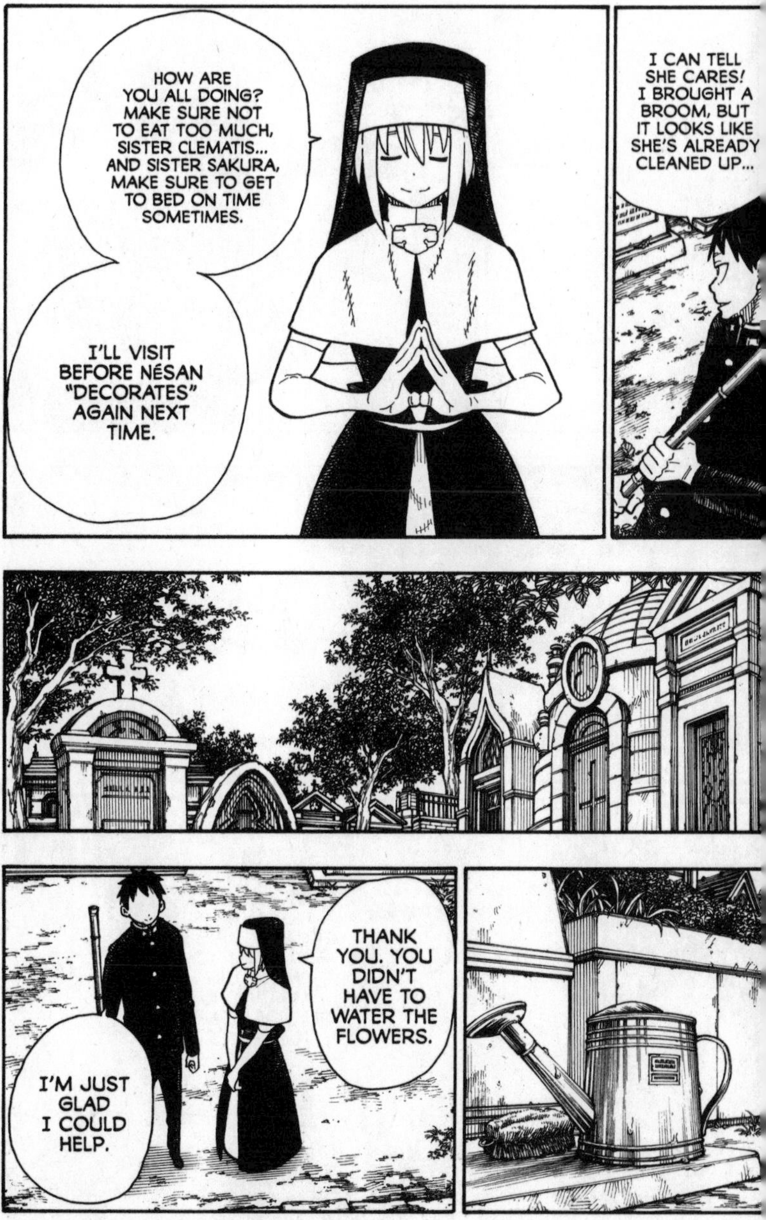
I CAN TELL SHE CARES! I BROUGHT A BROOM, BUT IT LOOKS LIKE SHE'S ALREADY CLEANED UP...
HOW ARE YOU ALL DOING? MAKE SURE NOT TO EAT TOO MUCH, SISTER CLEMATIS... AND SISTER SAKURA, MAKE SURE TO GET TO BED ON TIME SOMETIMES.
I'LL VISIT BEFORE NÉSAN "DECORATES" AGAIN NEXT TIME.
THANK YOU. YOU DIDN'T HAVE TO WATER THE FLOWERS.
I'M JUST GLAD I COULD HELP.

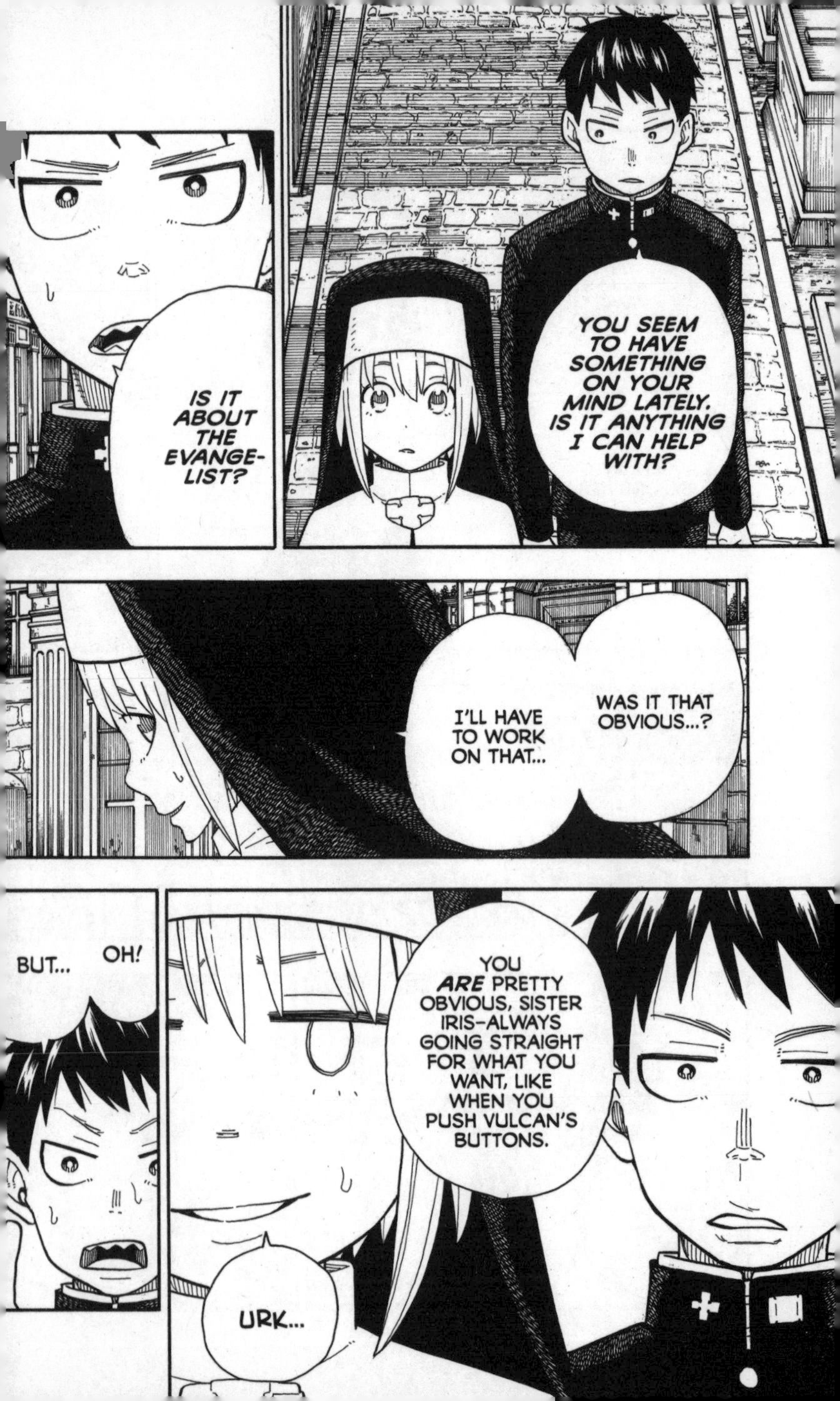
YOU SEEM TO HAVE SOMETHING ON YOUR MIND LATELY. IS IT ANYTHING I CAN HELP WITH?
IS IT ABOUT THE EVANGE-LIST?
WAS IT THAT OBVIOUS...?
I'LL HAVE TO WORK ON THAT...
YOU *ARE* PRETTY OBVIOUS, SISTER IRIS–ALWAYS GOING STRAIGHT FOR WHAT YOU WANT, LIKE WHEN YOU PUSH VULCAN'S BUTTONS.
URK...
OH!
BUT...

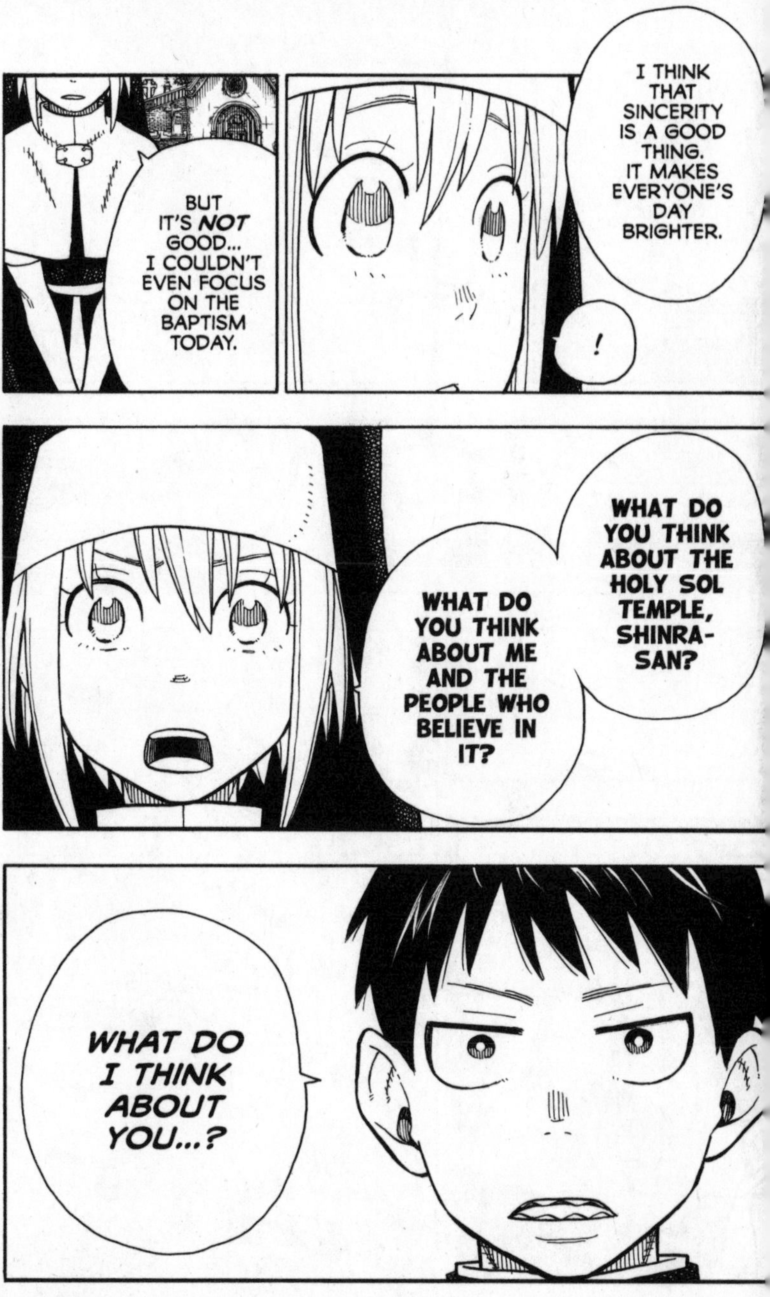
I THINK THAT SINCERITY IS A GOOD THING. IT MAKES EVERYONE'S DAY BRIGHTER.
!
BUT IT'S *NOT* GOOD... I COULDN'T EVEN FOCUS ON THE BAPTISM TODAY.
WHAT DO YOU THINK ABOUT THE HOLY SOL TEMPLE, SHINRA-SAN?
WHAT DO YOU THINK ABOUT ME AND THE PEOPLE WHO BELIEVE IN IT?
WHAT DO I THINK ABOUT YOU...?

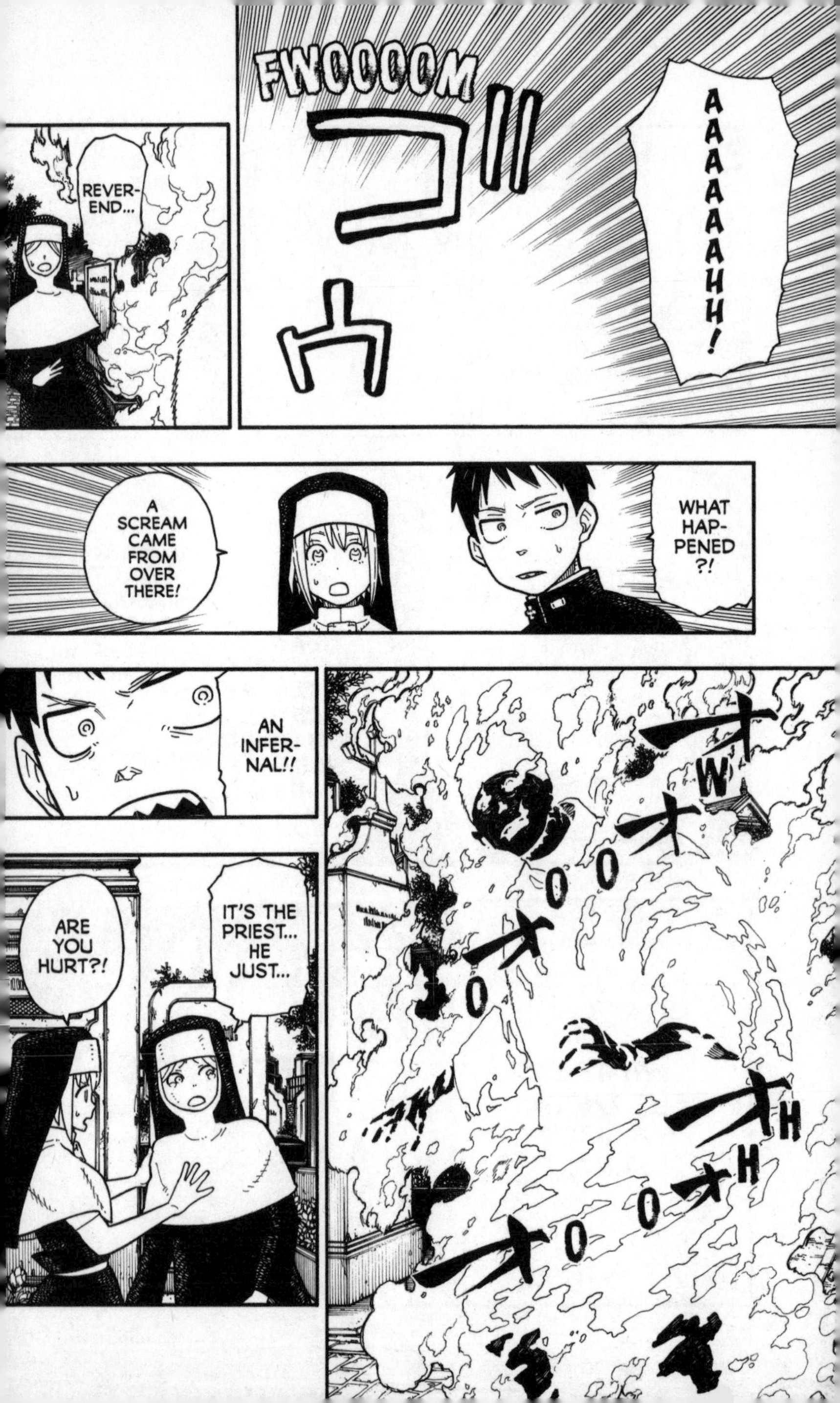
FWOOOOM
AAAAAAAHH!
REVEREND...
WHAT HAPPENED?!
A SCREAM CAME FROM OVER THERE!
AN INFERNAL!!
IT'S THE PRIEST... HE JUST...
ARE YOU HURT?!

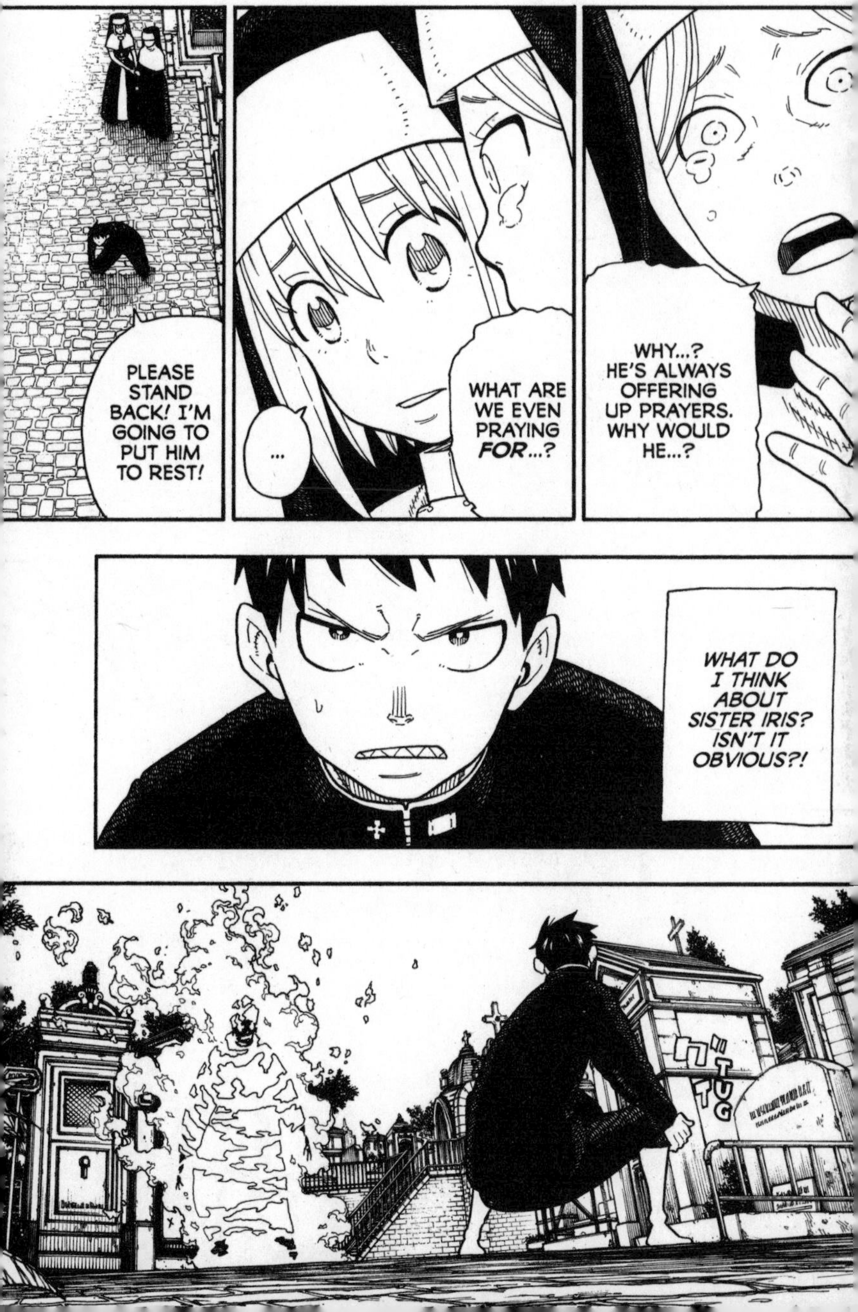
WHY...? HE'S ALWAYS OFFERING UP PRAYERS. WHY WOULD HE...?
WHAT ARE WE EVEN PRAYING *FOR*...?
...
PLEASE STAND BACK! I'M GOING TO PUT HIM TO REST!
WHAT DO I THINK ABOUT SISTER IRIS? ISN'T IT OBVIOUS?!
TUG

FIRE FORCE

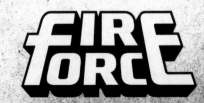

CHAPTER CL: SUNFLOWER

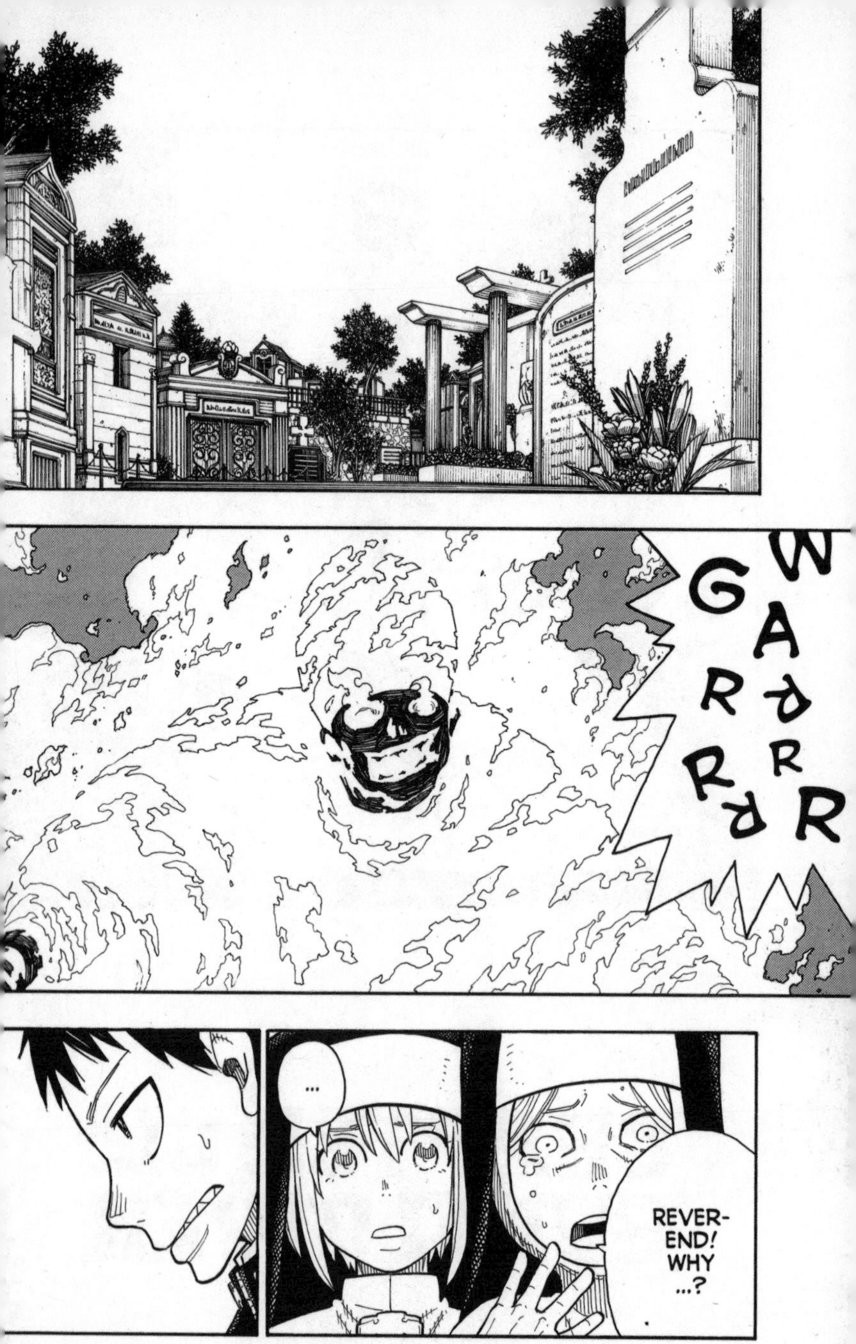
GWARRRRR
...
REVER-
END!
WHY
...?

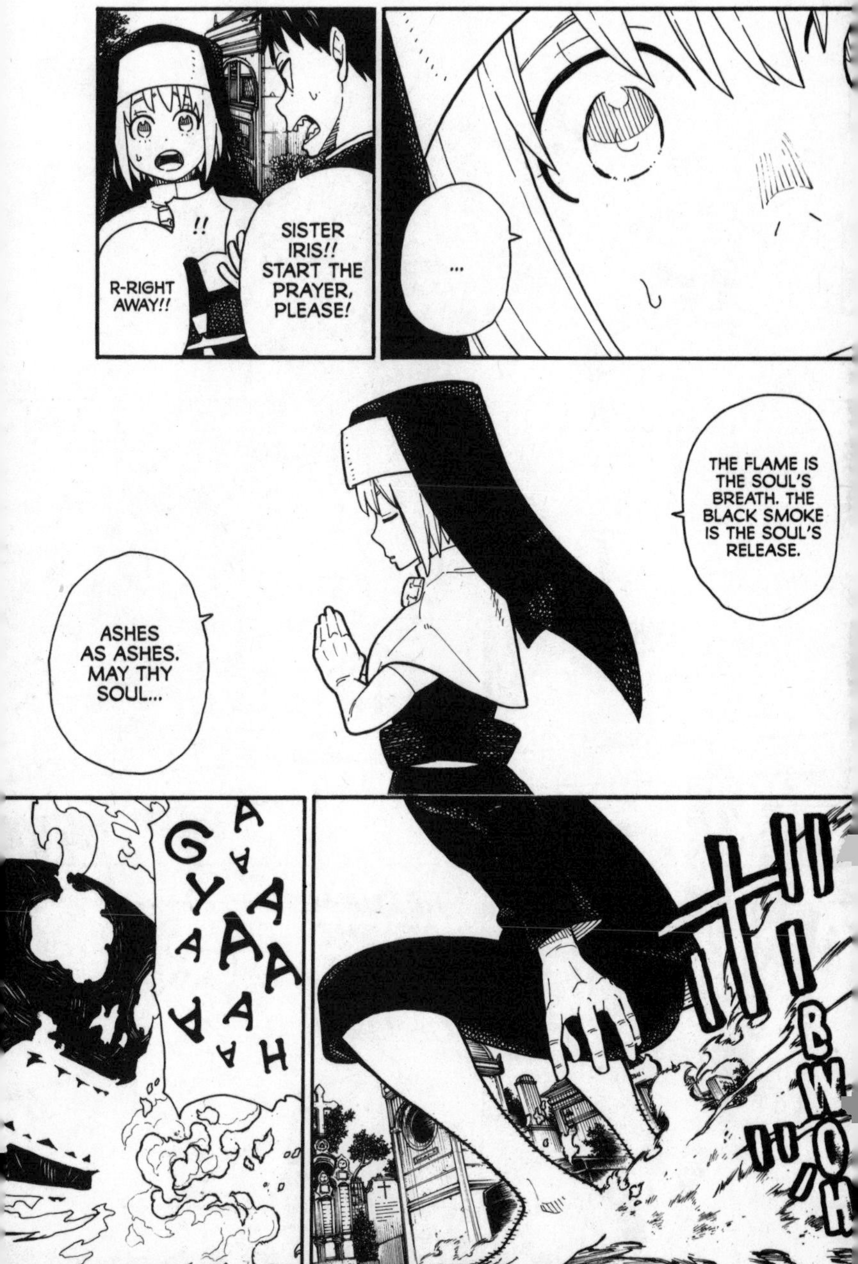
...
SISTER IRIS!! START THE PRAYER, PLEASE!
!!
R-RIGHT AWAY!!
THE FLAME IS THE SOUL'S BREATH. THE BLACK SMOKE IS THE SOUL'S RELEASE.
ASHES AS ASHES. MAY THY SOUL...

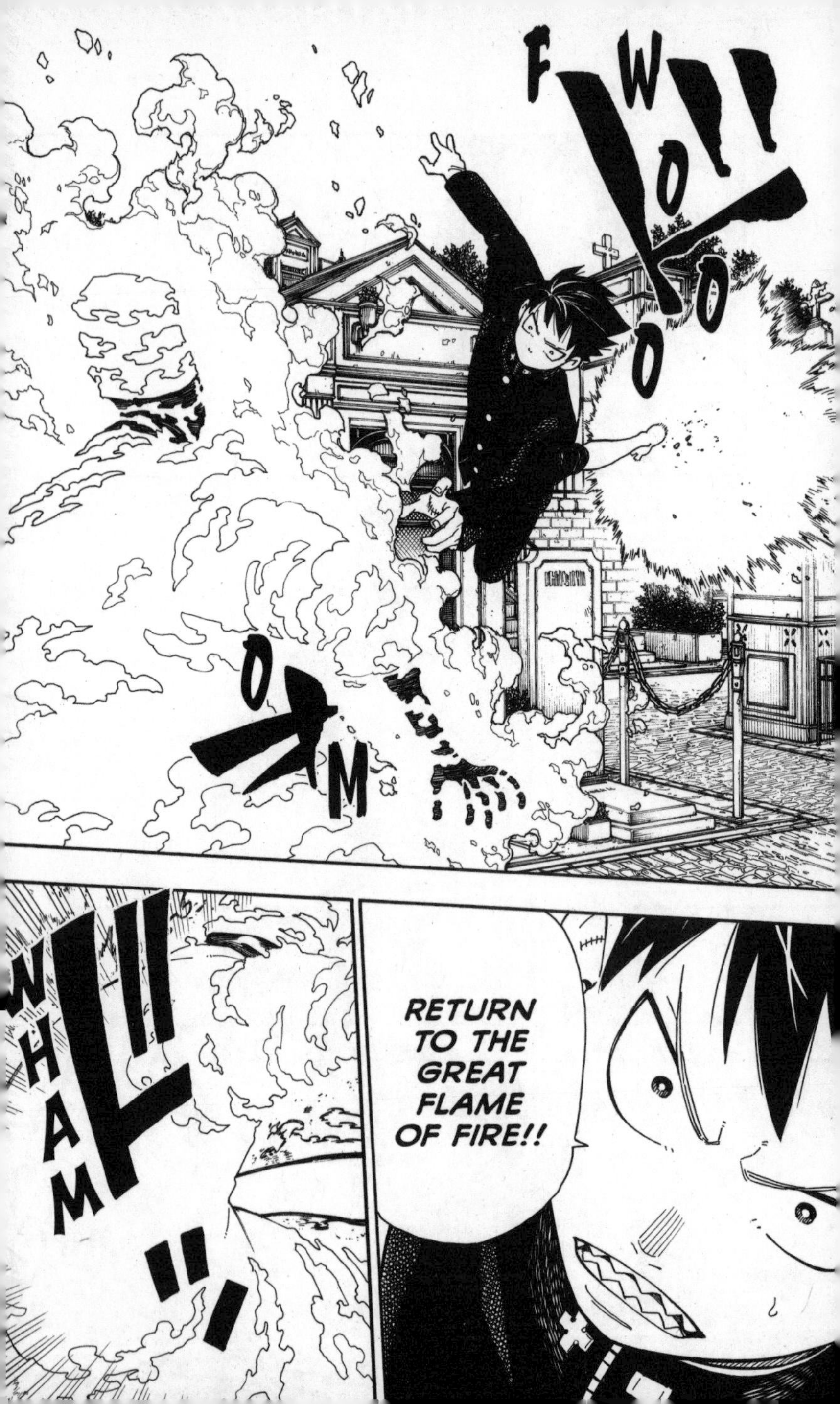
FWOOO!!
RETURN TO THE GREAT FLAME OF FIRE!!
WHAM!!

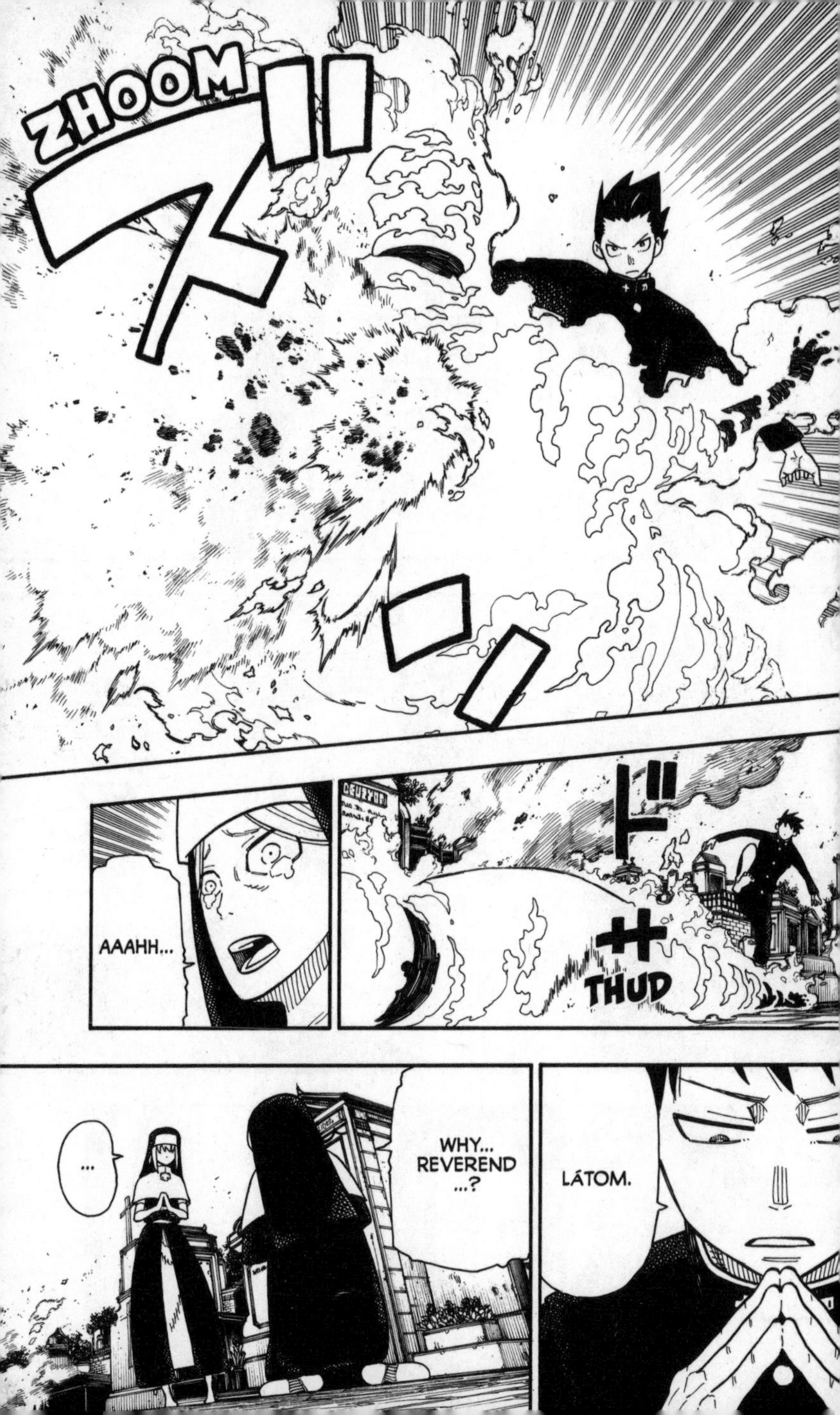
ZHOOM
THUD
AAAHH...
LÁTOM.
WHY... REVEREND ...?
...

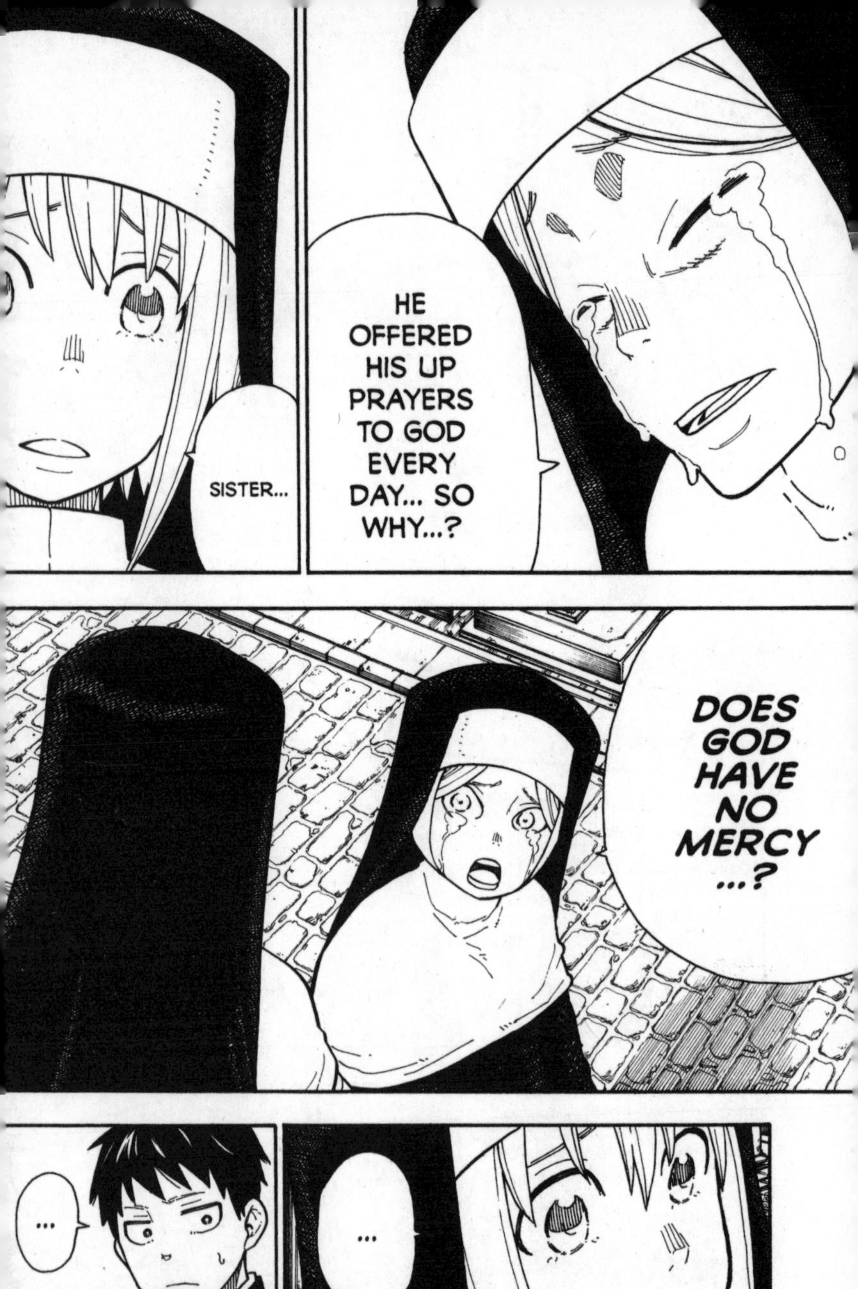
HE OFFERED HIS UP PRAYERS TO GOD EVERY DAY... SO WHY...?
SISTER...
DOES GOD HAVE NO MERCY ...?
...
...

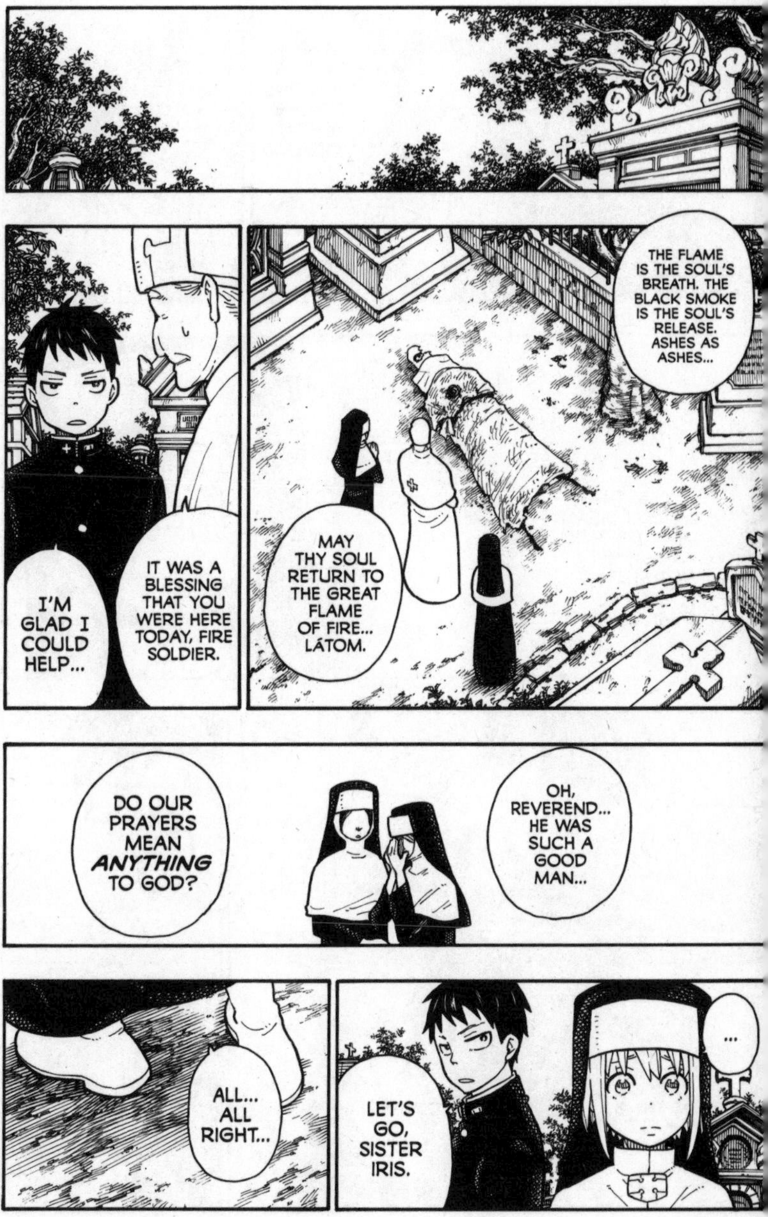

THE FLAME IS THE SOUL'S BREATH. THE BLACK SMOKE IS THE SOUL'S RELEASE. ASHES AS ASHES...
MAY THY SOUL RETURN TO THE GREAT FLAME OF FIRE... LÁTOM.
IT WAS A BLESSING THAT YOU WERE HERE TODAY, FIRE SOLDIER.
I'M GLAD I COULD HELP...
OH, REVEREND... HE WAS SUCH A GOOD MAN...
DO OUR PRAYERS MEAN ANYTHING TO GOD?
...
LET'S GO, SISTER IRIS.
ALL... ALL RIGHT...

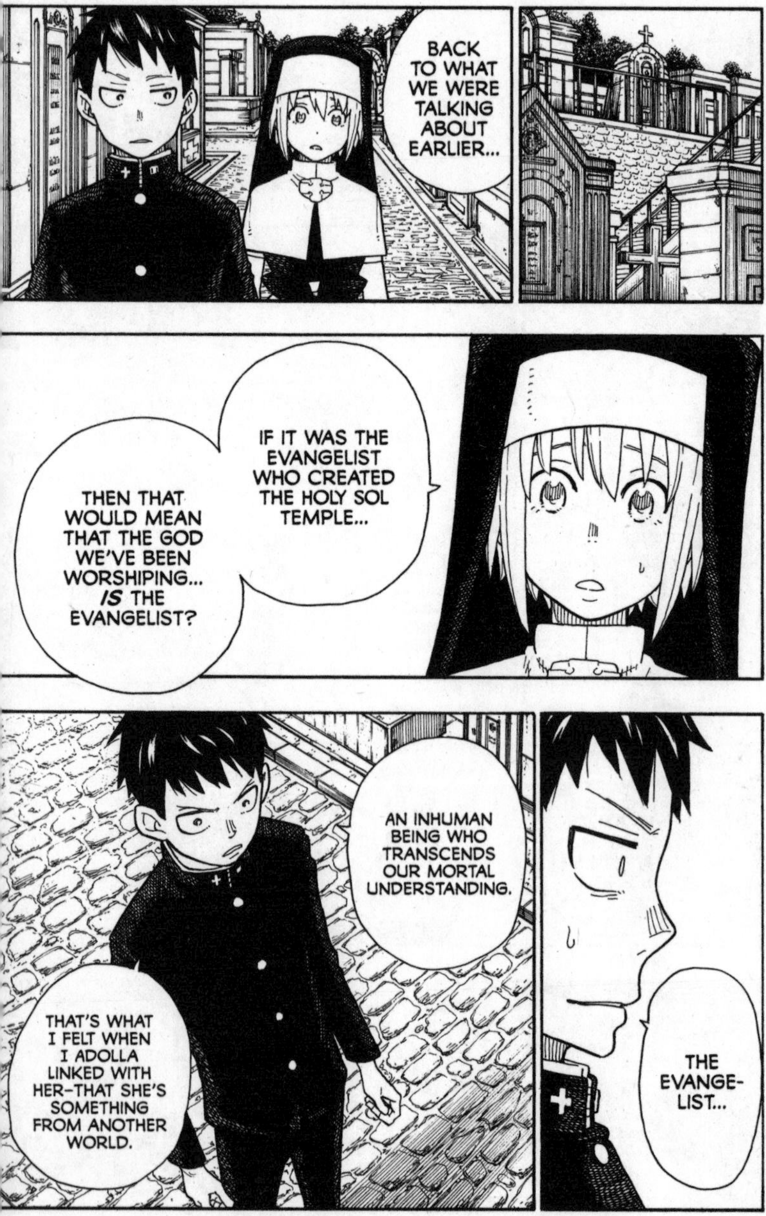
BACK TO WHAT WE WERE TALKING ABOUT EARLIER...
IF IT WAS THE EVANGELIST WHO CREATED THE HOLY SOL TEMPLE...
THEN THAT WOULD MEAN THAT THE GOD WE'VE BEEN WORSHIPING... *IS* THE EVANGELIST?
THE EVANGE-LIST...
AN INHUMAN BEING WHO TRANSCENDS OUR MORTAL UNDERSTANDING.
THAT'S WHAT I FELT WHEN I ADOLLA LINKED WITH HER—THAT SHE'S SOMETHING FROM ANOTHER WORLD.

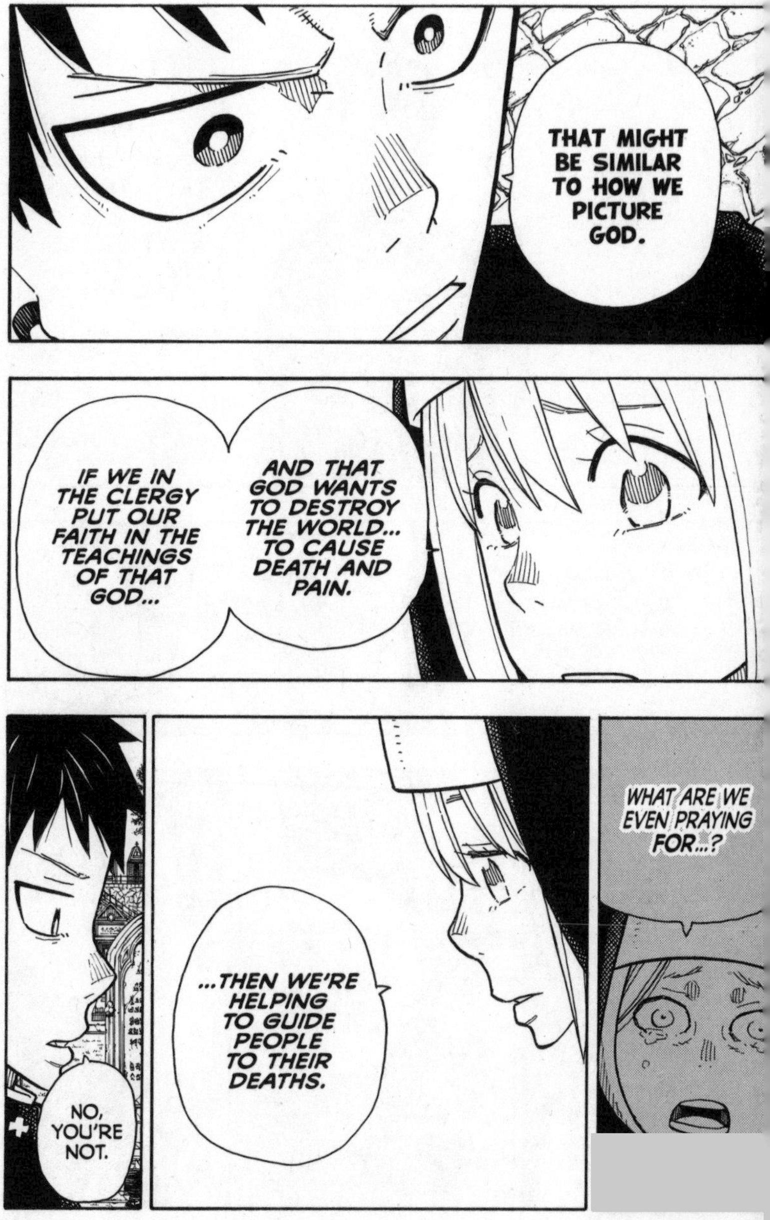
THAT MIGHT BE SIMILAR TO HOW WE PICTURE GOD.
IF WE IN THE CLERGY PUT OUR FAITH IN THE TEACHINGS OF THAT GOD...
AND THAT GOD WANTS TO DESTROY THE WORLD... TO CAUSE DEATH AND PAIN.
WHAT ARE WE EVEN PRAYING FOR...?
...THEN WE'RE HELPING TO GUIDE PEOPLE TO THEIR DEATHS.
NO, YOU'RE NOT.

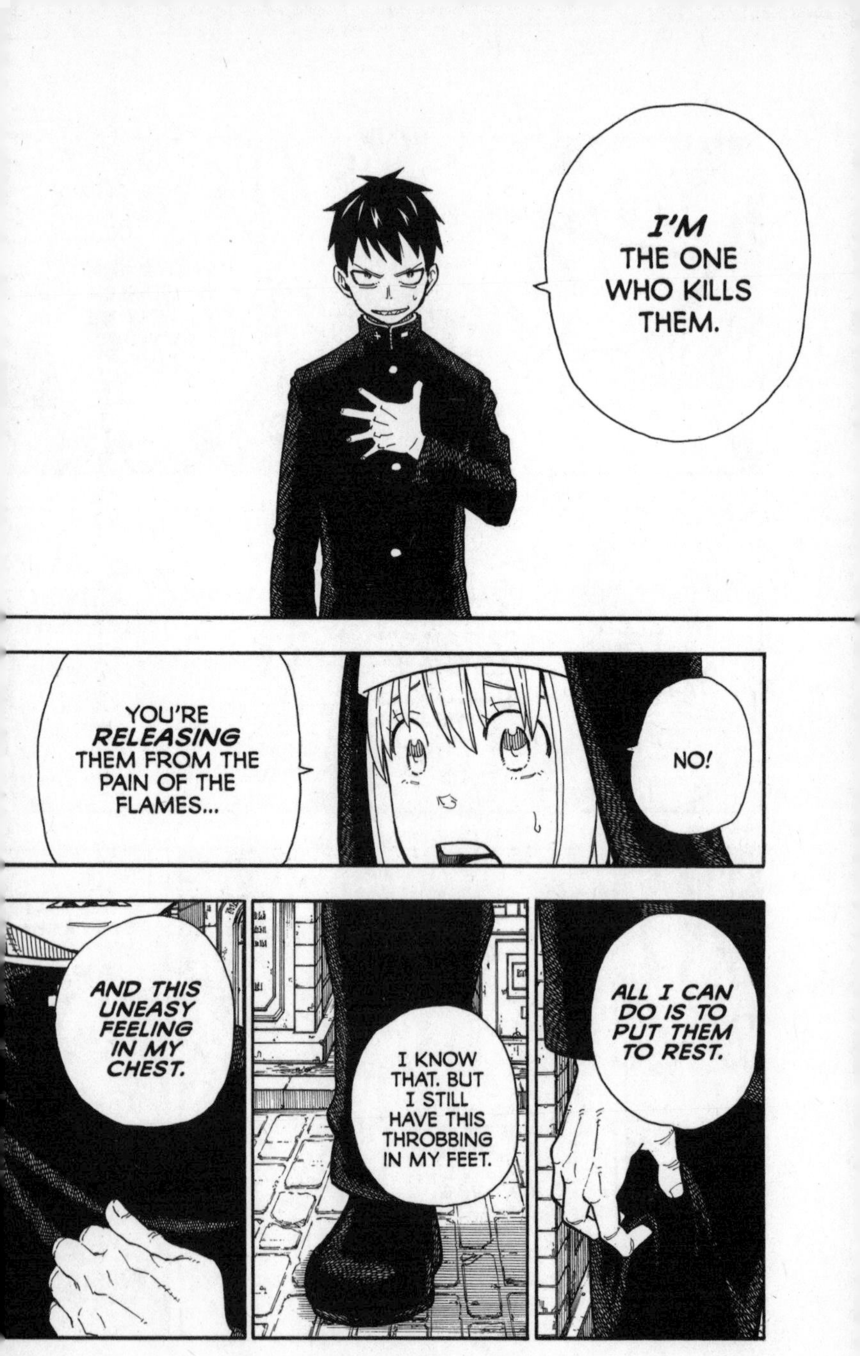
I'M THE ONE WHO KILLS THEM.
NO!
YOU'RE RELEASING THEM FROM THE PAIN OF THE FLAMES...
ALL I CAN DO IS TO PUT THEM TO REST.
I KNOW THAT. BUT I STILL HAVE THIS THROBBING IN MY FEET.
AND THIS UNEASY FEELING IN MY CHEST.

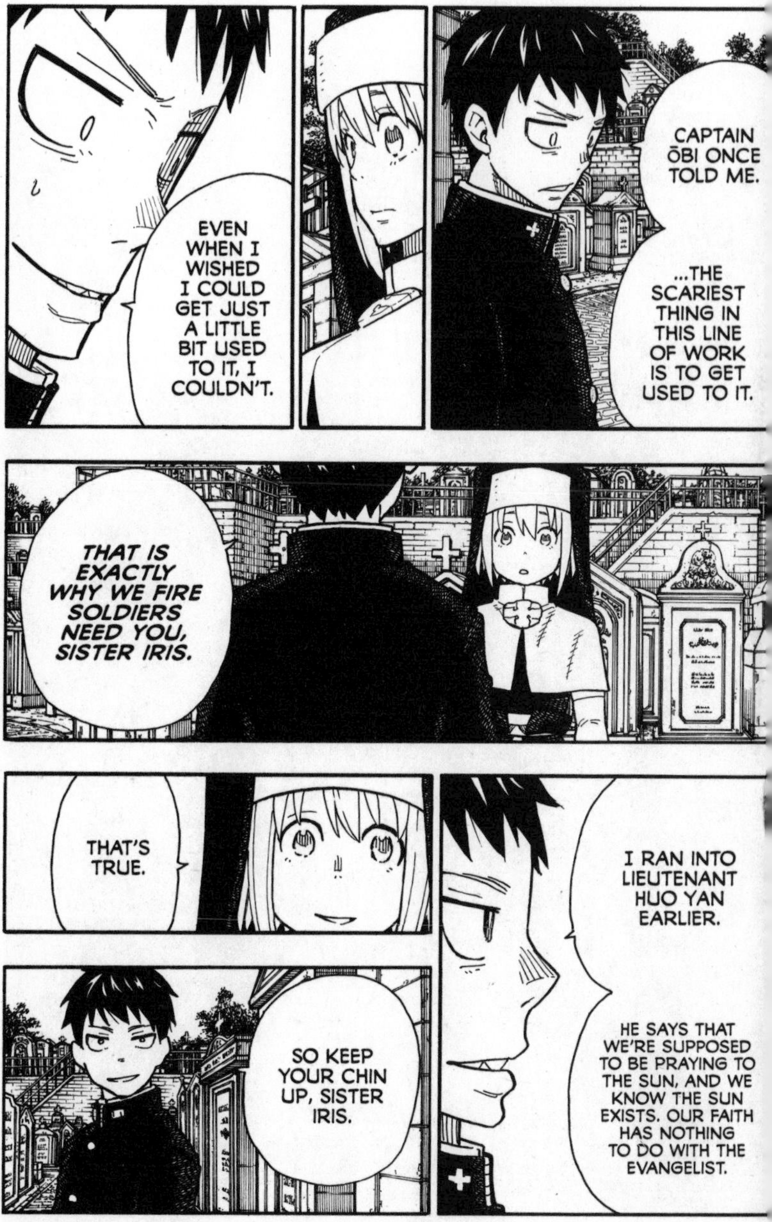
CAPTAIN ŌBI ONCE TOLD ME.
...THE SCARIEST THING IN THIS LINE OF WORK IS TO GET USED TO IT.
EVEN WHEN I WISHED I COULD GET JUST A LITTLE BIT USED TO IT, I COULDN'T.
THAT IS EXACTLY WHY WE FIRE SOLDIERS NEED YOU, SISTER IRIS.
I RAN INTO LIEUTENANT HUO YAN EARLIER.
HE SAYS THAT WE'RE SUPPOSED TO BE PRAYING TO THE SUN, AND WE KNOW THE SUN EXISTS. OUR FAITH HAS NOTHING TO DO WITH THE EVANGELIST.
THAT'S TRUE.
SO KEEP YOUR CHIN UP, SISTER IRIS.

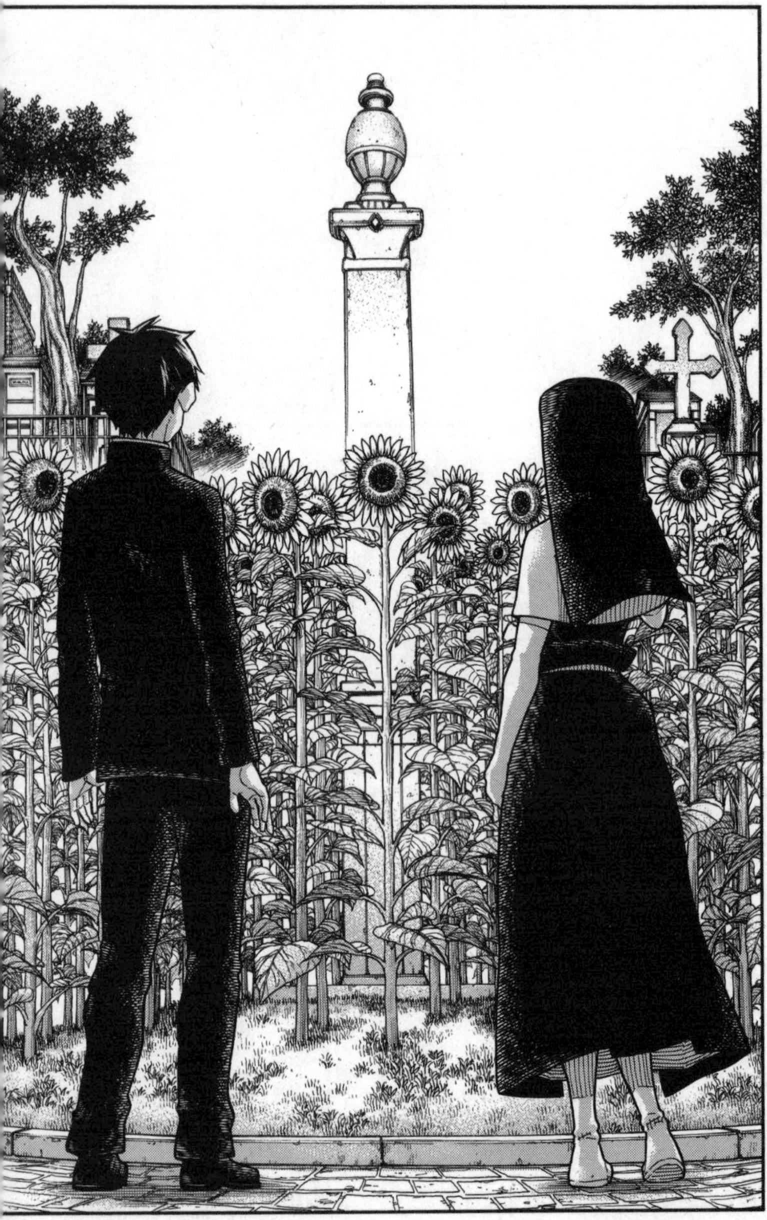

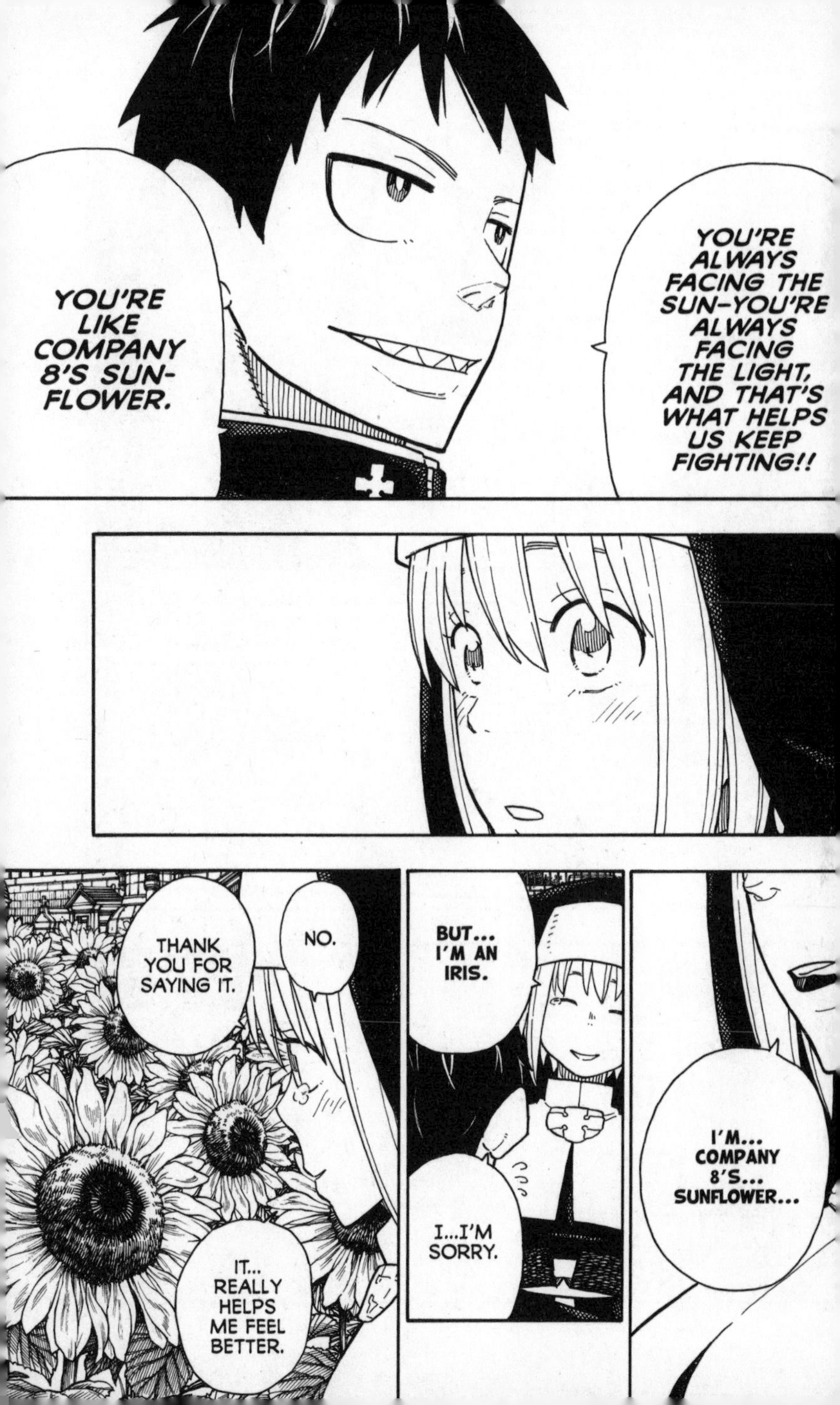
YOU'RE ALWAYS FACING THE SUN–YOU'RE ALWAYS FACING THE LIGHT, AND THAT'S WHAT HELPS US KEEP FIGHTING!!
YOU'RE LIKE COMPANY 8'S SUN-FLOWER.
I'M... COMPANY 8'S... SUNFLOWER...
BUT... I'M AN IRIS.
I...I'M SORRY.
NO.
THANK YOU FOR SAYING IT.
IT... REALLY HELPS ME FEEL BETTER.

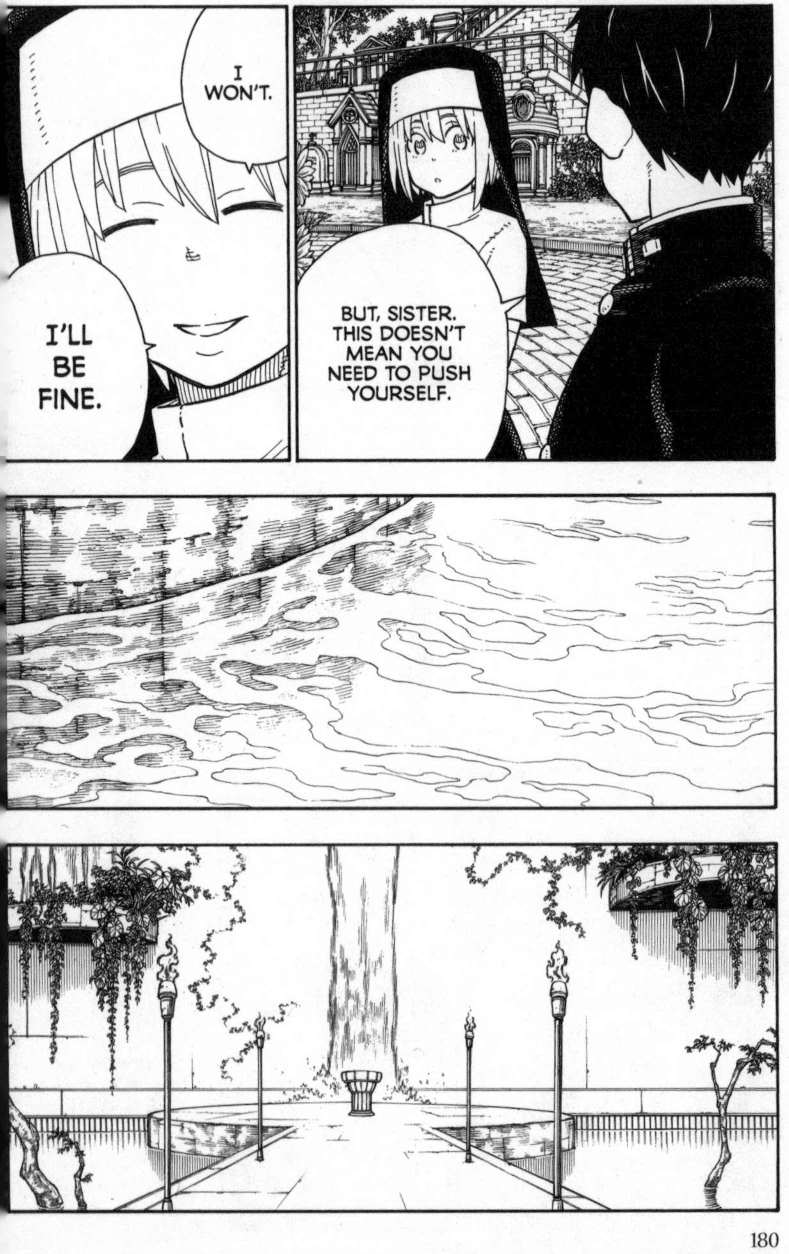
BUT, SISTER. THIS DOESN'T MEAN YOU NEED TO PUSH YOURSELF.
I WON'T.
I'LL BE FINE.

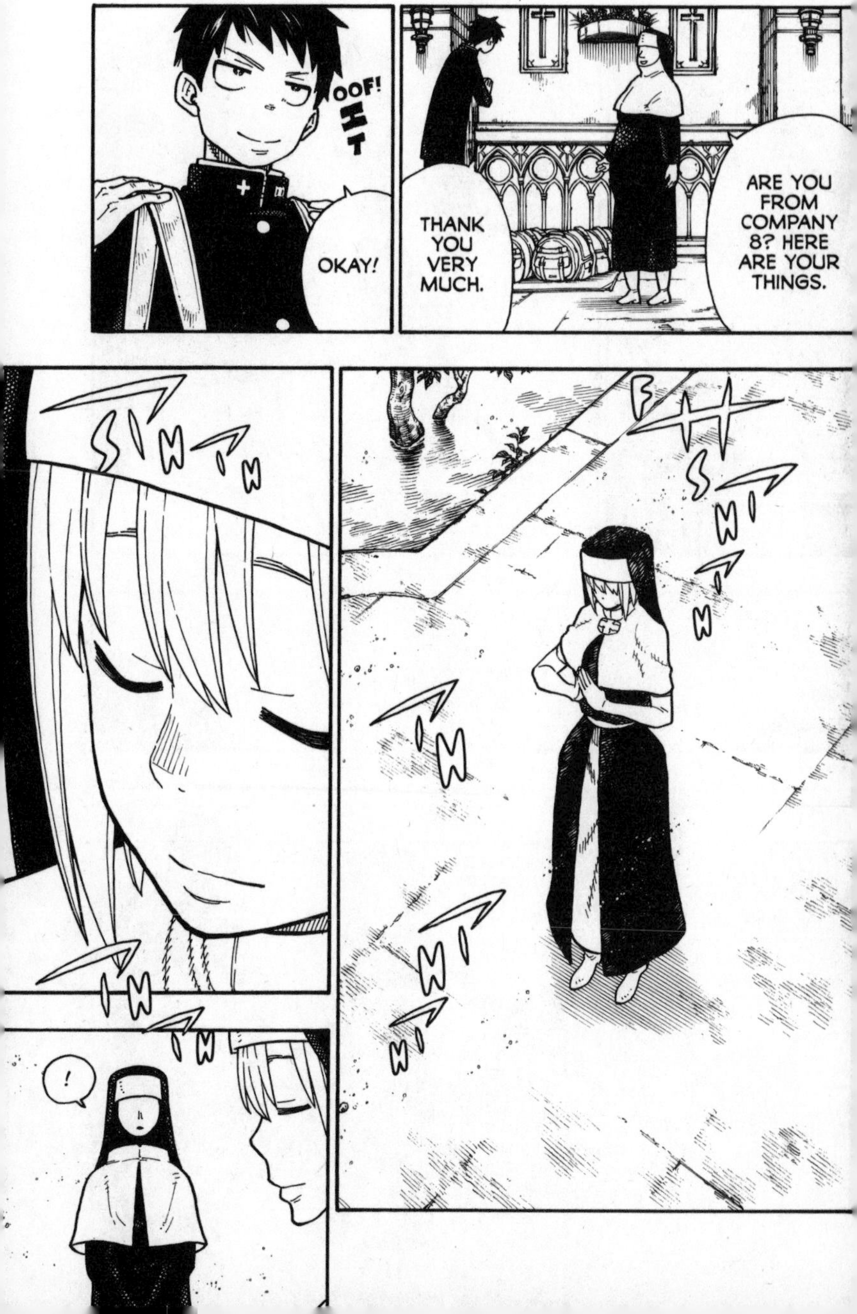
ARE YOU FROM COMPANY 8? HERE ARE YOUR THINGS.
THANK YOU VERY MUCH.
OOF!
OKAY!
!

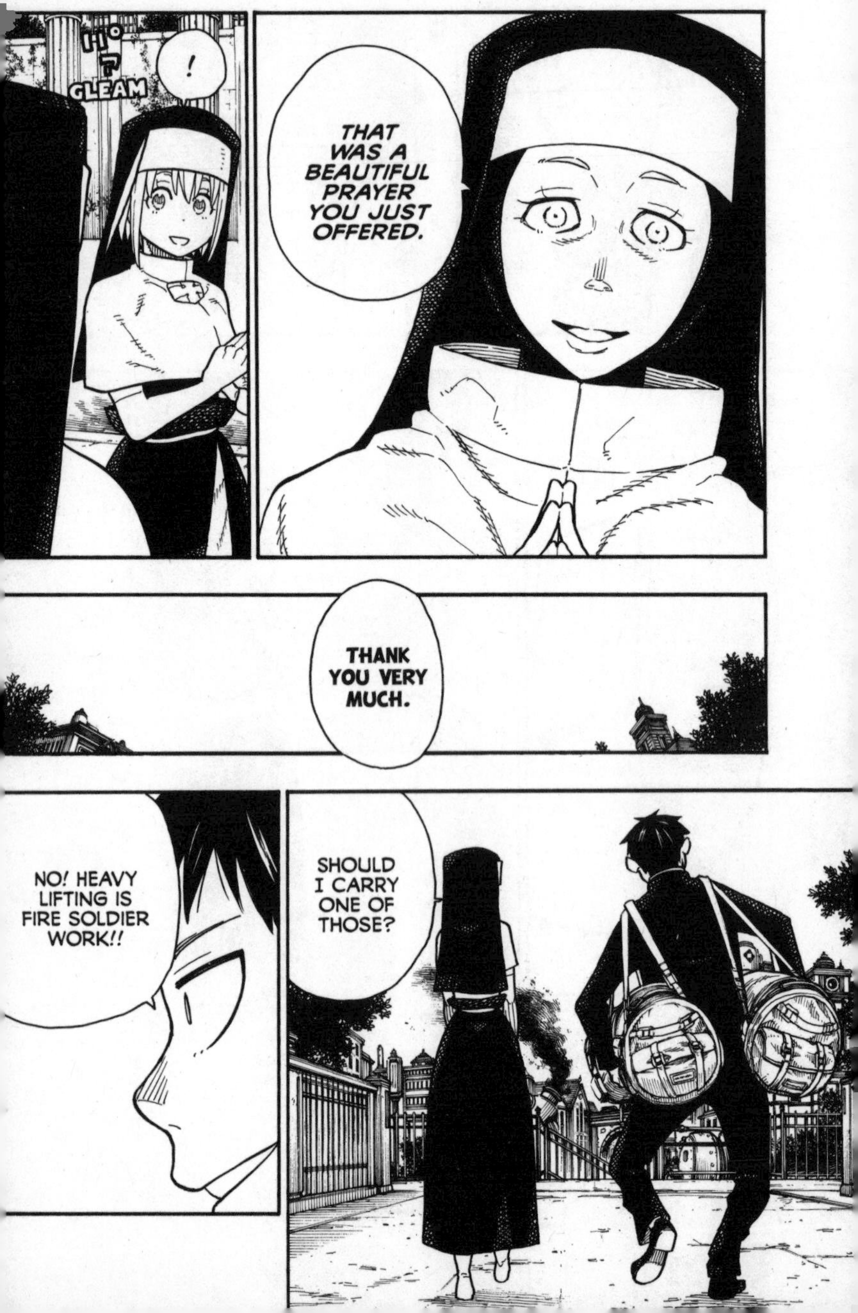
THAT WAS A BEAUTIFUL PRAYER YOU JUST OFFERED.
!
GLEAM
THANK YOU VERY MUCH.
SHOULD I CARRY ONE OF THOSE?
NO! HEAVY LIFTING IS FIRE SOLDIER WORK!!

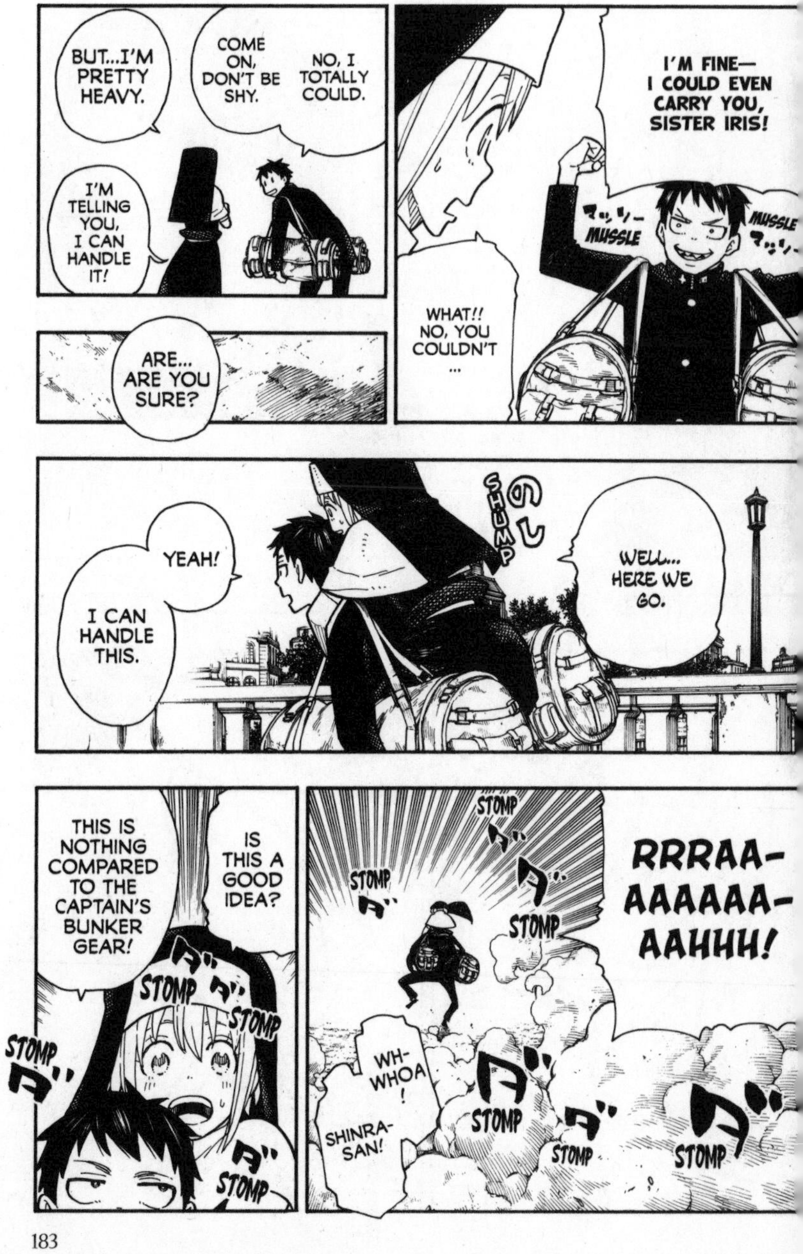
I'M FINE—
I COULD EVEN CARRY YOU, SISTER IRIS!
MUSSLE
MUSSLE
WHAT!! NO, YOU COULDN'T ...
NO, I TOTALLY COULD.
COME ON, DON'T BE SHY.
BUT...I'M PRETTY HEAVY.
I'M TELLING YOU, I CAN HANDLE IT!
ARE... ARE YOU SURE?
WELL... HERE WE GO.
SHUMP
YEAH!
I CAN HANDLE THIS.
RRRAA-AAAAAA-AAHHH!
STOMP
STOMP
STOMP
WH-WHOA!
SHINRA-SAN!
STOMP
STOMP
STOMP
IS THIS A GOOD IDEA?
THIS IS NOTHING COMPARED TO THE CAPTAIN'S BUNKER GEAR!
STOMP
STOMP
STOMP
STOMP

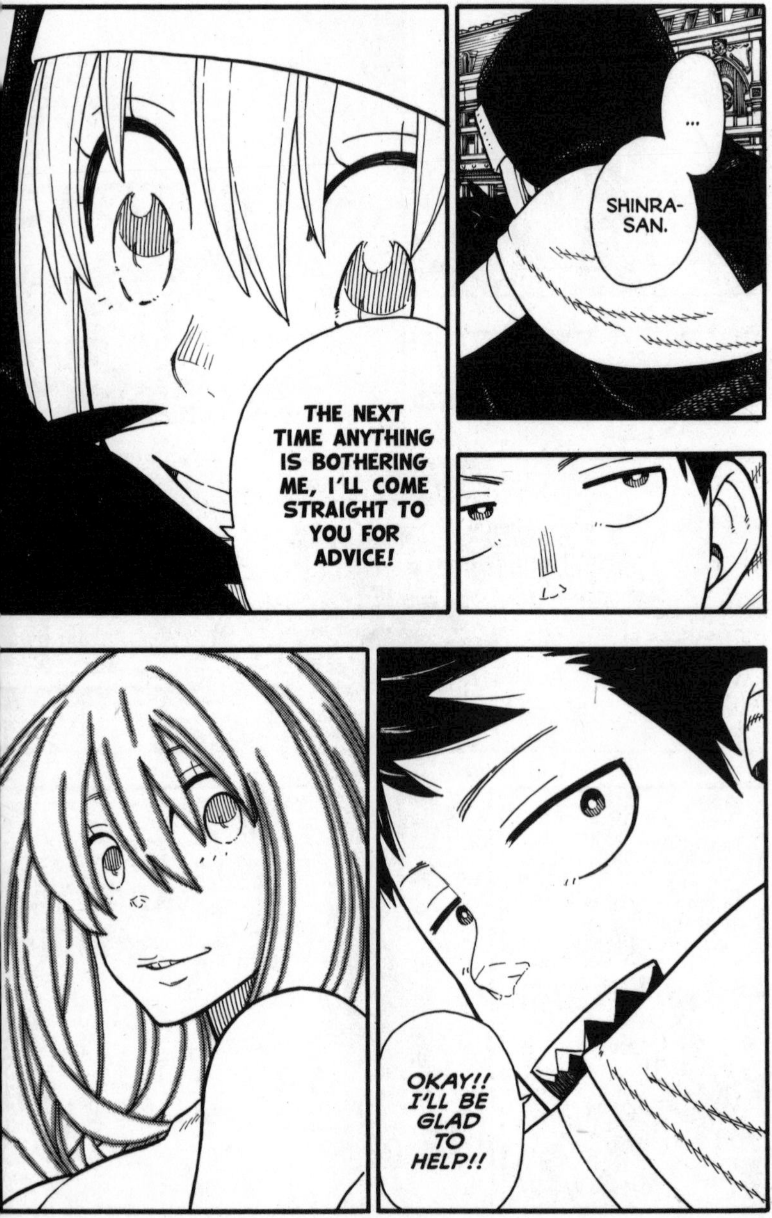
…
SHINRA-SAN.
THE NEXT TIME ANYTHING IS BOTHERING ME, I'LL COME STRAIGHT TO YOU FOR ADVICE!
OKAY!! I'LL BE GLAD TO HELP!!

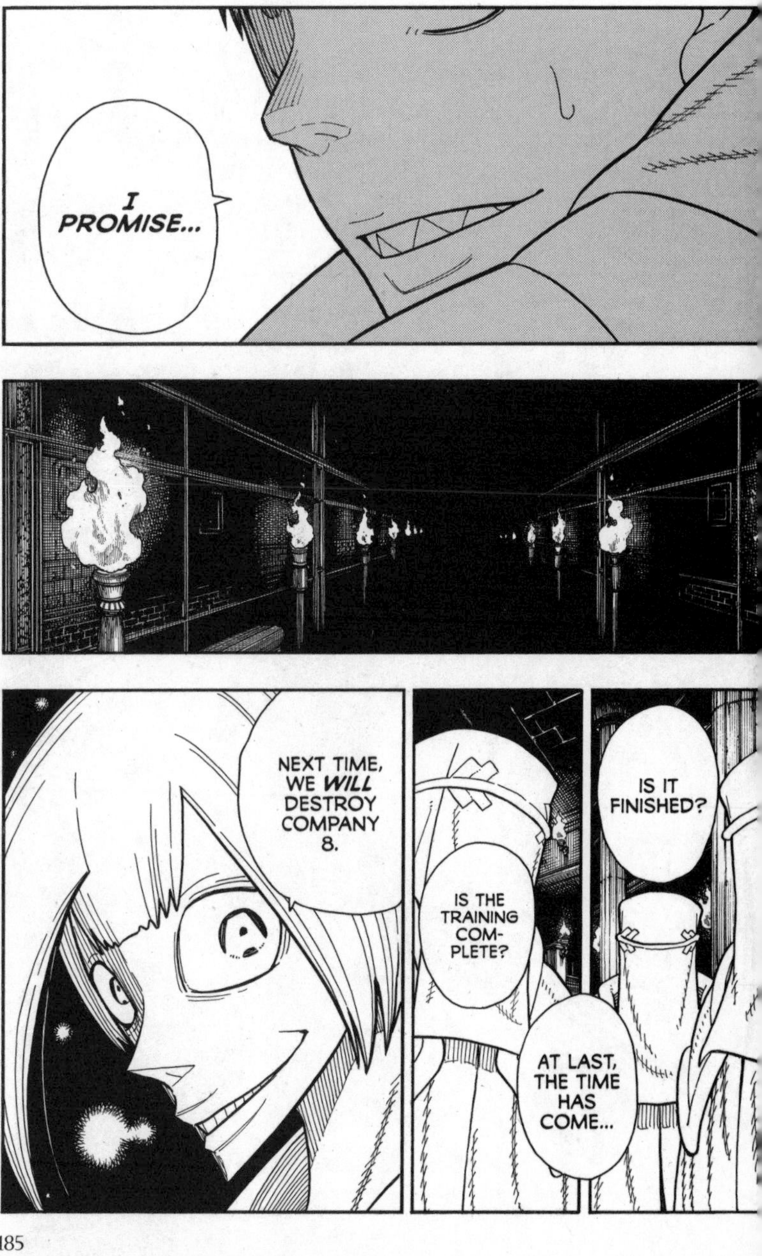
I PROMISE...
IS IT FINISHED?
IS THE TRAINING COM-PLETE?
AT LAST, THE TIME HAS COME...
NEXT TIME, WE *WILL* DESTROY COMPANY 8.

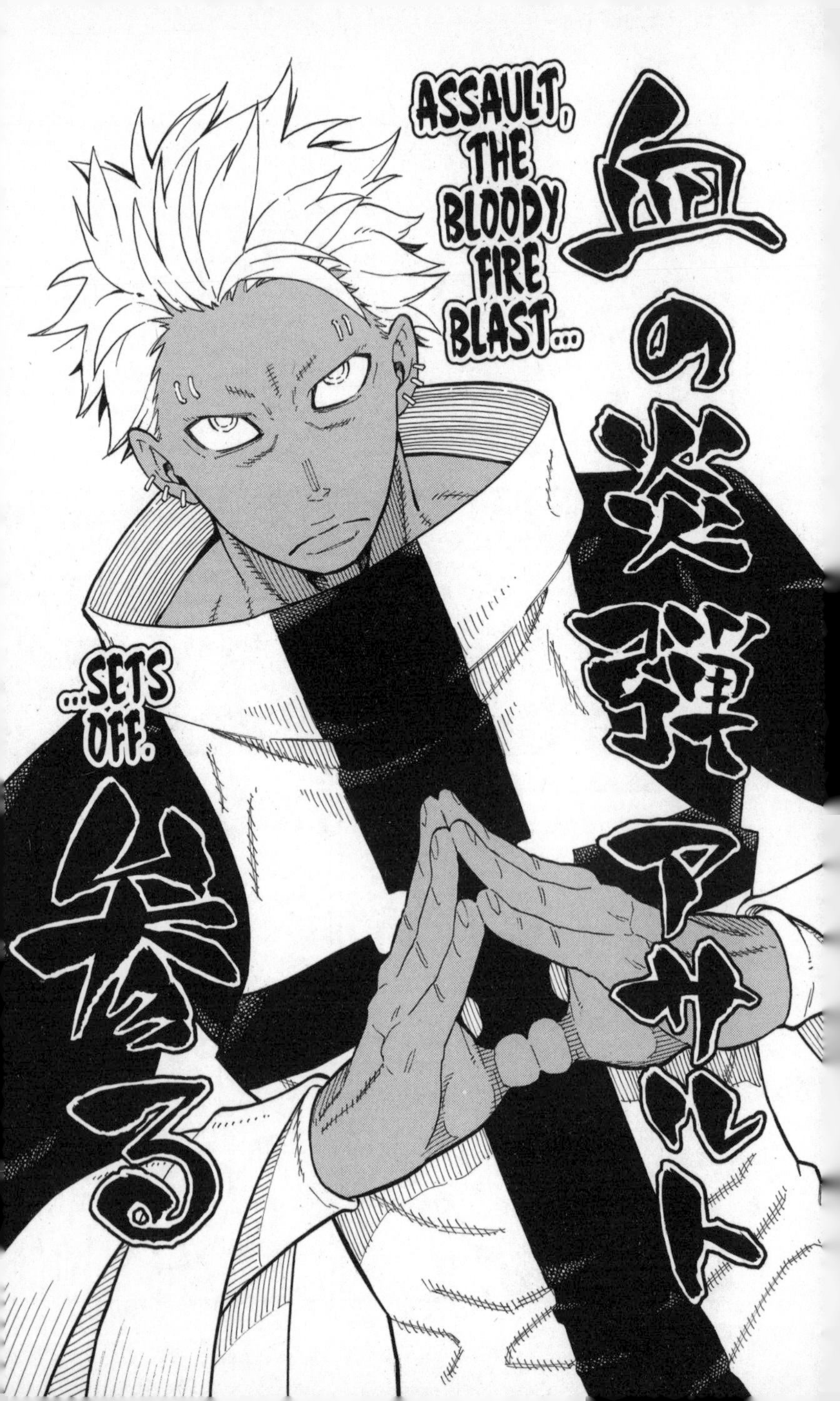
ASSAULT, THE BLOODY FIRE BLAST...
...SETS OFF.

TO BE CONTINUED IN VOLUME 18!!

Translation Notes:

Boys, don't be ambitious, page 87

This is a reference to a motto known all across Japan, which states, "Boys, be ambitious." These words are attributed to William S. Clark, the founder of the Sapporo Agricultural College in northern Japan. Legend has it, this was his parting advice as he left the school on horseback, and his words have lived on as a motto of encouragement in following one's goals and dreams—the sort of thing that leads people to become stronger.

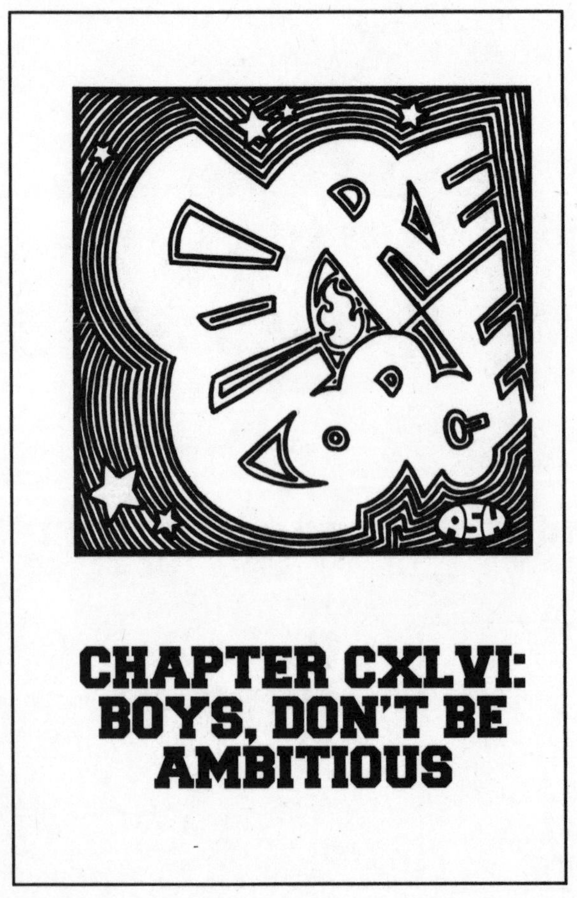
ASH

CHAPTER CXLVI: BOYS, DON'T BE AMBITIOUS

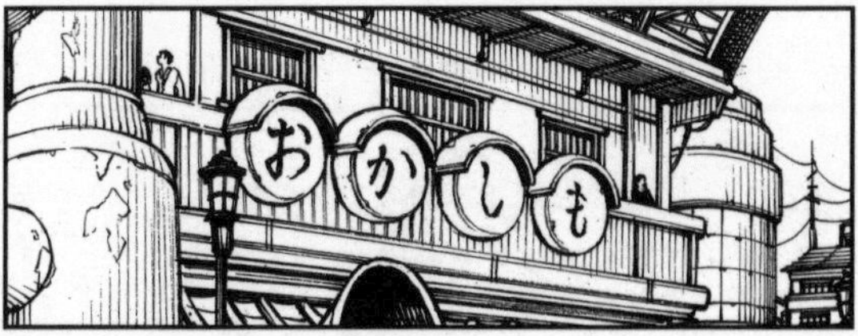
おかしも

Oh-ka-shi-mo, page 127

A Japanese mnemonic for emergency safety drills, most commonly taught in schools during fire drills. Each letter represents a directive: Don't push; don't run; don't chat; don't turn back.

Ready to get busy, hun, page 137

Perhaps in an attempt to mimic the Asakusa-speak so popular among Company 8, Iris here uses something called *kuruwa-kotoba* from the Edo period, meaning "red-light district words."

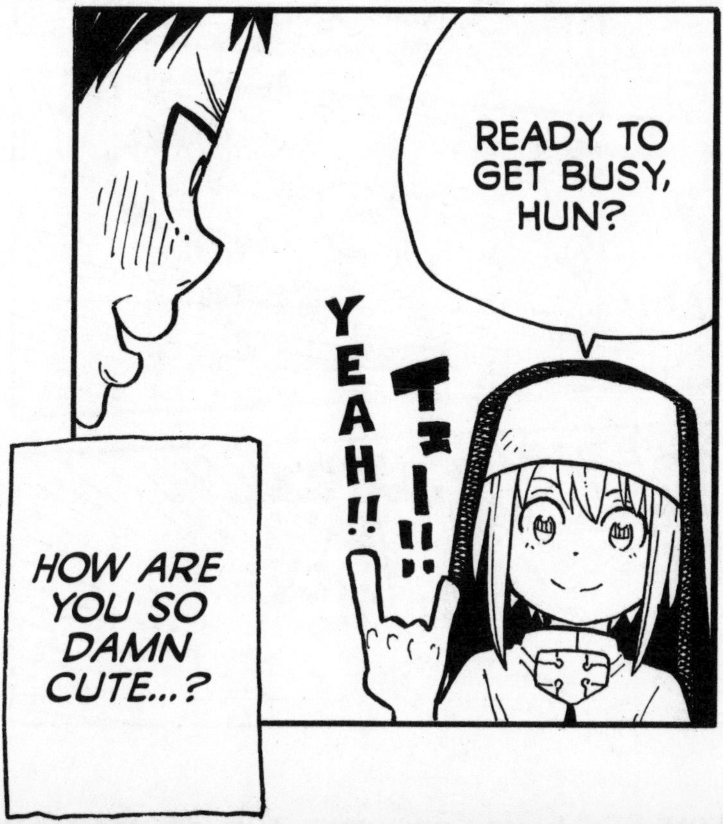
READY TO GET BUSY, HUN?
YEAH!!
HOW ARE YOU SO DAMN CUTE...?

AFTERWORD MANGA: ATSUSHIYA

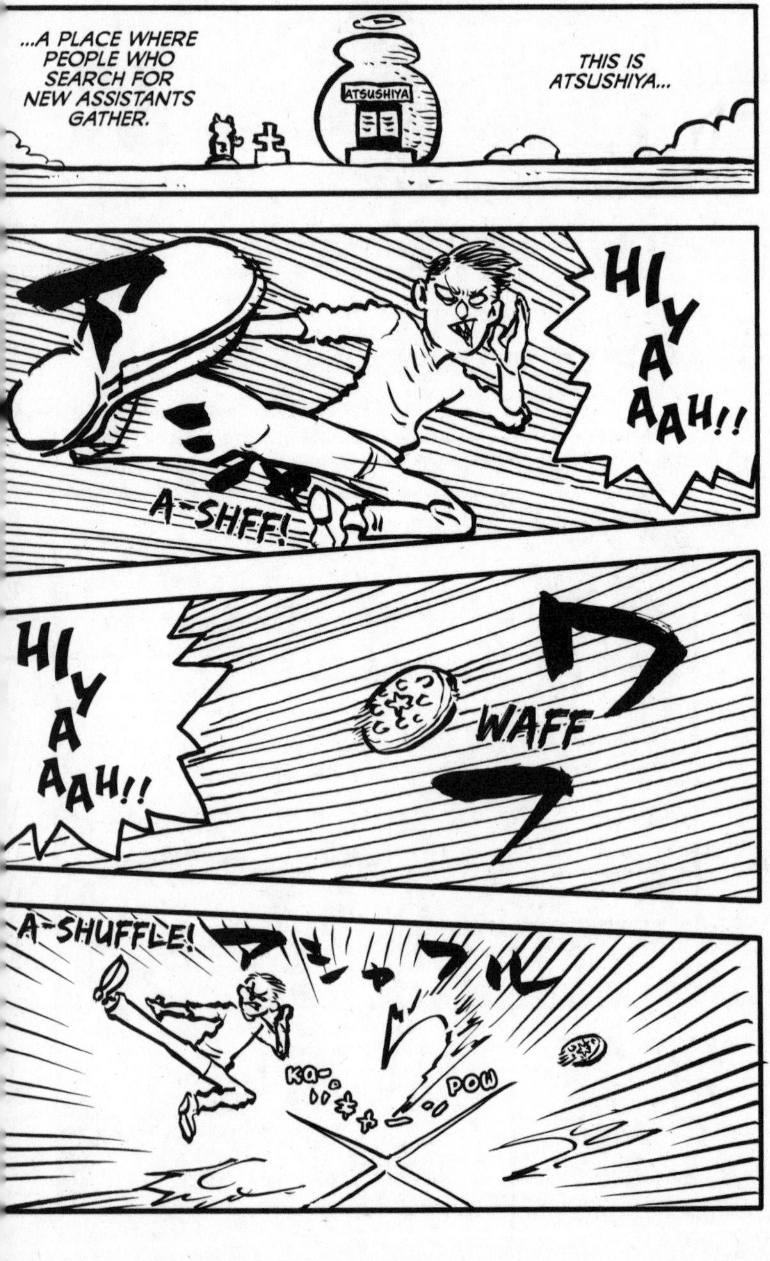
THIS IS ATSUSHIYA...
...A PLACE WHERE PEOPLE WHO SEARCH FOR NEW ASSISTANTS GATHER.
ATSUSHIYA
HIYAAAH!!
A-SHFF!
WAFF
HIYAAAH!!
POW
A-SHUFFLE!

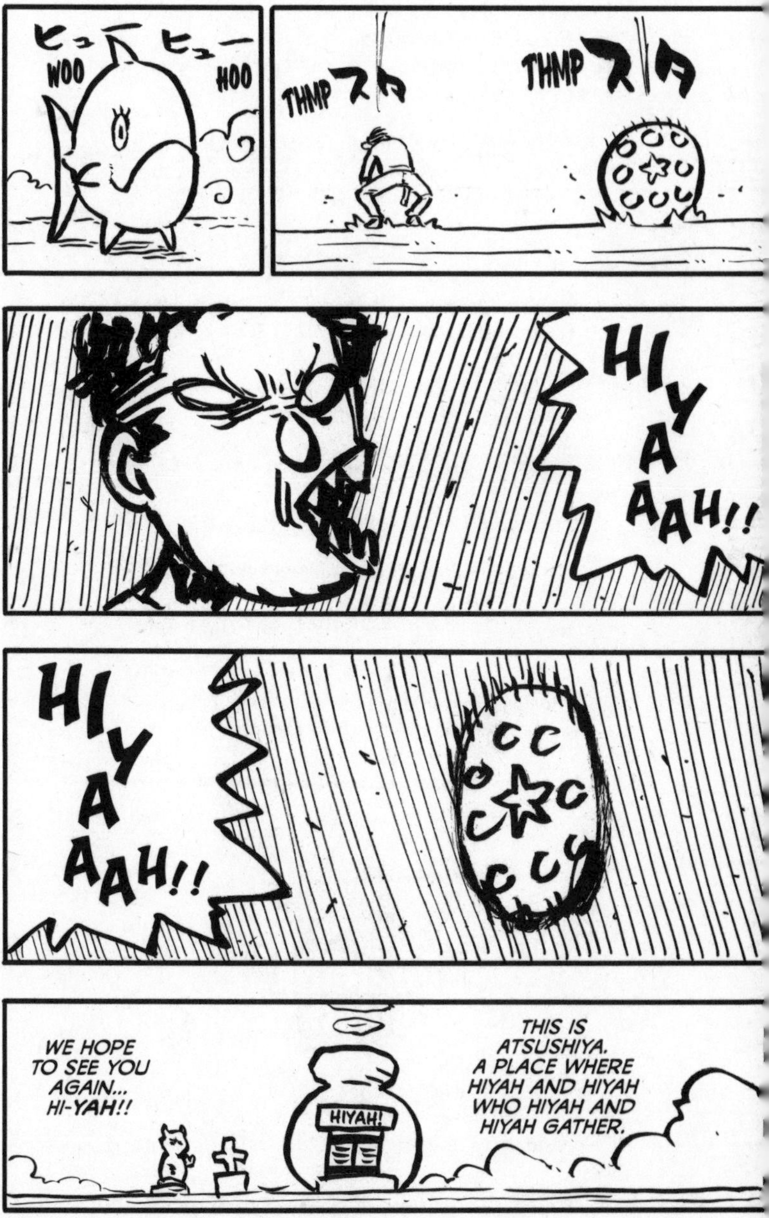

THMP スタ
THMP スタ
ヒュー
HOO
ヒュー
WOO
HIYAAAH!!
HIYAAAH!!
THIS IS ATSUSHIYA. A PLACE WHERE HIYAH AND HIYAH WHO HIYAH AND HIYAH GATHER.
HIYAH!
WE HOPE TO SEE YOU AGAIN... HI-YAH!!

A Kodansha Comics Trade Paperback Original
Fire Force 17 copyright © 2019 Atsushi Ohkubo
English translation copyright © 2019 Atsushi Ohkubo

Published in the United States by Kodansha Comics, an imprint of Kodansha USA Publishing, LLC, New York.

Publication rights for this English edition arranged through Kodansha Ltd., Tokyo.

First published in Japan in 2019 by Kodansha Ltd., Tokyo.

ISBN 978-1-63236-790-7

Printed in the United States of America.

www.kodanshacomics.com

9 8 7 6 5 4 3 2 1
Translation: Alethea Nibley & Athena Nibley
Lettering: AndWorld Design
Editing: Haruko Hashimoto
Kodansha Comics edition cover design by Phil Balsman

Publisher: Kiichiro Sugawara
Managing editor: Maya Rosewood
Vice president of marketing & publicity: Naho Yamada

Director of publishing services: Ben Applegate
Associate director of operations: Stephen Pakula
Publishing services managing editor: Noelle Webster
Assistant production manager: Emi Lotto